Law and the Business of Sport

David Griffith-Jones
LLB, of the Middle Temple, Barrister, FCIArB

Consulting editor
Adrian Barr-Smith   *MA, Partner: Denton Hall, London*

Butterworths
London, Edinburgh and Dublin
1997

United Kingdom	Butterworths a Division of Reed Elsevier (UK) Ltd, Halsbury House, 35 Chancery Lane, LONDON WC2A 1EL and 4 Hill Street, EDINBURGH EH2 3JZ.
Australia	Butterworths, SYDNEY, ADELAIDE, BRISBANE, CANBERRA, MELBOURNE and PERTH.
Canada	Butterworths Canada Ltd, TORONTO and VANCOUVER.
Ireland	Butterworth (Ireland) Ltd, DUBLIN.
Malaysia	Malayan Law Journal Sdn Bhd, KUALA LUMPUR.
New Zealand	Butterworths of New Zealand Ltd, WELLINGTON and AUCKLAND.
Singapore	Reed Elsevier (Singapore) Pte Ltd, SINGAPORE.
South Africa	Butterworths Publishers (Pty) Ltd, DURBAN.
USA	Michie, CHARLOTTESVILLE, Virginia.

A CIP Catalogue record for this book is available from the British Library.

ISBN 0 406 89035 8

Typeset by Kerrypress Ltd, Luton
Printed by Redwood Books, Trowbridge, Wilts

Foreword

One of the first lessons I learned after I arrived at the F.A. Premier League was that while it may be difficult to define precisely what is meant by 'sports law' there is no difficulty in defining the very important role that the law has in sport in the late 20th century. Nor do I believe that the role of the law in sport is likely to diminish in the early 21st century.

There is no area of the organisation of a professional league or of a professional sports club that does not bring that league or that club into contact with the law and legal issues many times each day. One has to be alert constantly to the very many areas of the law which are involved, and to the very many legal issues which have to be resolved. It is no surprise, therefore, that lawyers are increasingly involved in the organisation and administration of both leagues and clubs.

However, until David Griffith-Jones decided to remedy the situation, there was no one book to which one could refer for the answer to the daily problems which arise and upon which leagues and clubs require legal advice. Now the answers to those problems are at hand.

This is a book which stands by itself as a reference book, and for lawyers who have to work in and advise sporting bodies, it will be as invaluable as it is essential. I cannot imagine that any lawyer who is involved in the administration and organisation of a sports league or club will not want to keep this book very close to him or her.

I congratulate David Griffith-Jones and his team on their efforts in producing this book.

Peter Leaver QC

Preface

A moment's thought reveals that no discrete area of law exists to which can aptly be attached the label 'sportslaw'. Further reflection may lead to the conclusion that this is not altogether surprising, given that the very concept of 'sport' embraces many different activities with no discernible common denominator and no obvious defineable boundaries. Human activity is subject to the law in all its aspects and sport can plead no special exemption. Moreover, the last 30 years or so has seen a revolution in sport, with a steady and concerted move, to the regret of some, away from the amateur or 'corinthian' ethic towards professionalism. Such a move, to support it, has required the generation of money from sport and the growth of profession-alism has indeed produced a general and spiralling commercialisation of sport. In certain areas in particular, huge amounts of money are both earned from sport and poured into sport. Many individuals now make their living directly from sporting performance or competition. Some such individuals find that their sporting successes serve also to open doors to other commercial opportunities. Many other individuals and organisations are engaged in businesses which, whether wholly or partially, depend upon sport for the generation of their turnover. In such circumstances, it is inevitable that the disciplines of the law are often required, to protect, regulate and control the relationships involved, not simply within the conduct and administration of sport itself, but also within the businesses constructed in association with or on the back of sport.

Even in an earlier era, George Orwell was moved to declare[1]:

> 'Serious sport has nothing to do with fair play. It is bound up with hatred, jealousy, boastfulness, disregard of all rules and sadistic pleasure in witnessing violence: in other words it is war minus the shooting.'

To the extent that such a cynical view had elements of truth in 1945, with increased money now at stake how much more pertinent it is in modern times! Sport plays an important part in the economy of every developed nation. The public in the United Kingdom and elsewhere appears to have an insatiable appetite for sport, and there is an increasing number of people and organisations anxious to feed (and to feed off) that appetite, not the least of which are the television companies who not only have the capacity to bring top class sporting action into the home but who thereby provide substantial advertising and marketing opportunities for a wide range of other commercial interests. The 'business of sport' has developed to the point that it is surely now one of the largest commercial sectors in the world and one would accordingly expect the law increasingly to be deployed in its conduct. And so it has proved, with the relationship between sport and the

1 'The Sporting Spirit', December 1945.

law having moved on a steep upward curve for some years, to the point that barely a week now goes by without the media reporting some conflict within or related to sport where one of the parties has resorted, or threatened resort, to the law for its resolution.

This book attempts to analyse some of the commercial and other relationships involved in and around sport and to give some guidance towards an understanding of some of the more important legal implications of such relationships, particularly with a view to assisting those embarking on such relationships to make sensible provision for their conduct so as, hopefully, to minimise the risk of conflict. The field is potentially huge and, inevitably, any such attempt will be partial and any such guidance limited, given that the commercial tentacles of sport are ever expanding, and fresh and unexpected problems are always around the corner. I am only too aware that I have been able to make but brief incursions into many different areas of the law. But most of these areas have their own comprehensive jurisprudence recorded in other specialist works and it is hoped that, at least in many instances, the reader will gain a sufficient insight into the particular problems covered to enable him/her if not to be confident of the answers, then at least to be clear as to the appropriate areas of further research.

The task of producing a book such as this whilst also conducting a legal practice has proved as arduous as I was led to believe it would be. I could not have done it alone. I should like to record my sincere thanks to those many individuals who have provided me with the considerable support and assistance which I have been lucky enough to enjoy. Space precludes me from listing them all individually, but special mention must go to my colleagues in Devereux Chambers, especially Colin Wynter and Timothy Brennan who have used their specialist knowledge and expertise to contribute the chapters on insurance and tax respectively, to Malcolm Chapple who wrote the chapter on his specialist subject of intellectual property, to Rebecca Owen of Denton Hall who kindly reviewed the chapter on competition law, and especially to my consulting editor, Adrian Barr-Smith of Denton Hall, whose breadth of knowledge of the subject is second to none and whose expert advice and assistance across the whole field has proved quite invaluable. In spite of all such help which I have received, any glaring errors or omissions remain my responsibility alone - I would be glad to be alerted to them so that I may make amends in any future edition.

Finally, this book is dedicated to my wife and family, whose patience and understanding during the months of its gestation far exceeded the bounds of anything which I was entitled to demand of them.

David Griffith-Jones
Devereux Chambers

Contents

Table of statutes

Table of statutory instruments

Table of cases

H

I

J

K

L

S

T

Z

Decisions of the European Court of Justice are listed below numerically. These
decisions are also included in the preceeding alphabetical list.

Chapter 1

Liability for injury in sport

Introduction

The potential for liability of one form or another within a sporting context is as great as in any other context. Very often the relationship within which a particular incident occurs will be governed by the terms of a contract between the parties, in which case disputes arising from the incident may well fall to be determined according to the rights and obligations reserved to the respective parties by their agreement and the application thereto of general contractual principles. Any detailed examination of such principles is beyond the scope of this chapter which seeks to focus on non contractual liabilities which may arise within certain sporting relationships and on the scope and limitations of such liabilities derived from the sporting context within which the relationships are forged.

The cornerstone of most non contractual claims arising out of such relationships is the tort of negligence which involves a breach of a duty of care deemed to be owed by one person to another in certain circumstances. This chapter will therefore focus primarily on negligence and, in particular, will seek to identify in relation to particular categories of person operating within the sporting field respectively the circumstances in which such a duty is deemed to exist, to whom it is owed and the scope and limitations of any such duty so identified. In addition, where appropriate, certain other potential causes of action will briefly be considered.

The legal principles – negligence

On 26 August 1928 an unfortunate shop assistant, Miss Donoghue, drank from a bottle of ginger beer which she then found to contain the decomposed remains of a snail. She sued the maufacturers, complaining that she had been caused to suffer shock and gastroenteritis. In doing so, she was unwittingly embarking on a course which was ultimately to lead to the House of Lords laying the foundations of the modern law of negligence. Their Lordships (in *Donoghue v Stevenson*[1]) had to consider in what circumstances the relationship between individuals gave rise to a duty of

1 [1932] AC 562.

care, breach of which sounded in damages. Their decision (by majority), whilst fashioned by the facts of the case before them, was expressed in terms appropriate for general application. In one of the classic statements of legal principle known to the common law, Lord Atkin said[2]:

> 'The liability for negligence ... is no doubt based upon a general public sentiment of moral wrongdoing for which the offender must pay. But acts or omissions which any moral code would censure cannot in a practical world be treated so as to give a right to every person injured by them to demand relief. In this way rules of law arise which limit the range of complainants and the extent of their remedy. The rule that you are to love your neighbour becomes in law, you must not injure your neighbour; and the lawyer's question, Who is my neighbour? receives a restricted reply. *You must take reasonable care to avoid acts or omissions which you can reasonably foresee would be likely to injure your neighbour. Who then is my neighbour? The answer seems to be – persons who are so closely and directly affected by my act that I ought reasonably to have them in contemplation as being so affected when I am directing my mind to the acts or omissions which are called in question.'*

In so formulating the principle, Lord Atkin gave qualified approval to the earlier statements of principle emanating from Lord Esher, firstly (as Brett MR) in *Heaven v Pender*[3] and later in *Le Lievre v Gould*[4]. In the former case, he had said[5]:

> '... whenever one person is by circumstances placed in such a position with regard to another that every one of ordinary sense who did think would at once recognise that if he did not use ordinary care and skill in his own conduct with regard to those circumstances he would cause danger of injury to the person or property of the other, a duty arises to use ordinary care and skill to avoid such danger.'

In the later case, Lord Esher had added this qualification[6]:

> 'If one man is near to another or is near to the property of another, a duty lies upon him not to do that which may cause a personal injury to that other, or may injure his property.'

Lord Atkin took Lord Esher's qualifying remarks as being in line with the statement by AL Smith LJ in the same case[7]:

> 'The decision in *Heaven v Pender* was founded upon the principle that a duty to take care did arise when the person or property of one was in such proximity to the person or property of another that, if due care was not taken, damage might be done by the one to the other.'

Accordingly, Lord Atkin went on to say[8]:

> 'I think this sufficiently states the truth, if proximity be not confined to mere physical proximity, but be used, as I think it was intended, to extend to such close and direct relations that the act complained of directly affects a person whom the person alleged to be bound to take care would know would be directly affected by his careless act.'

2 At 580.
3 (1883)11 QBD 503.
4 [1893] 1 QB 491.
5 At 509.
6 At 497.
7 At 504.
8 At 581.

There are a number of features arising from the above statements of principle. In particular:

(i) a duty of care is owed to those who ought reasonably to be in contemplation as being affected by a particular act;

(ii) the duty itself is simply to take reasonable care to avoid injury to the person or property;

(iii) because the existence and practical content of the duty and the identification of the individuals to whom the duty is owed are dependent in part on the concept of reasonableness, the particular circumstances of any given case will determine whether or not a duty is established and, if so, whether or not breach of such duty can be shown.

The third of the above three points is of particular importance when it comes to considering the issue of liability within different particular fields. It is important to keep in mind that, in all fields, the principles of law to be applied are the same. What may, however, make a difference to the result of a particular case, are the circumstances within which those principles of law fall to be determined. Hence it is often said that the categories of negligence are never closed. Fresh circumstances are always arising and will continue regularly to arise in which a decision is called for as to whether or not the duty of care exists or has been breached. Indeed, in laying down the principles, Lord Atkin well recognised that they were of a nature that cases would inevitably arise in which it would be difficult to decide upon their application[9].

Application of legal principles in the sporting context

In the sporting context, whilst the issue of liability falls to be determined by reference to the above general principles of law, it is that very context which will often inform the decisions required in the application of those legal principles. Hence the decision on liability in relation to a blow inflicted by a punch or a kick may be different where the blow is landed in the context of some sporting conflict, in comparison with an identical blow inflicted on another occasion, such as in a public house. If, in an otherwise comparable situation, liability is to arise in the public house, but not on the playing field, the reason for the distinction in treatment lies not in the fact that different rules or principles of law are being applied in the two cases, but rather in the fact that the application of the principles of law involved depends upon the particular circumstances of the case being judged. This is because the principles of law are framed in terms of reasonableness and themselves require that all relevant circumstances are taken into consideration in their application.

The clear conclusion must be that it represents a fundamentally wrong approach to treat sport as though it were a special case, as though the ordinary principles of law have no application to it and to seek instead to identify particular and different principles appropriate for application in

9 See for example (at 582) his comments on the potential difficulty in deciding whether or not a particular relationship is sufficiently close to give rise to the duty.

sporting contexts. Any such approach is liable to lead to error and misconception.

The position was put succinctly in 1927 by Swift J in *Cleghorn v Oldham*[10] in giving judgment for the plaintiff who had been injured when struck by the defendant's golf club during a demonstration swing:

> 'Games might be, and [are], the serious business of life to many people. It would be extraordinary to say that people could not recover from injuries sustained in the business of life, whether that was football, or motor racing, or any other of those pursuits which were instinctively classed as games but which everyone knew quite well to be serious business transactions for the persons engaged therein.'

The correct approach is to understand that ordinary principles apply, whilst also recognising that such principles require that, in a sporting context (as in any other context), the circumstances derived from that context go into the melting pot when judging the issues of reasonableness which are inherent within the principles themselves.

Another feature of the central role of the concept of reasonableness within the established legal principles is that, because reasonableness depends upon all the circumstances, individual judgments as to what is reasonable may change with time. What was regarded as reasonable in years gone by, may later be deemed unreasonable (or vice versa) because of the changing times and the different circumstances which they may bring. This results in the possibility that, whereas a given case may have given rise to no liability in the past, liability may nevertheless be established in a similar case today. This is not because different principles are applied today, but because the circumstances in which the principles are applied (and in particular the public's perceptions of what is and is not acceptable behaviour) have changed. This may explain why, for example, there has been an increase in recent times in the number of claims for damages arising from incidents occurring in the sporting arena. In the past, violence on the playing field may have been regarded as simply part and parcel of the game and something to be accepted to a far greater extent than is now the case. That such violent conduct within a sporting context is now more generally deprecated is one of the circumstances likely to influence the judges called upon to determine whether particular instances give rise to legal redress.

It follows that it is fundamental to a proper understanding of the law of negligence to appreciate that the context of any incident being judged will help determine whether or not a duty of care can be established and, if so, whether or not it has been breached. The particular results of 'sports cases' which have come before the courts have depended in part upon the very sporting context within which the incidents concerned have occurred. In short, in 'sports cases', decisions on the issues of liability are likely to be fashioned by the particular sporting context within which they fall to be judged. It follows that any consideration of the application of established legal principles in a 'sports case' requires, first and foremost, an examination of those features of the sport in question which serve to identify the relevant sporting context within which such principles require to be applied. Such features will almost invariably have a significant bearing on the determination of the issues on which such a case depends. The point was re-iterated by the Court of Appeal in the recent case in which the liability of a rugby

10 (1927) 43 TLR 465 at 466.

referee was examined, *Smoldon v Whitworth*[11], when the court reviewed the authorities and again confirmed the principle in terms which, although related to the facts of the particular case before the court, are of general application:

> 'The level of care required is that which is appropriate in all the circumstances, and the circumstances are of crucial importance. Full account must be taken of the factual context in which [a referee exercises his functions]... .'

In the following parts of this chapter, therefore, although each section is devoted, as a matter of convenience, to the liability of particular categories of person within particular sporting relationships respectively, it should be remembered that, when it comes to issues of negligence, the *principles* to be applied are the same in each case. It follows that statements of principle in cases dealing with particular sporting relationships are likely to be worthy of application to other types of such relationship. Equally, it should be remembered that the features of a particular type of sporting relationship may well influence the particular decision in the application of such principles.

Liability of individual competitors to spectators and other onlookers[12]

In a seminal case, with important implications for issues of liability in many different types of sporting circumstances, the Court of Appeal considered the scope of a sporting competitor's duty in *Wooldridge v Sumner*[13], a case where a horse competing in the Horse of the Year Show at the White City had bolted from the arena and into the spectators, injuring a photographer. The photographer sued the rider in negligence. In his judgment, Diplock LJ highlighted the remarkable fact that [at that time] there was:

> 'An almost complete dearth of judicial authority as to the duty of care owed by the actual participants to the spectators.'

The Court of Appeal looked at the circumstances of the relationship between competitor and spectator and accepted that there was a sufficient degree of proximity between them to give rise to a duty of care on the part of the competitor. On the facts, however, the court decided that there had been no breach.

In rejecting the plaintiff's claim in negligence against the rider of the horse (and overturning the trial judge) Diplock LJ accepted that the rider had been guilty of an error of judgment, but went on[14]:

> 'That is not enough to constitute a breach of the duty of reasonable care which a participant owes to a spectator. In such circumstances something in the nature of a reckless disregard of the spectator's safety must be proved, and of this there is no suggestion in the evidence.'

11 [1997] ELR 115; on appeal [1997] ELR 249, CA.
12 It is not unknown for a spectator to be held liable to a competitor! In *Karpow v Shave* [1975] 2 WWR 159, a spectator intervened after a fight between two competitors, one of whom was his brother. He was held liable for a punch which broke the competitor's nose.
13 [1963] 2 QB 43.
14 At 72.

This apparent introduction into the law of negligence in a sporting context of a requirement that, for him to be liable, the defendant should have acted with recklessness might be seen as novel. In other (non sporting) contexts, an error of judgment or other similar lapse is often all that is required. It is, however, important to note that, properly understood, Diplock LJ was not purporting to modify the duty owed, which remained a duty simply to exercise reasonable care. Rather, he was indicating what was required, in the special circumstances of a particular type of sporting occasion, for a breach of that duty to be established. This is clear from an earlier passage, when he said[15]:

> '[Lord Atkin's statement of principle in *Donoghue v Stevenson*] does not purport to define what is reasonable care and was directed to identifying the persons to whom the duty to take reasonable care is owed. What is reasonable care in a particular circumstance is a jury question and where, as in a case like this, there is no direct guidance or hindrance from authority it may be answered by inquiring *whether the ordinary reasonable man would say that in all the circumstances the defendant's conduct was blameworthy* ... The law of negligence has always recognised that the standard of care which a reasonable man will exercise *depends upon the conditions under which the decision to avoid the act or omission relied upon as negligence has to be taken.*'

In this passage, Diplock LJ was not departing from established principles so as to make recklessness a prerequisite of liability in sports cases. Rather, he was simply identifying the practical content of the obligation to take reasonable care in the particular circumstances of the specific sporting context within which the issue of the defendant's liability required to be judged. This is clear from the passage where he went on to express his view as to what the reasonable man would say if asked to identify blameworthy conduct in such circumstances. He said[16]:

> 'A person attending a game or competition takes the risk of any damage caused to him by any act of a participant done in the course of and for the purposes of the game or competition notwithstanding that such act may involve an error of judgment or a lapse of skill, unless the participant's conduct is such as to evince a reckless disregard of the spectator's safety.'

In so expressing himself, Diplock LJ was doing no more than recognising that, as in all situations, the specific requirements imposed by a general obligation to exercise reasonable care depend upon all the circumstances. In the context of a competitive horse show, where the proper and accepted aim of the competitors was to attempt to win the competition, the Court of Appeal did not feel that mere errors of judgment were enough on which to found liability.

Elsewhere in his judgment, Diplock LJ illuminated the criterion of reasonableness further, by making it clear that, in such a case, the reasonableness of the defendant's actions cannot be judged in isolation. The spectator's expectations require to be considered as well. As Diplock LJ said[17]:

> 'The matter has to be looked at from the point of view of the reasonable spectator as well as the reasonable participant; not because of the maxim *volenti non fit injuria*, but because what a reasonable spectator would expect

15 At 66.
16 At 68.
17 At 67.

a participant to do without regarding it as blameworthy is as relevant to what is reasonable care as what a reasonable participant would think was blameworthy conduct in himself ... .'

In the two last quoted passages, Diplock LJ articulated a principle of fundamental importance to cases involving alleged negligence in the context, in particular, of a vigorous and competitive sporting occasion. The principle that spectators (and indeed others with a voluntary involvement, whether active or passive, in sport) must be taken to accept such risks as are 'inherent in' or 'incidents of' the game and that, accordingly, a competitor's duty of care does not extend to sheltering them from such risks is manifestly sound and uncontroversial. The broad principle was expressed in the United States of America by Chief Justice Cardozo in an entertaining and illuminating judgment in *Murphy v Steeplechase Amusement Co Inc*[18] when he said:

> 'One who takes part in such a sport accepts the dangers that inhere in it so far as they are obvious and necessary just as a fencer accepts the risk of a thrust by his antagonist or a spectator at a ball game the chance of contact with the ball ... the antics of the clown are not the paces of the cloistered cleric...'

It might be said, however, that it is less immediately obvious that the inherent risks which have to be accepted may embrace the risk of injury through errors of judgment and lapses in skill by individual competitors. But it is suggested that any sensible analysis confirms the sense of such a proposition, the validity of which, as will be seen below, is not confined to issues of liability simply between competitors and spectators but extends to all such issues arising out of the frenzy of sporting activity itself. Diplock LJ's reasoning, in *Wooldridge v Sumner*, was that everyone knows and spectators (and other interested parties) are taken to accept that a reasonable participant in a competitive sporting contest (of the kind there before the court) will be likely to be pushing himself to the limit in an effort to win that contest and, where the competition is fast moving, he will be likely to have to act and exercise judgments decisively and swiftly. The decisions made and actions taken by such competitors in 'the agony of the moment' or 'the heat of battle' (viz: in the 'flurry and excitement' of the competition itself) are, rightly, deserving of special allowance when it comes to such matters being judged by reference to the standard of reasonableness inherent in the criteria for legal liability. It is in the light of such considerations that a competitor in such a sporting event will only be likely to breach his duty, which however remains one of reasonable care, if he displays such a disregard for the safety of others (be they spectators, fellow competitors or others) that his actions may properly be categorised as *reckless*.

Sellers LJ expressed his judgment to similar effect[19]:

> '... provided the competition or game is being performed within the rules and the requirement of the sport and by a person of adequate skill and competence the spectator does not expect his safety to be regarded by the participant. If the conduct is deliberately intended to injure someone whose presence is known, *or is reckless and in disregard of all safety of others so that a departure from the standards which might reasonably be expected in anyone*

18 166 NE 173 at 174 (1929).
19 At 56.

pursuing the competition or game, then the performer might well be held liable
for any injury his act caused. There would, I think, be a difference, for
instance, in assessing blame which is actionable between an injury caused
by a tennis ball hit or a racket accidentally thrown in the course of play into
the spectators at Wimbledon and a ball hit or a racket thrown into the
stands in temper or annoyance when play was not in progress.'

The distinction drawn by Sellers LJ between injury caused by actions during
play and at other times, is simply a recognition that actions which are not
part of 'the heat of battle' and are outside the 'flurry and excitement' of the
competitive activity itself do not merit the same consideration.

Thus in *Payne v Maple Leaf Gardens Ltd*[20], a spectator at an ice-hockey
match recovered damages in respect of injuries sustained not due to an
ordinary incident of the game of ice-hockey but as a result of a fight between
two players. Further examples abound, particularly in the context of injuries
to fellow competitors[1].

Another case where the court had to consider the potential liability of a
competitor to a spectator was *Wilks (formerly infant) v Cheltenham Home
Guard Motor Cycle and Light Car Club*[2]. There, a motorcycling scrambler lost
control of his machine which left the course and injured two spectators. In
finding that the rider was not liable in negligence, the members of the Court
of Appeal gave their judgments in terms which cautioned against expressing
the test generally in terms of recklessness. Edmund Davies LJ articulated the
proper test to be applied in such circumstances in the following terms[3]:

'... the proper test is whether injury to a spectator has been caused by an
error of judgment that a reasonable competitor, being *a reasonable man of
the sporting world,* would not have made.'

This touchstone of 'the reasonable man of the sporting world' is a useful
gloss on the general expression of the test of negligence because it
immediately brings the circumstances of the particular sporting context into
the equation. The Court of Appeal plainly thought that a 'reasonable man of
the sporting world' who attended a motor cycle scramble as a spectator
expected the participants to be going all out to win and that, in such
circumstances, provided they played within the rules and did not act in an
obviously foolhardy way, such a person would not expect them to have any
particular regard for his safety and would simply accept the foreseeable risk
of injury inherent in the sport and its ordinary incidents. In the circumstances, the scrambler was held not to be in breach of his duty of care.

Of course, there is the potential for a competitor to cause injury to others
who are not strictly spectators but merely passers by. In general terms,
however, the test is the same. As always, what amounts to reasonable care
will depend on all the circumstances. Particular circumstances which may
well affect the equation include the extent, nature and likelihood of
foreseeable harm. It is no more than common sense to say that less should be

---

20 [1949] 1 DLR 369.
1 See, for example, *Cleghorn v Oldham* (1927) 43 TLR 465 in which the plaintiff was injured
   by the defendant demonstrating a golf swing otherwise than in the course of play. See also
   Harrison v Vincent [1982] RTR 8, discussed below primarily in relation to the liability of the
   promoters of a motor cycle race, in which however the rider of a motor cycle was held liable
   to his combination passenger for negligence not during the race itself but during the
   preparation of his machine beforehand.
2 [1971] 1 WLR 668.
3 At 674.

expected of a competitor to guard against small or insignificant risks than against substantial risks of significant injury/damage.

Hence, in *Bolton v Stone*[4], it was held by the House of Lords not to be unreasonable and negligent for cricketers to ignore the (albeit foreseeable) risks of injury and damage from the ball being hit out of the ground, in circumstances where the chances of injury etc were assessed as negligible, the ball having been so struck only about six times in 30 years. On the other hand, in a case where such blows were struck regularly each season, the Court held the cricketers liable[5].

Further, in *Brewer v Delo*[6] where a golfer hooked his ball off the tee and struck another player on the next fairway, it was held that the risk of injury had been so small that a reasonable man would have been justified in ignoring it and judgment was given for the defendant.

Liability of competitors/participants to each other

TRESPASS TO THE PERSON

Where it is alleged that injury was inflicted by one competitor upon another with intent (that is, deliberately), it may be that a cause of action in assault (trespass to the person) will be asserted. Such a claim asserts the inflicting of injury by the intentional application of force to which the 'victim' has not consented. This requirement of intent is quite specific. The kind of reckless behaviour which (as explained above in relation to claims by spectators) is generally required to establish a breach of the duty to take reasonable care in order to establish the tort of negligence will not suffice. As Lord Denning made clear in *Letang v Cooper*[7]:

> 'When injury is not inflicted intentionally, but negligently, I would say the only cause of action is negligence and not trespass.'

This additional requirement of intent (still coupled to the absence of consent) means, in the sporting context, that successful claims of assault will inevitably be very much rarer than assertions of negligence[8].

NEGLIGENCE

Having identified, above, that the general duty owed by a competitor to a spectator is the same duty as is owed by any individual to his 'neighbour' in any circumstances (one of *reasonable* care) and that the implications of such duty in its application to a spectator depend upon the sporting context within which the duty is exercised, it will readily be understood that it is the same general duty which is owed by a competitor to his fellow competitors. It follows that the principles enunciated in cases such as *Wooldridge v Sumner* and *Wilks v Cheltenham Cycle Club* discussed above in the context of claims

4   [1951] AC 850.
5   *Miller v Jackson* [1977] QB 966. See also *Hilder v Associated Portland Cement Manufacturers Ltd* [1961] 1 WLR 1434.
6   [1967] 1 Lloyd's Rep 488. Compare *Lamond v Glasgow Corpn* 1968 SLT 291. See also *Ellison v Rogers* [1968] 1 OR 501, *Clark v Welsh* 1975 (4) SA 469; on appeal 1976 (3) SA 484 and *Finnie v Ropponen* (1987) 40 CCLT 155.
7   [1964] 2 All ER 929.
8   See, however, *Lewis v Brookshaw* (1970) unreported, noted at 120 NLJ 413.

by spectators, are appropriate for application in cases between sporting participants. It follows further that, as with a spectator, a plaintiff competitor is taken to accept the risks of injury from the ordinary incidents of his particular sport, which may involve errors of judgment and failures of skill, especially where the sport requires decisions to be taken and skill to be exercised at extremes of physical endeavour. Thus it was said in a Canadian case, *Agar v Canning*[9]:

> 'The conduct of a player in the heat of the game is instinctive and unpremeditated and should not be judged by standards suited to polite social intercourse.'

It was on this basis that, in *McComiskey v McDermott*[10], the duty owed by a rally driver to his navigator was held to be to exercise such care as was reasonably to be expected of a driver going all out to win the rally. Manifestly, decisions taken in such circumstances would have to be judged in the context that they were taken in the 'flurry and excitement' of the event itself.

In recent years, such cases have arisen with increasing frequency and the reports and newspapers now abound with examples. In the landmark case of *Condon v Basi*[11] a footballer was held liable for breaking his opponent's leg in a tackle. Again, the Court of Appeal stressed the circumstances of the footballing context in identifying the particular implications of the general duty to take reasonable care. In doing so, Sir John Donaldson MR gave his approval to the words of Kitto J in the Australian case of *Rootes v Sheldon*[12]:

> '... the conclusion to be reached must necessarily depend, according to the concepts of the common law, upon the reasonableness, in relation to the special circumstances, of the conduct which caused the plaintiff's injury ... the tribunal of fact may think that in the situation in which the plaintiff's injury was caused, a participant might do what the defendant did and still not be acting unreasonably, even though he infringed the "rules of the game". Non-compliance with such rules, conventions or customs (where they exist) is necessarily one consideration to be attended to upon the question of reasonableness; but it is only one, and it may be of much or little or even no weight in the circumstances.'

The Court of Appeal also made it clear that the proper approach in such circumstances is to see whether or not the defendant acted with reasonable care in all the circumstances, rather than to ask whether or not the plaintiff should be taken to have consented to the manner in which the defendant had acted so as, thereby, to *excuse* the defendant's lack of care.

In other words, the issue of consent (in the sense of the acceptance of certain risks, namely those risks which are inherent in the game and its ordinary incidents) affects the practical implications of the duty to take

---

9   (1965) 54 WWR 302 at 304.
10 [1974] IR 75.
11 [1985] 1 WLR 866.
12 [1968] ALR 33. In that case a water skier sued the boat driver for damages arising out of an incident where the skier collided with an object, of which the driver had given no warning. The claim failed, the risk in question being held to be inherent in or part and parcel of the sport. A (Canadian) water skiing case where liability was established is *Pawlak v Doucette & Reinks* [1985] 2 WWR 588. There the driver of the tow boat, having first failed to establish that the plaintiff was a novice, had applied full power before the plaintiff was ready to start, causing the latter's fingers to become entangled in and severed by the rope. The driver's actions were held to fall outside the range of risks which the plaintiff was taken to have accepted in the circumstances.

reasonable care itself rather than provides a potential defence to an established breach of that duty. Logically this makes sense. The competitor is only liable to avoid inflicting injury upon his opponent by taking reasonable care, and what amounts to reasonable care depends upon all the circumstances, one of which is that he is competing against others who are, as 'reasonable men of the sporting world', expected to appreciate and accept the risk of injury occurring during the general run of play. Hence it is where the competitor steps outside the general run of play that the risk of injury will be less likely to be one which his opponents ought to be expected to accept. In such circumstances, the offending competitor is more likely to be held liable. Thus it was that Mr Basi was held liable for Mr Condon's broken leg, his sliding tackle having been adjudged to constitute 'serious foul play', to have been made in a reckless and dangerous manner (albeit without malicious intent), and to be worthy of a sending off.

The clear implication from *Condon v Basi* is that, in the case of contact sports such as football, rugby etc, it will be almost impossible to establish liability unless the actions of the defendant are outside the rules of the game. Indeed the Court of Appeal appeared to be saying that a breach of the rules is virtually a *necessary*, albeit not necessarily a *sufficient*, requirement for liability to attach. Again, there is nothing 'special' about sports cases in this regard. In various fields, it has regularly been held that the rules and standards laid down by professional bodies provide a good guide as to the standards of reasonabless expected of those who operate in the fields governed thereby[13].

Thus, in *Wright v Cheshire County Council*[14], for example, the fact that certain gymnastic activities were being conducted in a manner which was generally accepted, caused the Court of Appeal to overturn a finding of liability in respect of injuries caused.

Equally, the 'customs of the slopes' were one ingredient which went into determining the issue of liability in a skiing accident case in *Gilsenan v Gunning*[15].

That a breach of the laws of the game should not necessarily be sufficient, however, to establish liability as a matter of law is surely self evident. As has been seen above, the duty owed by a competitor is directed towards avoiding the risk of injury which his fellow competitors are not taken to have accepted by their very participation. The law cannot confine its assumption that competitors accept particular risks to risks of injury inflicted by action falling strictly within the laws of the game. Were the position otherwise, injuries caused by fouls of one form or another would be expected to give rise to legal liability with a frequency which would be quite intolerable. Foul play is, therefore, regarded *up to a point* as being part and parcel of the game, or as part of 'the culture of sport' and as something which the participants have to accept. No one would sensibly suggest that the duty of care owed by one competitor to another should extend to a duty never to commit a foul. There must come a point, however, where a line has to be drawn beyond which the risk of injury should not have to be accepted. Precisely where such line should be drawn is incapable of definition. All the circumstances of

13 See, for example, *Bolam v Friern Hospital Management Committee* [1957] 1 WLR 582; *Sidaway v Board of Governors of the Bethlem Royal Hospital* [1984] QB 493; *Gold v Haringey Health Authority* [1987] 2 All ER 888.
14 [1952] 2 All ER 789.
15 (1982)137 DLR (3d) 252.

each individual case will require to be considered. It is suggested, however, that in a game of high physical endeavour (such as rugby or football) it will be only in the case of a particularly bad foul, involving obviously blameworthy conduct[16], that it will be possible to prove a breach of the duty to take reasonable care by one of the participants in the game, thus rendering him liable for injury caused to a fellow competitor.

In certain sports, of course, part of the very object of the game is to land blows on one's opponent (with the inevitable consequence of causing injury of one form or another). Boxing is the obvious example. Plainly, in such circumstances, no action will lie in respect of such injury, at least where caused in accordance with the rules of the sport. A competitor in such a sport is taken to accept such risks, against which his opponent is not expected to guard. Once a competitor steps outside the rules (see the boxer Mike Tyson's bites of Evander Holyfield's ears) the potential arises for a possible claim. Thus, in *Lane v Holloway*[17], where the plaintiff challenged the defendant to a fight (after one of them had referred to the other's wife as a 'monkey faced tart'), in the course of which, however, the plaintiff was injured by a severe punch in the eye, the defendant was held liable, Lord Denning MR remarking that the defendant:

> '... went much too far in striking a blow *out of all proportion to the occasion.*'

Although that case was one where the cause of action was of assault and the discussion centred on the issue of consent[18], it is suggested that the concept of acting 'out of all proportion to the occasion' is a useful one when considering the nature and extent of a sportsman's liability to his opponents and fellow competitors. The point is that the further outside the rules of the game that a competitor goes, the more likely it is that he will be found to have committed an act the risk of which his fellow competitor should not be taken to have accepted as part and parcel of the sport or the culture thereof (and that he will be held liable for any injury caused by his actions) and the less likely it is that the injury will be regarded as having been caused by an ordinary incident of the game and as involving no breach of the duty to exercise reasonable care. In the context of competitive sport (in which things necessarily may happen very quickly and judgments are exercised in the 'flurry and excitement' of the contest), practical realities suggest that a participant has to act in flagrant breach of the rules (in a manner that is deliberate, reckless or at least foolhardy) before the courts are likely to show an inclination to fix him with liability for injuries caused.

The principles established in *Condon v Basi*[19], have been applied in recent times in two other well publicised football cases:

---

16 The temptation is to use terms such as 'recklessness', as was used by Diplock LJ in *Wooldridge v Sumner* (above). Such terms are apt, provided only that their use is not permitted to introduce confusion as to the extent of the duty owed. Such duty is always to exercise reasonable care in the circumstances. It is the circumstances of a particular sporting occasion which may sometimes require an element of recklessness to be proven if breach of that duty is to be established. See *Smoldon v Whitworth* [1997] ELR 115; on appeal [1997] ELR 249, CA.

17 [1968] 1 QB 379 at 388.

18 Whereas the question of consent is relevant in the tort of negligence (at least in the sporting context) to the practical content of the duty to take reasonable care, it may provide a defence to the tort of assault.

19 [1985] 1 WLR 866, above.

- In *Elliott v Saunders*[20], the Chelsea player Paul Elliott failed to establish that Dean Saunders, then of Liverpool, had acted with such a lack of care as to be in breach of his duty to exercise reasonable care in all the circumstances, when the defendant's tackle had severed the plaintiff's cruciate ligaments. In so holding, Drake J appeared to accept that the circumstances were such that the plaintiff would have had to have been able to establish that the defendant had been guilty of dangerous and reckless play to get home. He went on to accept the evidence of the defendant that he had raised his feet in the tackle at the last moment in an instinctive attempt to avoid probable serious injury to himself. Such instinctive reactions were not such as, in the learned judge's view, to give rise to liability in law, occurring as they did in the heat of battle. In following *Condon v Basi*, however, Drake J did not agree with the *obiter dictum* in that case that there might be a higher standard of care required of a player in, say, the Premier League than of a player in a local football match. The standard of care required in each case was the same, although, as he was at pains to point out, the nature and level of the match in question (and, accordingly, the standards of skill to be expected from the players) would form part of the factual context within which such standard fell to be applied. This is surely right.

- In *McCord v Swansea City Football Club*[1] Brian McCord, a former Stockport County player, succeeded in his claim that John Cornforth, captain of Swansea City, had acted negligently in challenging for a loose ball by sliding down onto one leg, whilst raising his other leg above the height of the ball. In the circumstances, Ian Kennedy J found that Mr Cornforth had acted in a way which was inconsistent with his taking reasonable care. The defendants were, accordingly, liable to the plaintiff for his broken leg which ended his professional career.

Similar principles apply in relation to sports where the activity involved is less strenuous or frenetic. In golf, for example, participants are required by the law to accept that wayward shots by others on the course constitute a risk which is part and parcel of the game and, within limits[2], has to be accepted.

Thus in *Clark v Welsh*[3], a player injured when a ball flew off the toe of another player's club had no redress, the offending player having been under no duty to prevent such an injury which derived from a risk inherent in the game itself[4].

On the other hand, in *Lewis v Buckpool Golf Club*[5], a wayward shot which struck a player on an adjacent green gave rise to liability in circumstances where the pursuer, a high handicap golfer (and therefore, perhaps, prone to

---

20 QB Transcript, 10 June 1994.
1   QB Transcript, 19 December 1996.
2   Such limits cannot be defined. Each case will depend upon all its circumstances. It is, however, suggested that the rules and etiquette of golf may often provide a guide as to what should and should not have to be accepted – see eg *Ellison v Rogers* [1968] 1 OR 501. Thus, for example, a player who drives before the party in front of him has cleared the green or has otherwise proceeded beyond his range is likely to receive scant consideration if his ball should strike and injure a player in such party – see eg *McVety v Mahoney* (1980) 25 AR 173.
3   1975 (4) SA 469; on appeal 1976 (3) SA 484.
4   See also *Feeney v Lyall* 1991 SLT 156n and *Potter v Carlisle and Cliftonville Golf Club Ltd* [1939] NI 114.
5   1993 SLT (Sh Ct) 43. See also *Ratcliffe v Whitehead* [1933] 3 WWR 447, *Whitefield v Barton* 1987 SCLR 259 and *Finnie v Ropponen* (1987) 40 CCLT 155.

poor shots), could easily have waited to allow the injured player to clear the green before hitting off the tee.

Similar principles apply elsewhere. In skiing, for example, certain dangers inherent in the sport, such as an occasional loss of control, have to be accepted. Thus in *Gilsenan v Gunning*[6] it was said:

> '... a skier's conduct has to be measured in relation to the circumstances of skiing ... It is in the light of the very nature of the sport that one must consider what the standard of care is that ought to be applied to skiers' conduct[7].'

Liability of sports promoters/organisers

The promoter or organiser of a sports event is not exempt from the obligation to exercise reasonable care which forms the foundation of the tort of negligence. In addition, however, he may face additional causes of action. In particular, if he is the occupier of the premises where the event is staged, an action against him may, in appropriate circumstances, be framed under the Occupiers' Liability Act 1957. Further, where the actions complained of are alleged to have interfered with another's use or enjoyment of land, or of some right in relation to land, the action may be framed in nuisance[8]. These additional causes of action will briefly be considered first.

NUISANCE

Whereas in a claim founded in negligence, the plaintiff's interest in avoiding injury is, in one sense, sacrosanct and the reasonableness of the defendant's actions is judged simply according to the steps which he could have taken to avoid causing injury to the plaintiff, in a claim founded in nuisance the reasonableness of the defendant's actions or activities are judged in balance with the rights of the plaintiff peaceably to enjoy (his) land. It is only if such actions or activities are adjudged unreasonable after balancing them against the defendant's competing interests that liability will be established. It is this balancing exercise which distinguishes nuisance from negligence[9]. As with negligence, however, all the circumstances have to be taken into account in judging the question of reasonableness. Particular considerations which are likely to be important include the extent, duration and seriousness of the alleged interference, the general nature of the locality and the ease with which the alleged interference might be curbed. Whether a nuisance has occurred will be a question of fact in each case.

6   (1982) 137 DLR (3d) 252 at 257. See also *Turanec v Ross* (1980) 21 BCLR 198.
7   To be pedantic, the court was guilty, in this passage, of confusing the *standard of care* (which was, as always, one of reasonableness) with the *practical content* of that duty in the circumstances of the case.
8   Where the rights infringed are to enjoyment of private land, the action is in private nuisance; where rights of access to or passage over the public highway are interfered with, the action lies in public nuisance.
9   For an examination of the distinctions between the torts of nuisance and negligence, see *The Wagon Mound (No 2)* [1967] 1 AC 617 at 639 and *Goldman v Hargrave* [1967] 1 AC 645 at 657.

In *Castle v St Augustine's Links Ltd*[10] damages were recovered by the plaintiff (who had the distinct advantage of represention by the 'dream team' of Sir Edward Marshall Hall KC and Norman Birkett) against a golf club as a result of being struck in the eye by a golf ball whilst using the highway adjacent to the course. The judge was influenced by his finding that balls had for some time and with regularity been sliced onto the highway in question.

On the other hand, in *Stone v Bolton*[11], the plaintiff, Bessie Stone, failed in her attempt to recover damages as a result of being struck by a cricket ball, on the grounds that there was no evidence that a cricket ball had ever previously hit or inconvenienced anyone on the road where the plaintiff had been standing. The fact that balls had previously, but only occasionally, been hit onto the road over a period of 30 years was insufficient to make the playing of cricket on the ground a public nuisance.

By contrast, in *Miller v Jackson*[12] the playing of cricket on a village green (which had been a feature of village life since the turn of the century) was held to amount to an actionable nuisance at the suit of the owners of an adjacent residence into whose garden balls had regularly been struck, even though the house in question was of relatively recent construction and had been acquired by the plaintiff only in 1972. Interestingly, however, in a dubious exercise of its discretion[13], the Court of Appeal discharged the injunction granted by Reeve J, the effect of which had been to prohibit further playing of cricket on the green, in deference to the interests of the other villagers. In this regard, the greater interest of the public was permitted to triumph over the hardship to individual householders, although damages were payable. Indeed, had the Court of Appeal felt able to do so, it would have determined that there was no actionable nuisance because the cricketers had been there well before the plaintiff. The court's hands were tied by binding authority, however, that such considerations did not provide a defence to a claim[14].

In either of the above cricket cases, the plaintiff's claims were additionally framed in negligence. Indeed, where physical injury is caused, it is likely that a claim in negligence will be determinative and that an additional claim founded in nuisance will add little to the plaintiff's prospects. The position may be different, however, where the interference alleged is through an assault upon the senses, for example by noise or smell. It is in such cases that the tort of nuisance is likely to be crucial.

Thus in *Stretch v Romford Football Club*[15], for example, the defendants were held liable for an actionable nuisance when they started speedway racing at their football stadium and, in *Kennaway v Thompson*[16], a motor-boat racing club was held liable in respect of the noise from its events[17].

---

10 (1922) 38 TLR 615.
11 [1949] 1 All ER 237 (affirmed on appeal as to nuisance, [1950] 1 KB 201, CA, and also on other grounds – [1951] AC 850, HL). See p 9 above.
12 [1977] QB 966.
13 See *Kennaway v Thompson* [1981] QB 88, below.
14 See *Sturges v Bridgman* (1879) 11 Ch D 852 and *Bliss v Hall* (1838) 4 Bing NC 183.
15 (1971) 115 Sol Jo 741.
16 [1981] QB 88.
17 Other examples include *Inchbald v Robinson* (1869) 4 Ch App 388 (circus); *Becker v Earl's Court Ltd* (1911) 56 Sol Jo 73 (a merry-go-round and other sideshows); *Thompson-Schwab v Costaki* [1956] 1 WLR 335 (brothel); *Dunton v Dover District Council* (1977) 76 LGR 87 (playground); *Laws v Florinplace* [1981] 1 All ER 659 (sex shop in a residential area).

THE OCCUPIERS' LIABILITY ACT 1957

The Occupiers' Liability Act 1957 imposes a duty of care on 'occupiers' of premises towards 'visitors' thereto. For this purpose, an 'occupier' is not simply someone in physical occupation but extends to anyone with control over the premises, and a 'visitor' includes anyone who comes lawfully onto the premises[18]. Thus the organiser or promoter of a sporting event, to the extent that he controls the venue where it takes place, owes a duty under the Act to everyone who attends the event, from competitors and spectators to broadcasters and vendors etc. Equally, it is not beyond the realms of possibility that, in appropriate circumstances, a sponsor or a governing body may have such a close involvement in the organisation of an event as to have sufficient control of the venue to be categorised as an occupier thereof for these purposes.

The duty owed by an occupier to a visitor is simply the 'common duty of care' namely:

'... a duty to take such care as in all the circumstances of the case is reasonable to see that the visitor will be reasonably safe in using the premises for the purposes for which he is invited or permitted to be there[19].'

It can be seen, therefore, that the scope of an occupier's duty is essentially the same as at common law[20], although the Act expressly articulates certain circumstances to be taken into account by providing[1] that an occupier must expect children to be less careful than adults and is entitled to expect people exercising their calling (including, it is suggested, sportsmen and women) to appreciate and guard against risks incidental thereto, where free to do so. Such circumstances are little more than common sense and are equally likely to be regarded as relevant in appropriate cases at common law.

Thus, for example, in *Morrell v Owen*[2], the organiser of a sporting event for the disabled was obliged to take account of the participants' disabilities in fulfilling its duty to take reasonable care for their safety, which duty (in its practical content) was accordingly more stringent than it otherwise would have been.

The correlation between the Act and the common law is further underlined by s 2(4)(a), which provides that a warning of danger will not absolve the occupier unless in all the circumstances the warning was enough to enable the visitor to be reasonably safe[3].

The duty extends to taking reasonable steps to protect visitors from forseeable risks of injury. Further, such risks may stem from the state of the premises itself or from the activities conducted thereon. This may be so even where the activities are unauthorised. In *Cunningham v Reading Football Club*

---

18 See ss 1(2) and 2(6) and, for example, *Wheat v Lacon & Co Ltd* [1966] AC 552. Trespassers are not covered by the Act (but see the Occupiers' Liability Act 1984 which accords limited rights to trespassers.)

19 See s 2(2).

20 See, for example, *Simms v Leigh Rugby Football Club Ltd* [1969] 2 All ER 923, in which a rugby league player failed in a claim both in negligence and under the Act, in respect of injuries sustained after being shunted by a tackle into a wall some seven yards from the touchline. See also *Gillmore v LCC* [1938] 4 All ER 331.

1 See s 2(3).

2 (1993) Times, 14 December.

3 See, for example, *Jones v Northampton Borough Council* (1990) Times, 2 May, where the defendant council was held not liable in respect of injuries caused at its sports centre through slipping on a wet floor during a game of five a side football, it having given due warning of the fact that water had leaked onto the floor.

Ltd[4], for example, a football club was held liable in claims by police officers injured whilst policing a match when fans ran amok. The fans in question had a violent reputation and trouble was manifestly foreseeable, and yet the club had taken no adequate steps to prevent them from obtaining missiles, in the form of pieces of concrete ripped from the terraces (which were in a poor state of repair). The fact that the degree of foreseeability was such that it was 'very probable' that the fans would seek to use such missiles, meant that the intervention of such fans in inflicting the injuries on the plaintiffs did not break the chain of causation between the club's breach of duty and the damage complained of[5].

Similarly, in *Hosie v Arbroath Football Club Ltd*[6], a football club was held liable in respect of injuries caused when a security door proved insufficiently robust to withstand the attentions of an unruly crowd which had surged at it.

NEGLIGENCE

The passages and citations above have shown how, when it comes to the liability of competitors in sport, fellow competitors and spectators are expected to accept the risks which are inherent in the particular sport. Promoters and organisers, on the other hand, are expected to take appropriate steps to minimise such risks where reasonably practicable, by the provision of safety measures of one form or another. For them, decisions affecting the safety of spectators and others are not taken in the flurry and excitement of the competition. On the contrary, the fact that the competitors cannot be expected to guard against such dangers as are inherent in such competition, is itself a feature of the circumstances which are likely to affect the extent to which the promoters or organisers may be expected themselves to provide appropriate protective measures. For example, whilst racing drivers are not expected to hold back from the extremes of their competitive endeavour in order to shelter the spectators from danger, the obvious dangers from their activities will be expected, within the limits of reasonable anticipation, to be minimised by sensible safety measures put into place by the promoters/organisers. The nature and extent of the measures required to be taken will depend upon all the circumstances, because, once again as always, the duty is simply to take such care as is reasonable to avoid forseeable accidents and injury. What amounts to reasonable care in each case will depend upon the context of the incident in question.

The position was well put in a New Zealand case, *Evans v Waitemata District Pony Club*[7], by Speight J:

> '... if a plaintiff is a paying customer at a spectator sport, there are certain duties owed to him by both organisers and competitors but those are not absolute. He may well have volunteered to accept such risks (for example, a flying cricket ball from a big hit) as no reasonable precautions on the part of the organiser or observation of care on the part of the competitor could be

4   (1992) 157 LG Rev 481.
5   See also *Home Office v Dorset Yacht Co Ltd* [1970] AC 1004; *Lamb v Camden London Borough Council* [1981] QB 625 and *Perl Ltd v Camden London Borough Council* [1984] QB 342.
6   1978 SLT 122.
7   [1972] NZLR 773 at 775. The case involved a claim by spectators at a pony club gymkhana who were injured when a tethered horse tethered to a fallen tree broke free and ran amok. The organisers were held liable for failing to provide a secure area where horses could be kept when not competing.

expected to prevent and such risks can be said to be within the type of danger that the customer is prepared to run. *But it must be apparent that a spectator[8] only recognises and accepts the risks which prudent management and control and sensible competition cannot be expected to avoid* ... Did the organisers fail to take sufficient precautions to make the area and the operations as safe as reasonable care and skill could achieve in the circumstances including the nature of the contest and the known vagaries of the ... animals and competitors likely to be engaged?'[9]

Further, according to the general principles of negligence enunciated by the House of Lords in *Donoghue v Stevenson*[10], the duty is owed to all those who ought reasonably to be in contemplation as being affected by the acts in question.

Thus, for example, in *Alcock v Chief Constable of South Yorkshire*[11], a case arising out of the Hillsborough disaster (at the home of Sheffield Wednesday Football Club), where 95 spectators at an FA Cup semi-final football match were crushed to death as a result of poor crowd control procedures, it was held by the House of Lords that a duty of care might be owed in appropriate (but limited) circumstances to prevent nervous shock (in the form of a recognisable psychiatric illness) even to those not present at the scene of such a disaster but who were linked to those who died by close 'ties of love and affection'[12]. As Lord Keith said[13]:

'It is common knowledge that such ties exist, and reasonably foreseeable that those bound by them may in certain circumstances be at real risk of psychiatric illness if the loved one is injured or put in peril ... .'[14]

In the event most of the claims failed, on the grounds either that the plaintiffs' relationship with those who died were insuffiently close or that their proximity to the disaster itself (through watching television, which generally did not dwell on depictions of the suffering of identifiable individuals) was too remote.

In *Hall v Brooklands Auto-Racing Club*[15], spectators injured when two racing cars crashed and left the track claimed damages from the organisers. In dismissing their claims, the Court of Appeal drew a helpful distinction between 'the dangers of the place' and 'the dangers of the entertainment'. The organisers of a sporting event are taken to owe a duty (in negligence, as occupiers and even, in relation to a spectator, under the contract by which

---

8 It is suggested, further, that this could equally be said of a competitor.

9 See also *Green v Perry* (1955) 94 CLR 606 and *Moloughney v Wellington Racing Club* [1935] NZLR 800.

10 [1932] AC 562, above.

11 [1992] 1 AC 310.

12 Another case arising from the Hillsborough disaster was *Hicks v Chief Constable of South Yorkshire* [1992] 2 All ER 65, in which the House of Lords rejected claims for pre death pain and suffering on behalf of two sisters who had been killed, in the absence of evidence of any specific injury suffered before the girls lost consciousness.

13 At 110.

14 The limitations of a claim in such circumstances, however, were made clear by the House of Lords. In particular, the close ties of love and affection must be proved by positive evidence and the fact of a particular blood or other relationship will not necessarily suffice alone, save perhaps in the case of the closest relationships such as a parent/child or husband/wife. Further, the psychiatric illness must derive through sight or hearing of the acts complained of (or their immediate results) – in the circumstances of this case, even exposure to pictures of the scene generally on the television was not enough, the broadcasts having avoided pictures of suffering by recognisable individuals.

15 [1933] 1 KB 205.

the spectator purchases his ticket to secure his right of entry) to take reasonable steps to guard against foreseeable risks from the condition of the premises where the event is staged, even where the danger in the condition of such premises derives from the fact that the event is being staged. In relation to the event or entertainment itself, however, in common with competitors themselves, the practical content of the duty to exercise reasonable care is fashioned by the tacit acceptance by all concerned of the risks which are incidental thereto. The duty in relation to risks from the conduct of a sporting event or occasion (as distinct from the condition of the premises in which the event is staged) was held not to extend to:

'... an obligation to protect against a danger incident to the entertainment which any reasonable spectator foresees and of which he takes the risk.'[16]

It was this principle which determined the result in *Murray v Harringay Arena Ltd*[17], where a spectator (a six year old boy) failed to recover damages for injuries sustained by a flying puck at an ice-hockey match. The arena in which the match had taken place was held to be as safe as was reasonably to be expected and the plaintiff's injury to have been the result of a danger inherent in the sport itself which the plaintiff was taken to have accepted and against which the organisers could not reasonably have been expected to guard.

Contrast, however, *Klyne v Bellegarde*[18], where a spectator at an ice-hockey match recovered damages for injuries sustained (from a hockey stick) whilst standing in an aisle alongside the rink which had no protective guards above the side boards. In these circumstances the organisers were held to have failed to take such steps as would reasonably have been expected to provide spectators with an arena where they would be protected from the obvious dangers to which they were liable to be exposed.

In *Harrison v Vincent*[19] the Court of Appeal found that the organisers of a motor cycle combination race were negligent and liable for the injuries caused to the plaintiff (the passenger in the first defendant's combination) when the first defendant's machine suffered brake failure, the first defendant missed a gear and the machine left the course via a slip road only to collide with a recovery vehicle which was protruding into the plaintiff's escape route some 40 metres up it. The brake failure was held to be the result of the first defendant's negligent preparation of the machine (for which the first defendant and his employers were liable). Further, however, the organisers were also held liable on the basis that they ought to have contemplated that a competitor might leave the course and need the slip road and that, in allowing the recovery vehicle (itself, no doubt, part of the safety regime) to park in a position of relative danger, they were in breach of their duty to take reasonable care. The injuries sustained by the plaintiff were not the result of any risk which was inherent in the sport which the plaintiff should be taken to have accepted[20]. Rather, they derived from the condition of the premises on which the event was staged through the dangerous positioning of the recovery vehicle. Significantly, the rules of the international federation

16 Per Scrutton LJ at 217.
17 [1951] 2 KB 529.
18 [1978] 6 WWR 743.
19 [1982] RTR 8.
20 See Watkins LJ at 19.

under whose auspices the race was organised provided for escape roads to remain unobstructed for 100 metres. As Sir John Arnold P said[1]:

> 'It is not of course conclusive that, because there is a general rule of this sort, every failure to comply with its terms in every circumstance would necessarily be negligent. Nevertheless, it is relevant to the matter that, if one is not to comply with such a rule, at least one must have a convincing reason for not doing so.'

It should be noted that many sporting and other bodies, in addition, publish codes of practice for the safe conduct of particular types of sporting event. It is likely that the extent of any compliance or non-compliance with any such relevant code of practice will be a material consideration in appropriate cases. Such codes may well be regarded as an indication of acceptable conduct and a measure of the kind of safety measures which reasonably ought to be taken to provide protection from foreseeable risks. In particular, a contravened provision in a code may make it difficult for an organiser to plead that an injury was caused by a risk which was inherent in the sport which spectators and others were obliged to accept and against which there was no obligation, in exercise of a duty of reasonable care, to guard[2].

Sir John Arnold P, in *Harrison v Vincent*[3], went on to make it clear that the fact that no other similar accident had ever occurred was no reason for not following the rule of the federation. In passing he made it clear that the test of reasonableness requires a person to take steps to reduce or eliminate real risks of which he knows or ought to know subject only to the qualification

> '... that it is justifiable not to take steps to eliminate a real risk if it is small and if the circumstances are such that a reasonable man, careful of the safety of his neighbour, would think it right to neglect it[4].'

It is suggested, however, that this qualification to the general principle (that risks which are reasonably foreseeable, and which are not to be regarded simply as the normal incidents of the sport in question, should be guarded against where practicable) should be treated with caution. It will be rare indeed that it will be held justifiable not to take steps to guard against a 'real risk'[5] and it may be that the better distinction is between 'real' or significant risks and minor risks. Thus the position was expressed, for example, by Lord Dunedin in *Fardon v Harcourt-Rivington*[6] in the following terms:

> 'If the possibility of the danger emerging is reasonably apparent, then to take no precautions is negligence; but if the possibility of danger emerging is only a mere possibility which would never occur to the mind of a

---

1 At 15.
2 See, for example, *Wright v Cheshire County Council* [1952] 2 All ER 789 and *Smoldon v Whitworth* [1997] ELR 115; on appeal [1997] ELR 249, CA.
3 Above.
4 Per Arnold P quoting from *The Wagon Mound (No 2)* [1967] 1 AC 617 at 642. See also *Bolton v Stone* [1951] AC 850 (above). See also *Simms v Leigh Rugby Club Ltd* [1969] 2 All ER 923, where a rugby club was held not liable for a player's broken leg, and where it was said (obiter) that even if there had been evidence to show that the injury had been caused by contact with the concrete retaining wall some seven yards from the touchline, the club would not have been liable as the risk was sufficiently improbable that it was not necessary to guard against it (note, however the words of disapproval of Arnold P in *Harrison v Vincent* (above)).
5 See for example *Whitefield v Barton* 1987 SCLR 259.
6 [1932] All ER Rep 81.

reasonable man, then there is no neglience in not having taken extraordinary precautions.'

Thus, for example, in *Gillon v Chief Constable of Strathclyde Police*[7], it was because the risk, although foreseeable, was minimal, that a police sergeant watching the spectators at a football match failed to recover damages in respect of injuries caused when a player, in losing control of the ball, cannoned off the pitch and collided with her.

Similarly, in *Bolton v Stone*[8], Bessie Stone's negligence claim in respect of her injuries after being struck by a cricket ball hit from the ground onto the highway failed because the risk of any such injury had been minimal, the evidence being that balls had only rarely reached such highway and that no one had previously been injured or otherwise inconvenienced[9].

Liability of coaches/referees/supervisors etc

Because a claim in negligence is founded upon the simple principle that the law requires the exercise of reasonable care to avoid injuring one's 'neighbour' and identifies one's neighbour as anyone who ought reasonably to be in contemplation as being affected by one's acts or omissions, it is immediately apparent that coaches, other supervisors and the like will be expected to exercise reasonable care in imparting their knowledge and skills to their charges.

For example, in *Pawlak v Doucette & Reinks*[10], the owner of a motor boat was held to owe a novice water skier a duty of care where he had taken it upon himself to supervise the water skiing activities.

Similarly, an individual who, for example, takes it upon himself to coach a pupil on how to effect a proper (and, therefore, 'safe') rugby tackle may expose himself to legal liability if he gets things wrong with the result that his charge is injured in a match. An example of such a case (which, however, failed on the facts) is *Van Oppen v Clerk to the Bedford Charity Trustees*[11] where a schoolboy unsuccessfully claimed damages from his school for injuries sustained in a rugby tackle, on the basis that he had never been taught how to tackle properly. Indeed that case suggests, rightly in view of the nature of the relationships involved between coaches and players (particularly where the players are young pupils to whom the coaches are, to some extent, 'in loco parentis'), that a coach may be liable through failure to give appropriate instruction (negligence by omission) as well as in the more obvious case of giving advice which is wrong. Thus, for example, a weightlifting coach who fails to advise as to the way in which to lift heavy weights so as to minimise the risk of back injury may find himself exposed to

---

7 (1996) Times, 22 November.
8 [1951] AC 850, above.
9 Compare *Miller v Jackson* [1977] QB 966, where the decision went the other way, the evidence being that balls were regularly hit out of the ground. In the circumstances it was held that the risk of injury had been of such significance as to have required additional protective measures. Equally, in *Lamond v Glasgow Corpn* 1968 SLT 291, liability was established in respect of injuries caused by a wayward golf ball, the evidence being that balls were frequently hit from the course onto a disused railway line (even though the plaintiff's was the first recorded accident).
10 [1985] 2 WWR 588.
11 [1990] 1 WLR 235.

liability when his charge sustains injury through the use of an unsafe technique. Hence, a schoolboy who broke his neck when diving from a starting block into the shallow end of a swimming pool succeeded in a claim for damages against his PE teacher who had failed to give him appropriate instruction on how safely to effect such a dive[12].

Similarly, in *Hedley v Cuthbertson*[13], a professional mountain guide was held liable for the death of his fellow climber because of his failure to take adequate safety precautions when proceeding with a manoeuvre. The decision was received with some dismay in the worlds of rock/mountain climbing and other inherently dangerous sports, partly because the manoeuvre was made urgent as a result of a perceived risk from a threatened rock fall. The basis of the judge's decision appears to have been his finding that the defendant had overestimated the potential danger posed by a rock fall, which (the judge also found) was unlikely. In the circumstances, the judge took the view that the guide's conduct had fallen below the standard to be expected of a competent mountain guide in the circumstances. In doing so, he was careful to point out that his decision was founded upon the special facts of the case, and ought not to be regarded as liable to open the floodgates to similar claims.

In Canada, the courts have equated the duty of a teacher-instructor to the standard reasonably to be expected of a parent. In a case where a pupil suffered a catastrophic accident during a gymnastics class, which was poorly supervised[14], the duty was expressed as follows:

> '... [the] common law duty to take care of this pupil during this activity in the manner of a reasonable and careful parent, taking into account the judicial modification of the reasonable and careful parent test to allow for the larger than family size of the physical education class and the supraparental expertise commanded of a gymnastics instructor.'[15]

A striking example of the application of the principles of negligence in this area is provided by the well publicised case of the referee held liable for injuries sustained by a front row forward in a collapsed scrummage in a rugby union colts game, *Smoldon v Whitworth*[16]. The publicity which that case earned has lead to a degree of anxiety, not to say hysteria, amongst referees up and down the country, which it is suggested, is largely misplaced. On the facts as found by the judge at first instance, the circumstances which lead to his finding of liability against the referee, which finding was upheld by the Court of Appeal, were extreme indeed. Liability was established only by reason of a combination of circumstances, which included the facts that:

(a)   the game in question was a colts (under 19) game;
(b)   the laws of the game, as applied to colts, had been specifically revised by the International Rugby Football Board to reduce the risk of such injuries, in particular by requiring that scrummages should be required to form according to a defined sequence of crouch-touch-pause-engage;

---

12 See *Gannon v Rotherham Metropolitan Borough Council* (6 February 1991, unreported). Interestingly, he also succeeded against the Amateur Swimming Association for failing to issue (to instructors) appropriate warnings as to relevant dangers.
13 QB Division, Dyson J, (20 June 1997, unreported).
14 *Thornton v School District No 57, Board of School Trustees* (1976) 73 DLR (3d) 35 at 57.
15 See also *Williams v Eady* (1893) 10 TLR 41, CA.
16 [1997] ELR 115 (Curtis J); on appeal [1997] ELR 249, CA.

(c)   the International Board and the defendant referee's own Society of Referees had issued, respectively, directives and minutes emphasising the importance of correctly following the crouch-touch-pause-engage procedure and the dangers inherent in not doing so[17];

(d)   prior to the scrummage in which the plaintiff sustained his injury, the referee in question had failed to apply and enforce those revised laws properly and the scrums had been allowed to 'come in hard' and this had lead to in excess of twenty collapsed scrummages[18];

(e)   the referee had failed to take appropriate steps to enforce the laws, even in the face of a warning from one of his touch judges that someone would get hurt if he did not step in and in the face of shouts from spectators and complaints from certain of the players.

The case was, therefore, an extreme one on the facts and should not lead to a flurry of referees prematurely hanging up their whistles. What is important about the case is that it underlines the fact that the principles of negligence are of universal application and that, accordingly, referees are not immune from their application[19]. As the Court of Appeal said:

'The case ... is also of concern to many who fear that the judgment for the plaintiff will emasculate and enmesh in unwelcome legal toils a game which gives pleasure to millions. But we cannot resolve the issues argued before us on the basis of sympathy or personal predilection. We must instead endeavour to apply established legal principles, so far as applicable in this novel field, in order to draw on that public wisdom by which the deficiencies of private understanding are to be supplied.'

The Court of Appeal went on, however, to underline once again the crucial fact that the established legal principles require that the factual context within which particular events take place will inform the content of any duty to take reasonable care. For this reason, it did not accept as well founded the argument that a finding in favour of the plaintiff would open the floodgates to numerous claims by injured players. On the contrary, the Court of Appeal warned that it would be difficult ever to establish liability:

'The level of care required is that which is appropriate in all the circumstances, and the circumstances are of crucial importance. Full account must be taken of the factual context in which a referee exercises his functions, and he could not be properly held liable for errors of judgment, oversights or lapses of which any referee might be guilty in the context of a fast moving and vigorous contest. The threshold of liability is a high one. It will not easily be crossed ... [the learned trial judge] did not intend to open the door to a plethora of claims by players against referees, and it would be deplorable if that were the result. In our view that result should not follow provided all concerned appreciate how difficult it is for any plaintiff to establish that a referee failed to exercise such care and skill as was

---

17 Interestingly, the Staffordshire Rugby Union Society of Referees had previously expressly recognised the risk that a referee might be held legally liable in negligence for any injuries caused if the procedures were not properly enforced.

18 Significantly, the defendant referee himself accepted in evidence that 25 collapsed scrummages (he did not accept there had been so many, but his evidence was rejected by the judge) would suggest that the laws were not being enforced and that he had lost control of the game.

19 It ought to come as no surprise that, in *Smoldon v Whitworth*, the judge expressly found that a referee does owe a duty of care to the players in the game under his charge. Indeed, the point had not been in issue between the parties.

reasonably to be expected in the circumstances of a hotly contested game of rugby football ...'

In a further passage of unquestionable logic, the Court of Appeal also distinguished the practical content of the duty of reasonable care as owed by a referee to the players from that owed by, say, a competitor to a spectator (as in *Wooldridge v Sumner*[20] and *Wilks v Cheltenham Home Guard Motor Cycle and Light Car Club*[1]):

'In [the latter] cases it was recognised that a sporting competitor, properly intent on winning the contest, was (and was entitled to be) all but oblivious of spectators. It therefore followed that he would have to be shown to have very blatantly disregarded the safety of spectators before he could be held to have failed to exercise such care as was reasonable in all the circumstances. The position of a referee vis-à-vis the players is not the same as that of a participant in a contest vis-à-vis a spectator. One of his responsibilities is to safeguard the safety of the players. So, although the legal duty is the same in the two cases, the practical content of the duty differs according to the quite different circumstances.'

It follows that, as always, all the circumstances must be taken into consideration when it is sought to hold a referee liable for injury sustained during the course of a game. As the Court of Appeal made clear, the 'threshold of liability' is a high one. Referees may take comfort from the fact that, if they know the laws of their game and simply seek to apply them in a reasonable manner, they should have little to fear[2]. In particular, as has already been seen in relation to the liability of competitors between themselves, an individual competitor is taken to have accepted the risk of injury occurring in the ordinary run of the game, even as a result of all bar the more serious and flagrant of fouls. Similarly, it seems clear that in ordinary circumstances a player will be likely to be able legitimately to complain of errors by the referee in only the clearest cases of incompetence[3]. But it has to be said that the age or other significant attributes of the players being refereed, is manifestly one of the circumstances to be taken into account in determining whether or not the referee has acted reasonably in all the circumstances – there is plainly less scope for the argument that a player must be taken to have accepted certain risks where the player is young and still learning generally about the game being played. In such a case the referee has a particular responsibility to see that the players in his charge are reasonably safe and are given appropriate protection. The same applies wherever the activities of children are conducted under supervision, in particular during school or other similar sporting activities[4]. Similarly, in a contact sport, where an adult coach participates in a demonstration or a practice game, his duty of care must take appropriate account of the difference in size and strength between himself and his students[5].

20 [1963] 2 QB 43, above.
1 [1971] 1 WLR 668, above.
2 A clear lesson to be derived from the decision, however, is that referees should know the laws and be aware of the dangers inherent in a failure to apply them.
3 See for example *Carabba v Anacortes School District No 103* 435 P 2d 936 (1967) and *Kline v OID Assocs Inc* 609 NE 2d 564 (1992).
4 See, for example, *Gibbs v Barking Corpn* [1936] 1 All ER 115; *Ralph v LCC* (1947) 111 JP 548; *Wright v Cheshire County Council* [1952] 2 All ER 789; *Conrad v Inner London Education Authority* (1967) 111 Sol Jo 684; *Fowles v Bedfordshire County Council* [1996] ELR 51 and *Thornton v Trustees of School District No 57* (1976) 57 DLR (3d) 438.
5 See for example, *Affutu-Nartoy v Clarke* (1984) Times, 9 February.

Volenti non fit injuria

The maxim '*volenti non fit injuria*' describes a defence to a claim in circumstances where it is shown that the plaintiff had consented to the breach of the duty of care which is alleged and had agreed to waive his right of action in respect thereof. It can be seen, therefore, that the defence is founded upon the concept of consent. Further, such consent may be express, but is usually implied from particular circumstances.

It is suggested that the maxim is not often likely to have any application to claims (at least those founded in negligence) in sporting contexts of the kind discussed in the preceding paragraphs. This is simply because, as has already been seen, the concept of consent or the acceptance of particular risks is already inherent in the identification of the practical content of the duty to exercise reasonable care in all the circumstances. Thus, as has been seen, in a sporting contest of one form or another, a competitor's duty to exercise reasonable care does not require him to avoid risks which are part and parcel of the game and its culture, such risks being taken as having been accepted (and consented to) by those willingly taking part in (or watching) the very same contest. It follows that, where such a risk materialises and results in injury, no breach of duty will be established to which the maxim '*volenti non fit injuria*' is needed to provide a defence. Further, if a breach of duty is established, the plaintiff will already have shown that the defendant's actions had gone beyond the indefinable line distinguishing between what was and was not part and parcel of the game to be accepted by all participants and that, accordingly, he had not consented thereto or accepted the risk of injury thereby.

It followed, for example, in the 'referee's case', *Smoldon v Whitworth*[6], that the Court of Appeal gave short shrift to the defendant's alternative defence that, in the event that he was held to have been in breach of duty by allowing continual collapsed scrums, the plaintiff had consented to the risk of injury of the type sustained by him by voluntarily playing in the front row of the scrummage and thereby participating in the collapses:

> '... this argument is unsustainable. The plaintiff had of course consented to the ordinary incidents of a game of rugby football of the kind in which he was taking part. Given, however, that the rules were framed for the protection of him and other players in the same position, he cannot possibly be said to have consented to a breach of duty on the part of the official whose duty it was to apply the rules and ensure so far as possible that they were observed.'

The point is that, whereas a competitor or participant accepts the risks which are inherent within his sport and accordingly negligence will not be established by a failure to avoid such risks, such a competitor or participant does not, through his participation, accept untoward risks, that is risks which are not inherent within (or 'part and parcel of') the sport and its culture.

There is no basis, therefore, for saying that a competitor or participant must be taken to have accepted the risk of injury caused by neligence. Thus in *White v Blackmore*[7], a case involving a claim by the dependents of a spectator killed whilst watching a jalopy race, Lord Denning MR said:

6 [1997] ELR 115; on appeal [1997] ELR 249, CA, see above.
7 [1972] 2 QB 651 at 663.

'No doubt the visitor takes on himself the risks inherent in motor-racing, but he does not take on himself the risk of injury due to the defaults of the organisers.'[8].

The Court of Appeal in *Smoldon* went on, however, to give an indication of a particular set of circumstances in which a '*volenti*' defence might yet call for consideration. If the plaintiff had been identified as a prime culprit in causing the scrummage to collapse, then it might have required some consideration as to whether or not, by his actions, he should have been taken to have consented to the risk of injury and to have waived his right of action against the referee for breach of his duty of care[9].

Exemption clauses

In certain sporting relationships and the potential liabilities arising therefrom, it may be necessary to consider the provisions of the Unfair Contract Terms Act 1977, which target 'business liabilities' namely liabilities arising from things done by a person in the course of a business (whether his own or someone else's) or resulting from the occupation of premises for business purposes[10].

Section 2 is directed at liability for negligence[11] and provides:

'(1)   A person cannot by reference to any contract term or to a notice given to persons generally or to particular persons exclude or restrict his liability for death or personal injury resulting from negligence.
(2)   In the case of other loss or damage, a person cannot so exclude or restrict his liability for negligence except in so far as the term or notice satisfies the requirement of reasonableness ... .'

Section 2 of the Occupiers' Liability Act 1984, however, introduced an amendment by providing that:

'Liability of an occupier ... for breach of an obligation or duty towards a person obtaining access to the premises for recreational or educational purposes, being liability for loss or damage suffered by reason of the dangerous state of the premises, is not a business liability of the occupier unless granting that person such access for the purpose concerned falls within the business of the occupier.'

It should be noted, however, that this exemption will not apply to the conduct of sporting events and activities as a business but will only catch the gratuitous use of land for recreational activity, in which case the fact that the occupier carries on some unrelated business will not prevent him from excluding his liability. Further, even in that event, the only liability which may be excluded or limited is for loss or damage arising by reason of the dangerous state of the premises.

8   See also *Cleghorn v Oldham* (1927) 43 TLR 465.
9   Query whether in such circumstances, however, the referee would still have been held to be in breach. Arguably the concept of consent, as used to define the content of his duty in the circumstances, might simply have been extended so as to absolve him from any obligation to the plaintiff in the first place, to take account of the fact that, in the circumstances, 'the game' which the plaintiff was choosing to play was a game which ignored the relevant laws relating to set scrummages.
10 See s 1(3).
11 For this purpose, 'negligence' means breach of any obligation, by contract or at common law, to take reasonable care or exercise reasonable skill and includes the common duty of care under the Occupiers' Liability Act 1957. See s 1(1).

Thus, in the case of professional sport at least, and wherever sport is being conducted as a business[12], liability in negligence for personal injury or death may not be excluded or restricted. This will apply, for example, to a sports promoter or event organiser[13], to the occupier of a particular sports stadium or other venue, to individual athletes or competitors, to coaches, referees governing bodies and, indeed, to anyone who potentially may have a liability to another in negligence.

In relation to negligence liabilities other than death and personal injury, exclusions and limitations of liability are only permitted to the extent that they satisfy the 'requirement of reasonableness'. This is defined in s 11 as follows:

'(1)   In relation to a contract term, the requirement of reasonableness ... is that the term shall have been a fair and reasonable one to be included having regard to the circumstances which were, or ought reasonably to have been, known to or in the contemplation of the parties when the contract was made ... .
(3)   In relation to a notice (not being a notice having contractual effect), the requirement of reasonableness ... is that it should be fair and reasonable to allow reliance on it, having regard to all the circumstances obtaining when the liability arose or (but for the notice) would have arisen....'

In determining whether a particular exclusion or limitation may be relied upon, a distinction is drawn between contractual provisions, which are judged for their reasonableness by reference to the circumstances when the contract was agreed, and other notices, which are judged according to the circumstances obtaining at the time of the alleged breach of duty. Further, no additional guidance is given as to the criteria to be considered when determining whether or not a provision satisfies the requirement of reasonableness as so defined[14] save that, by s 11(4), it is provided that where the provision purports to limit liability to a specified sum of money, particular consideration should be given to the defendant's available resources and to whether it was open to him to take out insurance. It is suggested that the relative extent to which insurance cover is readily available to the respective parties (otherwise than at prohibitive cost or on unreasonable terms) is something which will always be relevant to the requirement of reasonableness, as will such matters as the parties' respective resources, the extent to which the relevant provision was drawn to the attention of the affected party and the extent to which he had had any real

12 Amateur sport is not necessarily exempt from the provisions of the Act. Although the sportspersons themselves may be truly amateur (as distinct from in name only), nevertheless their performance may be carried out in the course of another's business. Thus, for example, an amateur team may perform at a venue to which spectators pay to gain admission. Certain circumstances may give rise to real issues as to whether or not actions take place 'in the course of a business'. The extent to which, for example, a charity may be regarded as conducting a business is open to question.
13 Thus the Unfair Contract Terms Act 1977 would, if enacted at the time, have changed the result of *White v Blackmore* [1972] 2 QB 651, where the organisers of a jallopy race avoided liability for the death of a spectator by reliance upon the exemption notices which they had posted at the scene.
14 This is in marked contrast to the requirement of reasonableness as applied, by ss 6 and 7, to contracts for the sale and supply of goods, where particular (non exclusive) guideline criteria are spelt out in Sch 2. They include such things as the parties' relative strengths of bargaining power, whether the provision was known (or ought reasonably to have been known) to the affected party and whether or not the affected party had any option but to agree to the contract.

option over exposing himself to the risk which the provision was designed to cover. As with the duty to exercise reasonable care itself, so the 'requirement of reasonableness' is sufficiently flexible to be capable of being moulded to suit the circumstances of any particular case. Indeed, the concept of reasonableness is such that no clear and binding principles beyond the wording of the Act itself can be derived from the cases[15].

Legislation for the protection of spectators and others

In addition to the common law rights of individual spectators and others to sue for injuries caused whilst following their chosen sport, stadium and other venue owners are required by statute to adhere to certain safety standards. Generally, breach of such health and safety legislation does not give rise directly to a cause of action at the suit of an injured individual, but the standards set by such statutes, and any subordinate legislation and codes laid down thereunder, may in appropriate circumstances be of crucial importance in setting particular benchmarks of good practice, according to which allegations of negligence and other actionable breaches of duty fall to be judged.

There are many applicable health and safety statutes and other regulations which are not specifically targeted at sport but which, nevertheless, are of sufficiently wide ranging application as to bring the conduct of sporting activity within their general sphere of application. The prime example is the Health and Safety at Work Act 1974[16] and its subordinate regulations. Such general legislation is not covered by specific discussion in this work, there being many specialist works to which the reader may refer if required[17]. Instead, this section seeks to provide the briefest of outlines on the more important aspects of the statutory health and safety regime which are specifically directed, in one form or another, at sport itself. As will be seen, most of the more significant legislation in this field has sprung from the experience of a number of catastrophic disasters[18].

In 1971 a stand collapsed at Ibrox Park, the home of Glasgow Rangers Football Club. Some 66 spectators died. As a result of this and other footballing disasters, and pursuant to the Wheatley Report, the Safety of

---

15 In this regard, see *George Mitchell (Chesterhall) Ltd v Finney Lock Seeds Ltd* [1983] QB 284, per Lord Denning MR at 299.

16 This Act imposes duties on employers, employees and the self employed. As its name implies, it is primarily concerned with safety within the workplace, but the duties imposed are not owed simply to employees and other 'workers' but extend to members of the public and others who may be affected by the work operation. It follows, for example, that where sport is concerned, spectators, competitors, officials, contractors and many others are all liable to be embraced by the protection contemplated by the Act.

17 The Sports Council also issues a Guidance Note on Health and Safety [ISBN 1-86078-0091] which provides a useful introduction to some of the relevant general legislation.

18 A further example in addition to those mentioned below is the Activity Centres (Young Persons' Safety) Act 1995 and its subordinate legislation (in particular SI 1996/771 and SI 1996/772) which was the product of the tragedy in Lyme Bay in March 1993 when four young canoeists on an adventure course drowned as a result of inadequate safety precautions. The legislation established a licensing regime, with effect from 16 April 1996, designed to ensure that the provision of adventure activities for young people is provided only by those with appropriate and up-to-date qualifications and experience.

Sports Grounds Act 1975 was introduced, with the aim of ensuring the safety of spectators at major sporting venues, most particularly football matches. As subsequently amended[19], it seeks to deliver its aim principally by setting up a detailed system of licensing and control[20], under which, in particular, the Secretary of State is able to 'designate'[1] any sports ground with a capacity in excess of 10,000, so as to require it to hold a current safety certificate issued by the local authority. By s 17, a sports ground is defined, for this purpose, as any place where sports or other competitive activities take place in the open air, and where accommodation has been provided for spectators, consisting of artificial structures or natural structures artificially modified for the purpose. Numerous designating orders have been made[2], so that, in particular, all qualifying football league, rugby union, rugby league and cricket grounds are now designated under the Act. Safety certificates for designated sports grounds may be 'general' or 'special'[3], the latter being concerned with particular events or a series of events. The Act grants wide information-seeking powers to the local authority[4], who may require specific measures to be taken to bring a ground up to an acceptable standard and attach other conditions[5] to the grant of a safety certificate. In practice, any safety certificate issued by the local authority will establish the maximum number of spectators who may be admitted to the venue in question. Further, the local authority may issue a 'prohibition notice'[6] in respect of a sports ground, or part of it, in the event that it considers that the admission of spectators involves or will involve serious risks. Such a notice may prohibit or simply restrict the admission of spectators pending the carrying out of specified remedial measures. In fulfilling its functions and giving consideration to the safety standards of individual sports grounds, a local authority will have regard to the non statutory code 'Guide to Safety at Sports Grounds' (generally known as 'the Green Guide'), the latest edition of which was published in 1990[7]. Such a code, as its name suggests, gives general guidance on safety matters and is likely to have significant evidential value in negligence and other similar claims.

Unfortunately, the Safety of Sports Grounds Act 1975, in its original form, proved ineffective to prevent the fire disaster at Bradford Football

19 In particular, the Act was amended by the Fire Safety and Safety of Places of Sport Act 1987.
20 In addition, by s 12, it creates a number of criminal offences where sports grounds are operated in a manner which contravenes the requirements of the regime established pursuant to the system of licensing and control.
1 See s 1(1) of the Act.
2 See SI 1976/1264, SI 1977/1323, SI 1978/1091, SI 1979/1022, SI 1980/1021, SI 1981/949, SI 1982/1052, 1983/962, SI 1984/942, SI 1985/1063 amended by SI 1988/1975 and SI 1996/2648, SI 1985/1064 and SI 1986/1296 both amended by SI 1992/607, SI 1987/1689, SI 1988/1975, SI 1992/607, SI 1996/4999 and SI 1996/2648.
3 See s 1(3).
4 See, for example, s 11 of the Act which empowers the Local Authority to enter a sports ground at any reasonable time for the purposes of inspection of it or making inquiries relating to it or examining/copying attendance and health and safety records.
5 By s 2, the Local Authority may impose such terms and conditions as it deems necessary to secure 'reasonable safety' at the sports ground in question, including terms and conditions which involve alterations and additions thereto. The power to attach conditions is a general one, but sub-s (3) specifically contemplates conditions as to the keeping of records relating to the attendance of spectators and to health and safety.
6 Under s 10, as substituted by the Fire Safety and Safety of Places of Sport Act 1987, s 23(1).
7 HMSO, ISBN 0-11-341001-8.

Club on 11 May 1985, in which 56 spectators died. This, together with a riot at Birmingham City Football Club's ground also in 1985, led to the Popplewell (interim) Report[8] and, after the Heysel Stadium tragedy in Brussels (again in 1985) in which 38 people were killed and 100 injured when spectators rioted, to the Popplewell (final) Report[9]. Popplewell J's conclusions, in turn, resulted in the Fire Safety and Safety of Places of Sport Act 1987 which amended the 1975 Act and the Fire Precautions Act 1971. In particular, by s 26, it introduced an important requirement, of wide potential significance, for a safety certificate for an individual stand[10] at any form of sports ground which is not 'designated' under the Safety of Sports Grounds Act 1975, if such stand provides covered accommodation for 500 or more spectators. Again, the issuing and regulation of such safety certificates is the function of the local authority, whose powers and obligations largely mirror those provided for by the 1975 Act. Thus, after the passing of the 1987 Act, virtually all of the medium to large grounds which host major spectator sports and which aspire to attract crowds of any significance are brought within a general system of licensing and control administered by the local authority (save for those which do not provide covered accommodation).

Sadly, this increasing list of safety legislation proved inadequate once again, and it was the Hillsborough disaster, on the 15 April 1989, at the home of Sheffield Wednesday Football Club, in which large numbers of spectators were crushed to death on an overcrowded terrace which resulted in the Taylor Report[11]. The Taylor Report urged, in particular, that the licensing regime under the Safety of Sports Grounds Act 1975 be used to require that all Football League stadia should be all-seater, with standing room only terraces being phased out progressively by 1999. The government was not prepared immediately to go that far, in view of the financial implications for smaller clubs. It did, however, pass the Football Spectators Act 1989 with the aims of controlling the admission of spectators at particular football matches (by means of both a national membership scheme and licences to admit spectators) and of providing for the safety of spectators at such matches, again through a licensing system. The scheme of the Act applies to football matches designated by the Secretary of State[12] and it has two main limbs. First, the Act established a national membership scheme, membership of which is a pre-requisite of lawful attendance, as an

---

8   HMSO 1985, Cmnd 9585 ISBN 0-10-19585-01.
9   HMSO 1986, Cmnd 9710 ISBN 0-10-197100-1.
10 By s 6(11), a stand, for this purpose, means an artificial structure providing spectator accommodation which is wholly or partially covered by a roof. Temporary structures are not included.
11 HMSO 1989, ISBN 0-10-1076525 (interim report); HMSO 1990, ISBN 0-10-109622-4 (final report).
12 Designation is by order under s 1(1) in relation to matches in England and Wales or s 14(2) in relation to matches elsewhere. Designation orders have been made under both sections. See SI 1993/1691, which designated all football matches at Wembley Stadium and the National Stadium Cardiff or at the grounds of clubs belonging to the FA Premier League or the Football League. SI 1990/732 and SI 1992/1554 designated matches outside England and Wales involving the England or Wales national teams, a club which is a member of the Football League or FA Premier League, or a club in England or Wales playing in a UEFA competition. The purpose of the designation of overseas matches is limited to the control and monitoring of attendance by fans under Part II of the Act.

'authorised spectator', at designated matches in England and Wales[13]. Secondly, the Act established the Football Licensing Authority which was charged with issuing and regulating licences, upon such terms as it considers appropriate, to admit spectators to any premises for the purpose of watching any designated football match[14]. Under s 11 of the Act, the Secretary of State is able, by order, to require the Football Licensing Authority to include in any licence to admit spectators specific requirements in respect of the seating of spectators at designated football matches. The Secretary of State has now exercised that power to impose an all-seater policy in respect of the grounds belonging to the clubs within the FA Premier League and the Football League[15]. A further function of the Football Licensing Authority[16] is to keep under review, and generally to police, the discharge of local authorities' functions under the Safety of Sports Grounds Act 1975 in relation to sports grounds at which designated football matches are played. In exercise of this function, the Football Licensing Authority is specifically empowered[17] to require a local authority to include in any safety certificate particular terms and conditions. Thus, for example, the Football Licensing Authority is able to impose upon local authorities requirements as to the seating of spectators which mirror those introduced by the Secretary of State under s 11.

13 See ss 2–7 of the 1989 Act. The objects and nature of the scheme are set out in s 5. Essentially, the scheme aims to regulate, control and monitor who may and may not attend as a spectator at designated football matches.
14 See s 10, which confers on the authority wide powers as to the conditions which may be attached to its licences.
15 See SI 1994/1666 and SI 1996/1706.
16 See s 13.
17 See s 13(2).

Chapter 2

Judicial regulation/control of sporting relationships

Introduction

It will be seen in later chapters how, in particular circumstances, the United Kingdom and European statutory regimes enable the courts to intervene in the conduct and administration of sporting activity. The opportunities for such intervention, however, are necessarily confined by the proper limits of the relevant statutory regimes themselves. In addition, the courts have displayed a readiness, albeit sometimes reluctantly, to allow the general principles of the common law to be used, and occasionally adapted, to control and regulate relationships of one form or another within the sporting field. Of course, where any such relationship is regulated by a contract, the fact that it operates within a sporting context provides no reason for general contractual principles not to apply. The courts will require the parties to behave within the confines of and to adhere to such principles and will grant appropriate relief at the behest of an aggrieved party able to establish breach (or threatened breach) of his contractual rights.

For example, an employed sportsperson is able to sue for damages in the ordinary way if his employment is wrongfully terminated without due notice. Any number of other types of contract with a sporting flavour provide further examples of how the express or implied terms of a contract may be used to provide the foundations of an action, whether to enforce specific obligations, to restrain infringement of rights or to provide relief (usually damages) in the event of a breach of duty. Such actions, in concept at least, are straightforward and untoward. Particular difficulty arises, however, where contentious issues are raised in the context of some relationship which has not been formalised within the confines of any immediately recognisable contract. In such a case, legal intervention may nevertheless be sought, but is sometimes declined by the courts on the basis that no established cause of action exists. In every case where the court is prepared to intervene or consider intervening, it does so by first identifying a justiciable cause of action. Sometimes this poses little difficulty – as will be seen in due course there are a number of well established means by which, depending on the circumstances, an aggrieved person can invite the court to intervene, under both European and/or United Kingdom domestic law. Indeed there is nothing particularly special about sport which renders access to the law any more difficult than in other fields. In theory the kind of problems which arise in all different fields of activity, commercial or

33

otherwise, may well arise within a sporting context of one type or another and it would be quite impossible to attempt to cover every potential cause of action in a work of this kind. Experience shows, however, that when it comes to the exercise or attempted exercise of established or asserted rights, obligations and powers in various common species of sporting relationships, a number of particular types of dispute are liable to surface. They can often be identified by reference to particular causes of action or areas of law, namely:

- contract
- freedom of competition (under European and UK domestic law)
- freedom of movement (principally under European law)
- statutory rights (eg racial and sex discrimination)
- restraint of trade
- Judicial Review; and Public law principles as applied by private bodies.

The topics of freedom of competition, freedom of movement, discrimination and contracts of employment, all have their own distinct jurisprudence and are dealt with in separate chapters below. But the potential for conflict within sport is such that an aggrieved individual may sometimes face problems in identifying the requirements necessary for relief under any such discreet topic and thus may find it difficult to establish any obvious and legally recognised avenue for redress. It is with such difficulties that this chapter is primarily concerned.

When the courts have been willing to intervene and to provide relief at common law, it has often been where the injured party has been able to establish, sometimes with a degree of artificiality, a form of contractual right. The broad nature and flexibility of contractual concepts has enabled the courts to intervene from time to time, in particular in the attempts made by individual bodies to regulate and control specific sporting activities. As will be seen below, the courts have been ready to regard the rules of such sporting bodies and associations as constituting contractual terms binding both the bodies themselves and their members, and have been prepared to consider appropriate relief either to force such bodies and associations to act within the limits of their powers under such rules and/or to compensate aggrieved members for breaches of the rules.

In the absence of an established breach of some contractual right, it will also be seen how the courts are sometimes willing to intervene under the doctrine of restraint of trade or even in some circumstances to recognise, in one form or another, certain principles borrowed from the field of administrative or public law, in particular the rules of natural justice. In this latter respect, it remains to be seen whether the new Labour Government's declared intention to introduce into United Kingdom law the provisions of the European Convention on Human Rights will provide a new avenue of legal recourse for aggrieved individuals. In particular, Article 6 underwrites (amongst other things) an individual's right to a fair trial in the determination of his civil rights and obligations.

In addition, the court will sometimes intervene to prevent unnecessary duplication of proceedings. Hence in *Conteh v Onslow Fane*[1], the court granted an injunction to the boxer, John Conteh, to restrain disciplinary proceedings being continued against him by the British Boxing Board of

---

1 [1975] CA Transcript 291.

Control pending the determination of an action by him against his former manager in which the court would decide certain legal issues upon which the disciplinary charges against Mr Conteh largely depended. The Court of Appeal decided, not surprisingly, that the court was better able to determine questions of law and so should take precedence over the Board's disciplinary proceedings. In so deciding, however, the Court of Appeal made it clear that it was only in 'special circumstances' that the court would interfere in the hearing of a complaint by a domestic tribunal.

Contractual relief

NATURE OF A CONTRACT

In formulating any contractual cause of action, certain important questions invariably need to be addressed. First, it is necessary to identify the contractual nature of the relationship in question – it is self evident that, without a contract, contractual remedies are not available. Secondly, it is necessary to identify and establish the relevant terms of the contract. These questions can, on occasion, give rise to difficulty.

It might be said that a contract is a bit like an elephant – you (usually) recognise one when you see it, but it is difficult to describe (let alone define). It might also be thought that, because a contract is generally readily recognisable, any description or definition is superfluous. In most circumstances, this may well be true, but contracts come in different shapes and sizes and there will always be particular relationships and situations which, whilst not strikingly recognisable as founded upon any obvious contract, nevertheless give rise to contractual rights and obligations. To cater for such circumstances, the essential features of a contract require to be identified. For present purposes, a contract can be said to exist where there is an agreement between at least two parties which involves the reciprocal giving and taking of 'consideration' (that is, something of value to the recipient) and which is intended to be legally binding. Hence a contract is in essence a 'bargain' and is to be distinguished from, say, a gratuitous promise[2].

THE FORMATION OF A CONTRACT

It is important also to understand the mechanism by which the law recognises a contract as being made. A contract is complete at the point where, one person having made a contractual 'offer' to another, the other 'accepts' the offer unconditionally. At that point, the terms of the contract are agreed and may not be added to (other than by further agreement). This may be significant, for example, in relation to contracts under which spectators gain admission to particular sporting events. It is important that all relevant terms should have been brought to the attention of the spectator, before he concludes the contract by agreeing to pay the price of his ticket[3].

---

2   A gratuitous promise is nevertheless enforceable if contained in a deed or other document under seal.
3   See eg *Olley v Marlborough Court Ltd* [1949] 1 KB 532; *Thornton v Shoe Lane Parking Ltd* [1971] 2 QB 163; *Dillon v Baltic Shipping Co* [1991] 2 Lloyd's Rep 155.

The printing of terms only on the admission ticket may not cause such terms to be part of the contract where, as in most circumstances, the ticket is issued after payment of the price and therefore after completion of the contractual bargain[4].

THE FORM OF A CONTRACT

Save in certain very limited (and for present purposes unimportant) circumstances, a contract does not require to be in any particular form. There is no requirement for the terms of a contract to be reduced into writing. A contrary belief appears to be prevalent, especially in the football world where club managers in particular are regularly described as working 'without a contract' simply because they have not yet signed a written contract (usually for a fixed term)[5]. Such managers (assuming they are working for reward) are nevertheless employed by their clubs pursuant to a contract – an oral contract – and owe and are owed the ordinary obligations which arise as between employer and employee. It follows that, if they are to comply with their contract, they must generally give due notice if they decide to leave and they are entitled to similar notice in the event that their club decides to dispense with their services[6] (unless the other party specifically waives the requirement for notice).

The existence of a contract may be inferred even where there are no communications expressly confirming agreement. The parties may signify their agreement otherwise than by communication, for example by their conduct. This will most obviously be so where one party simply promises to do X if the other does Y and the second party duly proceeds to do Y. The issue in each case is whether or not the parties have in fact signified their agreement to the bargain. This factual issue is not determined by the means by which they may have chosen to express agreement (unless, of course, in the negotiations, the parties have stipulated that an offer is only to be accepted by particular means).

THE TERMS OF A CONTRACT

As with contracts themselves, there are different types of terms of contracts:

– *Express terms*:   In particular, a contract may contain express terms, that is terms which are expressly articulated and agreed, whether orally or in writing.

– *Implied terms*:   Equally, the law will often recognise the existence of implied terms, of which there are three main categories:

4   The position may be different where the circumstances are such that it ought to have been appreciated that standard terms would be identified on the ticket.
5   It may be that the explanation is that most managers are ex players and that, as players, they became used to operating under administrative regulations which require player contracts to be in a specified written form.
6   The amount of notice required will depend upon what has been agreed. In the absence of express agreement, the contract requires simply that reasonable notice be given. Notice may be dispensed with in certain circumstances, in particular where the other party has been guilty of a serious (repudiatory) breach of contract.

(i) *Terms implied as a matter of law* – certain types of relationship themselves import particular obligations as incidents of the relationships themselves. The classic such relationship is an employment contract – the very nature of the relationship of master and servant is such as to imply particular obligations; in the case of the employee, for example, duties to serve with honesty, fidelity and obedience, duties to exercise reasonable skill care and competence and a duty not to abuse the employer's confidential information; in the case of the employer, a duty to pay wages/salary and duties to provide safe systems and a safe place of work; in the case of both employee and employer, a duty to preserve the bond of trust and confidence[7] which is at the heart of any relationship between master and servant. Such terms may be seen as incidents or 'badges' of the relationship in question.

(ii) *Necessary or obvious terms* – quite apart from terms which are implied as a matter of law as incidents of particular types of legal relationship, the courts also imply terms either which are thought to be necessary[8] to make the contract work as the parties must have intended or which are taken to have been so obvious (to all the parties) that they 'went without saying' when the contract was originally agreed.[9] Thus, an athlete who contracts without reservation to run in a particular race may well be taken impliedly to covenant that (to the best of his knowledge) he is/will be fit to do so; and a sports star who obtains commercial sponsorship may impliedly contract that he/she will not deliberately damage the image of the sponsor. Equally, where particular parties have contracted on a number of occasions such as to give rise to a 'course of dealing', the terms of such earlier deals will readily be implied into any further contract in that same course of dealing (in the absence of some contrary indication).

(iii) *Custom and practice* – evidence may be permitted that, in a particular trade, profession or relationship, a particular term is and invariably has been adopted and adhered to. In that event, the court may be prepared to assume that the parties in dispute impliedly agreed to such a term. It should be noted, however, that for such a term to be implied, it must be notorious, certain and reasonable, and not contrary to law.

Terms will not be implied in so far as they contradict any expressly agreed terms. Further, where a contract has been reduced to writing, any necessity for the implication of additional terms must derive from the content and context of the written contract itself. This so called 'parole evidence rule'

7 See, for example, *Woods v WM Car Services (Peterborough) Ltd* [1981] ICR 666, EAT; affd [1982] ICR 693, CA. In the Court of Appeal, Lord Denning MR caught the flavour of the term by saying that 'just as a servant must be good and faithful, so an employer must be good and considerate'. See also *Bliss v South East Thames Regional Health Authority* [1987] ICR 700, CA and *Imperial Group Pension Trust Ltd v Imperial Tobacco Ltd* [1991] ICR 524.
8 See *The Moorcock* (1889) 14 PD 64.
9 See *Shirlaw v Southern Foundries (1926) Ltd* [1939] 2 KB 206, CA; affd sub nom *Southern Foundries (1926) Ltd v Shirlaw* [1940] AC 701, HL.

generally prohibits reliance upon evidence as to extraneous matters (in particular as to the negotiations between the parties) in order, by implied term or construction, to put a gloss on what has been expressly agreed[10].

CONSIDERATION

Although a contract must contain an element of reciprocity, with the parties each giving and taking some form of valuable consideration, the bargain does not have to be an objectively good and fair one. Further, the concept of 'taking' consideration may be misleading in certain circumstances. For example, A may, in giving consideration to B, stipulate that the consideration to be given by B should be given to C. In such an example, A 'takes' consideration only in the sense that he takes it not for himself but for C. Such a tripartite arrangement (which confers no enforceable rights directly upon C) may arise, for example, in relation to sporting events which involve competitors, promoters, landowners, sponsors and broadcasters, where the interdependence of the various relationships may well involve a particular contract stipulating for the conferring of benefits upon a person who is not a party to the contract in question.

Provided the consideration has some value to the recipient, it will suffice. Further, such value does not have to be appropriate or even capable of measurement in financial terms, and simple reciprocal promises will suffice (I promise to do X if you promise to do Y; I agree to confer this benefit on you, in return for your agreement to confer that benefit on X).

REMEDIES FOR BREACH OF CONTRACT

All contractual causes of action are founded upon an assertion by an aggrieved party that another party either has not performed or intends not to perform the contract according to the terms agreed. The ordinary remedy for an actual breach of contract is damages. This involves the court in assessing the difference in financial terms between the injured party's actual position (in the light of the breach) and the position as it would have been had the defaulting party performed the contract (albeit upon the basis that such defaulting party would have chosen to perform his obligations to his own best advantage and, therefore, to fulfil only his minimum obligation under the contract[11]).

The dispute may arise in the context of a disagreement over what has been agreed, whether expressly or impliedly. In such circumstances, a court may, perhaps, in addition to awarding (or refusing) damages, make a declaration, thereby defining the extent and nature of particular rights or obligations under the contract. It may go further and make an order for specific performance, requiring a party to fulfill some or all of his obligations under the contract. Equally, in an appropriate case a court may be prepared to

10 See *Jacobs v Batavia and General Plantations Trust Ltd* [1924] 1 Ch 287, *Prenn v Simmonds* [1971] 1 WLR 1381 and *Reardon Smith Line Ltd v Hansen-Tangen* [1976] 1 WLR 989.
11 See *Lavarack v Woods of Colchester Ltd* [1967] 1 QB 278.

grant an injunction to restrain a continuing or threatened breach[12]. The procedural and substantive conditions for the grant of these kinds of order by way of relief for breach or threatened breach of contract are beyond the scope of this book and are, in event, subject to the court's discretion. They are all important potential weapons in the armoury of a party who alleges that he has sustained or is liable to sustain injury (whether financial or otherwise) by reason of an alleged breach or threatened breach of contract.

THE EXCLUSION/LIMITATION OF LIABILITY

A common feature of a formal written contract is that one party (usually the person tendering the contract as his 'offer') seeks to absolve himself from, or restrict his liability in the event of his breach. Such exemption or limitation of liability clauses come in different shapes and sizes and have led to significant jurisprudence in their interpretation and application, a comprehensive examination of which is beyond the scope of this work. Two points of particular importance, however, are worthy of special mention.

First, if the intention is to exclude liability for loss and damage caused through a party's own negligence, only the clearest indication to that effect will be effective[13]. Words which in terms expressly exempt the party from the consequences of negligence will manifestly suffice. In the absence of express words, the court will consider whether the words used are wide enough to include such exemption. If not, or if the position is unclear, negligence will not be excluded. If the words are indeed wide enough to exclude liability for negligence, however, they will only be effective to do so if, realistically, the damage intended to be excluded could only be inflicted through negligence – if the head of damage in question could be based upon some other ground, the court will be inclined to assume that it was not intended to exclude liability for negligence.

Second, in certain circumstances, the Unfair Contract Terms Act 1977 renders invalid clauses which purport to exclude or restrict liability. In particular, the Act targets 'business liability'[14], namely the liability either for acts done in the course of a business or arising from the occupation of premises for the purposes of a business. Thus in relation to attempts to exclude or restrict any such liability for damage resulting from negligence[15], s 2 invalidates such attempts altogether in relation to death or personal injury, and invalidates them in relation to other types of loss or damage save in so far as they satisfy the 'requirement of reasonableness', which is a requirement that:

---

12 The courts will generally not grant an order for specific performance or an injunction where the effect would be to enforce an obligation to provide personal service. See, for example, *A Schroeder Music Publishing Co Ltd v Macaulay* [1974] 1 WLR 1308, *Warren v Mendy* [1989] 1 WLR 853 and s 236 of the Trade Union and Labour Relations (Consolidation) Act 1992.
13 For the full test, see for example *Canada SS Lines Ltd v R* [1952] AC 192 at 208.
14 See s 1(3).
15 For these purposes 'negligence' means the breach of any obligation, whether by contract, at common law or under the Occupiers' Liability Act 1957 or the Occupiers' Liability (Northern Ireland) Act 1957, to take reasonable care or exercise reasonable skill – see s 1(1).

'the term shall have been a fair and reasonable one to be included having regard to the circumstances which were or ought reasonably to have been known to or in the contemplation of the parties when the contract was made.'

Further any attempt by a person to exclude or restrict his 'business liability' either where the contract comprises his written standard terms of business or where the other party is a 'consumer'[16] (viz: is not himself acting or purporting to act in the course of a business) is invalidated by section 3, again to the extent only that the exemption or limitation of liability clause fails to satisfy the requirement of reasonableness. Similarly, where one party is a consumer, the other party may not rely upon a term requiring the consumer to indemnify him in respect of his 'business liability' for negligence or breach of contract, subject again to the requirement of reasonableness.

INDUCING BREACH OF CONTRACT

It is worth noting that a breach of contract will not necessarily only give rise to a cause of action against the party in breach. The common law also recognises a quasi contractual or tortious cause of action against any third party who intervenes to induce or procure another to breach his contract. For such a cause of action to be complete, it must be established that the third party knowingly and intentionally caused the defaulting party to breach his contract and that he did so without reasonable justification or excuse[17].

Thus, in *Greig v Insole*[18], where the cricket authorities purported to ban Tony Greig and other players who had signed contracts with a rebel promoter, Kerry Packer, Mr Packer was able to rely on this particular cause of action on the basis that, as he alleged, the ban was an attempt by the authorities to persuade the rebel cricketers to renege on their agreements.

Similar arguments were advanced in the Australian Rugby League's 'Super League' case, *News Ltd v Australian Rugby Football League*[19] where Rupert Murdoch's News Ltd was held, on appeal, to have induced breaches of contract by encouraging 'rebel' rugby league clubs to breach their implied obligations to the ARL by allowing their contracted players to sign up with News Ltd's new 'Super League', at a time when they were already under contract to the ARL's competitions. News Ltd were held not to be liable in respect of breaches of further 'loyalty' agreements (under which the rebel clubs had purported to commit themselves to the ARL for some five years) only because such latter agreements were void under Australia's competition laws.

In *Warren v Mendy*[20] Frank Warren, the entrepreneur and boxing promoter/manager, sought injunctions to prevent the defendant from working with the boxer Nigel Benn, on the basis that Mr Warren already had an exclusive contract to promote and manage Mr Benn. The injunction which Mr Warren obtained was subsequently discharged, not because he could not establish the tort of inducing breach of contract, but simply on the grounds that an injunction is generally not granted where its effect is to require an individual to work for another in circumstances where the relationship

16 See s 12.
17 See *JT Stratford & Son v Lindley* [1965] AC 269, HL.
18 [1978] 1 WLR 302.
19 (1996) 139 ALR 193.
20 [1989] 1 WLR 853, CA.

between that individual and the other has irretrievably broken down[1]. In the circumstances, Mr Warren was left to pursue his claim in damages.

Restraint of trade

THE BASIC PRINCIPLE

It is a fundamental principle of the common law that individuals should be allowed to pursue their trade or business without interference. The doctrine is still best expressed by the well known words of Lord Macnaghten in *Nordenfelt v Maxim Nordenfelt Guns and Ammunition Co Ltd*[2]:

> 'The public have an interest in every person carrying on his trade freely: so has the individual. All interference with the individual's liberty of action in trading, and all restraints of trade of themselves, if there is nothing more, are contrary to public policy, and therefore void ... '

As is hinted by the qualification that restraints of trade, *if there is nothing more*, are contrary to public policy and void, the rule admits to exception. The passage quoted above continues:

> 'That is the general rule but there are exceptions: restraints of trade and interference with individual liberty of action may be justified by the special circumstances of a particular case. It is a sufficient justification, and indeed it is the only justification, if the restriction is reasonable – reasonable, that is, in reference to the interests of the parties concerned and reasonable in reference to the interests of the public, so framed and so guarded as to afford adequate protection to the party in whose favour it is imposed, while at the same time it is in no way injurious to the public.'

It follows that, as with many doctrines under the common law, the touchstone of validity is reasonableness. Further, as the quoted passage makes clear, it is not simply the interests of the parties which must be considered. In addition, the public interest must be taken into account. And, for what it is worth, it is well established that the onus of proof shifts as between matters of private and public interest. In *Esso Petroleum Co Ltd v Harper's Garage (Stourport) Ltd*[3] Lord Hodson stated that:

> '... the onus of establishing that an agreement is reasonable as between the parties is upon the person who puts forward the agreement, while the onus of establishing that it is contrary to the public interest, being reasonable between the parties is on the person so alleging ... The reason for the distinction may be obscure, but it will seldom arise since once the agreement is before the court it is open to the scrutiny of the court in all its surrounding circumstances as a question of law.'

What is more, although the doctrine of restraint of trade is most readily and regularly applied in the field of contract, it is of general application and may be used wherever private relationships are governed by rules, regulations or other terms which are calculated to stifle competition and restrict the conduct of trade or business.

---

1 See *Lumley v Wagner* (1852) 1 De GM & G 604; *Warner Bros Pictures Inc v Nelson* [1937] 1 KB 209; *Page One Records Ltd v Britton* [1968] 1 WLR 157.
2 [1894] AC 535 at 565.
3 [1968] AC 269 at 319.

In *Pharmaceutical Society of Great Britain v Dickson*[4], the principle was used to attack the rules of professional conduct adopted by the Pharmaceutical Society for registered pharmacists. Lord Wilberforce said[5]:

> 'It is of no materiality that members are not contractually bound to observe the rule ... The 'doctrine' of restraint of trade had never been limited to contractual arrangements ...'

RESTRAINT OF TRADE IN SPORT

The implications for sport of the ambit of the doctrine will immediately be clear. If the doctrine permitted challenge to the regulatory rules of a professional body with authority over a profession such as pharmacy, there should be no reason in principle why it should not equally apply to the regulatory regimes of other professions, and in particular to such regimes as are laid down by national and international sporting associations and federations. And so it has proved.

In the landmark case of *Eastham v Newcastle United Football Club Ltd*[6], Wilberforce J used the doctrine to declare void and unenforceable the then rules of the Football Association governing the retention and transfer of professional footballers. Under those rules a player registered with a particular club could be prevented from transferring to or playing for another club at the end of his contract, if his original club wished to retain him. In finding such rules to be an unreasonable restraint of trade and therefore void, Wilberforce J rejected a host of arguments designed to justify them[7]. In particular he did not accept that the rules were necessary to prevent the richer clubs acquiring the best players, in part because smaller clubs could secure the long term services of their players by offering longer term contracts. Nor did he accept that abolition of the rules would deter clubs from investing in the training and development of their players or lead to an anarchic system involving the poaching of players and a lack of cooperation between clubs. Significantly, Wilberforce J went on to accept that Mr Eastham was entitled to declaratory relief not simply against Newcastle United Football Club (with whom he had been in a contractual relationship and against whom he arguably might have been able to assert a contractual cause of action) but also the Football Association and the Football League with neither of whom, however, he had any obvious direct contractual relationship[8]. As he said[9]:

---

4   [1970] AC 403.
5   Ibid at 440.
6   [1964] Ch 413.
7   Interestingly, many of the self same arguments were deployed some 30 years later in *Union Royale Belge des Sociétés de Football Association ASBL v Bosman*: C-415/93 [1996] 1 CMLR 645. The ECJ did not feel that such arguments provided justification for the rules of footballing authorities under which clubs could effectively block the transfer of a player whose contract had come to an end unless the transferee club paid it a transfer fee. Such rules amounted to an unjustified and unlawful interference with the player's right of free movement under Article 48 the Treaty of Rome. The decision is discussed at length in the chapter on Freedom of Movement.
8   It is possible that, were a similar case to be considered today, it would be held that a player's necessary submission to, say, the FA's disciplinary regime gives rise to a sufficient contractual relationship under which the FA undertakes to administer such regime fairly and properly.
9   Ibid at 446.

'... the court has jurisdiction to grant a declaratory judgment, not only against the employer who is in a contractual relationship with the employee, but also against the association of employers whose rules or regulations place an unjustifiable restraint on his liberty of employment ...'

In the quoted passage, Wilberforce J referred to the court's jurisdiction simply to grant declaratory relief in cases where there is no contractual relationship such as might found, in addition, a claim for damages. It has since been made clear that, in such cases, the court may also be prepared, exceptionally, to go further and grant an injunction if necessary, either to give effect to the rights as declared or, on an interlocutory (temporary) basis, to hold sway until trial. In *Newport Association Football Club Ltd v Football Association of Wales Ltd*[10], Jacob J held that the right to claim a declaration was a sufficient cause of action to provide jurisdiction to grant ancillary relief (in particular an injunction) under s 37 of the Supreme Court Act 1981. In so concluding, he distinguished *The Siskina*[11], in which the House of Lords had previously suggested that, for jurisdiction to grant an interlocutory injunction, there had to be a pre-existing cause of action arising from the actual or threatened invasions of a legal or equitable right in the plaintiff.

In *Nagle v Feilden*[12], the Court of Appeal again confirmed the principle that the restraint of trade doctrine is not confined to contractual relationships. In particular, it extends to the rules of an association which exercises a virtual monopoly over a particular field of professional activity. In that case, the Court of Appeal overturned the court at first instance and refused to strike out a claim by a woman who had been refused a trainer's licence by the Jockey Club, pursuant to its practice of awarding such licences only to men[13]. In the course of his judgment, Lord Denning MR said[14]:

'The common law of England has for centuries recognised that a man has a right to work at his trade or profession without being unjustly excluded from it. He is not to be shut out from it at the whim of those having governance of it. If they make a rule which enables them to reject his application arbitrarily or capriciously, not reasonably, that rule is bad. It is against public policy. The courts will not give effect to it ... But if the rule is reasonable the courts will not interfere.'

In so concluding, Lord Denning MR placed reliance upon the case of *Faramus v Film Artistes' Association*[15] in which it had been stressed that an organisation with an effective monopolistic power over a particular field of activity, such that membership (or compliance with the rules) thereof is a pre-requisite to earning a living in that field, is subject to the restraint of trade doctrine at the suit of individuals who are prevented by the organisation from so earning a living. Lord Denning went on[16]:

'When a man is wrongly rejected or ousted by one of these associations, has he no remedy? I think he may well have even though he can show no

10 [1995] 2 All ER 87.
11 [1979] AC 210.
12 [1966] 2 QB 633.
13 The case was heard well before the passing of the Sex Discrimination Act 1975. It is likely that, today, any such practice in the field of professional sport would give rise to a cause of action under that Act. See Chapter 7, below.
14 [1966] 2 QB 633 at 644–645.
15 [1964] AC 925.
16 Ibid at 646–647.

contract. The courts have power to grant him a declaration that his rejection and ouster was invalid and an injunction requiring the association to rectify their error. He may not be able to get damages unless he can show a contract or a tort. But he may get a declaration and injunction ... The true ground of jurisdiction ... is a man's right to work ... When [such] associations exercise a predominant power over the exercise of a trade or profession, the courts may have jurisdiction to see that this power is not abused.'

In *Faramus* itself, the Court of Appeal had had no difficulty in holding that a rule of a closed shop trade union which precluded any person from becoming a member if he had ever been convicted of a criminal offence (however trivial) was unlawful as being in restraint of trade. Although the absence of a contract precluded an award of damages, the court was able to grant relief in the form of a declaration or injunction.

The authorities do not go so far as to say, however, that sporting associations or other organisations with monopolistic powers over particular fields of activity are not entitled to lay down qualifications for admission or to require adherence to particular standards of conduct or to prescribe regulations for the control of the activities in question. On the contrary, the Court of Appeal in *Nagle*, recognised the right of such associations/organisations generally to regulate their fields of activity. In doing so, however, they are obliged to observe certain basic requirements of the law, including the doctrine of restraint of trade. Any rules or requirements which restrict the way in which individuals may earn their living within a particular field of activity will be liable to be declared invalid and unenforceable save in so far as they are shown to be reasonable in relation both to the interests of the individuals concerned and to the wider public interest.

Hence, in a decision of Blackburne J in the ongoing saga of *Newport Association Football Club Ltd v Football Association of Wales Ltd*[17], the Welsh FA failed to establish that its rule, which restricted the right of Welsh clubs to be members of the English leagues, was no more than was reasonably necessary to protect the legitimate interests of the Welsh FA (in promoting the Welsh Football League)[18].

The cases already referred to show that the doctrine of restraint of trade is of such width as to permit those aggrieved to bring before the courts complaints of varying descriptions. We have already seen how the doctrine was brought into the forefront of the consciousness of the sporting world, by the decision in *Eastham v Newcastle United Football Club Ltd*[19], a case concerned with the regulation of transfers of the registration of professional footballers from one club to another. Although he declared the rules of the Football Association, as they were then constituted, void and unenforceable, Wilberforce J made it clear that he recognised that there was a justifiable need for the processes relating to the retention and transfer of players to be regulated and controlled by the governing body. His view was simply that the particular regime before him went too far. Whether judges today would be quite as readily disposed to accept the need for general controls, if such controls imposed significant restraints upon players' ability to 'trade', is

17 (12 April 1995, unreported).
18 Interestingly, in *Stevenage Borough Football Club Ltd v Football League* (1996) Times, 1 August, Carnwath J suggested that Blackburne J's decision might tend to mislead in that it failed to give sufficient weight to the distinction between the private interests of the parties concerned and the wider public interest.
19 Supra.

open to question[20]. In the southern hemisphere, a number of regimes of differing categories of stringency (but all, in one form or another, governing players' freedom to play their sport for whom and wherever they choose) have come under review and have tended to be struck down as unreasonable restraints of trade:

In *Buckley v Tutty*[1] the High Court of Australia declared invalid the rules applicable in New South Wales (but which were recognised by authorities in other jurisdictions both within Australia and elsewhere) which tied Rugby League players to clubs which held their registration and which prevented them from playing for other clubs without the registered club's consent (which, even if granted, might be made subject to payment of a transfer fee) even in circumstances where the players were no longer contracted to play for their registered club[2]. In a strong decision, the court made it clear that an injunction could be an appropriate remedy in such a case, which did not necessarily depend upon the plaintiff being linked to the defendant by contract, whether directly or even remotely through membership of his club.

In *Hall v Victorian Football League*[3], the rules of the 'Australian Rules' football authority in Victoria were declared invalid as they tied a player to the club in the area where he happened to reside (whether contracted to play for such club or not) unless the club consented to his release.

In *Hughes v Western Australia Cricket Association Inc*[4], the Australian ex test cricket captain, Kim Hughes, who had signed to play cricket in South Africa, successfully challenged the rules of the cricket authorities in Australia which purported to prohibit Australian cricketers from playing in any match not recognised or sanctioned by them[5].

In *Kemp v New Zealand Rugby Football League*[6], rules were struck down which purported to allow the New Zealand Rugby League authority, at its discretion and without limits of time, to prevent players from playing for clubs outside New Zealand.

Closer to home, in *Greig v Insole*[7], Slade J applied the restraint of trade doctrine to test the validity of the rules of the International Cricket Council

---

20 At the time of writing, the domestic footballing world was preparing for a fresh judicial examination of the modern regulatory regime applying to the transfer of players between domestic clubs, in the context of an action brought by the Wimbledon footballer Vinnie Jones. On this occasion, the reasonableness of such restraints as are still applied in the case of such transfers will fall to be considered in the light of the relaxation of such restraints in the case of transfers between clubs in different countries as a result of the decision of the ECJ in *Union Royale Belge des Sociétés de Football Association ASBL v Bosman*: C-415/93 [1996] 1 CMLR 645.

1 (1971)125 CLR 353.
2 See also *Adamson v New South Wales Rugby League* (1991) 103 ALR 319.
3 [1982] VR 64.
4 (1986) 69 ALR 660.
5 Other Australian cases where the rules of sports governing bodies have been attacked under the restraint of trade doctrine include *Adamson v West Perth Football Club Inc* (1979) 27 ALR 475 (registration and transfer rules) and *Barnard v Australian Soccer Federation* (1988) 81 ALR 51 (FIFA rules preventing soccer players from playing certain types of soccer).
6 [1989] 3 NZLR 463. See also *Blackler v New Zealand Rugby Football League Inc* [1968] NZLR 547 and *Adamson v West Perth Football Club Inc* (1979) 27 ALR 475 and *Re Adamson, ex p Western Australian National Football League* (1979) 143 CLR 190.
7 [1978] 1 WLR 302.

and duly declared invalid the restraints imposed upon those cricketers who had signed for Kerry Packer's 'rebel' circus.

No doubt similar arguments were deployed in the action, in 1997, which pitted the newly formed breakaway 'World Darts Council' and certain of its members against the established governing body, the 'British Darts Organisation'. The latter had been aggrieved at the breakaway and had seen fit to ban any WDC registered players from its competitions. In the event, the case settled, with the ban being lifted (and the WDC agreeing to change its name to the 'Professional Darts Council').

Sandra Gasser invoked the restraint of trade doctrine to sue the International Amateur Athletics Federation, alleging breach of her rights when she was suspended for failing a routine dope test after coming third in the women's 1500 metres at the World Championships in Rome in 1987. In addition to asserting that the IAAF's actions were ultra vires, she complained that the rules and regulations under which she was suspended were an unreasonable restraint of trade. In a decision which perhaps illustrates the court's general inclination to allow sporting bodies to regulate their own affairs (particularly when dealing with drugs cases) and which marks a clear reluctance to intervene in anything but the most extreme of cases, Scott J decided[8] that rules providing for suspension were, by definition, prima facie in restraint of trade even where the athlete was not paid by the regulatory body itself. As he said:

> '... in a sport which allows competitors to exploit their ability in the sport for financial gain and which allows that gain to be a direct consequence of participation in competition, a ban on competition is ... a restraint of trade.'

The lawfulness of the restraint depended upon the reasonableness of the rules in question, which went so far as to create an absolute offence and to impose a mandatory two year sentence of suspension. In coming to his decision to uphold the validity of the rules, which might be regarded as harsh in the context simply of the relationship between the sporting body and the individual athlete, Scott J had well in mind the importance to the public interest in general and the world of athletics in particular that the 'disease' of drugs in sport should be firmly dealt with. It was against that background that he held that the rules in question were not unreasonable.

Scott J had occasion again to consider the doctrine of restraint of trade, in a different sporting context (with different public interest considerations) a few years later. In *Watson v Prager*[9], he applied the doctrine to a contract between a professional boxer (Michael Watson) and his manager (Mickey Duff). He ruled that the (three year) contract was an unreasonable restraint of trade in that it gave to the manager (who also regularly acted as a promoter) the right to dictate the terms upon which the boxer should fight and the purse which he should receive; it also granted to the manager an option to extend the contract for a further period of three years on the same terms. The case is of particular interest in that the contract in question was in the form prescribed by the British Boxing Board of Control as the only terms to which a licensed boxer and his manager might agree. It was argued that it therefore represented a normal form of commercial relationship to which the doctrine of restraint of trade should not apply and with which the courts should not interfere. Scott J disagreed, holding that the public interest required an element of judicial supervision in such cases, particularly where

8 *Gasser v Stinson* (15 June 1988, unreported).
9 [1991] 1 WLR 726.

the terms of the contract were not freely negotiated but were imposed by some overriding authority and even where it was accepted that it was generally in the public interest that the authority should exercise careful regulatory control over the terms agreed between boxers and their managers, so as to prevent undue exploitation. Scott J distinguished between 'enlightened paternalism' and 'undue restraint of trade' and did not accept that an authority such as the British Boxing Board of Control necessarily and invariably 'knew best'. As he reiterated[10]:

> '*Nagle v Feilden* established in my judgment that where the rules or regulations of a body with power to control professional sport are restrictive of the ability of professionals within that sport to earn their living from the sport, the doctrine of restraint of trade applies. The restrictive rules or regulations must be franked by passing through the reasonableness gateway.'

In *Wilander and Novacek v Tobin and Jude*, two well known tennis players sought to challenge the rules of the International Tennis Federation under which they had been suspended after failing random dope tests. They sought interlocutory injunctions to stop the ITF from implementing the suspension or continuing with the disciplinary proceedings. They recognised that the validity of such rules depended upon their reasonableness and asserted (in certain respects boldly, in view of *Gasser*) that the rules providing for suspension were unreasonable on the grounds that they created absolute offences and provided for mandatory suspensions, that they imposed the burden of proof on the player (in effect to establish his innocence) and that the rules imposed a testing procedure without appropriate safeguards to ensure the integrity of the 'chain of custody' of the urine samples. Lightman J refused relief, holding[11] that the plaintiffs' case was unarguable on the facts. The Court of Appeal agreed[12]. However, the matter did not end there. In a subsequent hearing on 13 June 1996, Lightman J ruled[13] that the plaintiffs' claim could proceed to trial on new grounds, which he held to be arguable, which asserted that the rules were unreasonable in that they failed to provide for any appeal against suspension. The Court of Appeal duly struck out these new grounds too[14]. It did so, however, on the basis that the rules, when properly construed, did provide for a form of 'appeal'[15] and that, in any event, the players were adequately protected by their inalienable right to challenge their suspension by court proceedings[16].

RESTRAINT OF TRADE IN RELATION TO MEMBERSHIP CRITERIA

In *Stevenage Borough Football Club Ltd v Football League Ltd*, Carnwath J[17] and the Court of Appeal[18] had to consider the conditions imposed by the

---

10 Ibid at 747.
11 Transcript, Ch D 19 March 1996.
12 (1996) Times, 8 April.
13 [1997] 1 Lloyd's Rep 195.
14 [1997] 2 CMLR 346.
15 The Court of Appeal took the view that, although there was provision for only one disciplinary hearing, such hearing itself was the players' opportunity to challenge ('appeal') the findings of the testing procedure and the mandatory sentence which followed therefrom.
16 This last point may appear harsh, given the limited basis upon which an individual may challenge internal (private) disciplinary proceedings by court action.
17 (1996) Times, 1 August.
18 (1996) Times, 9 August 1997 9 Admin LR 109.

Football League for promotion of the winners of the GM Vauxhall Conference to the Football League's Division Three. The conditions included a requirement that the stadium of any club aspiring to promotion should have met certain standards by 31 December of the preceding season (viz: before the final positions in the Conference had been established). Stevenage won the Conference in the 1995/96 season and although it was able to give assurances (which were not doubted) that all necessary works would be completed by the start of the 1996/97 season, its stadium had not been up-graded by the due date of 31 December 1995 and it followed that it was unable to satisfy the Football League's rules of entry. Stevenage's argument, in part, was that it was unreasonable and unnecessary for the protection of the Football League's legitimate interests for it to have been required to expend the considerable sums which would have been necessary to bring its ground up to standard before it had won the Conference and, thereby, established the opportunity of entry to the Football League's Division Three. Stevenage also argued that certain financial stipulations for entry to the League were unnecessary. In relation to the conditions relating both to stadium eligibility and financial status, it argued, further, that they were not applied as stringently to existing Football League member clubs and that such discrimination rendered the rules (or their application) inherently unreasonable. In decisions which reflect the discretionary nature of any relief which may be granted in a case where the parties are not in a contractual relationship, both Carnwath J and the Court of Appeal declined to grant Stevenage declaratory relief, on the grounds that it had delayed until the end of the 1995/96 season before making application to the court. By that time, the die was already cast for the following season as a result of the application of the Football League's rules which had been well known to and apparently consented to by all parties throughout the conduct of the 1995/96 season. It was thought that it would not be right in those circumstances to upset the arrangements which had been put in place for the 1996/97 season by the Football League and its existing members (including Torquay United who would have been displaced from Division Three if the existing rules were to be relaxed and Stevenage were to be accepted for promotion.) As Millett LJ said:

> 'The inevitable consequence [of Stevenage's delay] was that [Stevenage] was compelled to ask the court not merely to declare the parties 'rights' for the future, but retrospectively to upset the basis upon which the previous season's competitions had been held ... the court should be extremely slow to accede to such an invitation.'

In dealing with the case simply on the basis of the court's discretion to refuse relief, the Court of Appeal emphasised that the case was not simply about whether or not Stevenage should be accorded membership of the Football League (by 'promotion' from the Conference) – if that had been the issue, it might have been hard to justify the complaint that Stevenage ought not to have waited until it had won the Conference before seeking relief from the court. The Court of Appeal, rightly, saw Stevenage's cause of action as being a general challenge to the validity of the Football League's rules for promotion and relegation to and from its Division Three. To put it bluntly, it was too late to change the rules of the game after the final whistle. In so concluding, the Court of Appeal was arguably acting in line with previous authority, for in *Esso Petroleum Co Ltd v Harper's Garage (Stourport) Ltd*[19] Lord Reid had said:

'... an agreement in restraint of trade is not generally unlawful if the parties choose to abide by it: it is only unenforceable if a party chooses not to abide by it.'

The point was that, although Stevenage was not yet in a contractual relationship with the Football League and indeed was seeking entry to such a relationship[20], it had known what the relevant rules were throughout the 1995/96 season, and had even signed a declaration consenting to them at the start of the season. It was against that background that the Court of Appeal was not prepared to countenance the grant of declaratory relief. In spite of this, Stevenage's court action had not (in the opinion of the Court of Appeal) been in vain, as it had established to the satisfaction of Carnwath J that the rules in question were indeed unreasonable and the Football League had therefore agreed that they would be changed for future seasons. For this reason and because of its view on Carnwath J's exercise of discretion, the Court of Appeal did not feel it necessary to consider whether or not Carnwath J had been right in his assessment of the validity of the rules. For his part, Carnwath J had accepted the approach of McGarry VC in *McInnes v Onslow Fane*[1] to the effect that in cases concerning individuals' attempts to gain admission to membership of a particular body, the courts should be slow to review the honest decisions of bodies exercising jurisdiction over sporting activities[2]. In general terms the public interest is served by the existence of a system of control imposed by regulatory bodies, although the public interest may still require that, for example, in certain circumstances a legitimate expectation[3] of admission or advantage should not be frustrated unfairly. As he said:

'... the precise legal analysis is less important than the substance of the principles applied. The *Nagle v Feilden* principle establishes, in my view, that if admission criteria are shown to be arbitrary or capricious in effect, whether because of the way in which they are formulated or in the way in which they are applied, they are in my view open to challenge. But the onus is on those who make the challenge to establish their case, and the court will give due weight to the judgment of the responsible bodies.'

Further, it is clear that Carnwath J took the view that, the greater the public interest in the particular field of activity, the less reluctant the court should be to intervene.

---

19 [1968] AC 269 at 297.
20 It is of passing interest that the rules of the Conference, with which Stevenage *was* already in a contractual relationship, had provisions for promotion which mirrored those of the Football League.
1 [1978] 1 WLR 1520.
2 See also *Cowley v Heatley* (1986) Times, 24 July, in which Miss Cowley, a swimmer originally from South Africa, failed to obtain an injunction to secure entry to the Commonwealth Games, as part of the England team.
3 Here, Carnwath J's reasoning borrowed much from the authorities dealing with the wider principle, considered below, under which the courts have occasionally felt able to intervene to prevent sporting authorities or other bodies from abusing their powers.

The abuse of power

INTRODUCTION

It will be seen further below that the willingness of the courts to invoke the doctrine of restraint of trade to permit challenge to the powers of sporting associations and other organisations even in the absence of a contractual cause of action may be seen as part of a wider principle of more general application, albeit of imprecise ambit. This is that the court will sometimes be prepared to intervene to prevent what it perceives as an *abuse of power* by any such association or organisation which purports to regulate a field of professional activity[4]. It will be seen that Lord Denning MR was in the vanguard of the development of such a general principle, although he did not always carry the rest of the judiciary with him quite as far as he would have liked.

For example, in *Breen v Amalgamated Engineering Union*[5], Lord Denning MR (in a dissenting judgment as to the result on the particular facts of the case) said boldly that similar principles should apply to associations exercising regulatory powers as apply to statutory bodies. Relying upon the controlling principles of administrative law as applied to the exercise of statutory powers he continued[6]:

> 'Does all this apply also to a domestic body? I think it does, at any rate when it is a body set up by one of the powerful associations which we see nowadays. Instances are readily to be found in the books, notably the Stock Exchange, the Jockey Club, the Football Association, and innumerable trade unions ... [Such] domestic bodies ... control the destinies of thousands. They have quite as much power as the statutory bodies of which I have been speaking. They can make or mar a man by their decisions, not only by expelling him from membership but also by refusing to admit him as a member: or it may be by a refusal to grant a licence or to give their approval ... The rules are in reality more than a contract, they are a legislative code laid down by [the domestic body] ... to be obeyed by the members. This code should be subject to control by the Courts just as much as a code laid down by Parliament itself ...'

As a result of the development of this wider general 'principle', borrowed from the realms of administrative law, cases which raise issues of restraint of trade very often also involve arguments founded upon the proper ambit of such wider principle.

GENERAL THEMES

A number of particular and often overlapping themes can be identified in the cases:

- The first (and the founding principle) is that the law requires such associations and bodies to act *within their powers or 'intra vires'* and the

---

4 The same does not seem to apply in the case of (truly) amateur sport, where the courts are unlikely to intervene, even in the case of a monopolistic organisation. The distinction was illustrated in *Currie v Barton* (1987) Times, 12 February, in which the court declined to intervene in the case of a ban imposed (without any form of hearing) upon an amateur county tennis player. The court made it clear that it would not consider arguments based upon natural justice where a player's right to earn a living was unaffected.
5 [1971] 2 QB 175.
6 Ibid at 190.

courts are often prepared to grant declarations (and sometimes injunctions) designed to secure that they do so.

- A second (and related) theme is that decisions which are taken purportedly in accordance with the rules of a particular body are sometimes *deemed* to be ultra vires and open to challenge on the basis that they are *incapable of being justified* on the available evidence.

- A third related theme relies heavily upon the *rules of natural justice* and a perceived requirement in certain circumstances that such associations and bodies, if their actions are to remain 'intra vires', should comply with such rules.

Judicial review and public bodies

As described above, these themes may be recognised as having been borrowed from established administrative or public law principles. The procedural instrument by which, in public law, such principles have been developed and are currently applied is 'Judicial Review' by the Divisional Court of the Queens Bench Division of the High Court of Justice. But that instrument, and access to the Divisional Court, is reserved for public law cases involving complaints about the abuse of power by government, organs of government and certain other *public* bodies. The exercise of power by such bodies is judged, in terms of its validity, by reference to the 'vires' of the person or body to whom the power is entrusted (see the first and founding principle referred to above, of which the second principle is an extension).

Further, when exercising certain functions, such bodies are expected to comply with the so called 'rules of natural justice' (see the third theme referred to above) which, for present purposes, are a set of general principles developed to ensure that the procedures by which certain important decisions are taken are fair – where the rules of natural justice apply, they establish particular standards with which the decision maker must comply if he is to arrive at a valid decision not open to challenge.

As developed in administrative law, the rules of natural justice can be expressed compendiously by two statements of general principle:

1. No man may be a judge in his own cause (*Nemo judex in re sua* – the rule against bias).
2. Judicial/administrative power should not be exercised to the detriment of another party without first hearing that other party (*audi alteram partem* – hear the other side or, more generally, the right to a fair hearing).

Further, in the case of discretionary powers, the validity of the particular decision resulting from the exercise of such power may also be attacked by showing that it was irrational, arbitrary or capricious (hence the second theme referred to above). In *Wheeler v Leicester City Council*[7] Leicester City Council was held by judicial review (at the suit of, amongst others, Peter Wheeler the well known rugby union England international hooker) to have acted unlawfully in refusing to allow Leicester RFC to use its facilities because three of the club members had played rugby (on tour with the

7 [1985] AC 1054 (HL overturning CA).

England team) in South Africa. The House of Lords held that the City Council's decision had been unreasonable and irrational and accordingly beyond its legitimate powers. In so finding, the House of Lords applied the well known test of '*Wednesbury unreasonableness*' derived from the earlier decision of the Court of Appeal in *Associated Provincial Picture Houses Ltd v Wednesbury Corpn*[8] in which Lord Greene MR had said[9]:

> 'It is true that the discretion must be exercised reasonably. Now what does that mean? ... [The word] has frequently been used and is frequently used as a general description of the things that must not be done. For instance, a person entrusted with a discretion must, so to speak, direct himself properly on the law. He must call his own attention to the matters which he is bound to consider. He must exclude from his consideration matters which are irrelevant to what he has to consider. If he does not obey those rules, he may truly be said, and often is said, to be acting 'unreasonably'. Similarly, there may be something so absurd that no sensible person could ever dream that it lay within the powers of the authority. *Warrington LJ in Short v Poole Corpn* [1926] Ch 66, gave the example of the red haired teacher dismissed because she had red hair. That is unreasonable in one sense. In another sense it is taking into consideration extraneous matters. It is so unreasonable that it might almost be described as being done in bad faith; and in fact all these things run into one another ...[10] The court is entitled to investigate the action of the local authority with a view to seeing whether they have taken into account matters which they ought not to take into account, or, conversely, have refused to take into account or neglected to take into account matters which they ought to take into account. Once that question is answered in favour of the local authority, it may still be possible to say that, although the local authority have kept within the four corners of the matters which they ought to consider, they have nevertheless come to a conclusion so unreasonable that no reasonable authority could ever have come to it. In such a case, again, I think the court can interfere. The power of the court to interfere in each case is not as an appellate authority to override a decision of the local authority, but as a judicial authority which is concerned, and concerned only, to see whether the local authority have contravened the law by acting in excess of the powers which Parliament has confided in them ...'

In *Wheeler v Leicester City Council*, of course, the court was concerned with an alleged abuse of power by a governmental, statutory or public body and accordingly was able to apply administrative law principles and, in particular, those established in *Associated Provincial Picture Houses Ltd v Wednesbury Corpn*.

Judicial review and private bodies

When it comes to the control of non-statutory, private, bodies, any basis for the court's intervention is less easily established. The difficulty derives from the fact that, traditionally at least, the availability of judicial review to control the abuse of power depends upon the question, not of whether the *effects* of exercise of the particular power are a matter of public interest, but whether

8   [1948] 1 KB 223.
9   Ibid at 229.
10   [1948] 1 KB 223 at 233–4.

or not the *source* of the power is derived from statute (or the prerogative[11]) so as to make the power truly 'governmental'. If such is not the source of a particular power, the traditional view in England has been that judicial review is not an available tool for its judicial control which, if available at all, requires some other cause of action to support it. According to this traditional view, if a sports governing body is not established by statute as an arm of government, its decisions are not amenable to judicial review as those of a public body.

The distinction between public and private law might be thought to be illogical and is not always clearly drawn in other jurisdictions. In Scotland, for example[12], in *Ferguson v Scottish Football Association*[13] Duncan Ferguson, the Scottish international footballer, was able to bring under judicial review the decisions of the Scottish Football Association's disciplinary committee and appeals tribunal (both essentially private bodies albeit exercising functions of public interest) by whom he had been censured and suspended for twelve matches as a result of an incident in a match between Glasgow Rangers and Raith Rovers. He succeeded in showing that such disciplinary measures were ultra vires, in the light of the restrictive wording of the Scottish Football Association's regulations which contained a lacuna which prevented the Association from dealing with incidents not seen and made the subject of a report by the referee. He obtained a declaration that the penalty was invalid and an order that it be rescinded.

Similarly, in New Zealand, the distinction between public and private law is less strictly marked. Thus in *Finnigan v New Zealand Rugby Football Union*[14], two individual plaintiffs with no connection with the NZRFU other than that they happened to belong to rugby clubs, were held to be entitled to challenge the decision of the latter body to send a representative team to South Africa. The New Zealand Court of Appeal took the view that, although the law recognised a distinction between private and public law decisions (especially in relation to an individual's right to challenge them) and although the decision in question was by a private and voluntary sporting association, the decision of the NZRFU was one of 'major national importance' such that 'a sharp boundary between public and private law [could not] realistically be drawn' and court intervention was permissible.

Equally, the Australian courts have shown a willingness on occasion to allow the traditional dividing line between public and private law rights to become blurred[15]. In *Forbes v New South Wales Trotting Club Ltd*[16], the court held amenable to review a decision of the defendant (which controlled the sport of trotting in New South Wales and owned a number of racecources) peremptorily to impose a ban on the plaintiff, a successful punter, barring his access to its courses. Intervention was justified on the basis that, although the defendant was not strictly a public body, its function was to control a 'public activity'.

Even in England, the traditional view that it is the source of the power which determines the availability of judicial review cannot now be taken as

---

11 See eg *R v Criminal Injuries Compensation Board, ex p Lain* [1967] 2 QB 864 and *Council of Civil Service Unions v Minister for the Civil Service* [1985] AC 374.
12 See also *St Johnstone Football Club v Scottish Football Association* 1965 SLT 171; *West v Secretary of State for Scotland* 1992 SLT 636.
13 1 February 1996, unreported.
14 [1985] 2 NZLR 159, 181 and 190.
15 See eg *Victoria v Master Builders Association* [1995] 2 VR 121.
16 (1979) 143 CLR 242.

comprehensively authoritative. In *R v Panel on Take-overs and Mergers, ex p Datafin plc*[17], Donaldson MR said:

'In all the reports it is possible to find enumerations of factors giving rise to the [judicial review] jurisdiction, but it is a fatal error to regard the presence of all those factors as essential or as being exclusive of other factors. Possibly the only essential elements are what can be described as a public element, which can take many different forms, and the exclusion from the jurisdiction of bodies whose sole source of power is a consensual submission to its jurisdiction.'

The *Datafin* case was rightly regarded as signalling a possible relaxation of the traditional understanding that the availability of judicial review is reserved for abuses of statutory or other governmental power. In the sporting field, however, it has not in practice lead to any material change in the courts' approach. In particular, and to the surprise of most commentators, it has not resulted in any decisions of sports governing bodies being held amenable to judicial review. The traditional limitations of judicial review have been the subject of attack in a succession of sports cases, both before and after *Datafin*, but in spite of occasional expressions of doubt or regret by different judges, they have emerged intact up to the level of the Court of Appeal.

In *Law v National Greyhound Racing Club Ltd*[18] the Court of Appeal refused to accede to an application to strike out a claim by originating summons which challenged a decision by the governing body of greyhound racing in the United Kingdom, the National Greyhound Racing Club to suspend the licence of a greyhound trainer for a doping offence. The plaintiff claimed that the suspension was ultra vires. The defendant maintained in support of its application to strike out the claim, that the plaintiff ought properly to have proceeded by way of judicial review. The Court of Appeal disagreed, pointing out that the NGRC's power derived not from statute or the prerogative but from contract. The exercise of such power was a matter of private, not public, law.

In 1989, in *R v Disciplinary Committee of the Jockey Club, ex p Massingberd-Mundy*[19] the applicant failed in an attempt to obtain judicial review of a decision by the Jockey Club, then the body governing horse racing in Great Britain, to disqualify him from acting in the capacity of chairman of a local stewards' panel. He claimed that the decision had involved a breach of the rules of natural justice.

In rejecting the claim, for want of jurisdiction, the Divisional Court felt constrained to follow *Law* and was not persuaded that the fact that the Jockey Club was established by Royal Charter was sufficient to embue its powers with the requisite public element. In teasing fashion, however, the court seemed to leave open a suggestion that certain limited decisions by the Jockey Club might yet be susceptible to judicial review. Roch J was impressed by the fact that the Jockey Club was in a position of national importance, able to exercise monopolistic powers in an area in which many persons earned their livelihood. He went so far as to say[20]:

'There may be cases where the authority of [the Jockey Club] will not be derived from a contract between them and the person aggrieved ... or

17 [1987] QB 815 at 838.
18 [1983] 1 WLR 1302.
19 [1993] 2 All ER 207.
20 Ibid at 224.

alternatively may not be derived wholly from a contract ... then the question, is [the act or decision complained of] susceptible to judicial review? may receive an answer different from that given by the court in *Law's* case.'

It is suggested, however, that Roch J went too far in suggesting that the issue may depend simply upon whether or not the power in question derives from contract. If any wider criteria for the application of judicial review is justified on the authorities than whether the source of the power is derived from statute (or the prerogative), the simple absence of a contractual relationship will surely not suffice alone[1]. Indeed, it seems doubtful that, in the case before him, there was any strictly *contractual* relationship between the Jockey Club and the applicant in any event.

Similarly, in *R v Jockey Club, ex p RAM Racecourses Ltd*[2] the Divisional Court was again invited to grant judicial review of a decision (not to allocate fixtures to the applicant's new racecourse) by the Jockey Club. The applicant relied upon the absence of any contractual relationship between itself and the Jockey Club, no doubt praying in aid the dictum of Roch J in *Massingberd-Mundy*. In fact the court rejected the application on its merits, but it went on to say, albeit with regret, that it felt bound by authority (in particular *Massingberd-Mundy*) to reject the attempt to bring the decision of the Jockey Club within the ambit of judicial review. In rejecting the application, the court was openly critical of the precedents by which it accepted it was bound, and expressed dissatisfaction that judicial review was not available. Simon Brown J noted[3] that the discharge of the Jockey Club's functions had, on occasion, 'strikingly close affinities' with the exercise of a statutory power of licensing and other 'sorts of decision-making that commonly are accepted as reviewable by the courts.' It is suggested that, to some extent, the whole debate may be regarded as somewhat academic. It was accepted by the court that the absence of judicial review was not likely to leave an aggrieved individual without remedy and that the applicant in the instant case could have brought proceedings by writ, claiming a declaration or injunction and relying upon the doctrine of restraint of trade. Simon Brown J's point was simply that, absent binding authority, he would have regarded the particular decision of the Jockey Club as *more appropriate* for scrutiny in judicial review proceedings than a writ action.

Whether he had been persuaded to a different point of view or not, Simon Brown J expressed the law in traditional terms, and without reserve, in a subsequent case, *R v Chief Rabbi of the United Hebrew Congregations of Great Britain and the Commonwealth, ex p Wachmann*[4], when he said:

'To attract the court's supervisory jurisdiction there must be not merely a public but potentially a governmental interest in the decision making power in question ... where non-governmental bodies have hitherto been held reviewable, they have generally been operating as an integral part of a

1 Donaldson MR referred, in *Datafin* (supra), to the possible 'exclusion from the jurisdiction of bodies whose sole source of power is a *consensual submission to its jurisdiction*'. Even such a test would exclude from judicial review many powers exercised outside the confines of a *contractual* relationship. Indeed, in *Massingberd-Mundy*, Neill LJ relied upon the Privy Council case, *Calvin v Carr* [1980] AC 574, in which the powers of the Australian Jockey Club were said not to be within the domain of public law in that their source was a 'consensual submission to the jurisdiction'.
2 [1993] 2 All ER 225.
3 Ibid at 247.
4 [1993] 2 All ER 249 at 254.

regulatory system which although itself non-statutory, is nevertheless supported by statutory powers and penalties clearly indicative of government concern.'

He went on to make the important point[5] that:

'... whether or not a decision has public law consequences must be determined otherwise than by reference to the seriousness of its impact upon those affected.'

This last quotation was in line with the words of Donaldson MR in *East Berkshire Health Authority, ex p Walsh*[6], when he had said that there was:

'... no warrant for equating public law with the interest of the public'.

When the Football Association announced its intention to establish the Premier League in 1991, the Football League sought to prevent it and applied for judicial review of the FA's decision. Not surprisingly, the application failed – in *R v Football Association Ltd, ex p Football League Ltd*[7], Rose J reviewed the authorities in some detail and expressly distanced himself from the reservations expressed, for example, by Simon Brown J and Roch J in *ex p RAM Racecourses Ltd* and *ex p Massingberd-Mundy* respectively. He held that the position was quite clear, although he accepted[8] that *Datafin* (supra) had indeed extended the scope of judicial review so as potentially to apply:

'... to a non-statutory body which exists otherwise than as a result of the exercise of the prerogative and that ... a body may be subject to judicial review if it regulates an important aspect of national life and does so with the support of the state in that, but for its existence, the state would create a public body to perform its functions'.

In his view, however, this extension to the scope of the jurisdiction did not have the result that such bodies as the Football Association, the Jockey Club, the British Boxing Board of Control and others should be regarded as amenable to the jurisdiction. In relation to the Football Association, Rose J went on[9]:

'Despite its virtually monopolistic powers and the importance of its decisions to many members of the public who are not contractually bound to it, it is ... a domestic body whose powers arise from and duties exist in private law only. I find no sign of underpinning directly or indirectly by any organ or agency of the state or any potential government interest ... nor is there any evidence to suggest that if the FA did not exist the state would intervene to create a public body to perform its functions. On the contrary ... a far more likely intervener to run football would be a television or similar company rooted in the entertainment business or a commercial company seeking advertising benefits such as presently provides sponsorship in one form or another.'

The issue finally came before the Court of Appeal in *R v Disciplinary Committee of the Jockey Club, ex p Aga Khan*[10], in which the Aga Khan sought judicial review of the Jockey Club's decision to disqualify his horse after it

5   Ibid at 255.
6   [1985] QB 152 at 164.
7   [1993] 2 All ER 833.
8   Ibid at 845.
9   *R v Football Association Ltd, ex p Football League Ltd* [1993] 2 All ER 833 at 848.
10 [1993] 1 WLR 909.

had won a race, the Oaks, on the grounds that its urine had subsequently been found to contain a prohibited substance. In confirming that the Jockey Club indeed was not susceptible to judicial review, the Court of Appeal confirmed that, even after *Datafin*, *Law v National Greyhound Racing Club Ltd*[11] remained good law. In particular, it was not persuaded to a different view by the arguments (a) that the jurisdiction of the Jockey Club was only nominally consensual in that any active participation in horse racing *required* consent to the operation of its rules, (b) that its powers were extensive and monopolistic, (c) that in certain circumstances its rules purported to enable it to exercise its powers over persons who had never submitted themselves to its rules[12], (d) that its influence over horse racing was to the benefit of the public or a significant section of the public, namely those who go to or bet on racing, and (e) that it was established by royal charter. Furthermore, Bingham MR expressed his conclusion in spite of accepting that, if the Jockey Club had not existed, the government would have been bound to create a public body to regulate horse racing[13]. In spite of this fact, he said[14]:

> 'But the Jockey Club is not in its origin, its history, its constitution or (least of all) its membership a public body. While the grant of a royal charter was no doubt a mark of official approval, this did not in any way alter its essential nature, functions or standing. Statute provides for its representation on the Horseracing Betting Levy Board, no doubt as a body with an obvious interest in racing, but it has otherwise escaped mention in the statute book. It has not been woven into any system of governmental control of horse racing, perhaps because it has itself controlled horse racing so successfully that there has been no need for any such governmental system and such does not exist. This has the result that while the Jockey Club's powers may may be described as, in may ways, public they are in no sense governmental.'

In delivering a concurring judgment, Hoffmann LJ expressly preferred the approach of Rose J in *R v Football Association Ltd, ex p Football League Ltd*[15] to that of Simon Brown J in *ex p RAM Racecourses Ltd*[16]. Pithily, Hoffmann LJ said:[17]

> 'I do not think that one should try and patch up the remedies available against domestic bodies by pretending that they are organs of government.'

Public law principles outside judicial review

The absence of judicial review as an available remedy in relation to the decisions of private bodies, does not mean that the *principles* developed within the public law jurisdiction have no application to such bodies. On the

---

11 Above.
12 For example, the rules gave power to warn off undesirables from race courses under the Jockey Club's jurisdiction.
13 It is of passing interest that, partly in response to criticisms that the Jockey Club was too unrepresentative to exercise the powers of a governing body, a new company, the British Horseracing Board, was formed by racing industry representatives to be the new governing body.
14 [1993] 1 WLR 909 at 923.
15 [1993] 2 All ER 833.
16 [1993] 2 All ER 225.
17 At 933.

contrary, in certain circumstances, the courts have been willing to control perceived abuses of power by non governmental bodies. To that end, they have been prepared to adapt and adopt certain public law principles so as to control the processes of certain monopolistic bodies, even where such bodies do not operate in a 'governmental' field. This willingness has only slowly been developed, and originally the courts tended to look only at whether or not the relationship in question was governed by a contract[18].

The traditional approach can be seen in *Maclean v Workers' Union*[19], in which the court made it clear that the basis upon which it would interfere with the disciplinary decisions of bodies such as a trade union, a members' club and certain professional bodies was a finding that the rules of such bodies constituted a contract between them and their members. The court also made it clear that there was some (albeit limited) scope for the implication of terms into that contract in order to ensure fair play. Maugham J set out the *general* rule as follows:[20]

> 'It is certain, therefore, that a domestic tribunal is bound to act strictly according to its rules and is under an obligation to act honestly and in good faith ... in such a case as a power of expulsion in a members' club it seems to me reasonably clear that the matter can only depend on contract express or implied ... a person who joins an association governed by rules under which he may be expelled ... has in my judgment no right of redress if he be expelled according to the rules, however unfair and unjust the rules or the action of the expelling tribunal may be, provided that it acts in good faith.'

This insistence upon compliance with contract did not mean, however, that the rules of natural justice could have no application. Whilst Maugham J was adamant that any such rules had to bow to the clear terms of the contract, he went on to recognise that, in the absence of clear and restrictive terms, certain principles of fair play would readily be implied (in accordance with and subject to ordinary contractual principles for the implication of terms). He went on to express the position in the following terms:[1]

> 'It is impossible to doubt that, if the rules postulate an inquiry, the accused must be given a reasonable opportunity of being heard. The phrase, 'the principles of natural justice' can only mean in this connection the principles of fair play so deeply rooted in the minds of modern Englishmen that a provision for an inquiry necessarily imports that the accused should be given his chance of defence and explanation ... But when it is sought to lay down elaborate rules, taken from decisions as to the Courts of law, and to apply them in such a case as the present, I think it is prudent to remember that these more or less artificial principles have no application except so far as they can be derived from a fair construction of the rules, and that the implication can only be made if it is clear that the parties ... must have intended it.'

Maugham J's approach in *Maclean* was apparently approved by the Court of Appeal in *Russell v Duke of Norfolk*[2], in which the rules of the Jockey Club, which provided for the withdrawal of a trainer's licence, were subjected to

18 It should be noted, however, that the courts have generally been prepared to entertain claims, at the suit of adversely affected individuals, that monopolistic organisations have acted strictly 'ultra vires'. See for example *Davis v Carew Pole* [1956] 2 All ER 524.
19 [1929] 1 Ch 602.
20 At 623.
1 At 624–5.
2 [1949] 1 All ER 109, CA.

scrutiny. In this decision, the precise ambit of which is far from clear, it was held as a matter of construction that before a licence could be withdrawn on grounds of misconduct, an inquiry complying with the rules of natural justice was impliedly required. The precise scope of the rules of natural justice, in such a context, depends upon the circumstances. As Tucker LJ said[3]:

> 'There are in my view no words which are of universal application to every kind of inquiry and every kind of domestic tribunal. The requirements of natural justice must depend on the circumstances of the case, the nature of the inquiry, the rules under which the tribunal is acting, the subject matter that is being dealt with and so forth.'

Denning LJ went further and took a first tentative step towards suggesting that, in cases where an individual's livelihood was at stake, the contract could not lawfully be framed in such a way as to exclude the implication of such a term.

It was no doubt a recognition of such principles which lead the Court of Appeal in *R v Disciplinary Committee of the Jockey Club, ex p Aga Khan*[4] to hold, when refusing to entertain an application for judicial review of a decision to disqualify the applicant's horse from the Oaks, that the denial of a public law remedy worked no injustice as the applicant could proceed by writ in any event. In particular, Hoffmann LJ said:[5]

> '... the remedies in private law available to the Aga Khan seem to me entirely adequate. He has a contract with the Jockey Club, both as a registered owner and by virtue of having entered his horse in the Oaks. The club has an implied obligation under the contract to conduct its disciplinary proceedings fairly. If it has not done so, the Aga Khan can obtain a declaration that the decision was ineffective ... and if necessary an injunction to restrain the Club from doing anything to implement it.'

In *Lee v Showmen's Guild of Great Britain*[6], the Court of Appeal again emphasised that the court's right to intervene in the business of a domestic tribunal is founded upon its jurisdiction to protect contractual rights. The case concerned the decision by the relevant Committee of a trade union of travelling showmen to fine and expel from its membership (for non payment of the fine) an individual which it had found guilty of unfair competition. In a shift of emphasis away from the more stringent approach of earlier decisions such as *Maclean*, and as presaged in *Russell*, Denning LJ invoked principles of public policy, one of which (as he put it) was 'the well known principle that parties cannot by contract oust the ordinary courts from their jurisdiction[7]', to support his view that[8]:

> 'Although the jurisdiction of a domestic tribunal is founded on contract, express or implied, nevertheless the parties are not free to make any contract they like ... The tribunal must, for instance observe the principles of natural justice. They must give the man notice of the charge and a

---

3 At 118.
4 [1993] 1 WLR 909.
5 At 933.
6 [1952] 2 QB 329.
7 See *Scott v Avery* (1865) 5 HL Cas 811.
8 At 342. In expressing his view, Denning LJ drew support from passages from the judgments in *Dawkins v Antrobus* (1881) 17 Ch D 615 at 630, *Wood v Woad* (1874) LR 9 Exch 190 at 196 and *Weinberger v Inglis (No 2)* [1919] AC 606 at 616.

reasonable opportunity of meeting it. Any stipulation to the contrary would be invalid. They cannot stipulate for a power to condemn a man unheard.'

Indeed, Denning LJ went further and held that, in the case of a domestic tribunal which sits in judgment on the members of a trade or profession, the court has an additional power to intervene, where the decision taken is shown to be incapable of being supported by the available evidence, in the sense that no reasonable person could sensibly have arrived at such a decision. In so holding, Denning LJ was borrowing from administrative law the concept of '*Wednesbury* unreasonableness'[9] and permitting its introduction into this particular (but related) field of private law[10]. In doing so, he was not purporting to depart from the established principle that the jurisdiction of the court to intervene is founded upon its right to enforce the contract between the parties. With that in mind, he saw this particular power of intervention as being founded upon the court's right to *construe* the terms of the contract and to enforce it according to that construction. His approach is clear from the following passage[11]:

'In most of the cases which come before such a domestic tribunal the task of the committee can be divided into two parts: firstly they must construe the rules; secondly they must apply the rules to the facts. The first is a question of law which they must answer correctly if they are to keep within their jurisdiction; the second is a question of fact which is essentially a matter for them. The whole point of giving jurisdiction to a committee is so that they can determine the facts and decide what is to be done about them. The two parts of the task are, however, often inextricably mixed together. The construction of the rules is so bound up with the application of the rules to the facts that no one can tell one from the other. When that happens, the question whether the committee has acted within its jurisdiction depends, in my opinion, on whether the facts adduced before them were reasonably capable of being held to be a breach of the rules. If they were, then the proper inference is that the committee correctly construed the rules and have acted within their jurisdiction. If, however, the facts were not reasonably capable of being held to be a breach, and yet the Committee held them to be a breach, then the only inference is that the committee have misconstrued the rules and exceeded their jurisdiction.'

In coming to his conclusion, Denning LJ recognised that many such domestic tribunals, albeit deriving their jurisdiction from private contractual relationships, were in a position of immense power, the exercise of which was liable to deprive individuals of their livelihood. Very often, the individuals concerned had had no real choice over whether or not to enter into the contract in the first place – if they wished to ply their trade, they had to join the club, union, or association. Denning LJ[12] saw no reason why the kind of principles applied to statutory tribunals in the administrative law field should not be adapted so as to apply to such (private) domestic tribunals. In both types of case the question of an individual's 'right to work' was at stake[13].

Denning LJ returned to the general theme which he had struck in *Lee,* in a later case, *Bonsor v Musicians' Union*[14]. He again stated that his task was to

9 See above.
10 See also *Esterman v National and Local Government Officer's Association* [1974] ICR 625.
11 At 345.
12 At 346.
13 At 343.
14 [1954] Ch 479.

construe the rules of the Musicians' Union as constituting a contract between the plaintiff and the union. But he went on to say[15]:

'... in approaching this question of construction, I desire to say that these rules are more a contract in theory than a contract in fact. In order for there to be a true contract, there must be the agreement of the parties freely made with full knowledge and without any feeling of constraint. That was not so here. The Musicians' Union was a closed shop. In order that a person should be allowed to work at his trade he had to sign a document agreeing to the rules. He had no option but to sign ... When one remembers that the rules are applied to a man in that state of mind, it will be appreciated that they are not so much a contract, as we used to understand a contract, but they are much more a legislative code laid down by some members of the union to be imposed on all members ... They are more like bye-laws than a contract ...'

The willingness of the courts to require adherence to the principles of natural justice in the conduct by governing bodies of their contractual relations with sports men and women, was illustrated once again by the interlocutory decision of Ebsworth J in *Jones v Welsh Rugby Football Union*[16]. There, a Welsh rugby union player, Mark Jones, and his club Swansea RFC, obtained an interlocutory injunction to restrain the WRU from activating a disciplinary suspension which it had imposed after Mr Jones had been involved in a fight during a match between his club and Ebbw Vale RFC. Although the very nature of an interlocutory decision means that Ebsworth J was not required finally to resolve the legal issues raised, she recognised the force in Mr Jones' argument that the WRU's procedures had been materially unfair in that they refused to countenance an accused player ever being legally represented at a disciplinary hearing, they did not allow for witnesses to be called or challenged by cross examination at such a hearing and they excluded the accused player from that part of the proceedings in which the disciplinary committee viewed a video of the incident under review. Such procedural 'defects' gave rise, in the judge's view, to:

'... an arguable case that the plaintiffs' right to defend themselves properly and effectively was denied them ...'

The learned judge went on to sound a general warning for all those concerned in the adminstration and regulation of sport, when she said:

'There are likely to be many people who take the view that the processes of the law have no place in sport and the bodies which run sport should be able to conduct their own affairs as they see fit and that by and large they have done so successfully and fairly over the years. It is a tempting and attractive view in many ways ... . However, sport today is big business. Many people earn their living from it in one way or another. It would, I fear, be naive to pretend that the modern world of sport can be conducted as it used to be not very many years ago.'

THE DISTINCTION BETWEEN 'FORFEITURE' CASES AND 'APPLICATION' CASES.

Thus far, most of the cases referred to have been cases involving decisions by bodies to expel existing members from membership or otherwise to penalise

---

15 At 485.
16 (1997) Times, 6 March.

them in some way. In such 'expulsion' or 'forfeiture' cases, it is generally relatively straightforward for the court to identify features of the parties' relationship as being sufficient to form the foundations of a contract and thereby to claim jurisdiction to intervene if thought appropriate. Often, however, decisions of monopolistic sporting or other professional bodies or trade unions etc will have the potential for equally draconian effects on an *aspiring* member's ability to earn a living within the field in question, by impeding such an individual's access to membership or to qualifications necessary to enable him to work within the field. The issue was bound to arise as to the extent to which the courts would intervene in such 'admissions' or 'applications' cases. As has been seen above, the absence of any contractual relationship does not prevent the law from intervening under the doctrine of restraint of trade, but the question remains whether such is the limit of the court's jurisdiction.

By 1966, Lord Denning MR was ready to take the arguments advanced in the 'forfeiture' cases a stage further so as to enable them to be applied to 'admissions' or 'applications' cases. In *Nagle v Feilden*[17], a case discussed above in relation to the doctrine of restraint of trade, he suggested that the true basis of the court's jurisdiction to intervene was not, after all, founded in any express or implied contract between the parties but was arguably determined by matters of public policy. He reviewed a number of the earlier cases, drawing no distinction between those founded upon the doctrine of restraint of trade (for which a contractual relationship was not necessary) and those others which had been held to depend upon whether or not some form of contract could be identified under which jurisdiction could then be established. In introducing his review he said this:[18]

> 'I quite agree that if we were here considering a social club, it would be necessary for the plaintiff to show a contract. If a man applies to join a social club and is black-balled, he has no cause of action because the members have made no contract with him. They can do as they like. They can admit or refuse him, as they please. But we are not considering a social club. We are considering an association which exercises a virtual monopoly in an important field of human activity. By refusing or withdrawing a licence, the stewards can put a man out of business. This is a great power. If it is abused, can the courts give redress? ... That is the question.'

In reviewing the authorities, Lord Denning MR questioned whether some might not have been decided differently in modern times[19]. Expressing a sentiment to which he returned subsequently[20], he referred to the tendency to base decisions on the existence of a contract, but went on[1]:

> 'But I think that could only be done by inventing a fictitious contract. All through the centuries courts have given themselves jurisdiction by means of fictions; but we are mature enough, I hope, to do away with them. The true ground of jurisdiction in all these cases is a man's right to work. I have said before, and I repeat it now, that a man's right to work at his trade or profession is just as important to him as, perhaps more important than, his

17 [1966] 2 QB 633. See p 43 above.
18 At 644.
19 An example of one such earlier case is *R v Lincoln's Inn Benchers* (1825) 4 B & C 855, in which it had been held that even a capricious refusal to admit to membership gave no right of redress 'because in fact there has been no violation of any right'.
20 See *Enderby Town Football Club Ltd v Football Association Ltd* [1971] Ch 591, below.
1   At 646.

rights of property. Just as the courts will intervene to protect his rights of property, they will also intervene to protect his right to work .. .When an association, who have the governance of a trade, take it upon themselves to licence persons to take part in it, then it is at least arguable that they are not at liberty to withdraw a man's licence – and thus put him out of business – without hearing him. Nor can they refuse a man a licence – and thus prevent him from carrying on his business – in their uncontrolled discretion ... .When those authorities exercise a predominant power over the exercise of a trade or profession, the courts may have jurisdiction to see that this power is not abused.'

Lord Denning MR was not alone in challenging the traditional distinction between 'forfeiture' and 'application' cases, based on the existence of a contract only in the former. Danckwerts LJ[2] also invoked principles of public policy when he said:

'... the courts have the right to protect the right of a person to work when it is being prevented by the dictatorial exercise of powers by a body which holds a monopoly ... . In the case of the Jockey Club there does not appear to be any check upon the exercise of their discretion, and unless some protection is provided for persons whose livelihood is involved, such persons are at the mercy of decisions which may be made capriciously and without any proper consideration of the merits of the case.'

Salmon LJ expressed similar views[3].

Of course the suggestion in *Nagle v Feilden* that the courts might invoke principles of natural justice to intervene even in 'application' cases in the absence of a contract was of limited authority. It was made in the context of an application to strike out the Statement of Claim and, properly understood, the Court of Appeal rejected the application simply upon the basis that it was arguable that the plaintiff did indeed have a cause of action. Further, the plaintiff's claim did not rely exclusively upon the rules of natural justice but was more appropriately framed under the doctrine of restraint of trade. Further, when in a subsequent case, *Edwards v Society of Graphical and Allied Trades*[4], Lord Denning MR justified the court's right to intervene in the decisions of a trade union (both as to 'expulsion' and 'admission') by reference to the fact that the union's approach was simply 'an unwarranted encroachment on a man's right to work', his brethren were not so forthright, preferring not to express a view in relation to 'application' cases.

Lord Denning returned to his theme that a contractual relationship was not a necessary requirement for the court to intervene in an appropriate case in *Enderby Town Football Club Ltd v Football Association Ltd*[5], in which he stated that the invention of some fictional contract should be put to one side and it should be recognised that the true justification for the court's intervention in these cases was public policy. In a graphic passage[6] he stated that he did not agree that:

'... public policy is an unruly horse [and] that no judge should ever try to mount it lest it run away with him.'

---

2 At 650.
3 See in particular at 652–654.
4 [1971] Ch 354.
5 [1971] Ch 591. See also Lord Denning's approach in *Breen v Amalgamated Engineering Union* [1971] 2 QB 175, in particular at 190.
6 At 606.

Rather, he believed that:

> '... with a good man in the saddle, the unruly horse can be kept in control. It can jump over obstacles. It can leap the fences put up by fictions and come down on the side of justice ... .'

The issue of the extent to which the court may intervene in 'application' cases, was before the court again in *McInnes v Onslow Fane*[7] in which the plaintiff sought to challenge the British Boxing Board of Control's refusal to grant him a boxing manager's licence. Megarry VC was prepared to accept that even in 'application' cases the court retained a jurisdiction to intervene 'in order to enforce the *appropriate* requirements of natural justice and fairness' but he went on to make it clear that those requirements were not the same as in an 'expulsion' case which necessarily involves the forfeiture of some existing right or position. 'Application' cases were, by definition, very different, in that they involved an application by an individual to a private body for a particular benefit or position which he had not hitherto held. In such cases, the furthest the court was prepared to go was to say that the body in question was under a duty simply to reach an honest conclusion without bias or caprice. In particular, there was no general obligation to grant any form of hearing before arriving at a decision to reject the application for a licence and the plaintiff was not entitled to reasons for his rejection. Megarry VC expressed his reasoning as follows[8]:

> '... I think that the courts must be slow to allow any implied obligation to be fair to be used as a means of bringing before the courts for review honest decisions of bodies exercising jurisdiction over sporting and other activities which those bodies are far better fitted to judge than the courts. This is so even where those bodies are concerned with the means of livelihood of those who take part in those activities. The concepts of natural justice and the duty to be fair must not be allowed to discredit themselves by making unreasonable requirements and imposing undue burdens. Bodies such as [the British Boxing Board of Control] which promote a public interest by seeking to maintain high standards in a field of activity which otherwise might easily become degraded and corrupt ought not to be hampered in their work without good cause. Such bodies should not be tempted or coerced into granting licences that otherwise they would refuse by reason of the courts having imposed on them a procedure for refusal which facilitates litigation against them ... . The individual must indeed be protected against impropriety; but any claim of his for anything more must be balanced against what the public interest requires.'

A similar reluctance to intervene in the activities of sports governing bodies was expressed by Browne-Wilkinson VC in *Cowley v Heatley*[9]. In refusing injunctive relief designed to secure the admission to the Commonwealth Games of Miss Cowley, a swimmer of South African extraction, the Vice Chancellor made it clear that, in his view:

> 'Sport would be better served if there was not running litigation at repeated intervals by people seeking to challenge the decisions of the regulating bodies'.

In his view, the court should only intervene to correct errors of law or in cases where the decision in question is manifestly absurd and unreasonable.

---

7 [1978] 1 WLR 1520.
8 At 1535.
9 (1986) Times, 24 July.

To every general rule, there is some exception, and Megarry VC, in *McInnes v Onslow Fane*, himself seemed to accept that even in an 'application' case, if the applicant could be said to have had a legitimate expectation of having his application granted, more especially if the decision is liable to take account of allegations of dishonesty or impropriety[10] so that a rejection of his application would involve some slur against the applicant's character, then his application should not be refused without first according him the right to be heard and to defend himself against the allegations. In such a case, the failure to accord such a right may well enable the court to intervene[11].

Carnwath J accepted the analysis of Megarry VC in *McInnes v Onslow Fane*[12] when, in *Stevenage Borough Football Club Ltd v Football League*[13] he felt able to consider intervening (in the event he exercised his discretion not to intervene) in the application of the rules of the Football League for admission to membership by promotion from the GM Vauxhall Conference to the Football League's Division Three, in circumstances where Stevenage Football Club, having won the Conference was nevertheless rejected for admission by the Football League.

Conclusion

As has been illustrated above, the principles upon which the court is prepared to intervene in the decisions of sporting authorities and other bodies have been developed over the years in different areas of the law. What emerges is that the relevant principles have merged between such different areas. Thus, the extent to which the court is prepared to intervene in any particular dispute depends less on the nature of the body whose decision is subject to challenge or whether the cause of action is framed in restraint of trade or by reference to the rules of natural justice, and more on the substance of the decision itself and the nature of the relationship between the decision maker and the aggrieved party. As was said by Cooke J in the New Zealand case of *Stininato v Auckland Boxing Association Inc*[14], a case concerning the Boxing Association's refusal of the plaintiff's application for a boxer's licence:

'As I see it, in this kind of case there is a meeting of the principles of natural justice or fairness (treating those terms as synonymous) and the principles as to unreasonable restraint of trade. The right to work in a chosen occupation or vocation is involved ... . I think that a refusal by the council of a professional boxer's licence application, for misconduct but without giving him any opportunity of answering the charge, is well capable of being regarded as an unreasonable restraint of trade and a breach of

10 In such a case, as in 'expulsion' cases, there is, in effect, a 'charge' against the applicant and a form of 'judicial' decision is required, for which the rules of natural justice are designed and equipped to cater. Thus in *Fisher v Keane* (1878) 11 Ch D 353 at 362–63, Jessel MR said of a committee (admittedly in a 'forfeiture' case) that it ought not 'to blast a man's reputation forever – perhaps to ruin his prospects for life without giving him an opportunity of defending or palliating his conduct'.
11 See for example *Breen v Amalgamated Engineering Union* [1971] 2 QB 175 and *Stininato v Auckland Boxing Association Inc* [1978] 1 NZLR 1.
12 Above.
13 (1996) Times, 1 August (Carnwath J); (1997) 9 Admin LR 109, CA.
14 [1978] 1 NZLR 1 at 24.

natural justice ... . In my opinion, proof of such allegations would give the court jurisdiction to grant a declaration; and in some cases an injunction would be appropriate.'

It can be said that, whether the principles of natural justice or restraint of trade are prayed in aid, the court will *more readily* intervene if the parties are in a contractual relationship and one of the parties is purporting to deprive the other of some existing right or advantage previously enjoyed ('forfeiture' cases). In so far as the parties are not in a contractual relationship and one simply denies the other admission to a contractual relationship or other advantage ('application' or 'admission' cases), it will be harder (but not necessarily impossible) to persuade the court to intervene, although it may be less hard where the aggrieved person can show that he had a legitimate expectation of securing the advantage in question or where the rejection is founded upon allegations of impropriety of one form or another.

What is quite clear is that the tests to be applied, however the cause of action may be framed, are sufficiently similar and flexible to require in each case that all the circumstances be taken into account. The touchstones of reasonableness and public interest so require in relation to restraint of trade, whereas, as has been seen, the so-called principles of natural justice or 'fairness' are not set in stone and require to be moulded to take account of the exigencies of the particular circumstances of their application. There is a danger in seeking too precisely to identify narrow statements of principle from the decisions in particular cases which invariably will have been determined in large part by their particular circumstances. The concepts of reasonableness, fairness and natural justice are, by their nature, broad and imprecise. Lord Reid put it nicely when, in *Ridge v Baldwin*[15] he said:

'In modern times opinions have sometimes been expressed to the effect that natural justice is so vague as to be practically meaningless. But I would regard these as tainted by the perennial fallacy that because something cannot be cut and dried or nicely weighed or measured therefore it does not exist. The idea of negligence is equally insusceptible of exact definition, but what a reasonable man would regard as fair procedure in particular circumstances and what he would regard as negligence in particular circumstances are equally capable of serving as tests in law, and natural justice as it has been interpreted in the courts is much more definite than that. It appears to me that one reason why the authorities on natural justice have been found difficult to reconcile is that insufficient attention has been paid to the great difference between various kinds of cases in which it has been sought to apply the principle.'

What is equally clear is that aggrieved persons are likely to seek to challenge the decisions of sporting authorities and other bodies with increasing frequency in the future. The doctrine of restraint of trade and the principles of natural justice will, in one form or another, inevitably be deployed by many such persons. Moreover, it is likely that litigants will seek to join such traditional causes of action with the less well known, newer, forms of 'Euro complaint' such as under Articles 85 and 86 (freedom of competition) and

15 [1964] AC 40 at 64–5.

48 to 66 (freedom of movement) of the Treaty of Rome[16]. Such causes of action are considered separately below.

In addition, it remains to be seen how the Government will implement its declared intention to introduce the requirements of the European Convention on Human Rights into United Kingdom domestic law. It seems likely that any such introduction will afford fresh avenues of recourse for aggrieved individuals. In particular, Article 6 requires that a fair trial be afforded to individuals, not simply in criminal proceedings, but also:

'In the determination of [their] civil rights and obligations.'

Moreover, it seems clear that the disciplinary and other proceedings[17] of sports governing bodies are likely to be regarded as often determining the civil rights and obligations of those falling within their jurisdiction[18] and thus to fall within the general principle enshrined in Article 6[19].

There can be little doubt that the jurisprudence in this area will develop further.

Postscript – an alternative to court action

We have seen above that there are limitations to the relief which the courts are prepared to contemplate. This, together with a commonly expressed and occasionally even chauvinistic belief that sports' disputes are not appropriate for resolution by judges who, it is said (often misguidedly), are ill equipped to understand the nuances of sporting relationships, often leads people to question whether there might not be some other mechanism which is more appropriate (and faster and/or cheaper) for healing rifts, adjudicating upon grievances and even imposing penalties. Sports governing bodies and other administrators are often heard to rail against a perceived and unwelcome 'intrusion' by the law into their (allegedly) private affairs, when their attempts to regulate a particular area of sporting activity are exposed to minute examination and exposure to public scrutiny in the context of contested litigation instituted by an aggrieved individual. Further, the

16 See, for example, *Wilander and Novacek v Tobin and Jude* [1997] 1 Lloyd's Rep 195 (Lightman J); revsd [1997] 2 CMLR 346, CA. Analysis of the decisions in this case (see the chapters on Freedom of Movement and Freedom of Competition) reveals how the limitations of such 'Euro complaints' are not dissimilar to those at common law. In particular, encroachments on the essential freedoms guaranteed by the Treaty of Rome may be permitted if justified by compelling reasons of the general interest provided that they comply with the principle of 'proportionality' and are no more intrusive than strictly necessary – see *Union Royale Belge des Sociétés de Football Association ASBL v Bosman*: C-415/93 [1996] 1 CMLR 645. A litigant may therefore find that he needs to address similar or related arguments, whether advancing a case under restraint of trade, natural justice or European law.

17 Examples are the grant of licences and even the admission to membership.

18 See for example, *Le Compte, Van Leuven and De Meyere v Belgium* (1981) 4 EHRR 1 and *H v Belgium* (1987) 10 EHRR 339. See also, for decisions relating to 'admissions' cases, *Konig v Germany* (1978) 2 EHRR 170; *Benthem v Netherlands* (1985) 8 EHRR 1; *Kraska v Switzerland* (1993) 18 EHRR 188 and *De Moor v Belgium* (1994) 18 EHRR 372.

19 Article 11 provides for 'freedom of association' and encompasses a right both to form *and to join* associations. For this purpose, however, the European Court of Human Rights has generally held that professional regulatory bodies are not 'associations' – see *Le Compte, Van Leuven and De Meyere v Belgium* (1981) 4 EHRR 1 (doctors) and *Bathold v Federal Republic of Germany* (1985) 7 EHRR 383 (veterinary surgeons).

vehemence of such pleas has not been extinguished by the courts' own recognition that such bodies must be allowed to perform their functions without undue interference and that their decisions should not be open to challenge otherwise than upon proof of one or more of the types of abuse to which reference has been made in the preceding paragraphs.

Whether or not it is possible rationally to defend a view of the law and the ordinary court processes as an unwieldy and unreliable mechanism which is simply inappropriate for sorting out sport's ills, it is inevitable that, as sport increasingly moves further into the era of professionalism, the inclination to resort to law in order to redress perceived wrongs, particularly those which result in significant financial consequences, will increase.

The first difficulty to be faced in finding an alternative to the court process is that any other mechanism of dispute resolution requires, in some form, the consent of the parties to the dispute. Such consent may, of course, be provided by an apparent acceptance of and adherence to the rules of the relevant governing body, to which all athletes/players are required to subscribe. We have already seen how such rules are regarded as being contractual in nature and, in the circumstances, as binding both the governing body and the participating sportsmen and women concerned. But it is clear that the concept of consent in such circumstances is problematic, in that it is often the case that, if a player or athlete wishes to compete in his or her chosen sport (or to compete in a particular event, tournament or championship), he or she simply has no effective choice but to subscribe to the rules in question. It follows that a rule which purports to require all disputes to be referred to some alternative form of resolution mechanism and to inhibit or prevent action by court proceedings may itself be open to attack, for example under the restraint of trade doctrine[20]. A recent example of such a rule is provided by the rules of entry to the Atlanta Olympic Games which required each athlete expressly to agree that all disputes should be submitted exclusively to a specially appointed arbitral system. Any athlete who wished to compete, had no choice but to sign up to such agreement. Whilst subject to much speculation, it is not understood that the validity of the 'agreement' comprised within such rules of entry was ever put to the test. The validity of any attack on such a rule (in the United Kingdom and other common law countries) would ultimately depend upon the application of the principles of established doctrines like restraint of trade, as previously discussed above, but the adjudication upon such validity would itself require court action. Thus one can see illustrated an important general principle at common law, namely that the jurisdiction of the courts cannot be ousted absolutely even by agreement.

Any agreement to refer disputes or differences to some body other than the ordinary courts is likely to be regarded as an arbitration agreement and, accordingly, to be governed by the law relating to arbitration. Today this means, in particular, the Arbitration Act 1996. That Act, by s 5, applies to

---

20 Other more dubious doctrines may also be brought into the equation. They include duress, undue influence and, possibly, inequality of bargaining power. Such doctrines, to the extent that they exist at all, rely upon a general principle which has the effect of negating apparent consent due to some vitiating circumstance rendering a bargain unconscionable. For a detailed examination of such 'doctrines', the reader is referred to the specialist works on contract. For present purposes, it is suggested that the general principle of unconscionability is one which may simply impact under the requirements of reasonableness within the doctrine of restraint of trade itself.

any arbitration agreement in or evidenced in writing[1]. For this purpose, insofar as the 'agreement' is provided simply by the rules or constitution of a sports governing body, then, provided that such rules or constitution are themselves in writing, the Act will apply[2].

The central principles enshrined in the Arbitration Act 1996 are identified by s 1. They include, fundamentally, that:

(a)   arbitration should be *fair* and by an *impartial* tribunal; and
(b)   *the court will not intervene* other than in defined circumstances.

FAIR AND IMPARTIAL

The requirement of fairness and impartiality is obvious but its express articulation in the Act is to be welcomed. In the workings of the Act, the requirement is delivered by the imposition of specific duties of fairness and impartiality on the arbitral tribunal itself[3]. In this connection, some of the jurisprudence developed under administrative law, in the context of judicial review, which has been discussed in detail above, has clear application to arbitration. In the world of sport, in particular, the requirement of fairness and impartiality serves to underline the stricture that arbitration does not provide governing bodies with a means of confining the resolution of all disputes to a mechanism over which they can properly retain control or influence. An arbitral process which effectively remains 'in house' abuses the principle of impartiality (and fairness). Indeed, it is suggested that a provision in the rules of a governing body which requires disputes to be finally determined by a body which is properly to be regarded as a part (or an affiliate) of itself does not provide an arbitration mechanism at all and so does not fall to be governed by the law relating to arbitration. Such a provision would not be accorded the primacy which the Arbitration Act 1996 recognises in the case of true arbitration agreements, under the second fundamental principle referred to above. In such cases, the ordinary rule which renders void contractual terms purporting to deprive individuals of their right of access to the court will apply[4].

It is the specific requirement of impartiality which lies at the heart of some of the perceived flaws (in the eyes of many) in the arbitral system established by the International Olympic Committee (IOC). Its creation, the Court of Arbitration for Sport (CAS), was founded in 1983 with the admirable purpose of:

---

1   The general provisions of the Act (see below for specific provisions relating to 'domestic arbitrations') apply to arbitrations in the United Kingdom. Certain provisions relating, in particular, to the court's powers also apply to other abitrations. For the specific details, see s 2.
2   See s 5(3).
3   See s 33.
4   See, for example, *Scott v Avery* (1856) 5 HL Cas 811, and *Baker v Jones* [1954] 2 All ER 553, a case concerning the rules of the British Amateur Weightlifters Association. See also *Lee v Showmen's Guild* [1952] 2 QB 329, *Enderby Town Football Club Ltd v Football Association Ltd* [1971] 1 All ER 215 and *St Johnstone Football Club Ltd v Scottish Football Association Ltd* 1965 SLT 171.

'Facilitating the settlement of disputes of a public nature arising out of the practice or development of sport, and, in a general sense, all activities pertaining to sport'[5].

In 1993 the constitution of CAS was revised after, in particular, a successful challenge in Spain to one of its awards on the grounds of an alleged lack of independence from the IOC itself. In particular, the IOC tried to distance itself from CAS by, together with the International Federations, creating the International Council of Arbitration for Sport for the purpose of administering CAS. However, the suspicion remains in certain quarters that, as a 'creation' of the IOC, albeit now at one stage removed, it is a 'creature' of the IOC and liable, if only in appearance, to favour the interests of its 'master'. To be fair, the IOC and CAS itself have gone to some lengths to try to dispel any suggestions or risk of bias[6], but suspicion is likely always to remain where an arbitral body is itself established by a governing body, especially where links with the governing body remain in place, whether through procedures for making appointments to the arbitral body, through provision for its funding or otherwise.

1997 has seen the start of an initiative to set up in the United Kingdom a British Sports Arbitration Panel. The initiative is being moved forward by the Central Council for Physical Recreation. Such a panel would provide a pool of independent expert arbitrators who would be available to determine such disputes relating to sport as would be referred to it. It is contemplated that, in the event of such a panel being finally established, many governing bodies would take steps to amend their constitutions and rules to permit or require particular types of dispute to be referred for arbitration to the panel or to provide for appeals against disciplinary or other decisions to lie with the panel. The aim is to keep the panel truly independent of the governing bodies themselves, both by the astute choice of arbitrators and by securing funding for the project which is not derived from the governing bodies themselves. If the project succeeds both in the establishment of the panel and in securing its aim of true impartiality, it will surely be a welcome development towards ensuring that more sports related disputes are resolved (hopefully speedily and without extravagant costs) by individuals who are seen as having the expertise and sympathy necessary for dealing with such matters.

THE COURT WILL NOT INTERVENE

The principle that the court will give way to an arbitration agreement is important but not absolute. The Arbitration Act 1996 distinguishes between 'domestic' and other arbitrations. A domestic arbitration is, broadly[7], one to which no party is a foreign national (or habitually resident outside the UK)

---

5 CAS Statute, Article 1. The Olympic Charter now provides that disputes connected with the Olympic Games should be referred exclusively to CAS.
6 By way of example, the ad hoc appointment of 'on the scene' arbitrators to deal with disputes as they arose at the Atlanta Olympic Games, appears to have passed sensible scrutiny (in relation to the impartiality criterion) by reason of the stature, quality and independence of the appointed arbitrators themselves. It should be said that the three adjudications of these arbitrators (re the eligibility of an Irish swimmer, the issue of an athlete expelled from the Olympic Village and the admitted use by certain Russian athletes of bromotan) all favoured the athletes directly involved.
7 The full definition appears at s 85.

or a foreign company and which provides for arbitration in the United Kingdom. By ss 9 and 86, the court will stay court proceedings in favour of an arbitration agreement, domestic or otherwise, unless satisfied that the agreement is null and void (as where, for example, it operates in unreasonable restraint of trade), inoperative, or incapable of being performed. In cases of domestic agreements, the court has a wider discretion, pursuant to s 86, and may additionally stay proceedings if persuaded that there are other sufficient grounds for not requiring adherence to the agreement. This wider discretion might permit it to be argued, for example, that a stay should properly be refused if there were cogent grounds for doubting the impartiality of the arbitral tribunal or where the proposed procedures were manifestly inappropriate. The general principle enshrined in s 1 of the Act (generally giving primacy to an arbitration agreement) strongly suggests that the court will not readily be persuaded to allow an action to proceed in the face of an appropriate agreement to submit all relevant disputes to arbitration.

Particular safeguards are contained within the Arbitration Act 1996 designed to ensure that arbitration is conducted properly. Thus, under s 24, the court retains a power to remove a particular arbitrator in certain circumstances; by s 32, it may rule on preliminary jurisdiction questions[8]; by s 45, in the absence of agreement to the contrary[9], it may be invited in certain circumstances[10] to make rulings on specific points of law. In particular, the Act gives specific powers to the court in relation to arbitral awards. Importantly, any party may challenge an award on the grounds of 'serious irregularity' affecting the tribunal, the proceedings or the award itself[11] or, in the absence of agreement to the contrary[12], may appeal on a point of law[13]. In addition, the court may set aside an award for lack of jurisdiction[14]. Finally, application may be made to the court for leave to enforce an arbitral award[15] as if it were a judgment or order of the court[16].

8 By s 30, the Act also gives power to an arbitral tribunal to rule on its own jurisdiction (in the absence of agreement to the contrary).
9 The contemplation of such contrary agreement provides a statutory inroad on the general principle that the court's jurisdiction over issues of law cannot be ousted by agreement. Note, however, that in the case of domestic arbitrations, any such contrary agreement must post-date the start of the arbitral proceedings in question – see s 87(1)(a).
10 In particular, no application may be made without the agreement of all parties or the arbitral tribunal itself.
11 See s 68, which defines 'serious irregularity' in broad terms, but one requirement is that the court must be satisfied that the irregularity in question has caused or will cause substantial injustice to the applicant.
12 By s 87(1)(b), any such contrary agreement is not effective in the case of a domestic arbitration unless entered into after the commencement of the arbitral proceedings themselves. Thus a blanket exclusion in a governing body's rules would not qualify (in relation to domestic arbitrations).
13 See s 69. The appeal requires leave, save by agreement of all parties. By s 70(2), the appellant must also first have exhausted his remedies under the arbitration process itself.
14 See s 67.
15 Note that Part III of the Act makes specific provision for the recognition and enforcement of foreign awards.
16 See s 66.

Chapter 3

Legal personality

In any situation where liability is alleged to attach in a sporting context, it will be necessary to consider not simply whether liability is established, but also to whom any such liability should attach[1]. The need for this second part of the equation derives in part from the fact that sporting bodies come in different shapes and sizes and the law does not recognise every kind of organised entity as having an identity or 'personality' which is itself able to attract legal rights and incur legal obligations[2]. In addition, in some circumstances the individual officers or members of a sporting body may themselves be exposed to personal liability arising from their exercise or purported exercise of, or their failure to exercise, powers on behalf of the organisation.

Different types of sporting bodies

Legal rights and obligations, and legal liabilities for infringement of rights or breach of obligations, can only attach to legal 'persons'. But sport and the business of sport may be conducted not simply by an individual or by separate individuals but also by groupings of individuals acting together and by any number of other entities. Such groupings and entities may comprise a corporation, a partnership or some other unincorporated association such as a members' club[3]. Other entities may be created by statute. An example of

---

1 Equally, where a right is asserted, it is necessary to identify who may properly assert it.
2 Even certain types of individual may not be recognised as having a sufficient legal personality to be capable of acquiring/enforcing rights or incurring obligations/liabilities. In particular, there are special rules relating to the extent to which minors (those under the age of 18) may be held liable in respect of particular obligations. The general rule is that, save in respect of contracts for necessary services or goods, and for apprenticeship, education/training and service (in respect of which contracts are enforceable if for the overall benefit of the minor), a contract with a minor is voidable at his option. The exception in relation to contracts of service, education or training is of obvious importance in sport. See, for example *Doyle v White City Stadium* [1935] 1 KB 110 in which a licence issued to a minor by the British Boxing Board of Control which bound the minor to adhere to the Board's rules was held to be enforceable, on the basis that such contract was a means which enabled the minor to earn a living and was ancillary to the contract which he had with his promoter. See also *Roberts v Gray* [1913] 1 KB 520 and *Denmark Productions Ltd v Boscobel Productions Ltd* (1967) 111 Sol Jo 715; on appeal [1969] 1 QB 699, CA. Minors may be liable in tort.
3 A proprietary 'club', in spite of its name, is no more than an operation run by its proprietor.

the latter is a trade union, which is a creature of (currently) the Trade Union and Labour Relations (Consolidation) Act 1992[4].

The extent and nature of any of these different entities' capacity to enter into legal relationships and the implications (in particular as to liabilities) of such relationships (both for the entity itself and its constituent elements, if any) vary according to how the entity is constituted and in particular as to whether it is constituted in such a way as to give it an identity recognised by the law as providing it with its own legal personality sufficient to attract rights and incur obligations in its own right rather than simply in the name of its constituent members. A detailed study of the concept of 'legal personality' is not apt for this book which here seeks simply to introduce a broad outline, sufficient only to draw attention to some essential distinctions and implications as between different types of organisation encountered in sport and related commercial fields.

– *Corporations:*

A corporation (a 'company' in ordinary parlance) may be constituted by charter[5], statute or registration under the Companies Acts. A registered company may be limited by guarantee or shares. In each case, the corporation has a legal personality which is distinct from its members or shareholders (if any) and its freedom to act or enter contractual or other relationships with legal consequences like any other individual is limited only by the terms of its own founding instruments. A corporation may only (properly) act within its powers or 'vires'. Thus the powers of a corporation established by charter are defined primarily by the terms of its charter, those of a statutory company by the provisions of its constituting statute and those of a registered company by the terms of its Memorandum and Articles of Association. A contract which does not fall within the powers and objects of a corporation's founding constitution is said to be 'ultra vires' the company and void, save that its validity is saved in favour of another contracting party dealing with the corporation in good faith[6]. The directors of a company owe fiduciary duties to the company, may not make any secret profits from their office and are subject to the constraints of the Companies Acts (both regulatory and adminstrative) and any relevant provisions as to their powers and rights contained in the company's constitution. A director may incur personal liability in certain circumstances, for example if he signs a cheque or other instrument on behalf of the company but without using the full and correct company name[7], where he purports to bind the company without due authority, where he fails to exercise the degree of skill, care and competence reasonably to be expected of him in the circumstances, where he acts in breach of particular requirements under the Companies Acts[8] or where he procures the company to act tortiously[9]

4   See s 1. By s 10, a trade union is said not to be a 'body corporate' but nevertheless to be capable of making contracts and suing and being sued in its own name.
5   The British Broadcasting Corporation provides an example of a corporation created by charter, as do certain professional organisations, such as the Institution of Mechanical Engineers and the Pharmaceutical Society of Great Britain. In the sports world, the sports councils were created by charter, as were certain governing bodies such as the Jockey Club.
6   See s 35 of the Companies Act 1985.
7   See s 349 of the Companies Act 1985.
8   See in particular the provisions designed to ensure fair dealing by directors, contained in Part X of the Companies Act 1985.
9   In this latter event, the procuring director may be personally liable as a joint tortfeasor.

It follows that, where a sports governing body or other sports organisation is constituted as a corporation, it will be recognised as a legal 'person' in its own right and will be capable of enjoying rights and attracting liabilities in its own name. Its officers and servants will generally be regarded as acting on its behalf and they will incur a personal liability only in circumstances where they have acted beyond their powers or otherwise improperly or where express statutory provision imposes such liability[10].

– *Unincorporated associations:*
As we have seen above, the distinctive feature of a corporation is that the very fact of incorporation is itself apt to provide an organisation with legal identity sufficient to constitute a recognisable personality distinct from its constituent elements, be they shareholders or other members. Thus the shareholders of a registered company are protected from personal liability in respect of the company's dealings, by the 'veil of incorporation' which may not generally be lifted or pierced. On the other hand, an unincorporated association is not recognised as having its own legal personality distinct from its constituents and therefore cannot usually sue or be sued[11], save where it has been accorded a sufficient status for that purpose by statute[12]. Thus a members' club which has not been registered as a limited company comprises, in terms of its legal personality, nothing more than its individual members acting collectively.

The constitution of such a club, assuming it has one, governs the relationships between its members, who are generally taken to have contracted with each other pursuant to its terms. Thus in *Clarke v Earl of Dunraven*[13], one yacht club member was held by the House of Lords to be entitled as a matter of contract to compensation for damage to his yacht caused by the yacht of another club member during a regatta, simply because the rules of the club so provided. On similar grounds, a court will restrain a club or other unincorporated association from expelling a member in a manner which is contrary to its rules[14].

Because an unincorporated association is no more than the sum of its constituent members, an individual member may have difficulty in

---

10 By way of example, in the area of health and safety, s 12(7) of the Safety of Sports Grounds Act 1975 imposes a personal (criminal) liability on any director, manager, secretary or officer who has consented to or connived at the commission of an offence under that Act or to whose neglect the commission of an offence is attributable. Similar provisions appear in s 36(8) of the Fire Safety and Safety of Places of Sport Act 1987 and s 24(1) of the Football Spectators Act 1989.

11 See *London Association for Protection of Trade v Greenlands Ltd* [1916] 2 AC 15; *London Griffiths v Smith* [1950] 2 All ER 662.

12 Certain associations may be accorded the status of an 'Industrial and Provident Society' under the Industrial and Provident Societies Acts 1965, 1968 and 1975. A members' club may qualify, for example, if it has the object of benefiting the community by providing recreational facilities. In such a case, registration as an Industrial and Provident Society accords a form of corporate status which gives rise to limited liability in relation to club debts. Other associations may register as 'Friendly Societies' under the Friendly Societies Acts 1974 and 1992, if their object is 'social intercourse, mutual helpfulness, mental and moral improvement and rational recreation'. A Friendly Society may be incorporated or unincorporated and registration will cause the association's assets to vest in trustees who are accorded limited liability in respect of the association's liabilities.

13 [1897] AC 59; see also *Harington v Sendall* [1903] 1 Ch 921.

14 See *Lee v Showmen's Guild of Great Britain* [1952] 2 QB 329.

establishing any cause of action against the association (in the form of the other members) in tort. In *Robertson v Ridley*[15], the Court of Appeal denied redress against a club at the suit of one of its members who had been injured by the defective state of the club's premises. It did so on the basis that an unincorporated members' club or its officers owed no duty to individual members except as may be provided by its rules. Although the Club's rules provided that the Chairman and Secretary were 'responsible in law for the conduct of the club' this was held not to be enough to impose on those officers any enforceable duty of care owed to the plaintiff. In the absence of special and clear provision in the rules[16], the officers were in the same position as ordinary members of which the plaintiff was himself one. In such circumstances, the members were no different from the plaintiff, and the plaintiff could not be held liable to himself. The position may be different where the breach of duty is committed by an individual member or officer to whom a specific responsibility has been clearly assigned by the other members and accepted by that individual. In such a case the individual may incur a personal liability[17]. Equally, in *Jones v Northampton Borough Council*[18], the Court of Appeal held that even without any clear and express allocation of liability by the rules, an officer or member may nevertheless incur a liability to other members if, when performing a task on behalf of the members, he is alerted to a specific danger to which he fails to alert those other members. In particular, where a member, in the course of booking a sports centre for a five a side football competition, learned of a dangerous wet patch on the playing surface, he was held liable for the injuries sustained by another member who duly slipped on the patch, for his failure to warn of the danger.

Relations between an unincorporated association and third parties are governed by the ordinary rules of agency. For example, an individual member who, or a committee which, purports to enter into a contract on behalf of an unincorporated club or other association will himself/itself be personally liable for its performance. The extent to which he/it will share such liability with, or be able to obtain contribution or indemnity from, the other members (or club funds) will depend upon the authority conferred upon him/it either specifically (pursuant to any procedure laid down in the constitution) or, in the case of an individual, by reason of any office held by him (again, as defined in the constitution). Further, if the members of an unincorporated association allow one or more of its members or officers to act as having appropriate authority on its behalf, a third party who is thereby lead to rely on such authority may be able to sue the members on the basis that the member or officer in question had 'apparent' or 'ostensible' authority to act as their agent. In so far as a member or committee of an unincorporated association is duly or apparently authorised to and does contract on behalf of the members generally, the body of members as a whole will be liable for the due performance of such contract and will be entitled to enforce it. In

---

15 [1989] 1 WLR 872. See also *Shore v Ministry of Works* [1950] 2 All ER 228.
16 In the case of a proprietor's club, the position is different. In such a case, the liability of the proprietor will follow ordinary common law and contractual principles.
17 See *Prole v Allen* [1950] 1 All ER 476; *Grice v Stourport Tennis Hockey and Squash Club*, (3 March 1997, unreported), CA.
18 (1990) Times, 21 May.

practice, enforcement is likely to be dealt with or directed against a small number of representative members authorised to handle such matters in a representative capacity on behalf of the membership[19]. The constitution of most such clubs provides for the management to devolve upon a committee with clearly defined powers. But it should be noted that, in the absence of special provision in the constitution, authority for one member, or even a general or management committee, to enter contracts so as thereby to pledge the credit of other members will not normally be implied. It follows that care needs to be exercised in drawing up club rules. The elected officers and management and other committees need to have their powers clearly spelled out if they are not to be at risk of exposure to personal liability without recourse to the membership generally[20].

– *Partnerships:*
A partnership is a form of unincorporated association. It can arise simply where two or more persons carry on a business together with a view to profit. As an unincorporated association, it has no legal personality beyond that of its constituent partners and has no capacity to litigate although procedural rules exist which enable the partners to sue and be sued in the firm's name[1]. Relations between the partners are governed by the terms of their partnership agreement and the Partnership Act 1890. Under that Act[2], all partners are jointly and severally liable for torts and frauds committed by any one of them against a third party. Equally, under the ordinary principles of agency[3], all partners are similarly liable in respect of breaches of contract entered into with the firm.

19 The rights and liabilities of the individual members are determined according to the ordinary rules of agency. Order 15, r 12 of the Rules of the Supreme Court enables a representative action to be brought against, or in the name of, a small number of sample members, provided that all members clearly have a common interest in the proceedings.
20 See *Cockerell v Aucompte* (1857) 2 CBNS 440, *Re St James' Club* (1852) 2 De GM & G 383 and *Wise v Perpetual Trustee Co* [1903] AC 139.
1 See RSC Ord 81.
2 See ss 10 and 12.
3 By s 5 of the Partnership Act 1890, every partner is an agent of the firm and his other partners. His acts in the ordinary course of business bind the firm and all the partners, save where a third party with whom he deals knows of his lack of actual authority.

Chapter 4

Freedom of competition

Introduction

EUROPEAN LAW

One of the major aims of the Treaty of Rome, which established the European Economic Community (now the European Union), was/is to ensure freedom of competition throughout the geographical area covered by it[1]. Articles 85 and 86 provide the chief means by which that aim is promoted[2]. Together they constitute the foundations of the European Community's policy in this area.

Article 85 attacks *decisions* and *concerted practices* generally which inhibit or prevent competition if they may affect trade between Member States.

Article 86 targets any so called *'abuse of a dominant position'* in the common market, or part thereof, again if it may affect trade between Member States.

Alleged breaches of either article may be investigated and, if established, dealt with by the European Commission[3], which has power to restrain breaches and impose fines. The articles also form part of the domestic law of individual Member States and are of direct effect within them, which means that alleged breaches are actionable in the domestic courts of each Member State[4]. In the ordinary case, alleged breaches will be more appropriate for determination by domestic courts rather than invoking the more unwieldy procedures of the Commission, and the Commission confirmed as much when, in February 1993, it published guidance notes in which it indicated that it intended only to concern itself with matters having particular political, economic or legal significance for the European Community and

---

1 Similar principles apply under the Agreement on a European Economic Area to Norway, Liechtenstein and Iceland. Certain other countries have their own agreements with the Community, affording analogous rights.
2 See also the Mergers Regulation (EEC No 4064/89) which makes provision for the Commission to investigate certain mergers and joint ventures (referred to as 'concentrations') and, depending upon their effect on competition, either to prohibit or validate them.
3 The Commission's powers are delegated from the Council by Regulation 17/1962.
4 *Garden Cottage Foods Ltd v Milk Marketing Board* [1984] AC 130; *Cutsforth v Mansfield Inns Ltd* [1986] 1 WLR 558.

that other complaints should be directed to the relevant domestic courts/
authorities in the individual Member States. This message was reinforced in
the Commission's XXVth Report on Competition Policy (1995).

PROPORTIONALITY

The principle of 'proportionality' is discussed in more detail below, in the
chapter on Freedom of Movement and the Right to Work. It also has
application in relation to the Community's competition rules. For present
purposes, it means that, to the extent that such rules allow derogations from
the fundamental freedoms provided for, a limitation to such derogations is
always that they should go no further than is strictly necessary to achieve the
legitimate purpose of the exception.

UK DOMESTIC LAW

In addition to the regime of European competition law which looks for
anti-competitive effects across international borders, there exists alongside it
a domestic structure of rules and regulations applicable to all arrangements
within the United Kingdom, whether they have international effects and
implications or not. Unlike most of its partners in Europe, the United
Kingdom has chosen not to model its domestic regulatory regime on
European law[5]. For UK traders (this includes those engaged in sport as a
business or who conduct their business in some way through or in
connection with sport) it is necessary to consider separately the two
disparate systems. The domestic structure is comprised largely within

- the Restrictive Trade Practices Act 1976 (which deals with agreements
  which restrict trade and so might be seen as targeting similar types of
  arrangement as Article 85)

- the Fair Trading Act 1973 (which deals with *mergers/monopolies* and so
  covers similar ground to Article 86)

- the Competition Act 1980 (which deals with *anti-competitive practices* by
  individual persons/groups and so bears some relation to Article 86 but
  targets effects on the market defined in a manner similar to Article 85)

- the Resale Prices Act 1976 (which deals with resale price maintenance).

UK law is administered in different respects by the Office of Fair Trading (in
particular the Director General of Fair Trading), the Department of Trade
and Industry and the Monopolies and Mergers Commission. Certain
specific issues are required to be determined by the Restrictive Practices
Court. Further, the UK legislation is 'overlapping' in the sense that the same
conduct may fall foul of more than one of the above Acts.

---

5   At the time of writing the new Labour Government has indicated that it intends to
    introduce a new Competition Bill, modelled broadly upon Articles 85 and 86 of the Treaty
    of Rome.

PART I: AGREEMENTS ETC WHICH RESTRICT TRADE

A. European law – Article 85

The prima facie prohibition under Article 85 is designed to outlaw cartels and other arrangements, the object or effect of which are anti-competitive in that they may prevent restrict or distort trade between Member States. To that end, Article 85(1) prohibits:

> '... all *agreements between undertakings, decisions by associations of undertakings and concerted practices* which *may affect trade between Member States* and which have as their *object or effect* the *prevention, restriction or distortion of competition* within the common market and, in particular those which:
>
> (a) directly or indirectly fix purchase or selling prices or any other trading conditions;
> (b) limit or control production, markets, technical development, or investment;
> (c) share markets or sources of supply;
> (d) apply dissimilar conditions to equivalent transactions with other trading parties, thereby placing them at a competitive disadvantage;
> (e) make the conclusion of contracts subject to acceptance by the other parties of supplementary obligations which, by their nature or according to commercial usage, have no connection with the subject of such contracts.'

For this prohibition to apply to a transaction, affirmative answers must be given to all of the following questions:

(a) Does the transaction involve *undertakings or associations of undertakings?*
(b) Does it amount to an *agreement, decision or concerted practice?*
(c) Does it involve *prevention, restriction or distortion of competition* in its *object or effect?*
(d) In particular, is it a transaction which *may affect trade between Member States?*

UNDERTAKINGS AND ASSOCIATIONS OF UNDERTAKINGS

The concept of an undertaking is not defined by the Article, but is a broad one. It includes any entity or enterprise (of whatever form[6]) which carries on activities of an economic nature[7]. It seems clear, therefore, that professional sports clubs (in so far as they are run on commercial lines, even if they are not profitable) will qualify. Further, the governing bodies of particular sports[8] (such as, for example, the Football Association) invariably amount, if not to undertakings in their own right, then to 'associations of undertakings'. Indeed, particular sports may include a number of distinct such associations, all of which are likely to qualify for inclusion amongst the bodies subject to the regulatory/prohibitory regime of Article 85 (see, in

---

6 Even individuals may qualify. See *Re RAI/UNITEL* [1978] 3 CMLR 306, where opera singers were held to be undertakings.
7 See *Pauwels Travel Bvba v FIFA Local Organising Committee Italia 1990* [1994] 5 CMLR 253 (package tours to the World Cup).
8 Sports which still operate on exclusively amateur lines may be excluded.

football for example, the Football Association, the FA Premier League, the Football League, the Scottish Football League, the Vauxhall Conference, UEFA, FIFA[9] etc).

AGREEMENTS, DECISIONS AND CONCERTED PRACTICES

Whilst the concepts of an agreement, a decision and a concerted practice may theoretically be separate and distinct, in practice they will frequently overlap. What is clear, is that the Article covers transactions across a very broad spectrum and any form of dealing between 'undertakings' is likely to be caught. No particular formality is required, and an arrangement which is not even binding in itself may well be included if, for example, it constitutes a 'concerted practice', which is a term which signifies simply some kind of (formal or informal) co-operation which is intended to produce (or does in fact produce) a common form of action or inaction.

Whilst, in relation specifically to 'associations of undertakings', and therefore sports governing bodies etc, it is only 'decisions' which are expressly covered[10], the general approach of the Commission (and the European Court of Justice) is such that a broad view should be taken as to what may qualify as a 'decision'[11]. Even non-mandatory recommendations and suggestions to members are likely to be regarded, in the context of the breadth of the Article as a whole, as amounting to 'decisions'. Further, it is thought likely that the governing constitutions of such bodies will themselves be regarded as amounting to or involving one or more 'decisions', so as to open them up to direct scrutiny[12].

Equally, and in any event, such bodies are likely to amount to or provide evidence of 'agreements'[13] between or 'concerted practices' by the constituent members of such bodies. In cases where there is any risk that the other features of Article 85 might be thought, actually or potentially, to apply[14], such bodies would be well advised carefully to consider and review the provisions of their constitutions, rules and recommendations.

PREVENTION, RESTRICTION OR DISTORTION OF COMPETITION

Again, the concepts of prevention, restriction and distortion of competition are not mutually exclusive and are used collectively to describe, and identify for potential prohibition, transactions which are, in any form, anti-competitive. The Article intends the description to be all embracing and goes on to provide some examples of transactions which will be caught.

---

9 Article 85 is not confined to activities of undertakings etc which are based within the European Community. The activities of all undertakings, wherever domiciled, are subject to its regime in so far as such activities impact in the defined anti-competitive way within the Community. See *A Ahlstrom Osakeyhtiö v EC Commission* [1988] 4 CMLR 901.
10 In addition, associations of undertakings may have a 'concerted practice', which is a free standing target of the Article.
11 See, for example, *Re Rolled Steel* [1980] 3 CMLR 193 (Rolled Steel).
12 See for example the decision in the case of a trade association in *Re National Sulphuric Acid Association Ltd* [1980] 3 CMLR 429.
13 See *Clarke v Earl of Dunraven* [1897] AC 59.
14 Do the rules have an anti-competitive effect or object? Do they have the potential to affect trade between Member States?

Included within such examples are cartel agreements, boycott agreements, market share agreements, research and development restriction agreements, bid rigging agreements[15], exclusivity agreements, franchising/licensing agreements. Indeed any form of agreement or arrangement which, directly or indirectly, seeks to impose price fixing, market sharing, impediments in access to markets, limitation/control of production or other activity or unrelated supplementary obligations may be caught, always remembering of course that the prohibition is activated only by a transaction which satisfies *all* qualifying requirements including that it may affect trade between Member States. In short, agreements, arrangements and understandings of any kind between competitors are at risk.

OBJECT OR EFFECT

The breadth of the prohibition is further illustrated by the fact that a relevant arrangement will potentially be caught either:

(a)   if its effect is anti-competitive in that it distorts, restricts or prevents competition even where such was never the intention; or alternatively (in theory[16])

(b)   where the intention is anti-competitive even though, in practice, no prevention restriction or distortion of the market is actually established.

THE 'RULE OF REASON'

One difficulty of interpretation which arises from the requirement that transactions must have an anti-competitive object or effect is whether an agreement containing relevant particular restrictive provisions is *necessarily* to be regarded as caught by the Article (assuming it qualifies in other respects). Some decisions suggest a negative answer where, for example, the agreement can be categorised in the round as being *pro-competitive* in spite of the restrictions. This line of reasoning, which owes a great deal to a doctrine developed under American anti-trust law known as the 'rule of reason', might be the case where it is clear that, but for the restrictions, the beneficiary of them would have chosen not to proceed with the agreement at all. Hence, in *Société Technique Minière v Maschinenbau Ulm GmbH*[17] the ECJ ruled that the grant of exclusive distribution rights was not prohibited in circumstances where the agreement enabled a new market (which was not devoid of competition) to be entered by the manufacturer and the provision of exclusivity was regarded as justifiable in that it went no further than was

---

15 Viz: agreements between competitors to take it in turns to bid for particular categories of contract.
16 In practice, the Commission will be unlikely to act in relation to arrangements which are not implemented in such a way as to have an anti-competitive effect, other than perhaps where the objective intent of the arrangement is blatant, as with a cartel agreement or an export ban. See for example *Viho Europe BV v Parker Pen Ltd* [1993] 5 CMLR 382.
17 56/65: [1966] CMLR 357.

necessary[18]. It may well be that this principle, the precise ambit of which is not clearly defined[19], but which is in line with the general principle of proportionality[20], may be prayed in aid by sports governing bodies and federations in appropriate circumstances. They may seek to show that their rules and dealings ought properly to be seen in the broad context of seeking to achieve, and actually achieving, full competition and that such restrictive provisions as they include are no more restrictive than is sensible and necessary in order to maintain such competition in an orderly fashion. It has to be said, however, that such bodies will place absolute reliance upon this 'principle' at their peril, in view of its questionable pedigree and imprecise ambit. They would be far better advised to seek exemption from the Commission under Article 85(3)[1]. A 'rule of reason' argument was deployed by UEFA, unsuccessfully in the opinion of Advocate-General Lenz, in *Union Royale Belge des Sociétés de Football Association ASBL v Bosman*[2]. Significantly, A-G Lenz tentatively accepted the legitimacy of the argument itself, rejecting it in the event only because he did not regard the restriction in question as being indispensable.

MAY AFFECT TRADE BETWEEN MEMBER STATES

In most sporting contexts, the issue of whether or not the transaction or arrangement under scrutiny is prohibited by Article 85 may well hinge upon whether or not it is liable to affect trade between Member States. In this connection, it is to be noted that most professional sports' bodies (and their clubs and associations) engage in (or facilite) 'trade' for this purpose. Trade is a wide concept[3] and there can be no doubt that, these days, sport very often means 'business'. It follows that deals, agreements, arrangements and understandings between sports clubs or other organisations located in different Member States are liable to have some cross-border trade implications. Equally the sports federations whose rules govern the playing of international competitions or other cross-border sport are prime targets

18 See also *Metro SB-Grossmärkte GmbH & Co KG v EC Commission*: 22/76 [1978] 2 CMLR 1 (selective distribution scheme); *LC Nungesser KG v EC Commission*: 258/78 [1983] 1 CMLR 278 (exclusive licence granted, where licensee was persuaded by the grant to invest in a risky venture and effect was to secure availability of new product); *Coditel SA v Ciné-Vog Films SA*: 262/81 [1983] 1 CMLR 49 (exclusive licence to exhibit film in one Member State); *Masterfoods Ltd v HB Ice Cream Ltd* [1992] 3 CMLR 830 (decision of Irish High Court upholding contractual restriction on ice cream retailers storing ice cream from manufacturers other than supplier of refrigeration unit). Note similar approach in UK by MMC in *Ice Cream* Cm 2524 1994, but beware more cautious approach in Europe – *Langnese-Iglo GmbH* 1993 OJ L183/9). See also *Gøttrup-Klim Grovvareforening v Dansk Landburgs Grovvareselskab AmbA*: C-250/92 [1994] ECR I-5641.
19 Equally, its precise relationship with Article 85(3) (see below) which permits exemption to be granted by the Commission in certain circumstances (including, for example, where the object is to achieve improved production/distribution) is not clear.
20 See, for example, *R v Intervention Board for Agricultural Produce, ex p E D & F Man (Sugar) Ltd*: 181/84 [1985] 3 CMLR 759, *Re Watson v Belmann*: 118/75 [1976] ECR 1185, *EC Commission v Germany*: 178/84 [1988] 1 CMLR 780, *EC Commission v United Kingdom*: 261/85 [1988] 2 CMLR 11, *Buet and Educational Business Services (EBS) v Ministère Public*: 382/87 [1989] ECR 1235, and *R v Minister of Agriculture Fisheries and Food, ex p Fedesa*: C-331/88 [1991] 1 CMLR 507.
1 See below.
2 C-415/93: [1996] 1 CMLR 645. The ECJ made no ruling on the issue. This important decision is discussed in detail below.
3 Opera singers engage in 'trade' – *Re RAI/UNITEL* [1978] 3 CMLR 306.

for scrutiny under Article 85. What is more, domestic transactions etc between clubs within one Member State will nevertheless be caught if such transactions are liable to have cross-border implications on the conduct of sporting business or 'trade'. Quite how far this kind of argument might be taken has yet to be made authoritatively clear, but it is surely not far fetched to suggest that rules or understandings which restrict how a particular sport is managed and controlled within one Member State may well impact on the way in which the sport generally or particular teams/clubs are able to compete in international competition.

A further feature of the wording of Article 85 is that a transaction will qualify, subject to the other requirements, simply if it *may* affect trade between Member States. This leaves open the possibility of transactions with no actual or established effect on trade between Member States nevertheless being prohibited[4].

EXEMPTIONS

Although Article 85 is phrased in wide, if not all embracing, terms (and Article 85(2) provides that any prohibited agreements or decisions are *automatically void*) there are a number of ways in which that widespread effect is or may be limited.

First, as has already been seen, it is only agreements, decisions or concerted practices which 'may affect trade between Member States' which are caught, leaving arrangements with no cross border trade implications to be governed solely by any applicable domestic law[5]. Even cross border transactions will be exempt, if their nature, size and significance is such as to be of no effect on trade between Member States.

Secondly, Article 85(3) makes provision for the prohibition to be declared (by the Commission) inapplicable if the arrangement in question:

'... contributes to improving the production or distribution of goods or to promoting technical or economic progress, while allowing consumers a fair share of the resulting benefit, and ... does not:

(a) impose on the undertakings concerned restrictions which are not indispensable to the attainment of those objectives;
(b) afford such undertakings the possibility of eliminating competition in respect of a substantial part of the products in question.'

In effect, Article 85(3) provides a mechanism for exempting[6] apparently prohibited arrangements where:

– they are shown to be beneficial (by improving production/distribution or promoting technical/economic progress);
– they give consumers a fair share of that benefit;
– they contain only essential restrictions; and

---

4 See eg *Windsurfing International Inc v EC Commission*: 193/83 [1986] 3 CMLR 489; *Cutsforth v Mansfield Inns* [1986[1 All ER 577. This principle is, however, subject to the de minimis rule which is discussed below.
5 In practice, the Commission generally has little difficulty in discovering appreciable effects on cross border trade.
6 It should be noted, however, that the fact that a particular arrangement is granted exemption under Article 85(3) will not provide it with corresponding protection from any liability under Article 86 – *Tetra Pak Rausing SA v EC Commission*: T-51/89 [1991] 4 CMLR 334.

– they do not give rise to the potential elimination of competition.

Further, exemptions under Article 85(3) may be granted either individually on specific application[7] or as 'block exemptions', by which categories of arrangement may be declared exempt[8]. Where such a block exemption is granted, regulations lay down the extent and nature of the exemption. In particular, they identify particular provisions which will be likely to be treated as attracting exemption. In addition, they identify provisions which, if included, will cause the agreement etc to lose such exemption as it otherwise might have attracted and it is important, therefore, to draft agreements with the terms of any relevant block exemption well in mind.

Thus far, only a few block exemptions have been granted. Most notable among them, for present purposes, is the exemption relating to Exclusive Distribution Agreements[9] by which (in broad terms) agreements for the exclusive distribution of goods may be exempt unless they result in the elimination of competition. Similarly, a block exemption exists in relation to Exclusive Purchasing Agreements[10]. Guidelines in respect of both such exemptions have been issued by the Commission[11]. Exemptions have also been granted in relation to Motor Vehicles[12], Patent Licences[13], Research and Development[14] and Franchises[15].

DE MINIMIS

In addition to the express provision in Article 85(3) whereby arrangements are granted specific exemption, it is now established that arrangements will only be deemed to be contrary to Article 85 where their (actual or potential) effect on competition and trade between Member States is found to be 'appreciable'[16]. This *de minimis* principle was fleshed out by the Commission, in 1986, when it published guidance[17] on the criteria for determining what is and is not 'appreciable' in this context, in its 'Notice concerning Agreements of Minor Importance which do not fall under Article 85(1) of the Treaty'[18]. That guidance suggests, broadly, that arrangements will probably not qualify for prohibition where the parties (together with certain

---

7 Individual exemptions are rare, very few being granted each year, for no other reason than pressure of work and time at the Commission. Realistically, in the sporting field, it is only the 'big issues' which are likely to be appropriate for an application for individual exemption. Such issues might, include the consideration of the constitution or other rules of particular governing bodies or federations.
8 Block exemptions, applying in specified circumstances, have been granted, for example, in relation to exclusive distribution or purchasing agreements, patent licences, research and development agreements, specialisation agreements and other types of agreement.
9 OJ 1983 L173/1.
10 OJ 1983 L173/5.
11 OJ 1984 C101/2.
12 OJ 1995 L145/25.
13 OJ 1996 L31/2.
14 OJ 1985 L53/5, amended by OJ 1993 L21/8.
15 Re franchises involving goods or services; OJ 1988 L359/46.
16 *Volk v Vervaecke*: 5/69 [1969] CMLR 273.
17 It should be noted that the Commision's guidance is no more than that. Strictly, it has no formal legal standing and any reliance upon it should therefore be cautious.
18 OJ 1986 C231/2, amended in OJ 1994 C368/20.

of their associated companies[19]) hold no more than 5% of the relevant market in the goods/services the subject thereof[20] and the annual turnover of such parties (and such associated companies) does not exceed (currently) 300 million ECU (approaching £250,000)[1].

The application of Article 85 in the sporting field

Contracts which are liable to require careful scrutiny are those which grant exclusive rights and those which grant rights in respect of a defined territory. In the sporting field, particular areas of vulnerability are broadcasting, ticketing, merchandising and sponsorship contracts as well as the contracts/arrangements inherent in the constitutions and other rules of individual sporting federations:

– *Broadcasting*
  In relation to broadcasting rights, it is clear that some form of exclusivity in the grant of such rights to a particular broadcaster is likely to be commercially very desirable in order to increase the value of such rights. Equally clear is the fact that exclusivity will tend to be regarded in most circumstances as restrictive of competition. It follows that any grant of exclusivity, whether general or territorial, whilst it may be commercially attractive and apparently reasonable, is at risk of being held to infringe Article 85(1) with the potential consequence of the grant itself being void. The Commission recognised this conundrum and has expressed the view consistently that the grant of broadcasting rights on an exclusive basis is not, of itself, necessarily objectionable. Thus, for example, in the Commission's decision in the *German Film Purchases* case[2], the grant of licences to a German television network giving it exclusive access to MGM films for a period of 15 years was granted exemption under Article 85(3), after provision for access by other broadcasters was agreed for short periods during the term of the licence. Further, Commissioner Van Miert set out the Commission's general approach in a written reply[3]:

  '... in the light of the specific characteristics of the television industry, the granting of exclusive television rights is in itself not contrary to Community competition rules. Exclusivity is normally an appropriate means to maintain the value of television programmes in terms of viewing figures and advertising revenues which they can attract. However, the competition rules apply to agreements on exclusive television rights which are *excessive in their scope and/or duration ...*'

19 Undertakings which must, for present purposes, be included in the equation are the parties themselves, undertakings in which they have more than a 50% stake, or which they have the right to manage and, correspondingly, undertakings which have more than a 50% stake in or the right to manage, any of the parties. Thus it is group market share which is regarded as important.
20 Identification of the market in question is plainly of great significance. It requires identification of the relevant products (which are not confined simply to the particular goods/services the subject of the particular arrangement, but include 'equivalent' goods/services) and the geographical area of the European market affected by the arrangement (see paragraphs 7 and 11–14 of the Notice).
1 In its 1995 Report on Competition Policy, the Commission indicated an intention to extend the limits of the de minimis rule.
2 OJ L284 3/10/89.
3 OJ 1989 L284/36.

This approach was reflected when the Commission belatedly considered the agreement which had granted British Satellite Broadcasting and the BBC exclusive rights to all Football Association matches for the period 1988 to 1993. It concluded that it would have been regarded as objectionable save only for the fact that British Satellite Broadcasting (by then merged as BSkyB) was a new entrant to the market. Generally, the Commission's view was that, in order to retain an appropriate degree of competition, contracts granting exclusivity in relation to matches with mass appeal should, as a rule of thumb, extend for no longer than one year. Such a view is thought by many to be unrealistic in that it gives little chance to the broadcaster to promote its coverage of the event or to help 'build' the event. It also gives to the seller little chance to make future financial plans and requires him to live effectively from hand to mouth.

The Commission went further, when in its *Eurovision* decision of 11 June 1993[4] it purported to grant an Article 85(3) exemption to the rules of the European Broadcasting Union which operated as a collective of public broadcasting authorities operating on a territorial exclusive licensing basis but with complicated sub licensing arrangements designed to give third party access to the centrally negotiated rights. The decision was arrived at only after painstaking negotiations and revisions to the Eurovision scheme. In particular, the decision confirmed that:

> 'Exclusivity is as a general rule considered to be necessary in order to guarantee the value of a given sports programme in terms of the viewing figures and advertising revenues which it can achieve.'

Further, this kind of approach to the competition rules is in line with decisions of the ECJ itself which have suggested that the grant of exclusivity within a single Member State is not of itself objectionable unless it gives rise to barriers to competition which are 'artificial or unjustified'[5]. In particular, it was said by the ECJ in *Coditel*[6] that it was for the national court in each case:

> 'To determine whether exercise of the exclusive right ... does not create artificial, unjustified barriers, having regard to the requirements of the ... industry, or the possibility of royalties exceeding a fair remuneration for the investments made, or an exclusive right for a period which is excessive by reference to these requirements, and whether generally the exercise of such right within a specified geographical area is not likely to prevent, restrict or distort competition within the Community.'

The Commission's general approach, however, suffered a setback as a result of the decision of the Court of First Instance in *Métropole Télévision SA v EC Commission*[7], in which the Commission's Article 85(3) exemption in the *Eurovision* case was annulled. In a judgment, the full rationale and implications of which are difficult to fathom, the CFI found that the Commission had failed to address all the issues which it ought to have done. In particular, it had not addressed the wider and

4   IV/32.150 – EBU/Eurovision System.
5   See, for example, *Coditel SA v Ciné-Vog Films SA*: 262/81 [1983] 1 CMLR 49. See also, albeit in a different context, *LC Nungesser KG and Eisele v EC Commission*: 258/78 [1983] 1 CMLR 278.
6   Ibid at para 19.
7   [1996] ECR II-649. Joined cases T-528/93, T-542/93, T-543/93 and T-546/93.

more general issues on the basis of which the exemption had been granted in the first place. In fact, the court did not go so far as to hold that no exemption was appropriate and Commissioner Van Miert has subsequently suggested that a further exemption to the EBU might readily yet be granted. It is suggested, further, that the CFI's decision ought not to signify an end to the kind of sensible and pragmatic approach exemplified by the Commission's original decision and the cases previously referred to. In modern day circumstances, with undertakings such as BSkyB and other commercial channels bringing considerable financial muscle to the sports broadcasting market, it is suggested that a group of public broadcasters such as the EBU needs to be able to flex its muscles collectively in order to compete effectively and that allowing it to do so would not significantly distort competition. The decision of the CFI, however, has inevitably thrown the industry into confusion and doubt. It is understood that the EBU has appealed to the ECJ, the decision of which will be awaited with anticipation[8].

In the meantime, it is apparent that broadcasting contracts which accord exclusive rights to a particular competition will at least need to be restricted in terms of scope and/or duration to be safe.

The Commission has also consistently expressed concern over UEFA's rule 14, regulation 8 of which purports to prohibit the transmission of football matches, within certain time periods, from one federation member's territory into that of another (the aim and asserted justification being to maximise crowds at football matches). As yet, the Commission has not seen fit to bring the issue to a head.

In the United Kingdom, some commentators advance the questionable argument that the prohibition on the grant of exclusive rights to 'listed events' under the Broadcasting Act 1996[9] serve to encourage competition. Further, after a protracted debate within the Community concerning a proposed revision of the Television without Frontiers Directive[10], the European Parliament and the Council finally reached agreement in June 1997 upon the terms of an amendment which expressly sanctions such an approach by individual Member States[11]. The amendment includes a requirement that any Member State which adopts such measures should notify the Commission, which is charged with the task of verifying that the measures taken are not incompatible with Community law.

– *Ticketing*:
Arrangements which impose restrictions on the purchasing of tickets outside an exclusive territory or which require the purchase of other goods or services (such as a travel package) in order to secure a ticket are all in the frame for prohibition. In a case concerned with the arrange-

8   It is thought that, ultimately, the Commission's approach is likely to prevail. In particular, a new 'mood' is arguably apparent amongst European legislators, as evidenced by the revisions, in 1997, to the Television Without Frontiers Directive (89/552/EEC amended by 97/36/EC) which had the effect of sanctioning protective measures to preserve the availability of coverage of important events on free television. These and other provisions in the Directive are discussed in Chapter 13, below.
9   See ss 97 to 105, replacing s 182 of the 1990 Act.
10 1989/552/EEC.
11 See 97/39/EC. The Broadcasting Act 1996 and the amended Directive are discussed in greater detail in Chapter 13, below.

ments for distributing tickets to the 1990 Football World Cup in Italy[12], the Commission upheld a complaint (under Articles 85 and 86) by a Belgian travel agent, over the fact that exclusive worldwide rights had been granted to one company for the distribution of tickets and travel packages (and that company had granted exclusive agencies in each of a number of Member States.)

- *Merchandising*:
In the case of *Danish Tennis Federation*, which was primarily concerned with Article 86, the Commission expressed the view that the designation by the Danish Tennis Federation of Penn, Slazenger and Tretorn tennis balls as 'official' was objectionable in that such designation implied that the balls were of superior quality (and was liable, thereby, to give them a competitive advantage over other balls) in circumstances where no technical criteria had been applied such as to mark them out as being better than others. The anti-competitive effect was increased by the DTF's requirement that only such 'official' balls be used in particular tournaments. The Commission's views caused the DTF to modify its arrangements under which manufacturers obtained a right to supply balls for its tournaments in return for financial support. All manufacturers were entitled to bid for such right each year and the use of the word 'official' was dropped so as to remove the implied suggestion of superior quality. The Commission has indicated an inclination not to challenge this revised arrangement[13].

In *Dunlop Slazenger International Ltd v EC Commission*[14], the use of official logos and initials on sports equipment, so as thereby to signify endorsement by a sporting federation or other respected organisation again came under scrutiny. Here, the manufacturers of tennis balls (and other items) caused official stickers to be attached to shipments to their authorised distributors in different parts of Europe. The Commission decided (and was upheld by the Court of First Instance) that this amounted to a breach of Article 85 in that the aim was not to distinguish such balls by reason of their technical properties, but to identify balls which came onto a particular geographic market otherwise than via their authorised agent within such market and therefore through unauthorised parallel import agencies. In this way, the manufacturer's designation of balls as 'official' was being used in order to support a ban imposed by the manufacturers on the trade in its balls between, in particular, the United Kingdom and the rest of Europe[15]. Further, the Commission asserted that:

> 'The concerted use, within the framework of an exclusive distribution agreement, of an intellectual property right with the sole aim of impeding parallel imports constitutes an infringement of Article 85(1).'

In particular, the marking on the balls was anti-competitive because it favoured the manufacturer's exclusive distributor network by suggesting that balls with such a marking were of superior quality and that their higher prices were justified, to the detriment of the goods imported

---

12 See *Pauwels Travel Bvba v FIFA Local Organising Committee Italia 1990* [1994] 5 CMLR 253.
13 1996 OJ C138/7.
14 T-43/92: [1994] ECR II-441 CFI.
15 The point was that the manufacturer charged higher prices for its balls in the United Kingdom than elsewhere.

through parallel channels. Such an arrangement amounted to a clear attempt to partition the European market and, as such, was contrary to Article 85[16].

- *Sponsorship:*
There are many ways in which a sponsorship agreement will limit or control production, the markets, technical developments or investments, or may share markets or sources of supply so as to bring them within the scrutiny of Article 85(1)(b) and/or (c). In particular, a degree of exclusivity will often be an essential feature of many kinds of sponsorship contracts. A sponsor of a particular event or competition, for example, will not readily spend his money unless he is assured that he will have access to the opportunities afforded him by his contract free from avoidable competitive activity. What the sponsor is buying is the right to distinguish himself from his competitors. The designation of 'sponsor' (or even 'official supplier' etc) enables him to bask in the reflected glory of the event or competition. It follows that he will require some form of exclusivity of use of any intellectual property rights associated with the event/competition, as well as specific exclusions of advertising and other promotional opportunities for his competitors. Without such protective provisions, sponsors are likely to be reluctant to come forward (and competition will, thereby, be inhibited rather than promoted). There is no reason to believe that this will not be recognised by the Commission. It is suggested that, as with broadcasters, a degree of exclusivity will not be regarded as automatically objectionable. The Commission will look at individual arrangements and judge them by reference to their scope, their duration, the extent to which they inhibit competition and, under the principle of proportionality, the extent to which they can be shown to be necessary. If the relationship goes beyond one simply of sponsorship, however, we have already seen[17] how the competition rules may be brought into play, particularly where products are designated 'official', where markets are effectively partitioned and where arrangements are put into place (for example by the licensing of intellectual property rights in different countries) to prevent parallel importing.

- *The constitutions etc of sporting federations:*
The *Danish Tennis Federation* case referred to above, is but one example where the rules of a sporting federation have been considered objectionable and contrary to European competition law (primarily, in that case, Article 86). The potential liability for the rules of such bodies to come under scrutiny in such a context is very great, given the fact that such rules are often designed, in part, to regulate the conduct of sport across inter-state boundaries and are likely to impose specific requirements and restrictions in the pursuit of the orderly conduct of sporting affairs. Particular examples of inappropriate restrictions might include rules which required the approval of new applications for membership by all existing members (or by a core group of members with an effective veto), or which imposed penal financial criteria or other deterrents upon applicants for membership, or which imposed particular limitations upon the way business should be conducted. Any rules will potentially be caught

16 For a similar example, also relating to tennis balls, see the Commission's decision in *Tretorn* 1994 OJ L378/45.
17 See p 90 above.

which require (or recommend) restrictions on prices, limitations on free-dom to trade with other businesses or between members, limitations on members' ability to advertise or otherwise to access the market. For exam-ple, Commissioner Van Miert has recently expressed the view that a ban by the Danish Football Union on all personal advertising agreements by its members in respect of products similar to those of its own sponsors may amount to an illegitimate restriction on competitive trading[18].

In *Union Royale Belge des Sociétés de Football ASBL v Bosman*[19] the Court of Appeal in Liege invited the ECJ to consider the rules applicable within Belgium (but emanating from UEFA and FIFA):

(a)   under which transfer fees could be demanded in the event of the transfer of a professional footballer from one club to another, even where his contract with the transferor club had ended (the transfer rules); and

(b)   which limited the number of foreign players which could be fielded by a club in particular matches (the foreign player rules).

The domestic court sought answers in relation to competition law (Articles 85 and 86) as well as under Article 48. In the event, the Court confined its consideration to Article 48, indicating[20] that, by reason of its answers under that Article, consideration of the competition aspects of the transfer and foreign player rules was rendered unnecessary. It is suggested, nevertheless, that the rules in question had very obvious implications under European competition law. The particular questions referred to the ECJ were as follows:

'Are Articles 48, 85 and 86 of the Treaty of Rome ... to be interpreted as:

(1)   prohibiting a football club from requiring and receiving payment of a sum of money upon the engagement of one of its players who has come to the end of his contract by a new employing club;

(2)   prohibiting the national and international sporting associations or federations from including in their respective regulations provisions restricting access of foreign players from the Euro-pean Community to the competitions which they organise?'

Advocate-General Lenz expressed the firm view, in his opinion to the Court, that both the transfer and the foreign player rules infringed Article 85 (but not Article 86, which is discussed in detail below). With reasoning which it is hard to fault, he concluded in particular as follows:

(a)   All professional clubs, however successful and whether profitable or not, are 'undertakings' in that they engage in economic activity[1], and the football associations/federations are, accordingly 'associa-tions of undertakings'[2].

---

18 1996 OJ C217/40.

19 C-415/93: [1996] 1 CMLR 645.

20 Paragraph 138.

1   See *Höfner and Elser v Macrotron GmbH*: C-41/90 [1993] 4 CMLR 306, paragraph 21; *Poucet v Assurances Générales de France (AGF) and Caisse Mutuelle Regionale du Lempuedoc-Roussillon*: C-159/91, *Pistre v Caisse Autonome Nationale de Compensation de l'Assurance Vieillesse des Artisans (Cancava)* C-160/91 [1993] ECR I-637, paragraph 17.

2   Paragraphs 254 to 257. Such associations etc may also be 'undertakings' in their own right in so far as they themselves engage in economic activity. Under the common law, the constitution of such an association is liable to be regarded as giving rise to a contract between its constituent members – see *Clarke v Earl of Dunraven* [1897] AC 59.

(b)   The rules in question involve 'decisions of associations of undertakings' and/or (to the extent that they represent the expression of the collective will of the members) 'agreements between undertakings'[3].

(c)   The 'decisions' or 'agreements' involved have (and, in any event are liable to have) an appreciable effect on trade[4] between Member States[5]. In the case of the transfer rules, A-G Lenz did not here distinguish, expressly at least, between cross border transfers and domestic transfers (whether involving a foreign player or not). It is suggested that, given the extent of cross-border competition within European football, any transfers which have (or might potentially have) an appreciable effect on competition in footballing terms are likely to be regarded as having such an effect on trade between Member States. On this premise, there is no basis for excluding from any analysis of the rules in question under Article 85, transactions which, in one sense or another are 'wholly internal' to one Member State (so as otherwise to benefit from the exemption determined by the ECJ in relation to Article 48).

(d)   A-G Lenz regarded it as 'perfectly clear'[6] that both rules restrict competition. As he said[7]:

> 'The rules on foreign players restrict the possibilities for the individual clubs to compete with each other by engaging players ... [the rules on transfers] replace the normal system of supply and demand by a uniform machinery which leads to the existing competition situation being preserved and the clubs being deprived of the possibility of making use of the chances, with respect to the engagement of players, which would be available to them under normal conditions.'

(e)   The rules could not be saved by arguments based upon the so called 'rule of reason' under which such restrictions of competition are balanced or evaluated against the asserted benefits thereof, in that they did not adhere to the principle of proportionality – the rules could not be justified as being indispensable for the attainment of the legitimate objectives of the Treaty, and the proper functioning of the market of professional football[8].

(f)   There is no basis for the argument that competition law does not apply to restrictions properly to be regarded as within the field of labour law[9].

---

3 Paragraphs 258 to 259.
4 Presumably the (primary) 'trade' in which professional football clubs engage is the provision of a service (an entertainment), namely the spectacle provided by the matches in which they participate. A-G Lenz expressed the view (paragraph 261) that all forms of 'economic relations between Member States' qualify as 'trade' for the purposes of competition law. See also *Züchner v Bayerische Vereinsbank AG*: 172/80 [1982] 1 CMLR 313.
5 Paragraphs 260 to 261.
6 Paragraphs 262 to 263.
7 Paraggraph 262.
8 Paragraphs 265 to 270.
9 Paragraphs 271 to 276. Although the discussion in *Bosman* was referable to EU/EEA player transfers inter-state, following the commencement of two further cases (one involving the Rumanian footballer, Georg Hagi) UEFA amended its rules to recognise that *Bosman* principles applied to transfers of players between Member States irrespective of the player's nationality.

Following on from *Bosman* a local court in Namur has referred further questions to the ECJ. In *Deliege v ASGC Ligue Francophone de Judo et Disciplines Associees & ASGC Ligue Belge de Judo*[10] the issue is:

> 'Whether or not rules which require a professional or semi professional or a person aspiring to such status to have been authorised or selected by his national federation in order to be able to compete in an international competition, and which lay down national entry quotas for similar competitions are contrary to Articles 59 to 66 and Articles 85 and 86.'

Of course, the rules of a sporting authority are likely to impose any number of restrictions which may be said to give rise to the prevention, restriction or distortion of competition. Unjustifiable restrictions on membership of or affiliation to such bodies may qualify[11], as may unfair disciplinary rules. An attempt was made to pray Article 85 (as well as Articles 59 and 86) in aid in challenging disciplinary procedures in *Wilander and Novacek v Tobin and Jude*[12]. The disciplinary rules in question were those under which two tennis stars had been suspended for failing drug tests. On the facts, however, it was held that the argument under Article 85 was unsustainable and should be struck out. This is not to say that the disciplinary processes of governing bodies are safe from scrutiny under Article 85, as the primary basis of the court's conclusion was simply that there was no coherent case advanced as to how, in the circumstances, competition was liable to be prevented, restricted or distorted[13]. In other circumstances, such an argument might have a significantly stronger cogency.

B. UK domestic law

This section seeks to examine that part of UK domestic law which is most akin to Article 85. Primarily, this means the Restrictive Trade Practices Act 1976. The Resale Prices Act 1976, which targets resale price maintenance agreements is also examined in brief. The Competition Act 1980, which targets certain activity which is identified as 'anti-competitive' (within the UK) in terms similar to those in Article 85 (namely practices which are liable to *restrict, distort or prevent competition*), is part of a domestic regime of which the Fair Trading Act 1973 (which targets transactions/situations akin to those dealt with by Article 86) forms another part. That regime targets

---

10 Case C-51/96: OJ 1996 C133/13.
11 See, for example, *La Cinq SA v EC Commission*: T-44/90 [1992] 4 CMLR 449. In *Stevenage Borough Football Club Ltd v Football League Ltd*, (1996) Times, 1 August, (Carnwath J); affd (1997) 9 Admin LR 109, CA, a challenge to the Football League's rules of entry was given short shrift at first instance, on the basis that there was no evidence that they were liable to have any appreciable effect on competition or trade between Member States (on the basis that clubs joining the League from the GM Vauxhall conference were hardly likely to be significant players in European competition). The point was not renewed in the Court of Appeal.
12 [1997] 1 Lloyd's Rep 195 (Lightman J). The case is discussed in detail in Chapter 5 below.
13 Lightman J was not impressed with the mere assertion that the competition which was liable to be affected was that 'between players affected by the elimination of those who are suspended and between tradesmen who earn a living from providing services to the public where and when tournaments are held.' This part of the decision was not the subject of appeal to the Court of Appeal.

defined practices, transactions and situations as worthy of investigation by the domestic authorities[14] without necessarily outlawing them. The Competition Act 1980, therefore, is examined as part of that regime, along with the Fair Trading Act 1973, after consideration in Part II below of Article 86.

Restrictive Trade Practices Act 1976

The object of the Restrictive Trade Practices Act 1976 is to outlaw agreements which prevent/distort competition in trade involving goods or services. Unlike European law, the Act focuses on the form or character of the agreement rather than its substance or effect, with the consequence that careful drafting will often take an agreement outside the ambit of restriction altogether even where its effect is undeniably anti-competitive.

The scheme of the Act provides that qualifying agreements are void, unless registered with the Office of Fair Trading which will, subject to an exception in s 21(2), refer it to the Restrictive Practices Court for a determination whether it is contrary to the public interest (as to which the onus is on the parties). By the exception in s 21(2), the Director General may, instead, recommend to the Secretary of State that the restrictions in question are not of sufficient seriousness to merit referral.

SPORT AND THE ACT

In 1980 the Office of Fair Trading gave advance warning to the world of sport by issuing a press release identifying particular categories of restriction in sporting contexts which it would be unlikely to regard as suitable for such a recommendation, namely those:

(a)   by which sport tried to regulate the level of admission charges;
(b)   which required a pooling of revenue from commercial sources;
(c)   which curtailed the ability to exercise individual rights;
(d)   which restricted the use of income.

All restrictions of the kind referred to should be registered. Thus, for example, agreements between clubs or requirements in a governing body's rules under which broadcasting rights are required to be sold collectively or centrally, thereby removing or curtailing the right (if any) of individual clubs to cut their own deals, would fall squarely within (c) above [and possibly (b)] and should be registered. Where such agreements or requirements involved the revenue from broadcasting to be pooled before being split according to some formula provided for, they would be likely, additionally, to fall within (b). Similarly, agreements or requirements as to the allocation of gate receipts would be likely to fall within (d) [and, perhaps, (b)] and provisions which sought to control ticket prices would obviously come under (a).

Qualifying restrictions which are not registered are void. Once registered, they are valid unless ruled otherwise by the Restrictive Practices Court.

14 Principally the Office of Fair Trading and/or the Monopolies and Mergers Commission.

The principal type of agreement which qualifies for compulsory registration is one which[15]:

(a)   is between two or more persons[16] carrying on business in the United Kingdom either[17]

(i)   producing, manufacturing or supplying goods[18]; or
(ii)   supplying services; and

(b)   contains one or more 'qualifying restrictions' by which two or more persons accept some specific limitation on their freedom to trade (other than a limitation on the very rights granted by the agreement itself).

'AGREEMENTS'

An 'agreement' for this purpose includes any kind of agreement or arrangement. No particular form is required and it does not have to amount to a legally enforceable contract as such[19]. It follows that the requirements and obligations contained in the rules and regulations of a sport's governing body, to which all subscribing members are required to agree and adhere, will qualify under the Act as an 'agreement' which relates to the supply of services[20].

'QUALIFYING RESTRICTIONS'

The 'qualifying restrictions', in the case of agreements concerning goods, relate to the following matters[1]:

(a)   prices, whether at point of sale/purchase or for resale;
(b)   the terms and conditions on which the goods are to be produced, manufactured or supplied/acquired;
(c)   the quantities/descriptions of such goods;
(d)   the processes to be applied to such goods;

15 Relevant agreements relating to goods are defined by s 6 of the RTPA 1976; agreements relating to services by s 11 and SI 1976/98 as amended by SI 1985/2044, SI 1986/2204, SI 1989/1082 and the Transport Act 1985.
16 Companies in the same group, and partners, are treated for this purpose as one person – RTPA 1976, s 43.
17 The two or more persons carrying on business need not be doing so in the same kind of business, save that they must both be engaged in businesses relating to goods or they must both be engaged in businesses relating to services. An agreement between a person who,say, supplies goods and one who supplies services will not be registrable.
18 The RTPA 1976 also applies to 'information' agreements, whereby provision is made for the disclosure of information on specified matters such as prices, costs, markets, terms and conditions etc. See s 7 of the RTPA 1976. The corresponding provision relating to agreements concerning services (s 12) has not been brought into force.
19 See s 43 of the RTPA 1976. See also *Fisher v Director General of Fair Trading* [1982] ICR 71; *Re Royal Institution of Chartered Surveyors' Application* [1986] ICR 550.
20 Under ordinary common law principles, a governing body's constitution (which is likely to require adherence to its rules and regulations) is liable to be regarded as a contract between its constituent members in any event – see *Clarke v Earl of Dunraven* [1897] AC 59.
1   See s 6(1) of the RTPA 1976.

(e)   the persons to, for or from whom, or the places in or from which, goods are to be supplied/acquired or processes applied.

Similar kinds of restriction qualify in relation to agreements concerning services[2].

Qualifying restrictions may be either positive (as in the case of exclusive purchasing agreements) or negative (as in agreements not to deal with particular persons or in particular areas). They may be express or implied (as in the grant of exclusive selling rights, which implies an obligation on the grantor not to sell in breach of that exclusivity, or where privileges are accorded upon compliance with conditions relating to restricted matters or where penalties are imposed for failure to comply[3]).

One important principle is that restrictions have been held not to qualify under the Act unless they curtail rights enjoyed otherwise than by dint of the 'agreement' by which they are imposed[4]. Thus a specific grant of rights which imposes limitations on the exercise of those very rights will not thereby involve the imposition of 'qualifying restrictions'. The agreement by which such a grant is made would not therefore be registrable under the Act and may properly be regarded simply as a grant of limited rights. It would seem to follow, for example, that a merchandising agreement under which a sporting club or federation grants licences to third parties permitting them to market their goods or services by association with the former's profile, perhaps with access to specific items of intellectual property, will not be registrable merely because the licence imposes restrictions on the manner of its exercise. By contrast, the position may be different where the licence imposes restrictions on the third parties' rights, for example, to take similar licences from others or on the nature or price of the goods which they may sell.

TRADE AND SERVICE SUPPLY ASSOCIATIONS

Special provision is made for agreements with and recommendations by trade or service supply associations[5]:

– A trade association is defined by s 43 as:

> 'A body of persons (whether incorporated or not) which is formed for the purpose of furthering the trade interests of its members or persons represented by its members.'

As has already been highlighted above, professional (and semi-professional) sport is or involves business. It follows that sports clubs are often involved in 'trade'. It also follows that the governing bodies and other representative bodies within sport (eg player 'trade unions' such as the Professional Footballers Association) are likely to be regarded as fulfilling the purpose (amongst others) of furthering the business or 'trade' interests of its member clubs and/or such interests of the players represented by such member clubs. Such bodies are liable to qualify as 'trade associations' for the purposes of the legislation.

– A service supply association is defined by s 16(1) as:

2 See s 11(2) of the RTPA 1976 and SI 1976/98.
3 See ss 6(3) and (4) and 17 of the RTPA 1976.
4 See, for example, *Re Ravenseft Properties Ltd's Application* [1978] QB 52.
5 See ss 8 and 16 of the RTPA 1976.

'any association (whether incorporated or not) if:

(a)   its membership consists wholly or mainly of persons ... who are either engaged in the supply of services ... or are employed by or represent persons so engaged; and

(b)   its objects or activities include the promotion of the interests of persons engaged in the supply of those services who are either members ... or are persons represented by such members.'

It is far from fanciful to suggest that sports clubs (whether professional or otherwise) are engaged in the supply of services. They may supply a service to the public, who pay to come and watch matches. Equally, a members' club may be said to provide services to its members in the form of the facilities which it offers. It also seems clear that the definition of a service supply association will include leagues such as the Football League and the FA Premier League as well as certain governing and other representative bodies[6].

– There is no reason, in theory, why a particular body should not qualify for regulation by the Act as being both a trade association and a service supply association. The consequences of a body falling within either or both definitions are as follows:

(a)   Any 'agreement' between that body and its members requiring or suggesting compliance with its rules will be caught[7]. Of course, as already mentioned, membership of the body may itself give rise to an express or implied 'agreement' between all the members which is likely to be caught in its own right.

(b)   Agreements made with that body and a third party are treated as being made with each of the members of that body[8], thereby rendering each member liable to the processes laid down by the Act in the event that such agreements qualify for registration.

(c)   Recommendations (express or implied) by that body (for example as to prices, charges or other appropriate terms and conditions) are treated as being subject to an agreement between members that such recommendations will be complied with even where they are not binding or even adhered to in practice[9].

EXEMPTIONS AND RELIEFS

The Act contains detailed provisions (in particular, ss 9 and 18 and Schedule 3) which have the effect of excluding certain types of agreement from the operation of the Act. In particular:

(a)   certain specific *restrictions* are disregarded for the purposes of determining whether or not agreements are registrable[10]; they include, for example, restrictions which relate only to the goods or services which

6   Many such bodies' objects will surely include promoting the interests of their members.
7   See ss 8(1) and 16(2) of the RTPA 1976.
8   See ss 8(1) and 16(2) of the RTPA 1976.
9   See ss 8(2)–(5) and 16(3)–(6) and *Re Birmingham Association of Building Trades Employers' Agreement* [1963] 2 All ER 361.
10   See ss 9 and 18 of the RTPA 1976.

are supplied under the agreement[11] (save where such restrictions are accepted as between more than one supplier or recipient) and restrictions designed to secure compliance with standards approved by, for example, the British Standards Institute;

(b)   Schedule 3 lays down a detailed raft of measures which *may*[12] exempt categories of *agreement*, namely

   (i)   exclusivity agreements;
   (ii) know-how agreements;
   (iii) certain intellectual property agreements;
   (iv) agreements with overseas operations;

(c)   agreements certified as important to the national economy (according to specified criteria) are exempt from registration[13];

(d)   provision is made for approving certain price limit agreements which are thereupon exempt from registration[14];

(e)   agreements relating to the services of particular occupations, professions and businesses may be exempt[15];

(f)   qualifying agreements may not be referred to the Restrictive Practices Court where the Director General of Fair Trading obtains exemption from the Secretary of State on the grounds that the qualifying restrictions are not 'significant'[16].

Due to their intricacy and complexity, a full examination of these exemptions and reliefs must be left to the specialist works on the subject. Any attempt to bring a particular restriction or agreement within any of them, will require strict adherence to their detailed terms.

PUBLIC INTEREST

Agreements which require to be registered and which are not protected by one or other of the forms of exemption or relief specified, are liable to be referred by the Director General of Fair Trading to the Restrictive Practices Court. There, it is for the parties to establish that each of the qualifying restrictions is in the public interest according to one or more of the set criteria or 'gateways' provided by the Act[17]. These are, broadly speaking, that:

(a)   the restriction is reasonably necessary

   (i)   to protect the public;

11 As in the case of a supply contract which imposes resale price obligations. Such obligations may, however, be caught by the Resale Prices Act 1976.
12 To qualify for exemption, the agreement must comply strictly with the qualifying criteria laid down, as to the detail of which see Sch 3 to the RTPA 1976.
13 See s 29(1) of the RTPA 1976.
14 See s 30(1) of the RTPA 1976.
15 See ss 11, 13 and Sch 1 to the RTPA 1976; SI 1976/98.
16 See s 1(2) of the RTPA 1976. The kind of agreement which regularly and readily attracts such dispensation (depending upon the circumstances) includes certain types of joint venture agreements, standard terms and conditions or codes of practice recommended by trade or service supply associations, group buying agreements.
17 See ss 10 and 19 of the RTPA 1976.

(ii) as a defence against competitive measures taken by third parties in the industry;

(iii) to permit the negotiation of fair terms with a dominant user or supplier;

(iv) maintain other legitimate restrictions;

(b) removal of the restriction would be likely

(i) to deprive the public of specific and substantial benefits;

(ii) seriously and persistently to increase local unemployment;

(iii) significantly to damage exports;

(c) the restriction does not (and is unlikely to) restrict or discourage competition to any material extent.

CONCLUSION

In spite of an increasing tendency in disgruntled individuals to seek legal redress in disputes within a sporting context, and thereby to attempt to establish, enforce or challenge asserted 'rights', as yet no particular jurisprudence has developed in relation to the application of the Restrictive Trade Practices Act in the sporting commercial field. Indeed, it is likely that many organisations in such a field (in this, sport would not be alone) will have no idea even that their agreements, understandings and practices may involve a registration requirement. Many 'agreements' which ought to have been registered will simply not have been. In most cases, of course, life will proceed as normal and the conduct of sporting relationships will survive in blissful ignorance of the requirements of registration (as indeed it will of other legal obligations). What is clear, however, is that the cat is now out of the bag and the Restrictive Trade Practices Act is likely increasingly to be seen as providing one of a number of means of opening up particular arrangements to scrutiny, whether through proceedings in the Restrictive Practices Court to examine the public interest aspects or by disgruntled individuals asserting that particular agreements are void for want of registration.

An example of the latter situation arose when, in 1996, Stevenage Borough Football Club Ltd sought to challenge the Football League's rules which purported to deny them entry to the third division after they had won the GM Vauxhall Conference. The case gave rise to a host of issues and was eventually decided by reference to issues relating to restraint of trade and to principles governing the grant of injunctions[18]. Interestingly, one of the arguments originally presented by Stevenage was that the Football League's rules were apt to be governed by the Restrictive Trade Practices Act, that the rules of entry and other particular rules included certain 'relevant restrictions', that all such restrictions had not been registered and that accordingly they were void. In spite of their apparent force, such arguments were not ultimately pursued, no doubt for good tactical reasons, but the very fact that they surfaced at all should serve as a shot across the bows of not simply the Football League but all bodies charged with the function of managing and regulating particular sports. It is suggested that such bodies should

---

18 *Stevenage Borough Football Club Ltd v Football League Ltd* (1996) Times 1 August (Carnwath J); affd (1997) 9 Admin LR 109, CA.

scrutinise their rules[19] and constitutions with care. It is likely that within them there will be found provisions which arguably amount to 'relevant restrictions'. If so, then unless the argument can readily be dismissed, any want of registration will be likely to undermine the authority of the governing body itself. The message must surely be – if in doubt, register. The failure to register renders the restrictions void.

Of course, registration will lead to scrutiny by the Director General of Fair Trading who is liable to decide to refer the matter to the Restrictive Practices Court for a determination as to the public interest. This is what has happened in relation to the FA Premier League's (registered) rules regulating the centralised collective sale of the broadcasting rights relating to League matches and the contracts with BSkyB and the BBC which resulted therefrom. The court is not expected to pronounce until the second half of 1998 at the earliest.

Resale Prices Act 1976

The Resale Prices Act 1976, as its name suggests, regulates agreements or arrangements intended to enforce minimum resale prices and may have application in a sporting context, in particular in relation to merchandising arrangements made by individuals, clubs, federations and manufacturers. There are no specific provisions of special application to sport and this section simply provides a brief overview of the scheme of the Act. In that context, the Act (which only applies to the sale of goods and not to the supply of services) targets:

(a)   agreements or arrangements between suppliers and dealers which seek to establish minimum resale prices[20];

(b)   witholding supplies from a dealer who has sold or is likely to sell the supplier's goods at below the suppliers resale price[1];

(c)   collective agreements between two or more suppliers to withhold supplies from, to offer supplies on unfavourable terms to, or otherwise to seek to penalise dealers who resell or have resold at a cut price or who refuse to agree to maintain their prices at a particular level[2];

(d)   collective agreements between two or more dealers to boycott, discriminate against or otherwise seek to penalise suppliers who supply or have supplied otherwise than subject to a resale price provision or who fail to ensure that such provision is adhered to[3].

Agreements or provisions which qualify under the Act are unlawful and may not be enforced[4]. The Director General of Fair Trading may investigate and has the power to seek injunctions if necessary.

---

19 It is not simply their rules which may expose such bodies to risk. In the case of a trade or service supply association, any recommendations by management may be caught.
20 See s 9 of the RPA 1976.
1   See s 11 of the RPA 1976.
2   See s 1 of the RPA 1976. Note that s 3 makes it unlawful for a supplier or dealer to recommend arrangements of the kind prohibited.
3   See s 2 of the RPA 1973. See also the preceding note about recommendations.
4   See ss 1(1) and (2), 2(1) and (2), 9(1) and (2) and 11(1) of the RPA 1976.

EXEMPTIONS

The Act makes provision for particular agreements or provisions to be exempt or partially exempt from prohibition, including:

(a) provisions in exclusive dealing sale of goods agreements between not more than two persons[5];
(b) the withholding of supplies from a dealer who is thought to have used such goods as a loss leader[6];
(c) where the Restrictive Practices Court has made a specific exemption order, which it may do on application[7] by reference to defined public interest criteria[8].

MONOPOLIES AND OTHER ANTI-COMPETITIVE PRACTICES

A. European law – Article 86

Whereas Article 85 prohibits certain types of concerted action by more than one person, Article 86 targets action by a single undertaking (or group of undertakings) in that it seeks to outlaw anti-competitive practices by undertakings which hold a dominant position in the market. It does so by prohibiting:

'any abuse by one or more undertakings of a dominant position within the common market or in a substantial part of it ...'

As under Article 85, the prohibition only extends to 'abuses' which:

'May affect trade between Member States.'

The questions which need to be addressed, in order to identify whether or not the prohibition in Article 86 applies are as follows:

(a) Is one or more *undertaking* involved?
(b) Does the undertaking (or do the undertakings) hold a *dominant position* within the *common market or a substantial part of it?*
(c) Is there any *abuse* of that dominant position?
(d) May it affect *trade between Member States?*

UNDERTAKINGS

The concept of an 'undertaking' has already been addressed in relation to Article 85 above. It has the same meaning for the purposes of Article 86. One particular feature of the prohibition in Article 86 is that it targets abuses not simply by individual undertakings, but also by groups of two or more

---

5 See s 5 of the RPA 1976. The exemption relates to collective agreements by suppliers and dealers (see ss 1 and 2 referred to above).
6 See s 13 of the RPA 1976. The exemption relates to s 11 liability, referred to above.
7 Application may be made under ss 16 or 17 by the Director General of Fair Trading, any supplier of relevant goods or any trade association of such suppliers – see s 15 of the RPA 1976.
8 See s 14 of the RPA 1976. Here, the exemption relates to agreements and other arrangements/practices between suppliers and dealers under ss 9 to 11, as referred to above.

undertakings. It follows that arrangements between competitors (whether formal or otherwise) may qualify as an abuse, where the undertakings concerned may be said *collectively* to hold a dominant position in the relevant market. This may well be so in the case of joint ventures. It may also be so, for example, in the case of undertakings within a particular trade association or, in the sporting context, individual clubs operating under the auspices of a particular governing body, regulatory authority or federation. The rules and dealings of such bodies may be challenged under Article 86 (to the extent that they satisfy the other requirements thereunder). It might be argued, for example, that a sporting governing body of which all clubs operating within the sport concerned were obliged (formally or as a matter of practicality) to be members, was a dominant 'undertaking' within Article 86, both in its own right and as a collective of the separate 'undertakings' constituted by its member clubs. Any liability under the Article in such a case would depend upon whether or not the rules or other activities of the federation amounted (a) to an abuse of its relevant dominant position which (b) was liable to affect trade between Member States.

DOMINANT POSITION WITHIN THE MARKET

The concept of a 'dominant position' is not defined. It signifies a position from which a significant degree of influence may be exerted on the market in question, to the extent that (within the market as a whole or within a substantial part of it) the undertaking (or undertakings) may be regarded as a market leader, or one which has sufficient muscle to be capable, substantially, of acting independently of the competition and of its customers. Hence, in *United Brands v EC Commission*[9] it was said that a dominant position implies:

> 'a position of economic strength....which enables [an undertaking] to prevent effective competition being maintained in the relevant market by affording it the power to behave to an appreciable extent independently of its competitors, customers and ultimately its consumers.'

It follows that market share is generally all important. But, before issues of dominance can be addressed, the relevant market needs carefully to be identified, by reference both to the appropriate definition of the relevant product or service[10] and to the appropriate geographical area concerned. Further, having defined the market, the percentage of that market which it is necessary to have captured in order to qualify as holding a 'dominant position' within it will vary depending upon all the circumstances, such as the nature and maturity of the market itself, the number and size of the players within it, its physical size etc.

---

9   27/76: [1978] 1 CMLR 429 at paragraphs 64 to 65.
10 In this regard it will not necessarily be sufficient to identify the individual product/service the subject of the transaction/operation under scrutiny. The degree of interchangeability as between different individual products/services may be an important factor in identifying the relevant 'product market'. See *Hoffmann-La Roche & Co AG v EC Commission*: 85/76 [1979] 3 CMLR 211.

ABUSE

The concept of an 'abuse' is also not defined, but the article gives some general examples, by providing:

'Such abuse may, in particular, consist in:

(a)   directly or indirectly imposing unfair purchase or selling prices or other unfair trading conditions;

(b)   limiting production, markets or technical development to the prejudice of consumers;

(c)   applying dissimilar conditions to equivalent transactions with other trading parties, thereby placing them at a competitive disadvantage;

(d)   making the conclusion of contracts subject to acceptance by the other parties of supplementary obligations which, by their nature or according to commercial usage, have no connection with the subject of such contract.'

Such examples are not exclusive, and the categories of 'abuse' are not closed. Any conduct which affects the structure of competition within the market or which prejudices customers will suffice, unless it can be objectively justified in accordance with the principle of proportionality.

Particular examples of practices by an undertaking in a dominant position which, depending upon all the circumstances, may constitute an 'abuse' under Article 86 are as follows:

(a)   any practice which is designed to exclude competitors or inhibit their access to or success in the market[11];

(b)   the imposition of terms of supply which require the purchaser to take other, unconnected, goods or services in addition to those primarily the subject of the contract, or which grant to the supplier the right to control the further marketing of the goods supplied[12];

(c)   a refusal to supply to particular customers, perhaps as a 'disciplinary' measure[13];

(d)   terms which preclude or deter the customer from taking supplies from any other supplier either directly[14] or indirectly[15] (eg by offering lower prices in return for exclusivity);

(e)   loyalty rebates whereby inducements are given to those who take a certain percentage of their requirements from the particular supplier[16];

(f)   predatory pricing arrangements whereby a market leader sets his prices at a level designed not to make a profit but to deter the competition[17];

(g)   discriminatory pricing arrangements whereby, for example, special deals are offered to the customers of competitors or within a particular area[18] or to prevent customers moving to a competitor[19];

(h)   import or export bans.

---

11 See *Elopak Italia Srl v Tetra Pak (No 2)* [1992] 4 CMLR 551.
12 See *Hilti v EC Commission:* T-30/89 [1992] 4 CMLR 16.
13 See *United Brands Co v EC Commission:* 27/76 [1978] 1 CMLR 429.
14 See *Re European Sugar Cartel, Cooperatieve Vereniging Suiker Unie UA v EC Commission* [1976] 1 CMLR 295.
15 See *Hoffmann-La Roche & Co AG v EC Commission:* 85/76 [1979] 3 CMLR 211.
16 See *Hoffmann-La Roche & Co AG v EC Commission:* 85/76 [1979] 3 CMLR 211.
17 See *AKZO Chemie BV v EC Commission:* C-62/86 [1993] 5 CMLR 215.
18 See *United Brands Co v EC Commission:* 27/76 [1978] 1 CMLR 429.
19 See *Hilti AG v Commission:* T-30/89 [1992] 4 CMLR 16.

As to whether or not the activities of a dominant sporting authority are likely to be regarded as an 'abuse', the issue will of course depend upon the particular circumstances of each case. Such authorities may draw some comfort, however, from the Commission's general approach to the control of individual sports as expressed in a written answer by Commissioner Van Miert[20], during the fallout from the *Bosman* decision[1]:

> 'In principle, each club must be free to join with others, in accordance with its own interests, to organise its sporting activity. Nevertheless it is generally acknowledged that the most effective institutional structure for promoting sport is the creation of a single federation in each Member State and a single international federation for each sport. Consequently, it needs to be ascertained in each practical situation the extent to which it is legitimate or practicable for more than one federation to govern autonomously a particular sport or a variant of that sport with a view to improving its quality for the benefit of clubs players and spectators. It may be that problems will arise in connection with the rules of competition set out in the Treaty where the stronger federation at national or international level hampers the setting up of another federation. The extent to which the rules of competition are to apply in such situations has still to be determined in the proper context of each practical situation.'

The message would appear to be that de facto monopolistic authorities are accepted as generally permissible, provided that the power derived from such de facto monopoly is not used to squash fledgling alternatives, whereupon each case will be examined on its merits. An example of the sort of arguments which might arise is provided by the recent Australian case concerned with the setting up of a rival to the established Australian authority in Rugby League. In *News Ltd v Australian Rugby League*[2], the full Federal Court in Sydney allowed an appeal against injunctions imposed upon Rupert Murdoch's News Ltd which had set up a rival 'Super League', on the grounds that commitment and loyalty agreements which the Australian Rugby League had procured from its clubs (and with which the ARL complained that News Ltd had wrongly interfered) were void as amounting (under the Australian Trade Practices Act 1974) to a 'contract, arrangement or understanding', a crucial purpose of which was to restrict the supply of teams and players to the rival Super League and thus to stifle competition[3].

MAY AFFECT TRADE BETWEEN MEMBER STATES

Of course, there may be many instances of arrangements or practices of the type referred to which do not fall foul of Article 86 at all, simply because they have no effect on trade between Member States (as to which see the discussion above in relation to Article 85).

---

20 12 April 1996, OJ 1996 C217/87.
1 *Union Royale Belge des Sociétés de Football Association ASBL v Bosman*: C-415/93 [1996] 1 CMLR 645. The competition issues of this decision are discussed at pp 92 and 106.
2 (1996) 139 ALR 193.
3 Similar arguments might be envisaged under European law, in respect of both Article 86 (abuse of a dominant position) and Article 85 (agreements and concerted practices liable to prevent, restrict or distort competition). Under domestic law, one can imagine arguments that the ARL and its clubs had engaged in an 'anti-competitive practice' for the purposes of the Competition Act 1980 (see below).

EXEMPTIONS

An arrangement or practice is either an 'abuse of dominant position' under Article 86 or it is not. Unlike Article 85, there is no provision for exemptions within Article 86, where the very concept of an 'abuse' is apt itself to rule out legitimate activity. Hence proof that an arrangement or practice is objectively justified will prevent it from amounting to an 'abuse', rather than exempt it from the consequences of being such an 'abuse'.

The application of Article 86 within the sporting field

We have already seen how, in *Union Royale Belge de Sociétés de Football Association ASBL v Bosman*[4], the ECJ was invited to consider the transfer rules and the foreign player rules by reference to competition law as well as to Article 48. In the event, it declined to do other than to rule on the matter under Article 48. As with Article 85, Advocate-General Lenz addressed the issues under Article 86. On this occasion, however, he expressed the opinion that the rules in question did not breach Article 86[5]. He indicated that UEFA is not to be regarded as occupying a dominant position in the market in that, properly regarded, the rules of UEFA were simply the representation of an agreement between the clubs (as being the entities most closely involved in the employment of players). In his view, Article 86 had no application.

To the extent that an association's rules do *truly* reflect the wishes of its members, the logic of A-G Lenz's argument is understandable. Whether UEFA's rules can in truth be accepted as such a reflection of the wishes of (all) its affiliated associations, let alone the individual clubs throughout Europe, however, is perhaps stretching a point. Certainly it would be a bold, if not rash, approach for any sporting authority to rely upon A-G Lenz's opinion in this respect, and simply to proceed upon the assumption that it did not qualify as a dominant undertaking for the purposes of Article 86.

A-G Lenz did recognise, and this must surely be right, that the clubs affiliated to UEFA might be said *collectively* to occupy a relevant dominant position. He went on to dismiss the argument that the clubs had abused any such collectively dominant position[6]. He did so on the basis that, in relation to the rules in question, there was no question raised which concerned

> 'The power in the market which the clubs taken together [had] against competitors, customers or consumers.'[7]

It is suggested that, at least in relation to club rather than international football, this approach is questionable. It may be correct in relation to competitors, in that it is not part of the clubs' intent to exclude other clubs altogether. But the logic of the argument is less clear in relation to 'customers or consumers'. In particular, in relation to the football fan or spectator, the clubs collectively reign supreme. Without them, there would be no professional football. The clubs' position in regard to them, therefore, is not simply dominant, it is omnipotent. Further, the idea that the fans/spectators have no interest in and are unaffected by the transfer or

4   C-415/93: [1996] 1 CMLR 645. See p 92 above.
5   Paragraph 282.
6   Paragraphs 283 to 286.
7   Paragraph 286.

foreign player rules[8] is one which does not bear scrutiny. Such rules play an important part in determining the entertainment value of the matches served up to the public by the clubs, in that they materially affect the competitiveness of individual teams.

It is suggested, therefore, that A-G Lenz dismissed the application of Article 86 altogether too readily and that there remains a very real question as to whether or not the football authorities, or their constituent clubs, were indeed guilty of an 'abuse' by the imposition of the rules in question.

It is further suggested that, given the position under Articles 48 and 85, it would be difficult to resist the conclusion that an 'abuse' was indeed involved. In this regard, it is worthy of note that the Commission has indicated that it would be unlikely to grant an exemption *from Article 85* (under Article 85(3)) in respect of rules which also breached Article 48[9]. In such circumstances, it is suggested that the compelling view is that rules which infringe Article 48, and which have some anti-competitive effect under Article 85 which is not apt for exemption under Article 85(3), are liable to be regarded as an 'abuse' for the purposes of Article 86.

It should be noted that A-G Lenz did not rule out the application of Article 86 to sports clubs/associations in all circumstances. On the contrary, he was simply considering the particular questions posed in the *Bosman* case. Indeed, in two passages which ought to sound significant warnings, he made it clear that Article 86 may well need to be considered in relation, for example, to broadcasting rights. Thus, in paragraph 282, he said:

> 'If ... the present case concerned the question of the marketing of television rights for the UEFA Champions League, one would plainly have to consider the market position of UEFA, which organises and markets that competition.'

Equally, when addressing the collective muscle of the clubs, he said[10]:

> 'There would be ... [a question to consider under Article 86] ... if ... the clubs themselves acted as a group to market the television rights for their matches.'

The Commission's approach to the collective and exclusive marketing of television broadcasting rights to sports events has been addressed in relation to Article 85 above.

B. UK domestic law

Under UK domestic law, provision exists for the regulation of, inter alia, monopolies (under the Fair Trading Act 1973) and other anti-competitive practices by single firms (under the Competition Act 1980). Unlike Article 86, such provisions are concerned with the market within the United Kingdom. Unlike the Restrictive Trade Practices Act 1976, the scheme of the Acts is not to render void unregistered restrictive provisions. Rather, they impose a structure under which qualifying transactions/situations are liable

---

8 In paragraph 286, A-G Lenz surprisingly suggested that the rules were not an abuse of the clubs' dominant position because 'only the relationship between the clubs and their players is affected' by such rules.

9 In this respect A-G Lenz agreed with the Commission's position.

10 Paragraph 286.

to investigation (by the Office of Fair Trading and/or the Monopolies and Mergers Commission) and report, whereafter they may be banned or have terms attached. Further, in the course of any such process of investigation and report, there exists the opportunity for negotiation and agreement.

In so far as these aspects of the law are of relevance to the world of sport, it is likely to be the governing bodies who are principally affected. In particular, the scheme of the two Acts referred to is such as to enable the Director General of Fair Trading to investigate particular public interest concerns in relation to the way in which particular sports are organised within the United Kingdom. It is for that reason that this section finds a place in this book. It is not thought appropriate, however, to do more than to provide a general outline of the scheme of the Acts in question.

Fair Trading Act 1973

The Fair Trading Act 1973 regulates monopolies and mergers.
A transaction qualifies as a 'merger' for this purpose where:

(a)   two or more enterprises[11] cease to be distinct enterprises[12]; and
(b)   either the gross assets of the business taken over exceeds £70M[13] or the merging enterprise controls (as buyer or seller) at least 25% of the relevant market (or a substantial geographical part of it)[14].

A situation qualifies as a 'monopoly' under the Act where[15]:

(a)   a company or group of companies control (as buyer or seller) at least 25% of the relevant market[16] (a 'scale monopoly'); or
(b)   a number of (non group) companies which, together, control at least 25% of the market as above, so conduct their affairs as to prevent restrict or distort competition (a 'complex monopoly').

It will be appreciated how the ruling bodies of individual sports might be said to constitute relevant 'monopolies' where their governance is apt to control the market in which the sporting services of their constituent members is supplied.

DGFT INVESTIGATION AND/OR REFERENCE TO THE MMC

Where qualifying transactions/situations occur, they are not necessarily outlawed. Rather, they are liable to trigger initial investigation by the Director General of Fair Trading, who may deal with the matter by proposing to the Secretary of State that appropriate undertakings be given

---

11 At least one must be in the UK or controlled by a UK company. An 'enterprise' includes 'the activities or part of the activities of a business' (s 63 of the FTA 1973) and is to be distinguished from the assets of the business.
12 See s 64 of the FTA 1973.
13 See s 64(1)(b) of the FTA 1973 and SI 1994/72.
14 See s 64(2)–(3). The problem of market definition, here, is acute.
15 See ss 6 and 7 of the FTA 1973.
16 The relevant market relates to the supply of any particular description of goods or services within the UK or (per s 9 of the FTA 1973) part of the UK.

and accepted[17]. Otherwise, he (or the Secretary of State) may refer the case to the Monopolies and Mergers Commission for detailed examination[18]. The Commission may, in effect, sanction the transaction or situation; alternatively it may decide that it is not in the public interest and refer it to the Secretary of State who may veto the transaction or impose terms upon its continuing[19].

RELEVANT MARKET

When reviewing any particular case, it is necessary to consider the appropriate definition of the relevant market. As under Article 86, this entails looking at the particular goods or services involved and analysing their characteristics to see whether they themselves determine the 'product' aspect of the market or whether substitutes may be available such as to suggest a widening of the appropriate definition. Where, for example, particular goods are readily capable of being substituted by other comparable goods, the relevant market will be defined so as to include such substitutes. It is suggested, however, that in the case of markets involving the supply of services in the form of the playing of sport (and thereby entertaining the fans), it would be inappropriate to define the relevant market by reference to sport generally and to argue that the service of one sport is interchangeable with that of another. On the contrary, it would surely be right to regard each sport as a discreet product and to consider the delivery of sporting entertainment as involving a number of different markets. Whilst there may be a number of genuine all round sports fans, many tennis fans may have no interest in football and the follower of motor sport may be far from captivated by bowls.

It is also necessary to consider whether the relevant market is the whole, or only part, of the UK (or both).

THE PUBLIC INTEREST

The criteria by which judgments as to the public interest are made include all the relevant circumstances, and in particular the desirability of[20]:

(a)   maintaining/promoting effective competition within the United Kingdom;
(b)   promoting the interests of consumers, purchasers and other users in relation to price, quality and choice;
(c)   promoting reductions in cost and the development/use of new techniques/products;
(d)   facilitating the entry into existing markets of new competitors;

---

17 See ss 56A–56G, added by the Deregulation and Contracting Out Act 1994, s 8(2). It is to be noted that, once undertakings have been accepted, they are binding and enforceable at the suit of any injured third party or the Director General of Fair Trading – see s 93A of the FTA 1973, as inserted by the Companies Act 1989 and amended by the Deregulation and Contracting Out Act 1994, Sch 11, paragraph 2(3).
18 See ss 50 and 51 of the FTA 1973.
19 See s 56 and Sch 8 of the FTA 1973.
20 See s 84 of the FTA 1973.

(e)   maintaining and promoting the balanced distribution of industry and employment within the United Kingdom; and

(f)   maintaining and promoting competitive activity in markets abroad by domestic producers and suppliers.

EXEMPTIONS

When any investigation is carried out, no account is taken of any provisions in the agreement under investigation which render the agreement liable to registration under the Restrictive Practices Trade Act 1976[1].

Competition Act 1980

The Competition Act 1980 provides a focused mechanism for the investigation of the anti-competitive effects of particular practices. To that end, it targets 'anti-competitive practices'. The scheme of the Act is similar to that under the Fair Trading Act 1973[2] in that qualifying practices are not outlawed per se but are liable to be investigated by the Director General of Fair Trading who may seek and accept undertakings[3] or refer the case to the Monopolies and Mergers Commission which then decides whether an 'anti-competitive practice' is established and, if so, whether it operates against the public interest[4]. The Commission reports to the Secretary of State who may veto the practice or impose terms[5].

'ANTI-COMPETITIVE PRACTICES'

A person engages in an 'anti-competitive practice' if[6]:

> 'In the course of a business [he] pursues a course of conduct which, of itself, or when taken together with a course of conduct pursued by persons associated with him, has or is intended to have, or is likely to have the effect of restricting, distorting or preventing competition in connection with the production, supply or acquisition of goods in the United Kingdom or any part of it or the supply or securing of services in the United Kingdom or any part of it.'

1 See s 10(2) of the FTA 1973.
2 Under the Fair Trading Act 1973, however, any investigation covers the relevant market as a whole, whereas an investigation under the Competition Act 1980 will focus on the particular practice of the particular company in question.
3 See s 4 of the CA 1980, as amended in particular by the Deregulation and Contracting Out Act 1994, s 12(4). As under the Fair Trading Act 1973, any such undertakings are binding and enforceable at the suit of any injured third party or the Director General of Fair Trading – see s 93A of the FTA 1973, as inserted by the Companies Act 1989 and amended by the Deregulation and Contracting Out Act 1994, Sch 11, paragraph 2(3).
4 The criteria for judging the public interest are, by s 7(6) of the CA 1980, those contained in s 84 of the Fair Trading Act 1973, as to which see p 109 above.
5 See s 10 of the CA 1980. The Secretary of State's powers are essentially the same as under the Fair Trading Act 1973, which is discussed above.
6 See s 2 of the CA 1980.

It follows that, potentially, all forms of exclusionary and exploitative conduct may be caught[7]. There are, however, a number of points to note:

– The Act targets a *course of conduct*. Arguably, a single act will not suffice. Equally the conduct concerned need not amount necessarily to 'misconduct'. The fact that the conduct in question is designed to achieve legitimate aims (even to protect against unfair competition) will not prevent it from qualifying as an anti-competitive practice[8]. Thus, once again, the activities of sports' governing bodies may potentially provide prime targets for investigation in so far as it might be argued that they may have an effect on competition.

– The Act requires consideration of action taken either alone or together with *associated persons*. A person is associated with another[9] if one is subject to the (direct or indirect) control of the other[10] or if they are both members of the same group. In relation to corporate bodies, an ability materially to influence policy is treated as control for this purpose. This opens up the possibility of investigation not simply of the activities of sporting authorities themselves, but, for example, their relationships with third parties such as merchandisers, sponsors and broadcasters.

– The relevant conduct must have the effect of *restricting, distorting or preventing competition*, which is the same concept as that applied by Article 85 and which is discussed above. Where a sports' governing body enjoys the effective control of its particular sport, it will be almost axiomatic that some of its actions, rules and requirements will be liable, to the extent that they may be categorised as a 'course of conduct', to affect competition in this way.

EXEMPTIONS

Businesses whose annual turnover is less than £10m and whose share of the relevant market is less than 25% are exempt from investigation[11].

Conduct which is required or envisaged by an agreement which is required to be registered under the Restrictive Trade Practices Act 1976 is not regarded as an anti-competitive practice[12].

Conclusion

In the United Kingdom, those who engage in 'trade' (which, as has been explained, includes many who are engaged, directly or indirectly, in the

---

7 See generally the discussion of Article 85 of the Treaty of Rome above.
8 See *Sheffield Newspapers Ltd* Cmnd 8664 (1982), paragraphs 7.5–7.13.
9 See s 2(6) of the CA 1980.
10 It is enough if the control is exercised by the other only in combination with other group companies. See the reference to 'interconnected bodies corporate' in s 2(6) of the CA 1980, a phrase which derives from s 137(5) of the FTA 1973. Hence one group company with no direct link with a third party will be associated with that third party where the group as a whole is able to exercise control over the third party.
11 See SI 1980/979 and SI 1994/1557.
12 See s 2(2) of the CA 1980.

'business' of sport) are faced with a barrage of complicated legislative provision both from Europe and under the domestic regime. In particular:

(a) Agreements, understandings and practices which prevent, restrict or distort competition may be caught. If trade between Member States is liable to be affected, Article 85 may outlaw the activity and the agreement etc may be void; if no inter-State trade implications arise, it may nevertheless be registrable under the Restrictive Trade Practices Act 1976 for a reference to the Restrictive Practices Court for consideration of the public interest (if not registered, it may simply be void); alternatively, it may be liable to investigation and subsequent control under the Competition Act 1980, as to which the touchstone is, once again, the public interest. Of course a particular agreement may have to be considered under both Article 85 and the Restrictive Trade Practices Act 1976 or the Competition Act 1980.

(b) Monopolistic activity with inter-State trade implications may be struck down as an 'abuse' under Article 86; domestic activity (whether with inter-State trade implications or not) may be subject to the investigation and control procedure of the Fair Trading Act 1973.

(c) Activity or agreement the object of which is to maintain resale prices, may fall foul of Articles 85 and/or 86 (where there are implications for inter-State trade) and may be outlawed by the Resale Prices Act 1976.

The requirements of the competition laws of both Europe and the United Kingdom are detailed, difficult and of wide ranging potential effect. Furthermore, they are often ignored even in the more traditional and 'mainstream' commercial contexts. It is hardly surprising if they are frequently flouted by sporting organisations which traditionally have taken the view that they are engaged in activities which are different or special, and are deserving of protection from the rigours of commercial law. The time has surely come, however, where ignorance can no longer be said to be bliss. Those who conduct the 'business of sport' itself or whose business is associated with sport, will ignore the principles outlined in this chapter at their peril.

Chapter 5

Freedom of movement and the right to work

Introduction

One of the fundamental rights enshrined in European law is the right of the nationals of Member States to move freely between Member States in order to find work throughout the Community and to do so without discrimination[1]. As a principle, it is plain that such a right has significant implications for sports men and women. The tenor of the right finds expression throughout the Treaty of Rome and in particular in Article 6[2] which introduces a general prohibition against discrimination on grounds of nationality, and in a series of Articles designed to preserve such right in particular circumstances, each involving economic activity in different working situations, namely:

- Articles 48 to 51 which provide a right of free movement for employees between Member States;

- Articles 52 to 58 which introduce the so called 'right of establishment', designed to permit businesses of one Member State to set themselves up ('establish') in any other Member State; and

1 Similar rights also apply under the Agreement on a European Economic Area to nationals of Norway, Liechtenstein and Iceland. Further, limited rights may also arise in relation to other nationalities pursuant to agreements between the EC and third countries. The European Union has Association Agreements with Turkey, Bulgaria, the Czech Republic, Hungary, Poland, Romania and Slovakia and Co-operation Agreements with Algeria, Morocco and Tunisia. Further agreements are under negotiation with Slovenia and some Middle Eastern countries. In the United Kingdom, foreign nationals from countries outside the EEA generally require a work permit before they can take up employment here (unless they are from a Commonwealth country and have a grandparent born in the United Kingdom, or they are the spouse or dependent child of a permit holder). Such permits are issued under the Immigration Act 1971 by the Overseas Labour Service within the Department of Education and Employment. Application is made by the prospective employer. For sportsmen and women, a special form 'WP3' has to be completed (for professional footballers, an additional form 'WP4' is also required). The criteria require that the individual in respect of whom an application is made should have established international credentials and be able to make a significant contribution to sport in this country. Permits are issued for limited periods (usually up to a maximum of 12 months) to named employers and in respect of particular positions. It follows that they are not transferable and any proposed new employer must submit his own fresh application.
2 The Treaty of Rome (1957) has been amended on a number of occasions, in particular by the Maastricht Treaty which, inter alia, renumbered certain articles and changed its name from the EEC Treaty to the EC Treaty. References herein are to the Treaty as so amended. Article 6, for example, was previously Article 7.

113

– Articles 59 to 66 which recognise a right freely to provide services between Member States.

In addition, subsidiary legislation in the form, in particular, of Council Directives, fleshes out the bones of the general Treaty provisions. For example:

– In relation to the free movement of employees, the main implementing legislation is comprised in Council Regulation 1612/68 and Council Directive 68/360.

– In relation to individuals or others seeking to set themselves up in business or to provide a service, the principal subsidiary measures are found in Council Directive 73/148.

– Certain of the more pertinent further provisions are contained, for example, in Regulation 1251/70 and Council Directive 75/34 (both dealing with the right to remain in a Member State after ceasing employment etc), and in Council Directives 64/221 and 75/35 (both dealing with a derogation from the freedoms, on grounds of public policy, security and health).

General

The whole raft of measures identified above is generally referred to by reference to the generic principle of 'freedom of movement' and the scheme of regulation under each set of provisions is broadly similar. Indeed, in *Re Royer*[3], the European Court of Justice made it clear that the above Articles, together with their subsidiary legislation, whilst sometimes framed in different terms, are based upon identical principles. The Court is generally not particularly concerned to identify under precisely which set of provisions a particular case properly falls, provided that it is clear that it must indeed be covered by one of them[4].

The aim of such provisions has been described by the European Court of Justice[5] as being:

'... to facilitate the pursuit by Community citizens of occupational activities of all kinds throughout the Community, and [to] preclude measures which might place Community citizens at a disadvantage when they wish to pursue an economic activity in the teritory of another Member State.'

In reality, a close examination of the terms of the relevant articles and the supporting legislation reveals two distinct strands giving rise to two separate, but linked, principles of fundamental importance[6]:

(a)   *The first and general principle* is that the nationals of all Member States should be free to cross inter-state boundaries in order to ply their trade (whether as employees or otherwise);

3   48/75: [1976] 2 CMLR 619.
4   See also *Roux v Belgium*: C-363/89 [1993] 1 CMLR 3 and *Walrave and Koch v Association of Union Cycliste Internationale*: 36/74 [1974] 1 CMLR 320.
5   In *R v Immigration Appeal Tribunal*: C-370/90 [1992] ECR I-4265 at para 16, quoting from *Stanton and SA Belge d'assurances l'Etoile 1905 v INASTI*: 143/87 [1988] ECR 3877.
6   Hence, in due course, it will be seen for example that Article 48(1) articulates the first, general, principle and Article 48(2) the second.

(b) *The second, subsidiary, principle* is that, in relation to work related matters, there should be no discrimination as between nationals of different Member States.

The distinction between these two principles is clear from the celebrated case of *Union Royale Belge des Sociétés de Football Association ASBL v Bosman*[7] which is discussed in detail below. It is less immediately clear whether the second principle may be regarded as a free standing right to work free from discrimination, or one which is accorded only to those who exercise their right, under the first principle, to work in a foreign Member State. The judgment of the ECJ in *Bosman*, suggests that the second principle is only triggered by exercise of the right under the first principle. On this basis, the second principle would accord no rights to those who remain at all times working within *their own Member State* and the principle of 'freedom of movement' would not affect issues with no cross border implications, as to which Member States would be free to regulate their own affairs. If this is right, the second principle may be seen as one designed simply to prevent one particularly obvious impediment to the main principle of freedom of movement *between Member States*. As such, it may be viewed as an adjunct to the first principle.

Further, it is important to note that the concept of discrimination, which lies at the heart of the second principle referred to, is not an essential feature of the first principle. Again, this was finally established in *Union Royale Belge des Sociétés de Football Association ASBL v Bosman*[8]. It follows that provisions which have the effect of inhibiting the nationals of Member States from crossing inter-State boundaries to ply their trade (whether as employees or independent contractors) are generally prohibited, regardless of whether such provisions are themselves discriminatory as between the nationalities of different Member States.

By contrast, the feature which runs through those provisions which give rise to the second principle is one which prohibits discrimination on grounds of nationality. Hence, under the second principle, individuals cannot generally complain if they are frustrated in the exercise of their rights to ply their trade (within individual Member States) by laws, procedures or other requirements which do not discriminate in their application or effect between nationals of different Member States. Put another way, it remains legitimate to require foreign nationals to conform to the standards and requirements laid down for nationals in the home Member State, provided, of course, that such provisions do not covertly[9] mask a form of indirect discrimination against foreign nationals (as, for example, in a requirement that an individual should have resided in the home Member State for a qualifying period or should hold a qualification from or equivalent to that granted in the Member State in question[10] before being able to take a particular form of employment, to engage in particular self employed activities or to provide particular services).

Finally, in considering individual situations, it is important to understand the general approach which is adopted by the Commission and the court to the interpretation and application of the principles referred to in this chapter. Such an approach seeks to be an essentially pragmatic one. The

---

7 C-415/93: [1996] 1 CMLR 645. See p 126 below.
8 C-415/93: [1996] 1 CMLR 645.
9 See eg *Sotgiu v Deutsche Bundespost*: 152/73 [1974] ECR 153.
10 See for example *UNECTEF v Heylens*: 222/86 [1989] 1 CMLR 901 (discussed at p 133 below).

letter of a particular article may, on occasions, be sacrificed on the altar of efficiency and common sense. In particular, 'freedom of movement' is interpreted so as not to mean 'carte blanche' or 'free for all', and 'public interest' requirements are recognised as occasionally having the effect of validating particular inhibitions on the general freedom. Rules, regulations and requirements which impinge on the right to freedom of movement may sometimes be permitted in order to secure and preserve overriding and essential public interests. This apparent validation of restrictions seems to fall outside the ambit of the wording of the provisions themselves and it is only in extreme cases that it will be accepted as applying. Indeed the cases suggest that restrictions will escape the general prohibition only where they measure up to certain minimum standards. Generally speaking, restrictions may be allowed only where[11]:

(a)   they are not directly discriminatory in themselves[12];
(b)   they serve a public interest which is objectively important (such as, for example, consumer protection, the maintenance of particular standards, the protection of public morals etc);
(c)   they are effective in achieving the objective sought; and
(d)   they go no further than is strictly necessary to achieve that objective[13].

Proportionality

The last of the above requirements reflects a principle of general application to all measures which inhibit the exercise of fundamental freedoms enshrined in Community law. The principle is that of '*proportionality*' and may be expressed as meaning that the means employed must be proportionate to the object to be achieved thereby. It is encapsulated, in one form[14], in Article 3(b) of the Treaty:

'Any action by the Community shall not go beyond what is necessary to achieve the objectives of this Treaty.'

It is because of this principle of proportionality that, even where restrictions on particular freedoms are potentially acceptable, it is not enough for a national legislative or other rule making body to *believe* that a particular restrictive measure is necessary to achieve a purpose permitted under European law. The restriction has to be shown to be *objectively necessary* to achieve that purpose and to go no further than strictly necessary to do so, so as not disproportionately to affect any particular objectives of the Community[15].

---

11 See generally *Stichting Collectieve Antennevoorziening Gouda v Commissariaat voor de Media*: C-288/89 [1991] ECR I-4007 and *EC Commission v Netherlands*: C-353/89 [1991] ECR I-4069. Both cases concerned restrictions placed in Holland upon the transmission of programmes and television advertising from abroad. In each case the restrictions were held not to be justified by the overriding requirement of some essential public interest.
12 See *Van Binsbergen v Bestuur van de Bedrijfs-vereniging*: 33/74 [1975] 1 CMLR 298.
13 See *Re Choquet*: 16/78 [1979] 1 CMLR 535 and *Van Binsbergen* (above).
14 In this form the principle is, strictly, that of 'subsidiarity'. The two principles, however, serve the same object.
15 See, for example, *R v Intervention Board for Agricultural Produce, ex p E D & F Man (Sugar) Ltd*: 181/84 [1985] 3 CMLR 759, *Re Watson and Bellmann* [1976] ECR 1185, *EC Commission v Germany*: 118/75 [1988] 1 CMLR 780, *EC Commission v United Kingdom*: 261/85 [1988] 2 CMLR 11, *Buet v Ministere Public*: 171/84 [1989] ECR 1235 and *R v Minister of Agriculture, Fisheries and Food, ex p Fedesa*: C-331/88 [1991] 1 CMLR 507.

This principle of proportionality is of particular importance when it comes to the regulation of sporting activity by sporting authorities. All such authorities, for example, exercise a disciplinary function and reserve the right in certain circumstances to impose sanctions, for example, in the event that an individual fails a dope test. Manifestly, such disciplinary rules are a potential impediment to the right of free movement. A suspended athlete of one Member State, for example, is deprived of the opportunity to ply his trade in other Member States and, theoretically, may complain of a breach of his rights under Articles 48, 52 or 59. Such was one of the very complaints levelled against the International Tennis Federation by the tennis players Mats Wilander and Karel Novacek, when they challenged the disciplinary action taken against them for allegedly taking prohibited drugs. Their case was not that it was not open to the ITF to operate disciplinary proceedings in drugs cases. On the contrary, they recognised the legitimacy of a sports authority seeking to regulate the activities of its members in the public interest. They argued, however, that because any disciplinary action involving a ban or suspension interfered with the right of free movement, it was incumbent upon the ITF to regulate its disciplinary process in accordance with the principle of proportionality and, therefore, to ensure that such process restricted the right of free movement only in a manner and to an extent that was strictly necessary. Any unreasonable elements within the process could not be said to be strictly necessary and would lead to an infringement of the fundamental right. Under such an argument, Messrs Wilander and Novacek sought to challenge the disciplinary proceedings against them both in the manner of its conduct (they complained in particular as to alleged failures in the testing procedure) and as to what they asserted to be a lack of any effective right of appeal[16]. Their arguments under proportionality, therefore, were similar to their arguments as to whether the process amounted to an unreasonable restraint of trade. In the event, the arguments were struck out by the Court of Appeal. They were struck out, however, on the basis that they had no reasonable prospects of success on the facts as presented[17]. Importantly, the arguments did not fail *in limine*. In particular, Lightman J, at first instance[18], recognised that, as the disciplinary rules of the ITF arguably[19] did fall within the ambit of Article 59 by:

> '... effectively banning exercise of [the players'] fundamental right to play at tournaments within the Community ...'

16 In this latter respect, the players relied heavily upon the Anti-Doping Convention of 1989 inter alia of the Member States of the Council of Europe which recognised that a right of appeal was a fundamental right of a sportsman under suspicion.
17 *Wilander and Novacek v Tobin and Jude* [1997] 2 CMLR 346, CA. In particular, the Court of Appeal took the view that the rules in question *did* provide a sufficient form of 'appeal' (in that the disciplinary hearing was itself an appeal against the results of the dope test) and that, in any event, a disgruntled player's right to proceed by court action was a sufficient safeguard in the circumstances.
18 [1997] 1 Lloyd's Rep 195. The Court of Appeal did not overturn Lightman J's approach in this respect.
19 In a subsequent case, *Edwards v British Athletic Federation* [1997] 30 LS Gaz R 29, Lightman J concluded that the rules of the IAAF, to which the BAF subscribed and which imposed a mandatory four year ban for a first doping offence, were *not* within Article 59, in that they were designed to regulate the manner in which sport is conducted and that the economic consequences of such a ban were simply an 'incidental and inevitable bye product' of a necessary rule against cheating. Similar arguments could no doubt have been deployed in favour of a finding that (as was accepted) the rules in question were proportional.

they were (arguably):

> 'void unless [they] can be justified on grounds of public policy, public interest or public health' ...

and that:

> 'restrictions on freedom of movement are compatible with Community law only if they are justified by compelling reasons of the general interest and comply with the principle of proportionality.[20]'

Lightman J relied upon the formulation of the principle of proportionality as it had been put by the ECJ in *Gebhard v Consiglio dell'ordine degli Avvocati e Procuratoria di Milano*[1], which he held to be equally applicable to the testing provisions in the rules of a sports association:

> '... measures liable to hinder or make less attractive the exercise of fundamental freedoms guaranteed by the Treaty of Rome must be applied in a non discriminatory manner, must be justified by imperative requirements in the general interests, must be suitable for securing the attainment of the objective which they pursue and must not go beyond what is necessary in order to attain that objective.'

The message for governing bodies should be clear. Their right to regulate their sports and to impose discipline where appropriate is accepted. But the manner in which they choose to proceed may be open to challenge in so far as it interferes with the right of free movement, in which case they will have to be able to show that the measures taken go no further than is necessary to attain their legitimate objectives in accordance with the public interest.

Article 48 – freedom of movement for employees

THE FIRST PRINCIPLE

The backbone of the right of nationals of Member States to work anywhere within the Community (the first principle referred to above) is provided (for employees) by Article 48, para 1 of which articulates the first principle by providing simply as follows[2]:

> 'Freedom of movement for workers shall be secured within the Community ...'

THE SECOND PRINCIPLE

The Article then goes on, in para 2, to articulate the second principle which both amplifies and extends that general right, by making it clear that the right granted by Article 48 is not simply one of free movement in order to find work, but extends to protect those who find work in a foreign Member State (or are looking for it) from discrimination on grounds of nationality. Paragraph 2 provides:

20 See also *Union Royale Belge des Sociétés de Football Assocaition ASBL v Bosman*: C-415/93 [1996] 1 CMLR 645 at para 104 and A-G Lenz's opinion at para 190. *Bosman* is discussed in detail at p 126 below.
1 C-55/94: [1996] 1 CMLR 603.
2 Paragraph 4 makes it clear that the article does not apply to employment in the public service.

'Such freedom of movement shall entail the abolition of any discrimination based on nationality between workers of the Member States as regards employment, remuneration and other conditions of work and employment.'

EXTENT OF THE RIGHT OF FREE MOVEMENT

Paragraph 3 identifies certain limits to and examples of the right(s) granted by Article 48, by providing:

'It shall entail the right, subject to limitations justified on grounds of public policy, public security or public health[3]:

(a) to accept offers of employment actually made;
(b) to move freely within the territory of Member States for this purpose;
(c) to stay in a Member State for the purpose of employment in accordance with the provisions governing the employment of nationals of that State laid down by law, regulation or administrative action;
(d) to remain in the territory of a Member State after having been employed in that State, subject to conditions which shall be embodied in implementing regulations to be drawn up by the Commission.'

The subsidiary implementing legislation in Reg 1612/68 also distinguishes the two principles respectively. Article 1 provides:

'(1) Any national of a Member State shall ... have the right to take up an activity as an employed person and to pursue such activity within the territory of another Member State ...
(2) He shall in particular have the right to take up available employment in the territory of another Member State with the same priority as nationals of that State.'

There are a number of important points of principle to emphasise about Article 48:

– First, it has long been established that Article 48 has direct effect and can be enforced by individuals in the domestic courts of Member States[4].

– Secondly, Article 48 applies to workers. It accords to all workers the right to freedom of movement between Member States (the first principle) and the right to equality of treatment, free from discrimination on grounds of nationality, in all employment matters (the second principle). A worker is not defined in the Treaty, but the fact that Article 48 allies the concept of a worker to that of employment makes it clear that the rights conferred by Article 48 are accorded to those who are employees or potential employees[5]. This is confirmed by the terms of Regulation 1612/68 (see Article 1 quoted above). Furthermore, Article 48 applies to

---

3 For an elaboration upon the derogation from the right upon grounds of public policy, security or health, see Council Directive 64/221.

4 *EC Commission v France*: 167/73 [1974] 2 CMLR 216; *Walrave and Koch v Association Union Cycliste Internationale*: 36/74 [1974] 1 CMLR 320; *Van Duyn v Home Office*: 41/74 [1975] Ch 358; *Donà v Mantero*: 13/76 [1976] 2 CMLR 578.

5 Someone who is actually or potentially engaged in economic activity in return for wages will qualify – *Hoekstra v Bestuur der Bedrijfsvereniging voor Detailhandel en Ambachten*: 75/63 [1964] CMLR 319. See also *Levin v Secretary of State for Justice*: 53/81 [1982] 2 CMLR 454, and *R v Ministry of Agriculture, Fisheries and Food, ex p Agegate Ltd*: C-3/87 [1990] 1 CMLR 366.

employees wherever they carry out work for remuneration irrespective of the sphere within which they are working[6]. Hence sports persons who qualify as employees fall within Article 48[7]. It should be noted, however, that the concept of 'employment' may not coincide with that under domestic law. In *Lawrie-Blum*, for example, the European Court said[8]:

> 'The essential feature of an employment relationship is that for a certain period of time a person performs services for and under the direction of another person in return for which he receives remuneration.'

It follows that, in certain circumstances, individuals who are regarded under domestic law as self employed might nevertheless qualify as employees under European law. Generally, however, it is assumed that the self employed are catered for by Articles 52 and 59 and, in practical terms, the distinction is of no importance, the Court taking the view that in any given case it is not necessary to determine whether the individual in question is better dealt with under Article 48 or, say, Article 59[9].

– The nature and extent of the rights accorded by Article 48 are amplified in particular by Council Regulation 1612/68 which, broadly and repetitively, requires absolute equality of treatment as between nationals of Member States. For example, Article 1(2) (see above) accords to nationals of any Member State 'the same priority' in employment matters as nationals of the host State; Article 3 provides that domestic laws, practices and procedures which impose discriminatory conditions in employment matters simply 'shall not apply'; and Article 7 requires nationals of other Member States to be accorded the same treatment as home nationals in relation to all employment conditions and opportunities.

– Further, the rights granted by Article 48 are subject to the exceptions referred to in paragraph 3, and accordingly discrimination in employment matters may be permitted on grounds of public policy, public security or public health[10]. In practice, exceptions on grounds of public policy are likely to prove difficult to establish and employers and others potentially affected by Article 48 should rely upon paragraph 3 with caution.

– Finally, it is now clear that Article 48 may not be invoked in relation to matters which are regarded as 'wholly internal' to one particular Member State. The precise extent of this exception to or exemption from the application of Article 48 is not entirely clear, and is discussed in more detail below, but it is suggested that it means that Article 48 will not directly assist the nationals of a Member State working within that Member State who have not exercised their right to work in another

---

6 *Lawrie-Blum v Land Baden-Wurttemberg*: 66/85 [1987] 3 CMLR 389.
7 *Walrave and Koch v Association Union Cycliste Internationale*: 36/74 [1974] 1 CMLR 320; *Donà v Mantero*: 13/76 [1976] 2 CMLR 578 and *Union Royale des Sociétés de Football Association ASBL v Bosman*: C-415/93 [1996] 1 CMLR 645.
8 See paragraph 17.
9 See, for example, *Walrave and Koch* (above).
10 See generally Council Directive 64/221, Article 3 of which provides that public policy and public security grounds must relate exclusively to the personal conduct of the individual concerned (Article 2 makes clear that economic reasons will not suffice); Article 4 identifies particular diseases etc which justify exclusion.

Member State[11].Whether the limitation extends beyond such a situation has been the subject of some debate, but it is suggested that any such debate is of limited if not academic interest in relation to the position within the United Kingdom which has, in the Race Relations Act 1976, its own well established scheme of domestic anti discrimination laws which prohibits all discrimination on the grounds of race in relation to employment in any event[12]. That domestic scheme of anti-discrimination laws is considered in more detail below, but it is worth noting at this stage that the suggestion from certain quarters, post *Bosman*, that sporting authorities could properly persist, in the United Kingdom, with restrictive rules in relation to certain categories of individual (eg nationals of non Member States) or certain categories of transaction (eg transfers between clubs within the United Kingdom) is one which is designed to institutionalise the very kind of discrimination (direct or indirect) which is targeted by the Race Relations Act 1976.

RIGHT OF RESIDENCE

The right to move freely between Member States in order to find and follow employment, in order to be effective, must imply with it the right to reside in any Member State where that employment is found or to be sought. This implied right is confirmed by Regulation 1612/68 which also extends the right to the family of the worker in question[13]. In this regard, the members of an individual's family extend to the spouse[14], 'descendants' under the age of 21 and other descendants/relatives who are dependants[15]. Further, Regulation 1612/68 enables the members of the 'worker's' family also to take up employment within the same Member State without discrimination even if not a national of any Member State[16].

Finally, the right to reside throughout the Community includes the right to remain in a Member State in certain circumstances after termination of employment through retirement or incapacity[17].

Article 52 – 'freedom of establishment'

Rights broadly akin to those provided to employees by Article 48 are accorded to other individuals, companies and other entities by means of Article 52 which purports generally to abolish:

11 See eg *R v Saunders*: 175/78 [1979] 2 CMLR 216 and *Volker Steen v Deutsche Bundespost*: C-332/90 [1992] 2 CMLR 406. See also the discussion in the context of the *Bosman* case at p 130 below.
12 It should be noted, further, that the Race Relations Act 1976 outlaws any form of racial discrimination and is not confined to discrimination as between nationals of Member States.
13 See also Council Directive 68/360 which requires Member States to abolish all restrictions on the movement and residence of relevant nationals of Member States and of members of their families.
14 The concept of a 'spouse' has been interpreted by the ECJ, in good modern fashion, as including an unmarried cohabitee. See *Netherlands v Reed*: 59/85 [1987] 2 CMLR 448.
15 See Article 10 of Regulation 1612/68.
16 See *Gül v Regierungspräsident Düsseldorf*: 131/85[1987] 1 CMLR 501.
17 See generally Commission Regulation 1251/70 and Council Directive 90/365.

'... restrictions on the freedom of establishment of nationals of a Member State in the territory of another Member State ...'

The article goes on to elaborate the freedom by providing:

'Freedom of establishment shall include the right to take up and pursue activities as self employed persons and to set up and manage undertakings, in particular companies or firms ...'

Hence the article is aimed at those who wish to 'establish' or set themselves up in business in a foreign Member State[18].

Article 56 makes provision for exceptions on grounds of public policy, health or security. Further, subsidiary legislation by and large mirrors that passed in relation to 'workers'[19] giving rise to a similar raft of measures, as described above, designed to eliminate all forms of discrimination as between nationals of different Member States who work or wish to work on a self employed basis. Hence, for example, a Dutch lawyer with Belgian legal qualifications could not be prevented from practising in Belgium by Belgian laws which purported to restrict such practice to Belgian nationals[20].

The move against discrimination has been taken a stage further by the passing of a host of harmonisation Directives directed towards the compulsory, but regulated, recognition across inter-State boundaries of particular professional qualifications. Such measures are beyond the scope of this work, but include many different professions from retailers to lawyers to different types of medical practitioner. No such Directive has been issued specifically in relation to sports men and women[1].

Article 59 – freedom to provide services

Similarly, the Treaty[2] requires that nationals (individuals or companies) of Member States should be free to provide (*and receive*[3]) services throughout the Community across inter-State boundaries. Article 59 provides:

'... restrictions on freedom to provide services within the Community shall be ... abolished ... in respect of nationals of Member States who are established in a State of the Community other than that of the person for whom the services are intended ...'

'Services' are said, by Article 60, normally to involve the payment of remuneration and to include activities of an industrial or commercial character as well as the activities of craftsmen and the professions. Paid sports men and women are therefore included and it is now clear that it

---

18 See *R v Secretary of State for Transport, ex p Factortame Ltd*: C-48/93 [1996] 1 CMLR 889.

19 See in particular Council Directives 73/184, 64/221 and 75/34.

20 *Reyners v Belgium*: 2/74 [1974] 2 CMLR 305; see also *Thieffry v Conseil de l'Ordre des Avocats à la Cour de Paris*: 71/76 [1977] 2 CMLR 373 (another lawyer), *Patrick v Ministre des Affaires Culturelles*: 11/77 [1977] 2 CMLR 523 (architect), and *Van Ameyde v UCL*: 90/76 [1977] 2 CMLR 478 (insurance claims investigator).

1 The process of step by step harmonisation eventually lead to a general Council Directive (89/48) for the Recognition of Higher Education Diplomas Awarded on Completion of Professional Education and Training of at least Three Years Duration. See also Decision 92/51 on professions not requiring higher education qualifications.

2 See also Council Directives 73/184, 64/221 and 75/34.

3 See *Luisi and Carbone v Ministero del Tesoro*: 286/82, 26/83 [1985] 3 CMLR 52.

matters not whether they are employees (Article 48) or self employed (Article 59). In each case the protection is the same[4].

Further, although some form of remuneration is generally required to bring Article 59 into play, it should be noted that it matters not from whom such remuneration comes. It is not a requirement that the recipient of the service in question should be the person making the payment[5].

Again, the aim is the elimination of discrimination between nationals of different Member States operating (or seeking to operate) from any Member State. Further, the close relationship between the right to provide services and the right of establishment for the self employed is recognised by Article 66 which applies the provisions of Articles 55 to 58 in each case. As indicated above, Article 56 provides for exceptions on grounds of public policy, security or health.

Freedom of movement and the right to work for sports men and women

INTRODUCTION

Sport is now big business. More and more people are earning their living, wholly or in part and with differing degrees of success, through participation in sport. Where they do so (or attempt to do so), they will either be employed or self employed or they will be providing (or seeking to provide) some form of service. The various rights of free movement (together with the associated rights of no discrimination) provided under the Treaty of Rome, in particular by Articles 48, 52 and 59, will catch within their ambit all such persons who are nationals of Member States of the European Union and who seek to engage in their particular sporting activity outside their own Member State[6]. In this regard, and in the face of frequent and plaintive protestations and entreaties to the contrary by certain sporting authorities, sport is regarded by the law as being no different in principle from any other gainful occupation. In recent years, this feature of sport has become increasingly well established, in particular by means of a number of important cases which have come before the European Court of Justice.

THE CASES

In 1974 a domestic court in Utrecht referred to the ECJ various issues which had arisen, in the context of the sport of motor-paced bicycle riding, in a dispute between two professional pacemakers and (principally) the governing body of the sport, the Union Cycliste Internationale (UCI). The issues related to UCI's rule that such pacemakers had to be of the same nationality

---

4 See for example *Walrave and Koch v Association Union Cycliste Internationale*: 36/74 [1974] CMLR 320.
5 See *Bond van Adverteerders v Netherlands*: 352/85 [1989] 3 CMLR 113, where the transmission of radio and television programmes to broadcasters in Holland by cable operators elsewhere was covered by Article 59 even though the payment was made by cable subscribers and not the recipient broadcasters.
6 Similar rights apply to certain other nationals, such as those from Norway, Liechtenstein and Iceland under the Agreement on a European Economic Area.

as the cyclists whom they were pacing. The ECJ was asked to pronounce upon the validity of the rule, within the context of Articles 7[7], 48 and 59, together with Regulation 1612/68. A number of important principles were established by the judgment of the ECJ in *Walrave and Koch v Association Union Cycliste Internationale*[8]:

First, the court confirmed[9] that the practice of sport is subject to Community law where it constitutes an economic activity within the meaning of Article 2[10] and that where such activity is conducted by paid sports men and women it is governed by Articles 48 to 51 (in the case of employees) or the parallel provisions of Articles 59 to 66 (in the case of sports men and women acting otherwise than as employees). This is on the basis that sports people who are not employed under contracts of employment are to be regarded as providing services and therefore to be caught by Articles 59 to 66. The court could equally have referred to Articles 52 to 58, to cover cases of sportspeople who seek to ply their trade by actually setting themselves up or 'establishing' in a foreign Member State. The court confirmed that there was no distinction to be drawn between employees and other sports men and women, save as a matter of form in relation to the particular Articles of application. In particular, all such provisions have direct effect and may be enforced by individual (professional and semi-professional) sports men and women.

Moreover, such sports men and women may rely upon the rights accorded them by, in particular, Articles 48, 52 and 59 to challenge the rules of their sporting associations[11].

Importantly, the ECJ determined that it had jurisdiction to adjudicate upon the validity and effect of the rules of even an international sports federation in so far as they are intended to have application to activities within the European Community. In this regard it is to be noted that the AUCI comprised in its membership national associations, both amateur and professional from over 100 different countries, most of whom were not members of the Community. This was not seen by the ECJ as an obstacle to its adjudication. It held that the provisions of European law applied to relationships which were entered into or which had effects within the Community[12].

Because the Treaty is concerned with economic activity, the Court admitted an exception to its general determination, in the case of matters which are of *purely* sporting relevance. The way it expressed such exception was to say[13]:

'This prohibition however does not affect the composition of sports teams, in particular national teams, the formation of which is a question of purely sporting interest and as such has nothing to do with economic activity.'

The true extent of the exception, as thus expressed, was far from clear. It was certainly no surprise that the ECJ should have striven to make provision which

---

7   Article 7 was renumbered by the Maastricht Treaty and is now article 6 which, as seen above, prohibits discrimination between nationals of different Member States.
8   36/74: [1974] 1 CMLR 320.
9   Paragraph 5.
10 Article 2 defines the objectives of the Community as being 'to promote throughout the Community a harmonious development of economic activities, a continuous and balanced expansion, an increase in stability, an accelerated raising of the standard of living and closer relations between the States belonging to it'. The subsequent articles provide the means of securing such objectives and have to be interpreted in the light of Article 2.
11 Paragraphs 17 to 25.
12 Paragraph 28.
13 At paragraph 8.

was apt to exclude rules for the selection of national teams. On one reading, however, this formulation extended to the selection of teams in any circumstances[14]. Further, the particular distinction drawn by the ECJ, in this case between the performance of economic activity and the selection of teams, might be regarded as an unsatisfactory and artificial method of achieving a sensible aim, as it is undoubtedly the case very often that individuals who compete even in representative teams are paid to do so. Such individuals cannot sensibly be said not to be engaging in economic activity simply because they are part of a team representing their country. The formulation of the exception by the ECJ, therefore, left a lot to be desired.

Not surprisingly, the ECJ's ruling meant that the application of the rule of the AUCI which restricted the nationality of pacemakers was capable of breaching Articles 7, 48 and/or 59. Whether or not it did so in a particular case, would depend upon whether the application of the rule fell within the admitted exception for selection criteria based on purely sporting considerations. This question would have to be determined by the domestic court. The essential question for that court, therefore, was whether or not pacemaker and cyclist comprised a team (competing in an international team event), in which case the ECJ's admitted exception to the prohibition against discrimination would permit the criteria for selection to be based upon nationality. It is no surprise that a competition for international teams should involve only teams made up of nationals from the same nation and that the rules of entry should so specify.

The ECJ revisited the above principles in 1976 in *Donà v Mantero*[15], a case involving the rules of the Italian Football Federation which, at that time, operated an effectively closed shop open only to players of Italian nationality[16]. Once again the court confirmed that such rules were subject to (and incompatible with) Articles 7, 48 and 59. The court sought, further, to refine or redefine the exception, in the case of matters of purely sporting relevance, which it had admitted in *Walrave and Koch*. It stated[17] that rules were permissible which operated to exclude foreign nationals

> 'From participation in certain matches for reasons which are not of an economic nature, which relate to the particular nature and context of such matches and are thus of sporting interest only, such as for example matches between national teams from different countries.'[18]

This re-articulation of the exception admitted in *Walrave and Koch* went some way towards clarifying its extent. In particular:

(a) the example given of matches between national teams from different countries suggests that the exception does not extend to selection of all teams but only representative ones;

(b) this formulation of the exception avoids the pretence that the activity of members of representative teams is not to be regarded as

14 As will be seen below, in *Bosman* it was made clear that the exception should be confined to representative teams.
15 13/76: [1976] 2 CMLR 578.
16 The rules, to which all competitive matches in Italy were subject, required all players to be affiliated to the Federation. Such affiliation, however, was only open (subject to limited exceptions) to Italian nationals.
17 At paragraph 14.
18 In *Bosman* (see p 126 below), Advocate General Lenz expressed the view (at paragraph 140 of his opinion) that this formulation (which was repeated by the ECJ in *Bosman*) confined the exception to matches between national or other representative teams.

'economic'; rather, it appears to require that the *justification* of the exclusion of foreign nationals be on non-economic and purely sporting grounds.

The implications for professional sport in the European Community of the above decisions of the ECJ were, or ought to have been, quite clear. The ECJ had authoritatively ruled that the activities of paid sportspersons and national and international sports associations and federations were not above, but were subject to, European law. Such activities required to be conducted in conformity with the regulatory regime established by and under the Treaty of Rome. Significantly, however, the reaction of certain sporting authorities was neither appreciative nor conciliatory. On the contrary, the reaction of some such authorities was, to some extent, chauvinistic and confrontational. UEFA, for example, embarked upon a course to see how best the law could be circumvented rather than to embrace the principle, now well established and enshrined in European law, that the regulation of professional sport had to be conducted within the confines of particular well defined legal principles of general application. This failure readily to embrace the application of the rule of (European) law in the field of professional sport and the stubborn adherence to the view that sport should be regarded as, in some way, above the law may be seen as being largely responsible for the events which followed, culminating (thus far) with the case of *Union Royale Belge des Sociétés de Football Association ASBL v Bosman*[19].

In *Bosman*, the ECJ had to consider two particular aspects of the regulatory regime applied to professional football derived from the controls imposed by the relevant governing federations, FIFA and UEFA:

- The first aspect was the rule by which a club could demand a fee for the transfer to another club of a player whose contract with the transferor club had come to an end.
- The second was the rule which placed restrictions on the number of foreign players who could be fielded by a club in particular matches[20].

The case arose when Mr Bosman, a Belgian professional footballer, declined a new contract (on substantially reduced terms[1]) from his Belgian club, SA Royal Club Liegeois (RC Liege) which then frustrated his attempts to join a club in France, Dunkerque, because of (apparently unfounded) concerns over whether the French club would be able to pay the appropriate transfer fee. When, in accordance with the rules of the Belgian FA, RC Liege suspended Mr Bosman, he was left without a professional home and without income. He sued RC Liege and the Belgian FA and obtained interim injunctions which, in theory, freed him to play for other clubs. Although he was taken on for short periods by at least three clubs (one as far afield as Club Saint-Denis on the island of Réunion which, apparently, is in the Indian Ocean near Madagascar) he complained (with some apparent justification, according to the Belgian court) that he was the subject of an

---

19 C-415/93: [1996] 1 CMLR 645.
20 The particular rule in question was the so called '3+2 rule', under which a team could field three foreigners together with another two who had been playing in the country in question for at least five years. Interestingly, this rule itself derived from a 'Gentlemen's Agreement' between the Commission and UEFA in 1991. As will be seen, the ECJ took the view that such agreement did not have the effect of legitimising the rule.
1 The terms offered were the minimum wage prescribed by the rules of the Belgian FA.

informal boycott amongst mainstream clubs in Europe. In the course of the domestic proceedings, various parties were added, including Dunkerque, UEFA and certain professional footballers unions. When the Court of Appeal in Liege finally referred matters to the ECJ, the stage was set for a battle fundamentally between sport and the law.

The particular questions referred to the ECJ in Bosman were as follows:

'Are Articles 48, 85 and 86 of the Treaty of Rome ... to be interpreted as

(1) prohibiting a football club from requiring and receiving payment of a sum of money upon the engagement of one of its players who has come to the end of his contract by a new employing club;
(2) prohibiting the national and international sporting associations or federations from including in their respective regulations provisions restricting access of foreign players from the European Community to the competitions which they organise?'

Although the questions in relation both to transfer fees and eligibility of foreign players were framed by reference to Articles 85 and 86 as well as Article 48, in the event, the ECJ only felt it necessary to adjudicate upon the issues in relation to Article 48. Further, in the light of the previous case law and the preponderance of academic opinion, the decision of the ECJ, when it came, ought generally to have surprised no one. The court decided as follows:

'1. Article 48 of the EEC Treaty precludes the application of rules laid down by sporting associations, under which a professional footballer who is a national of one Member State may not, on the expiry of his contract with a club, be employed by a club of another Member State unless the latter club has paid to the former club a transfer, training or development fee.
2. Article 48 of the EEC Treaty precludes the application of rules laid down by sporting associations under which, in matches in competitions which they organise, football clubs may field only a limited number of professional players who are nationals of other Member States ...'[2]

A number of features of the court's reasoning are worthy of note. First, once again the ECJ confirmed[3] (in the face of objection, in particular from UEFA) that Article 48 is applicable to the rules laid down by sporting associations. In doing so, it rejected a host of objections (some artificial and even far-fetched) which had been raised during the proceedings. In particular:

(a) The court firmly rejected the plea, inherent in many of the objections, that sport was in some way special and did not fall to be judged by the standards appropriate of application in other fields of economic activity[4].

---

2 The court went on to limit the effect of its judgment in relation to transfer fees by providing, in effect, that it should only apply to future transactions or to cases (such as that of Mr Bosman) where the principles established by the judgment had already been asserted. Surprisingly (since judgment was handed down in the middle of a European season) no temporal limitation was allowed in relation to the foreign player rules.
3 Paragraphs 69 to 87.
4 UEFA raised the question whether Article 48 was appropriate for solving the problems of sport. Advocate General Lenz took the view that this was a political question and simply did not arise. In his view (confirmed by the court) professional football is an economic activity and *therefore* Article 48 applied to it. See his opinion at paragraph 130.

(b)   It rejected the idea[5] that only the major clubs could be said to be carrying on an economic activity. On the contrary, the focus on the business of the clubs (and the nature, size and success of such business) was inappropriate, Article 48 (in contradistinction to Articles 85 and 86) making no reference to the concept of an 'undertaking'. All that was required, for Article 48 to apply, was that individual footballers should be in gainful employment. As the court said[6]:

> 'Article 48 of the Treaty ... applies to rules laid down by sporting associations ... which determine the terms on which professional sportsmen can engage in gainful employment.'

(c)   It made no difference that the rules in question governed the business relationships between clubs rather than, directly, the employment relationships between such clubs and the players, on the basis that such rules adversely affect the ready availability of employment opportunities and thereby constitute an obstacle to freedom of movement for workers[7]. Hence, in relation to the transfer rules, the court rightly made the point[8] that it was immaterial that the rules included specific provision that the business relationship between the two clubs involved should extend no influence on the activity of the player. The court recognised the reality of the situation, namely that the requirement to pay a transfer fee was liable to deter clubs from engaging in transfer activity and thereby to restrict the opportunities for players to move.

(d)   The court rejected the argument that the transfer and foreign player rules were but incidents in the exercise by the clubs and governing bodies of their 'freedom of association', a freedom underwritten by Article 11 of the European Convention for the Protection of Human Rights[9] and that Article 48 ought not to be used as an instrument to curtail that fundamental right. The argument, which had some superficial attraction, was that the rules and regulations of international sports federations were designed to maintain order so as to ensure that sports persons of whatever affiliation or club might compete under standard conditions and that such restrictions as the rules and regulations applied should not be regarded, against that background, as being constraints on the liberties of individual sports men and women. The flaw in the argument which the court identified was that the rules in question were simply not a *necessary* feature of the parties' freedom of association[10]. Again, therefore, the court was adopting a pragmatic approach and, perhaps, looking to see whether the rules could be justified on sporting grounds.

5   Paragraphs 73 to 74.
6   Paragraph 87.
7   Paragraphs 75 and 100.
8   Paragraph 101.
9   Article 11 provides as follows: '(1)Everyone has the right to freedom of peaceful assembly and to freedom of association with others ... (2) No restrictions shall be placed on the exercise of these rights other than such as are prescribed by law and are necessary in a democratic society in the interests of national security or public safety for the prevention of disorder or crime for the protection of health or morals or for the protection of the rights and freedoms of others ...'
10   See the discussion on the principle of proportionality at page 116 above.

(e)   The court also (again) rejected the argument (advanced on this occasion under the principle of subsidiarity[11]) that, in effect, private sporting associations, as opposed to public authorities, were not subject to Article 48 at all, holding that the protection of the article extends to rules of whatever nature aimed at the collective regulation of gainful employment[12]. In rejecting the argument, the ECJ also impliedly reaffirmed the principle that the rules of a sporting association or federation, even one such as UEFA or FIFA (based in a non-Member State with national associations from other non-Member States included in its membership), are subject to European law in so far as any activities conducted thereunder occur within the Community.

(f)   Also dismissed out of hand[13] was the argument that Mr Bosman's case was a matter of a purely internal nature, involving a Belgian player, his Belgian club and the transfer rules laid down by the Belgian FA. This extraordinary argument was rejected on the basis (which might have been thought to have been blindingly obvious to all concerned) that Mr Bosman's complaint related to the frustration of his attempts to move from his Belgian club to a French club.

(g)   In relation to the foreign player restriction, the ECJ rejected the argument that Article 48 did not apply because the restrictions only applied to the actual *fielding* of foreign players in matches rather than the *employment* of foreign players (as to which there was, in theory, no direct restriction under the rules). It did so on the (again obvious) basis that a restriction on participation rights is likely in practice to amount to a restriction on the employment of foreign players, in that employers will be deterred by such a rule from employing individuals who are restricted in the matches in which they may actually participate.

One feature of the court's decision which was new and less expected was that it defined the scope of Article 48 in a way which made it clear that the first principle thereunder (freedom of movement) did not itself require there to be established any element of discrimination (which is, of course, an essential feature of the second principle under Article 48). As the court said[14]:

> 'Provisions which preclude or deter a national of a Member State from leaving his country of origin in order to exercise his right of freedom of movement ... constitute an obstacle to that freedom even if they apply without regard to the nationality of the worker concerned.'

In a passage in which it again adopted a pragmatic approach, but in which it also demanded adherence to the principle of proportionality, the court recognised[15] that the rules of a sporting association might escape the

---

11 In this regard, the principle of subsidiarity was said to be one which required interference by the Commission and the ECJ to be confined to what is strictly necessary. As mentioned earlier, the principle is very similar to the principle of proportionality.

12 Paragraphs 81 to 86.

13 Paragraphs 88 to 91.

14 Paragraph 96. The court also referred to *Masgio v Bundesknappschaft*: C-10/90 [1991] ECR I-1119, paragraphs 18 to 19.

15 Paragraph 104.

prohibition of Article 48 where justified by pressing reasons of public interest, provided that:

(a)   such reasons pursued a legitimate aim compatible with the Treaty of Rome; and

(b)   they went no further than was strictly necessary to achieve that aim.

The *precise* ambit of this apparent exception to Article 48 [and its relationship with Article 48(3)[16]] was not made clear, but the court rejected the argument that the rules in question fell within it.

It is noteworthy, and may be of some comfort to sporting authorities generally, that the court did not decide that the football authorities were not entitled to establish a regulatory system with the aim of protecting clubs from the ravages of an unrestrained market. In particular, it accepted[17] as legitimate the asserted aims of (a) maintaining a balance between clubs by preserving a degree of equality and uncertainty as to the results of matches between them (the level playing field argument) and (b) encouraging the recruitment and training of younger players. Requiring rigorous adherence to the principle of proportionality, however, the court did not regard the transfer rules as being no more than was necessary to achieve such ends, but considered that the asserted objectives could be achieved by other means less intrusive on the principle of freedom of movement[18]. In relation to the first objective, such means, according to AG Lenz, might include measures such as collective wage agreements and/or the redistribution of club revenue from gate receipts and the sale of broadcasting rights.

Further, in relation to the second asserted objective, the court did not accept that it justified the transfer rules, on the basis that the transfer fees in issue were not calculated in any way by reference to any training or development costs which may have been incurred[19].

As for the foreign player rule, on the facts before it, the ECJ rejected the argument that it was justified in order to maintain the link between individual clubs and their Member States or to create a pool for national teams or to maintain a competitive balance between clubs[20].

A further feature of the *Bosman* decision of particular interest is the confirmation by the ECJ that Article 48 is not concerned with matters which are 'wholly internal' to an individual Member State. Although the court rejected the argument that Mr Bosman's case fell within the exception, the court said[1]:

> '... the provisions of the Treaty concerning the free movement of workers, and particularly Article 48, cannot be applied to situations which are wholly internal to a Member State, in other words where there is no factor connecting them to any of the situations envisaged by Community law.'[2]

Because it was abundantly clear that the facts of Mr Bosman's case did not, by any stretch of the imagination (albeit apparently not UEFA's), involve a

---

16 Article 48(3) admits particular categories of exception on the grounds of public policy, security or health.
17 Paragraph 106.
18 Paragraphs 109 to 110.
19 Paragraph 113.
20 Paragraphs 122 to 135.
1 Paragraph 89.
2 See also *Morson and Jhanjan v Netherlands*: 35, 36/82 [1983] 2 CMLR 221 and *Steen v Deutsche Bundespost*: C-332/90 [1992] 2 CMLR 406.

situation wholly internal to Belgium, the court did not see fit to articulate further the criteria by which a situation is to be judged to determine whether it is or is not 'wholly internal' so as to fall within the expressed exemption. Some footballing authorities, and UEFA in particular[3], have expressed the view that, for example, all transfers between clubs within a single Member State (whether or not involving a foreign player) fall within the exemption. It is suggested that this is at once a bold and probably an incorrect view and that a foreign player seeking to move between two clubs within a host Member State would be entitled to claim the protection of Article 48 on the basis that he was (still) seeking to ply his trade in a Member State of which he was not a national.

At first sight, the rationale behind this exemption, for wholly internal matters, from the second principle under Article 48 (the prohibition against discrimination) is puzzling. Were the transfer rules to be retained for application in the case of strictly domestic transfers (viz: the transfer of 'home' nationals between two 'home' clubs) it is hard to understand why a 'home' national could not legitimately complain that he was the subject of discrimination on grounds of nationality, in that he could only transfer to a 'home' club which was willing to pay a transfer fee, whereas a foreign player would be free to move without such a requirement. Such discrimination is sometimes referred to as 'reverse' discrimination and is generally a well recognised concept. The judgment of the ECJ[4] seems to make it clear, however, that Article 48 does not apply to protect 'home' nationals from such (reverse) discrimination. The reasoning for this conclusion would appear to be that the rationale behind the second principle (prohibition against discrimination) is simply to further the objectives, in a particular manner, of the first principle under Article 48 which is aimed at ensuring the freedom of movement for *foreign* nationals[5]. This reasoning is supported by the wording of (for example) Regulation 1612/68, Article 1 of which provides:

> '... any national of a Member State shall....have the right to take up an activity as an employed person and to pursue such activity within the Territory of another Member State ...'

Such reasoning would also seem to confirm that Article 48 does indeed apply wherever a foreign national is involved (even in a transfer between clubs located within one Member State)[6].

---

3 See UEFA press statement of 17 January 1996.
4 Paragraph 89.
5 On this basis, it might seem that a national of one Member State seeking to return from a foreign club to a home club would not be protected (but see note 6).
6 This appears to be confirmed also by *Steen v Deutsche Bundespost*: C-332/90 [1992] 2 CMLR 406, in which the ECJ confirmed that Article 48 is aimed at discrimination against workers from other Member States and does not apply to the nationals of the host Member State *who have not exercised the right to freedom of movement*. This suggests, further, that an individual who has exercised his right to freedom of movement but then seeks to return to work in his home Member State *can* claim the protection of Article 48 (or the equivalent articles). This would seem to be the conclusion to be drawn also from *R v Immigration Appeal Tribunal and Surinder Singh*: C-370/90 [1992] ECR I-4265, *Knoors v Secretary of State for Economic Affairs*: 115/78 [1979] 2 CMLR 357 and *Broekmeulen v Huisarts Registratie Commissie*: 246/80 [1982] 1 CMLR 91. In particular, in *Singh*, a British national who had worked for a time in Germany was held to be entitled to invoke her freedom of establishment rights against the United Kingdom upon her return, suggesting that a Member State must treat its own nationals who have moved abroad to work at least as well as nationals from other Member States.

Even in a strictly domestic transfer situation, the inability of a 'home' national to claim the protection of Article 48 will not necessarily deprive that individual of redress. On the contrary, he/she may well be able to rely on the provisions of other Articles in the Treaty, such as Article 85, which targets action which affects competition in inter-state trade and the scope of which has already been considered above. After all, a system which permits transfer fees for domestic transactions but outlaws them for inter-state deals is liable to distort the market generally in a manner calculated to infringe Article 85[7].

Equally, it may be the case in the United Kingdom that a court would now[8] look favourably upon the argument that the transfer rules constituted an unreasonable restraint of trade and were, therefore, void and unenforceable[9].

In addition, it should not be forgotten that, in the United Kingdom, all forms of racial discrimination in relation to employment matters[10] is rendered unlawful by the Race Relations Act 1976. The kind of discrimination which singled out 'home' players for adverse treatment in comparison with foreign players would surely be at risk of being held to be unlawful under that Act, the provisions of which are discussed in more detail below. In particular, it is suggested that it would be difficult to justify such differential treatment[11] in view of the ECJ's reasons for rejecting similar arguments advanced in support of UEFA's rules under Article 48.

In short, it is suggested that, within the United Kingdom at least, the rules which entitle a transferor club to a transfer fee on the transfer of a player whose contract has come to an end should generally be regarded as unlawful. In so far as the football authorities have failed thus far to abolish their rules relating to 'domestic' transfers, it is suggested further that they are treading on dangerous ground.

Finally, the ECJ confirmed[12] in *Bosman* that Article 48 does not apply to rules which exclude foreign players from *particular* matches by reason of the *nature and context* of such matches where such rules are of sporting interest only. The court therefore preferred the formulation of this exception which it had advanced in *Donà v Mantero* (supra) to that which it had originally articulated in *Walrave and Koch v Association Unions Cycliste Internationale* (supra)[13]. Such formulation gave as an example of what was intended, matches between National teams from different countries. There can be

---

7   This is likely to be so in spite of the fact that the consequence of such a system would be that cross-border transfers would be liable to *increase*. In this regard, see *Etablissements Consten SARL and Grundig v EC Commission*: 56, 58/64 [1966] ECR 299.

8   Times change, and it is suggested that there is some reason to think that a modern judge might take a different view of the transfer system from that expressed by Wilberforce J in *Eastham v Newcastle United Football Club* [1963] 3 All ER 139, when the registration and transfer system then applied in football was adjudged to be 'not so very objectionable'. At the time of writing, the Wimbledon footballer, Vinnie Jones had commenced proceedings in which he challenged the legitimacy of the current transfer rules.

9   Such an argument would be especially cogent where only certain individuals ('home' nationals) were singled out for the application of the rules.

10 It should be noted that for this purpose 'employment' is subject to an extended definition and includes a contract personally to execute any work or labour – see s 78(1) of the Race Relations Act 1976.

11 Under s 1(1)(b) of the Act.

12 Paragraph 127.

13 In *Bosman*, Advocate-General Lenz recognised that the precise legal basis for the exception in the case of representative teams (the justification for which he regarded as obvious and convincing) was hard to identify and he expressly chose not to do so because it was clear that it did not apply in any event. See his opinion at paragraph 139.

little doubt that the formulation is apt also to cover matches between other teams which may *properly* be described as representative (of, say a town or a county).

UEFA initially sought, after *Bosman*, to draw inappropriate comfort from this exception, by maintaining that the ECJ's ruling on the foreign players rule had no application to its club competitions because the clubs involved should be regarded as representing their countries. Such an extreme argument does not survive detailed scrutiny as a matter of common sense[14] and, in any event, the court in *Bosman* considered and rejected arguments which sought to link individual clubs with the Member States in which they happened to be located[15]. The court was also at pains to repeat[16] the warning from *Donà v Mantero* that:

> '... [the] restriction on the scope of the provisions in question must remain limited to its proper objective.'

Were any other approach to be adopted, so the court thought:

> 'Article 48 would be deprived of its practical effect and the fundamental right of free access to employment which the Treaty confers individually on each worker in the Community rendered nugatory.'

Another case which illustrates the court's pragmatic approach to the enforcement of the rights of free movement and the prohibition against discrimination (and which also provides a good example of potential indirect discrimination) is *Union Nationale des Entraineurs et Cadres Techniques Professionels du Football v Heylens*[17]. There, a Belgian national working as a football trainer in France was prosecuted for allegedly infringing French criminal law by practising without a qualification recognised by the French authorities, who had refused to accept his Belgian diploma. The Lille court referred the matter to the ECJ which recognised that, as a matter of practicality, it was justifiable for Member States to lay down particular qualifications which they would recognise as enabling individuals to follow particular occupations and to require production of a diploma or other certificate attesting to the attainment of a particular standard. However, because such a requirement involved in practice a restriction on the effective exercise of the rights granted by eg Article 48, it was important, in recognition of the principle of proportionality, that it should only be implemented in a way which was fair and reasonable so as not *unnecessarily* to deprive individuals of the practical benefit of such rights. The procedures for assessing the equivalence of foreign qualifications had to be sound and objective. Furthermore, because of the importance of the right to freedom of movement, the court decided that any restriction of the kind in question would have to accord to the individual an *effective* right of challenge, by some form of judicial review, to any decision which inhibited his exercise of such right[18]. For any such right of challenge to be effective, the individual would require to have a sufficient knowledge of the relevant facts and reasons which had lead to the restriction being imposed upon him.

---

14 It was swiftly abandoned by UEFA.
15 Paragraphs 131 to 134. Again, the court's reasoning borrows from the principle of proportionality.
16 Paragraph 127.
17 222/86: [1989] 1 CMLR 901.
18 See also *Johnston v Chief Constable of the Royal Ulster Constabulary*: 222/84 [1986] 3 CMLR 240.

It followed that the French authorities' failure to give reasons for their refusal to recognise Mr Heylen's Belgian qualification was liable[19] to prove fatal to their asserted right to prevent him from plying his trade in France.

Finally, as has already been mentioned above, in *Wilander and Novacek v Tobin and Jude*[20], the application of the right of free movement was considered in the context of a sports' association's rules for investigating possible doping offences. The importance of this case has already been underlined above, under the principle of proportionality. Lightman J, however, derived a number of propositions from *Bosman*. His formulation provides a useful reminder of certain important principles[1]:

'i   Articles 48 and 59 are to the same substantive effect. The distinction between them lies in their respective areas of operation. The activities covered by Article 48 are within, whilst the activities covered by Article 59 are outside, the ties of a contract of employment ...

ii   The EC Treaty confers fundamental rights to freedom of movement and freedom to provide services and (subject to one qualification to which I will subsequently refer) Articles 48 and 59 prohibit all restrictions on those freedoms.

iii   Sport is subject to Community law in so far as it constitutes an economic activity within the meaning of Article 2.

iv   The rules of sports' associations are subject to Community law, and so are the activities of professional sportsmen in the nature of gainful employment.

v   Associations enjoy a fundamental right to freedom of association and eg to draw up the rules for the practice and organisation of their sport; but that cannot justify the adoption of rules restricting individual rights conferred or protected by the EC Treaty.

vi   Articles 48 and 59 extend to the rules of associations aimed at regulating gainful employment in a collective manner, and any limitation on the right to gainful employment or to provide services must be justified on grounds of public policy, public security or public health ...

vii   Restrictions on freedom of movement are compatible with Community law only if they are justified by compelling reasons of the general interest and comply with the principle of proportionality ...'

In *Wilander* itself, Lightman J was only required to determine whether or not the players' arguments were legitimate. He ruled, in particular, that it was *arguable* that the rules of the ITF which imposed sanctions on players guilty of a doping offence did fall within Article 59. On appeal, the Court of Appeal did not feel it necessary to adjudicate upon the point, but expressed sympathy with the governing bodies' argument that Article 59 does not apply to rules designed to affect the manner in which sport is conducted, even where their exercise has economic consequences. The issue arose for decision in a later case, *Edwards v British Athletic Federation*[2], again before Lightman J. The case concerned the rules of the International Amateur Athletics Federation, to which the BAF subscribed, which provided for a mandatory ban of four years for a first doping offence. The rules also provided for early reinstatement of a banned athlete, but only in exceptional circumstances. Such discretionary reinstatement was generally applied in

19 It was ultimately a matter for the Lille court to decide the matter in the light of the ECJ's preliminary ruling on the ambit of Article 48.
20 [1997] 1 Lloyds Rep 195 (Lightman J); revsd [1997] 2 CMLR 346, CA.
1 [1997] 1 Lloyds Rep 195 at 203.
2 (Lightman J) [1997] 30 LS Gaz R 29, Ch D.

the case of athletes from countries where a four year ban for a first offence was established to be unlawful (for example, the sprinter Katrina Krabbe who successfully argued before the German courts that a ban in excess of two years was disproportionate and unlawful under German law). The British athlete, Paul Edwards, argued that his four year ban (and the refusal of the request for reinstatement) was discriminatory and an unjustified interference with his freedom to work, under Articles 59 to 66. On this occasion, Lightman J recalled that the ECJ in *Bosman* had made it clear that sport is subject to Community law only insofar as it constitutes an economic activity and that it does not apply to the purely sporting aspects of sporting activity. On the basis (which was common ground between the parties) that the four year rule itself was reasonable, justified and proportional, he felt able to hold[3] that:

> '[The rules in question] merely regulate the sporting conduct of partici-
> pants in athletics. They are designed to ban cheating by taking drugs and
> thus secure a level playing field for all participants in the sport ...
> Necessarily the imposition of the sanction may have serious economic
> consequences for those who breach the rules ... [but] this is a merely
> incidental and inevitable bye product of having the rule against cheating. A
> rule designed to regulate the sporting conduct of participants does not
> cease to be such a rule because it does not allow those who break it to earn
> remuneration by participating in the sport for what is (by common
> consent) an appropriate period.'

It remains to be seen, in some future case, whether or not the ECJ (or Court of Appeal) will endorse such an interpretation. It will be recalled that, in *Bosman*, the only guidance which it gave to the 'sporting interest only' exception to the application of Article 48 (freedom of movement) related to representative teams, for which selection based upon nationality is not to be regarded as objectional. It is far from clear that the ECJ would share Lightman J's view that some disciplinary rules do not fall within the ambit of those parts of Community law designed to preserve freedom of movement and freedom of competition, where such rules are designed (and are apt) to deter cheating. It may be more likely that the European Court would consider the lawfulness of such rules by reference to the established criteria of public interest and proportionality rather than to a blanket exemption from the application of Community law under any such 'sporting interest only' exception.

Conclusion

The cases referred to above show clearly that the ECJ rightly takes the view that wherever economic activity takes place, it is governed by, and those engaging in the activity are subject to and can claim the benefit of, the fundamental principles involved in the so called 'freedom of movement', 'freedom of establishment' and 'freedom to provide services'. Further, the cases referred to are not strictly 'sports cases' at all. Indeed, such nomencla-ture feeds the myth that sport somehow stands in a special position and is worthy of special consideration in the application of the Treaty rules which

---

3 He also held that the authorities' approach was not discriminatory in that it simply involved a recognition of the sovereign laws applicable within individual Member States.

are, however, of general application. As previously mentioned, professional sport means *business* which means *economic activity* which is precisely what is governed by, in particular, Articles 48, 52 and 59 of the Treaty of Rome. Employers, sporting federations, both national and international, governing bodies and indeed everyone involved in professional or semi-professional sport need to be aware that they are concerned with an economic activity which falls within the ambit of the regulatory and protectionary regime which has been discussed in this chapter. Increasingly this means that, to the extent that they have not already done so, sporting authorities may need urgently to change their approach and, in many cases, to revise their rules so as to bring them into line with the objectives of the Treaty and to ensure that any restrictions imposed on the right of free movement[4] are capable of being justified according to the general public interest and go no further than is necessary in accordance with the principle of proportionality.

The broad ranging potential effect of these European measures is such that it is likely that *Bosman* will prove not to be the last word on the subject in a sporting context. For example, in *Lehtonen & ASBL Castors Canada Dry Namur-Braine v Belgian Basketball Federation*[5] the ECJ has been asked by a Brussels court to adjudicate under Articles 6 and 48 (also under Articles 85 and 86) upon the rules of a sporting federation which prohibit participation in a competition of a player engaged after a specific date, in circumstances where the reasons advanced to justify such a rule include the need to prevent undue distortions of the competition itself.

Further, in *Deliege v ASGC Ligue Francophone de Judo et Disciplines Associées & ASGC Ligue Belge de Judo*[6] the issue referred to the ECJ is:

> 'Whether or not rules which require a professional or semi professional or a person aspiring to such status to have been authorised or selected by his national federation in order to be able to compete in an international competition, and which lay down national entry quotas for similar competitions are contrary to Articles 59 to 66 and Articles 85 and 86.'

Of course the 'freedoms' the subject of this chapter have a wide scope of potential application, extending far beyond the activities of individual sports men and women, and the regulation of such activities. When teams compete abroad, they collectively, and their owners individually, are exercising their freedom to provide their services abroad. Impediments placed in the path of clubs wishing to play matches in other Member States could therefore give rise to a complaint under Article 59. Equally, a club which wished to move from one Member State to another, but still wished to compete in the competitions within the first Member State, might well be entitled to pray in aid Articles 52 (right of establishment) and 59 (right to provide services) in so far as the rules of any relevant governing body placed restrictions upon such club's right to do so[7].

4   As has been seen (see *Wilander* above), disciplinary rules and procedures themselves may well involve an incursion into the right of free movement.
5   Case C-176/96.
6   Case C-51/96, OJ 1996 C133/13.
7   This scenario is not as far fetched as it might initially appear, in view of the recent flirtation by Wimbledon Football Club with the idea of moving to Dublin! Interestingly, the suggestion that Wimbledon might move to Scotland (or that Glasgow Rangers might join the English FA Premier League) would arguably not involve any attempt to exercise any of the so called 'freedoms', there being no (European) cross border implications of such a move.

Equally, rules which prevent or inhibit broadcasters from transmitting sports programmes or coverage into other Member States are likely to require close scrutiny under Article 59. For example, in *Stichting Collectieve Antennevoorziening Gouda*[8] and *EC Commission v Netherlands*[9], restrictions placed in Holland on the transmission of television programmes and advertising from abroad were held to involve a breach of Article 59 which, on the facts, could not be justified (and therefore excused) by any overriding requirements of public interest[10]. The lesson from such cases, together with those previously mentioned, is that wherever organisations involved in sport provide (or receive) a 'service' or employ 'workers' or facilitate the employment of self employed competitors, there is likely to be scope for the application of the raft of measures described in this section under the general description of 'freedom of movement'. That freedom requires, wherever possible, the removal of artificial barriers to the conduct of the economic activity in question. Where barriers are inevitable in order to secure some legitimate object, they must accord with the principle of proportionality.

8   C-288/89: [1991] ECR I-4007.
9   C-353/89: [1991] ECR I-4069.
10 See also *Bond van Adverteerders v Netherlands*: 352/85 [1988] ECR 2085.

Chapter 6

Racial discrimination

Introduction

We have already seen how, in European law, the generic principle of 'freedom of movement' has the particular effect in certain circumstances of prohibiting discrimination within individual EC Member States against nationals from other Member States. When dealing with events in the United Kingdom, it is important to look beyond the confines of European law before deciding upon the lawfulness of any potentially discriminatory action. This is because, unlike many of its European partners, the United Kingdom has, in the Race Relations Act 1976, its own well established domestic statutory regime designed to outlaw discrimination on racial grounds in a number of defined circumstances. Further, the Race Relations Act 1976 goes further than European law in its approach. Whereas the anti-discrimination regime in European law (where it applies) is itself discriminatory in only being concerned with discrimination between nationals of different Community Member States, the Race Relations Act 1976 targets discrimination on grounds of race generally, regardless of the particular race or nationality of the persons involved.

It follows that, in the field of sport, and in particular in the establishment, conduct and regulation of relationships within sport, a weather eye needs to be kept on the requirements of the United Kingdom's own anti-discrimination statutory regime as well as ensuring compliance with the stipulations of European law. It is suggested that the fact that the United Kingdom has its own domestic regime which extends beyond the confines of the limited European principle of 'freedom of movement' in its application, is something which has often been forgotten, particularly by those responsible for administering and regulating particular sports within the United Kingdom and for bringing their regulatory rules into line with the implications of, for example, the decision of the European Court of Justice in *Union Royale des Sociétés de Football Association ASBL v Bosman*[1]. The need for compliance with the domestic requirements of the Race Relations Act 1976 is all the more important, since the cap on awards made thereunder has been lifted. Given the earning power of top sportsmen and women, an established breach of the Act could well, in certain circumstances, give rise to a very substantial claim.

---

1 C-415/93: [1996] 1 CMLR 645. This case is extensively discussed in Chapters 4 and 5, above.

'Racial discrimination' under the Race Relations Act 1976

The Act, in Part I, first defines what it means by 'racial discrimination' and then, in subsequent Parts, identifies particular circumstances where such discrimination is unlawful, stipulates particular enforcement procedures and provides for certain exceptions. It follows that not all 'racial discrimination' is rendered unlawful by the Act. For any action or activity to be unlawful under the Act it must both comprise 'racial discrimination' as defined and occur on a prohibited occasion or in prohibited circumstances (it must also not fall within any of the exceptions provided for).

The starting point should always be the definition of 'racial discrimination'. Once that is established, the question then arises as to whether, in the circumstances, the discrimination in question is unlawful.

Section 1 of the Act identifies two types of discrimination, generally known respectively as 'direct' and 'indirect' discrimination:

– *Direct discrimination*[2] occurs where:

> on racial grounds, [a person] treats [another] less favourably than he treats or would treat other persons.'

For this purpose 'racial grounds' means[3] grounds of colour, race, nationality or ethnic or national origins.

– *Indirect discrimination* is more complex or subtle. It occurs, for example, where an unjustifiable hurdle is put in the way of access to a benefit and it is significantly more difficult for foreigners (or black people) to get over the hurdle than it is for white British nationals (or vice versa). Specifically, the Act[4] identifies this type of discrimination as occurring where:

> '[a person] applies to [another] a requirement or condition which he applies or would apply equally to persons not of the same racial group as that other but
> (i) which is such that the proportion of persons of the same racial group as that other who can comply with it is considerably smaller than the proportion of persons not of that racial group who can comply with it; and
> (ii) which he cannot show to be justifiable irrespective of the colour, race, nationality or ethnic or national origins of the person to whom it is applied; and
> (iii) which is to the detriment of that other because he cannot comply with it.'

DIRECT DISCRIMINATION

It can be seen that direct discrimination, in concept at least, is relatively straightforward and ought in theory to be easily avoided in practice, although it should be noted that the Act is not specifically concerned with the purpose or motive of the person allegedly discriminating (although a

2   See s 1(1)(a).
3   See s 3(1).
4   See s 1(1)(b).

racial motive will inevitably be fatal[5]) but, rather, with the effects of his actions and the causative link between such effects and the race of the person accorded the 'less favourable treatment'. Provided it is understood that the individual's race need not be the only cause of the less favourable treatment in question[6], the question may generally usefully be asked[7], 'would the action (the 'less favourable treatment') have occurred *but for* the individual's race?'

INDIRECT DISCRIMINATION

Indirect discrimination is a concept which raises all kinds of potential traps for the unwary. Again, motivation, purpose and intention are of no consequence, save only insofar as they may bear upon the question of whether a particular 'requirement or condition' for access to a particular benefit can be justified[8]. Further, the scope for inadvertent discrimination is considerable, as indirect discrimination occurs, by definition, in circumstances where a 'requirement or condition' is imposed on individuals in an even handed way regardless of their race. Further, any form of condition, test or criterion which is liable to affect a person's qualification, eligibility or acceptance for access to a particular benefit or advantage may well qualify as a 'requirement or condition' for the purposes of the Act, simply if it is liable in practice to have a significantly disproportionate impact on people of a particular race (or of particular races).

One particular criterion of eligibility which frequently surfaces in sporting contexts, for example, is a requirement of residence for a particular period in a particular country (say, England) or area. Such a criterion may not be directly discriminatory, in that (unlike a positive requirement that, say, all applicants/participants must be English) it may be satisfied by individuals whatever their race or ethnic origins. In the United Kingdom, however, such a criterion would almost certainly qualify as a 'requirement or condition' for the purposes of indirect discrimination under the Act as, inevitably, foreigners are considerably less likely than British nationals to have the requisite period of residence.

Similarly, a requirement that an individual should have a professional/trade/sporting qualification or certification from, say, an English institution or organisation, whilst it may be applied to all individuals regardless of their race and so not be directly discriminatory, is likely to be regarded as a qualifying 'requirement or condition' for the purposes of indirect discrimination under the Act, in that it will have a significantly disproportionate impact in practice on people who are not English. Whether it, or any other such qualifying 'requirement or condition' actually amounts to indirect

5 By contrast, a worthy motive will not, of itself, provide a defence. See eg *James v Eastleigh Borough Council* [1990] IRLR 288, HL; *R v Commission for Racial Equality, ex p Westminster City Council* [1984] IRLR 230.
6 See eg *Owen and Briggs v James* [1982] IRLR 502, CA.
7 See eg *James v Eastleigh Borough Council* [1990] IRLR 288, HL.
8 It is also the case that, where unlawful indirect discrimination is established, no compensation will be awarded where it is established that the requirement or condition was not applied with the intention of treating the aggrieved individual unfavourably on racial grounds – see ss 56(1)(b) and 57(3). Note, however, that an intentional application of the requirement or condition with knowledge of the discriminatory effect will undermine any such contention, per *JH Walker Ltd v Hussain* [1996] ICR 291, EAT.

discrimination in a given situation will then depend upon whether it is justifiable and whether or not the aggrieved person can comply with it.

As for justification, two points are worthy of note. First, the issue of justification is judged by an objective standard (is the requirement or condition reasonably necessary?) and demands that the discriminatory effects of the requirement or condition be balanced against the reasonable needs of the person applying it[9]. Secondly, the words of the statute insist that the requirement or condition must be justifiable irrespective of the race etc of the person to whom it is applied. This means, for example, that a requirement which is itself inherently discriminatory cannot be justified. Thus a requirement that an applicant for a post or other benefit should be a member of a particular organisation will be one which cannot be justified if membership of the organisation is open only to those of a particular race.

Finally, when considering the final piece of the jigsaw and assessing whether or not an individual has suffered a detriment, the concept of whether or not he/she can comply with the requirement or condition is a liberal one. A theoretical capability of compliance will not suffice. What the Act looks for is whether or not the individual can comply in practice, that is in a sensible and practical fashion, having regard to the normal standards of behaviour for individuals such as (and of the race of) the person concerned. Accordingly, for example, a Sikh would be able to say that he cannot comply with a requirement that no headwear be worn or that hair be kept short[10].

Racial discrimination in sport

As has already been pointed out above, the Race Relations Act 1976 does not outlaw all racial discrimination in all circumstances. Rather, it identifies particular circumstances and spheres of activity in which it prohibits such discrimination. Many such circumstances and spheres will be found in sporting environments and relationships of one form or another and it follows that sporting 'employers', regulatory authorities and other bodies operating within a sporting field will ignore the provisions of the Act at their peril.

Parts II and III of the Act identify the main spheres of activity which are targeted by the Act. In particular, Part II deals with discrimination by employers (s 4) and by certain other persons such as trade unions (s 11), certain professional bodies etc (s 12) and those who provide vocational training (s 13). Part III prohibits discrimination in education (s 17), in the provision of goods, facilities or services (s 20), and in the management of premises (s 21). Part III also prohibits particular types of discrimination by certain associations of persons, where the discrimination relates to membership terms, access to benefits, facilities or services or by the imposition of any detriment.

DISCRIMINATION IN 'EMPLOYMENT'

The first point to note in relation to the Act's treatment of discrimination in 'employment' is that, for this purpose, 'employment' is not confined to

---

9 See *Webb v EMO Air Cargo (UK) Ltd* [1993] IRLR 27, HL; *Hampson v Department of Education and Science* [1989] IRLR 69, CA.
10 See *Mandla v Dowell Lee* [1983] IRLR 209, HL.

employment under a contract of service but extends[11] to employment under a contract of apprenticeship or, more significantly, a contract *personally to execute any work or labour*[12]. It follows, in the sporting world, that not only do the provisions of the Act relating to 'employment' embrace relationships such as those between a professional sporting club and the players which are on its books (employed under contracts of service), but they apply with equal rigour to *all* situations where a sports man or woman is contracted to perform. For example, if one accepts (as is undoubtedly the case) that a professional sports man or woman when playing his/her sport, engages in 'work', it follows that a golfer, tennis or any other player who is contracted to play in a tournament or other competition agrees 'personally to execute work' and is thereby caught and protected by the provisions in the Act which deal with 'employment'.

Section 4 targets 'employment' at point of entry, during its currency and at termination. It does so by rendering unlawful any racial discrimination by a person in relation to 'employment' in Great Britain[13]

(1)   by s 4(1), at point of entry:

'(a) in the arrangements he makes for the purpose of determining who should be offered that employment; or
(b) in the terms on which he offers him that employment; or
(c) by refusing or deliberately omitting to offer him that employment.'

(2)   and by s 4(2), thereafter

'(a) in the terms of employment which he affords him; or
(b) in the way in which he affords him access to opportunities for promotion, transfer or training, or to any other benefits, facilities or services, or by refusing or deliberately omitting to afford him access to them; or
(c) by dismissing him or subjecting him to any other detriment.'

It can be seen from the quoted provisions that the areas of employment in which racial discrimination is prohibited are all embracing. Any racial discrimination as defined (see above) which occurs in relation to the grant or denial of contracts to professional sports men or women is liable to be regarded as unlawful. It follows, for example, that an English professional football club may not lawfully adopt a policy of only employing English players. Equally, subject to the particular circumstances of the case[14], it is suggested that an English club which operated a form of quota system, being prepared to employ foreign players only up to a limited number (or offering foreign players restricted opportunities or other benefits in comparison to their comparable English counterparts) would be likely to be acting unlawfully. In this regard, it goes without saying [but the position is expressly articulated by s 3(4) of the Act] that, in drawing comparisons between individual players, it is necessary to compare like with like. For example, an English player of exceptional skill may properly command a higher fee or other advantageous consideration by comparison with a lesser foreign

11 See s 78(1).
12 A contract is regarded as one personally to execute work or labour, if its dominant purpose requires the provision of personal work. See *Gunning v Mirror Group Newspapers Ltd* [1986] ICR 145.
13 See ss 4(1) & (2) and 8(1).
14 In particular, much would depend upon the scope of the exemption provided by the less than clear provisions of s 39 which is dicussed below.

player. In such circumstances the advantage afforded the English player would not be 'on grounds of his race' and there would be no direct discrimination. Equally, if there were any issue of indirect discrimination, then, provided that the differential was properly attributable to differences other than race, it is unlikely that there would be any liability. In the latter case, even if the situation satisfied the other elements of the test for indirect discrimination, the 'employer' would seek to establish justification.

A further example of potentially unlawful racial discrimination which is almost certainly committed on a regular basis albeit without any malevolent intent is the practice by certain tournament organisers in Britain of offering playing contracts (or other inducements) to British players in preference to others[15], or of reserving a number of tournament places for British players (regardless, say, of whether their ranking alone would merit their selection) or of offering enhanced terms to such players. Such practices are of dubious pedigree and, in many circumstances, are likely to be regarded as unlawful racial discrimination. In such cases, the discrimination would be likely to be regarded as both direct and indirect and to be actionable at the suit of a foreign player who could show that he had been disadvantaged in consequence. Further, whilst a complaint of indirect discrimination may be resisted by arguing justification, no such defence applies in the case of direct discrimination.

The outlawing of racial discrimination in the employment field is subject to one particular exemption which is of particular importance in the present context. It is provided by s 39 in the following terms:

> 'Nothing in Parts II to IV shall render unlawful any act done by an employer whereby a person discriminates against another on the basis of that other's nationality or place of birth or the length of time for which he has been resident in a particular area or place, if the act is done:
>
> (a) in selecting one or more persons to represent a country, place or area, or any related association, in any sport or game; or
> (b) in pursuance of the rules of any competition so far as they relate to eligibility to compete in any sport or game.'

Although the exemption provided by s 39 is specific in its application to the field of sport, it should not be regarded as an absolute exception for sport to the prohibition against racial discrimination. On the contrary, it is of strictly limited application. In particular:

(a)   It only protects acts 'done by an employer'. Whilst, as has been seen, the concept of 'employment' and accordingly that of an 'employer' is a wide one, s 39 will provide no protection for those who fall foul of the provisions in the Act which deal with discrimination otherwise than by 'employers' (as to which see below).

(b)   Whilst the *aim* of the exemption is clear (in (a), to allow selection for what might colloquially be termed 'representative' teams; in (b), to allow 'employers' lawfully to enter teams or individuals for particular competitions which themselves restrict entry to those satisfying particular discriminatory eligibility requirements) the precise ambit of

---

15 The Act also applies where the 'employer' is someone other than the tournament organiser himself. If the 'employer' contracts to supply the players to the tournament organiser, whilst s 4 only applies to the 'employer', s 7 correspondingly is apt to prohibit racial discrimination by the organiser.

its terms as drafted is unclear and has yet to be tested. For example, what is covered, in (a), by the concept of a 'related association'? It is suggested that a national or county sports association/organisation which selects a team to represent it rather than the nation or county itself would be covered but that, for example, an ordinary club (which is representative of nothing other than the club itself and its members but which might be said to be 'related' to a 'place or area' by dint simply of its geographical location, its name and perhaps even its following), would not.

(c) As for the provisions in (b), they might appear at first sight to be relatively straightforward. However, whilst they exempt the actions of an 'employer' in following the rules of a particular competition, they do not address the *lawfulness of the rules of the competition themselves*. To the extent, therefore, that there may be a right of action (otherwise than under s 4) against those who set and/or administer those rules, which action would target such persons otherwise than in their capacity, if any, as 'employers' (see below), s 39 will not protect them.

(d) In so far as s 39 may provide, on its face, a wider exemption than that permitted (in respect of the nationals of EC Member States) under the principle of 'freedom of movement' discussed in Chapter 5 above [see eg Article 48(3)], it should, where possible, be restrictively construed so as to coincide with the requirements of European law generally and Article 48 in particular. Under European law, there is no special provision made for employers or anyone else in the sporting field. The tendency, therefore, ought to be to interpret s 39 restrictively, especially where nationals of EC Member States are concerned.

DISCRIMINATION BY TRADE UNIONS AND OTHER MEMBERS' ORGANISATIONS

Section 11 of the Act makes it unlawful for certain members' organisations to discriminate in relation either to applications to join them or to their treatment of members. The section heading makes it clear that Parliament had trade unions particularly in mind, but it has wider application and is apt to catch any number of bodies within the sporting world, in that it applies[16] to:

'... an organisation of workers, an organisation of employers, or any other organisation whose members carry on a particular profession or trade for the purposes of which the organisation exists.'

Whilst a 'worker' is not defined by the Act, he or she is manifestly someone who 'works' and, within the general scheme of the Act, should be equated with someone who is 'employed', whether under a contract of service/ apprenticeship or a contract personally to execute work or labour[17]. Organisations such as the Professional Footballers Association, the Rugby Union Players Association and other sporting 'trade unions' are, therefore, all subject to the prohibitions against racial discrimination in section 11. In addition, the concepts of an 'organisation of employers' and an organisation

16 See s 11(1).
17 See the definition of 'employment' in s 78.

whose members carry on a particular profession or trade for the purposes of which the organisation exists, are of extremely wide potential application. They would seem to embrace organisations such as the Football Association, the FA Premier League, the Rugby Football Union and even the international sporting federations such as UEFA, FIFA, the IAAF and possibly even the IOC, at least to the extent that such organisations are significantly concerned with professional rather than amateur sporting activity[18].

The scheme of the section generally follows that in relation to employment[19] and, accordingly, any organisation which is caught by s 11 may not discriminate (contrary to s 1[20]) either[1]:

(a)   in the case of a non-member:

> '... in the terms on which it is prepared to admit him to membership, or ... by refusing, or deliberately omitting to accept, his application for membership'; or

(b)   in the case of an existing member:

> 'in the way it affords him access to any benefits, facilities or services, or by refusing or deliberately omitting to afford him access to them, or ... by depriving him of membership, or varying the terms on which he is a member, or ... by subjecting him to any other detriment.'

It follows that sporting trade unions, associations of employers of sports people and organisations of persons engaged in professional sport which exist for the purposes of such sport should be vigilant to prevent discrimination, whether direct or indirect. They must ensure that their rules, for example, do not directly favour members/applicants of any particular race or nationality and, insofar as they favour them indirectly (by providing for criteria which have a disproportionate impact on one race over another) that they are justifiable on grounds other than race.

DISCRIMINATION BY 'QUALIFYING BODIES'

Section 12 of the Act is of particular significance to the sporting world. It is directed[2] at so called 'qualifying bodies', namely any:

> 'authority or body which can confer an authorisation or qualification which is needed for, or facilitates, engagement in a particular profession or trade.'

Importantly, the word 'confer' includes a renewal or extension and the concept of an 'authorisation or qualification' embraces, inter alia[3]:

> 'recognition, registration, enrolment, approval and certification.'

Thus, for example, the British Judo Association was held to be a 'qualifying body' for the purposes of the corresponding provision in s 13 of the Sex

18 Insofar as such bodies are concerned only with amateur sport, they may not be caught by s 11. That is not to say that they are exempt from the prohibition against racial discrimination under the Act. It may well be the case that such bodies will be caught by other provisions, including in particular s 25, to which reference is made below.
19 See above.
20 See above.
1   See s 11(2).
2   See s 12(1).
3   See s 12(2).

Discrimination Act 1975 in as much as it determined who should and should not be allowed to act as a referee[4].

Any such 'qualifying body' discriminates unlawfully for the purposes of the Act where it does so:

> 'in the terms on which it is prepared to confer ... [the] authorisation or qualification, or ... by refusing, or deliberately omitting to [confer it], or ... by withdrawing it ... or varying the terms on which [it is held].'

In these days where particular sports are often regulated by individual monopolistic governing bodies, with whom players may even be required formally to be registered before they may play their particular sport or do so without significant restriction, s 12 has wide potential application. For example, a governing body such as the Football Association or the Rugby Football Union which seeks to impose a rule which has the effect of discriminating against foreign players, is liable to fall foul of s 12. Further, if such discrimination is direct (such as where foreign players are simply banned or made subject to a quota system) it will be unlawful. Indirect discrimination, on the other hand (such as is inherent in a rule which requires players from overseas to serve a period of residence before being allowed to play) will be unlawful only insofar as it cannot be justified on objective grounds. It is suggested, however, that it will often be difficult to establish such grounds of justification. In particular it should be remembered that the grounds relied upon must establish justification irrespective of the race of the individuals concerned and that, accordingly, justification will not be established where the grounds relied upon are themselves discriminatory. A requirement of a period of residence (or any other requirement or condition) will not be justifiable where the grounds for such a criterion are to prevent an influx of foreign players. Rules which are designed to preserve, say, the English game for English players, whether wholly or substantially, are almost certainly liable to give rise to a cause of action at the suit of any foreign player adversely affected thereby.

Any sports governing body which is not yet alive to either the existence or the implications of the prohibition against discrimination in s 12 would be well advised to examine its rules and the manner of their application with some care.

DISCRIMINATION BY OTHER BODIES

Many decisions by sporting bodies, if discriminatory under s 1 of the Act, will be open to legal challenge in accordance with the procedures appropriate in relation to the bodies already described, namely employers, trade unions and other members' organisations and so called 'qualifying bodies'. It may be, however, that a particular person, body or organisation does not exactly fit within the definitions of any such body. That does not mean that such person, body or organisation has carte blanche to operate discriminatory practices with impunity. On the contrary, the Act targets many other descriptions of person, some of which may overlap with those already described, but within at least one of which any particular person etc is often likely to find a home. Thus the Act targets discrimination, for example:

---

4 See *British Judo Association v Petty* [1981] ICR 660, EAT.

- by those who are concerned with the provision of *vocational training* (s 13);
- by bodies involved in *education* (ss 17, 18 and 19);
- by those concerned with the *provision of goods, facilities or services* to the public or a section of the public (s 20) [interestingly, in a case of alleged sex discrimination under the corresponding provisions in s 9 of the Sex Discrimination Act 1975, Lord Denning MR expressed the view, obiter, that the Football Association was concerned with providing facilities to the public in that it provided 'a system of leagues and membership of individuals in those leagues'[5]];
- by those concerned with the disposal or *management of premises* (s 21); and
- in a general sweeping up provision in section 25, by:

> '... any association of persons (however described, whether corporate or unincorporate, and whether or not its activities are carried on for profit) if:
>
> (a) it has 25 or more members;
> (b) admission to membership is regulated by its constitution ...; and
> (c) it is not an organisation to which section 11 applies.'

SPECIFIC, SUPPLEMENTARY, UNLAWFUL ACTS AND THE POTENTIAL LIABILITY OF SPORTS' GOVERNING BODIES

It has to be recognised that most sports played within the United Kingdom are played in other parts of the world as well and that the conduct of such sports even within the confines of the United Kingdom is often regulated, directly or indirectly, by one or more International Federation to which the domestic regulatory authority is affiliated, whether through 'membership' or otherwise. To some extent, the rules of the domestic authority may be prescribed by the relevant International Federation. Insofar as any such prescription ties the hands of the domestic authority and requires it to operate a rule or otherwise to act in a manner which is unlawful in that it constitutes racial discrimination contrary to one or more of the sections already outlined, such prescription will not be likely to afford the domestic body with a defence to a complaint under the Act. Further, the International Federation may itself be liable. Such liability may arise in a number of ways. First, it may be directly liable in its own right under one of the provisions already discussed. What is more, the Act contains a number of provisions designed to catch third parties in such circumstances, one or more of which is likely to provide an avenue of redress against the International Federation:

- section 30 provides that:

> 'it is unlawful for a person ... who has authority over another person, or ... in accordance with whose wishes that other person is accustomed to act, to instruct him to do any act which is unlawful [under the Act] or procure or attempt to procure the doing by him of any such act.'

Proceedings for breach of s 30 may only be brought by the Commission for Racial Equality, pursuant to s 63.

---

5 See *Bennett v Football Association Ltd* CA Transcript No 591.

- section 31 targets those who 'induce' or attempt to 'induce' others to act unlawfully under the Act, and it should be noted that, for this purpose, 'induce' means simply 'persuade or prevail upon'[6]. As with s 30, proceedings for breach of s 31 must be brought by the Commission for Racial Equality under s 63.

- section 32 makes express provision for vicarious liability of employers for acts done by their employees in the course of their employment[7] and of principals for (authorised) acts done by their agents.

- section 33 is concerned with those who knowingly aid another to act unlawfully under the Act.

- section 28 is a different type of provision and operates on a more general level, in that it enables the Commission for Racial Equality, after conducting an investigation under s 48[8], to intervene by issuing a non-discrimination notice under s 58[9], in order to prevent what are referred to as 'discriminatory practices'. Such a practice is defined as meaning[10], in effect, the application of a potentially unlawful indirectly discriminatory requirement or condition. Where a person either applies such a requirement or condition, or where he operates in such a way that it is clear that such a requirement or condition will be applied by him should the circumstances for its application arise, he acts unlawfully[11]. It follows from the nature of the beast that, unlike most other prohibitions under the Act, no aggrieved or disadvantaged person is required in order for the unlawful act to occur and the Commission may act simply where it sees the potential for individual persons to be disadvantaged by indirect racial discrimination.

THE ROLE OF THE COMMISSION FOR RACIAL EQUALITY

The Commission for Racial Equality was established by s 43 of the Race Relations Act 1976. Its functions are[12] to work towards eliminating racial discrimination, to promote equality of opportunity and good relations between persons of different racial groups and to review the workings of the Act. In pursuit of those purposes it may provide financial or other assistance both to organisations with similar aims[13] and to aggrieved persons in the preparation for and conduct of proceedings[14]. It may also undertake or fund

---

6 See *Commission for Racial Equality v Imperial Society of Teachers of Dancing* [1983] ICR 473.
7 In such cases, it is a defence for the employer to show that he had taken all reasonably practicable steps to prevent either the specific act in question or acts of that description. Whether or not something is done 'in the course of employment' is, in this context, a question of fact to be decided 'as a layman would decide it' and without reference to the restrictive tests appropriate for determining vicarious liability in other fields – see *Jones v Tower Boot Co Ltd* [1997] ICR 254.
8 See below.
9 The nature and scope of non-discrimination notices are discussed below.
10 See s 28(1).
11 See s 28(2).
12 See s 43(1).
13 See s 44.
14 See ss 65 and 66.

research[15], and issue codes of practice relating to equal opportunities and the elimination of discrimination in employment[16].

One of the Commission's most important functions is to conduct formal investigations pursuant to s 48. This function accords to the Commission wide ranging and theoretically draconian powers, under sections 49 to 52, to intrude into the affairs of individuals and other bodies, to obtain information and to make recommendations and reports. In addition, the Commission has powers of enforcement under ss 58 to 64 and, in particular, may issue a non-discrimination notice[17] requiring any unlawful act or discriminatory practice in question to stop, in which event, subject to an appeal under s 59, the person concerned must comply or face possible further proceedings and a possible injunction under s 62.

CONCLUSION

It will readily be seen that the scope for challenges under the Race Relations Act 1976 to particular decisions, rules and practices in the sporting world is very considerable. In particular, the 'employment' (both actual and contemplated) of sports persons, whether on a one off basis (for a particular event or competition) or for an extended period (as with a contract between a player and his club or team) brings with it the specific obligations not to discriminate either directly on grounds of 'race' or indirectly through the unjustified application of requirements or conditions with a disproportionate effect on different 'races'. Furthermore, the rules of sports governing bodies should be scrutinised for any discriminatory effects in their application in the United Kingdom. Any such discriminatory effects, whether actual or merely potential, are liable to cause problems both for the governing bodies themselves and for any subsidiary bodies such as employing clubs which operate under and in accordance with such rules. Such problems may surface through direct legal action by a disadvantaged individual or by general or specific (accusatory) investigative action by the Commission for Racial Equality.

It is suggested that there are particular categories of rules which operate within a number of sporting fields which are of dubious pedigree in the context of the requirements of the Race Relations Act 1976. Some have already been mentioned. In particular, any criterion for eligibility to play a particular sport within the United Kingdom should be carefully examined for any disproportionate effect on foreign players. Further, any rules which are liable to have a disproportionate effect on foreign players *or British nationals* in their ability to play or to continue to play without restriction in the United Kingdom should similarly be examined. We have already seen, for example, that the football authorities initially reacted to the decision of the European Court in *Union Royale Belge des Sociétés de Football Association ASBL v Bosman*[18] by relaxing the transfer rules in relation to EU/EEA 'out

15 See s 45.
16 See s 47. The current code was introduced by the Race Relations Code of Practice Order 1983, SI 1983/1081. Such a code is not mandatory of application and imposes no legal obligations directly. It is intended to provide practical guidance as to good practice and its provisions are admissible in proceedings under the Act [see, for example s 47(10) and (11)].
17 See s 58. Note that non-discrimination notices are entered on a public register maintained by the Commission.
18 C-415/93: [1996] 1 CMLR 645. This case is extensively discussed in Chapter 5 above.

of contract players' only in relation to cross frontier transfers so as to comply with the narrowest interpretation of the decision itself, leaving many of the old restrictions in place in relation to cross border transfers of non EU/EEA players and to transfers of players between clubs situated within a single Member State. It is suggested that such differential treatment, whilst it may arguably provide a legitimate response to particular concerns under European law, is fraught with potential danger within the conduct of football in the United Kingdom and may well not survive a legal challenge under the United Kingdom's own domestic laws and that one such challenge could well be under the Race Relations Act 1976[19]. One argument would surely be that:

(a) for a player to qualify, on a transfer to a British club, for the benefit of a 'free transfer', he must satisfy the 'requirement or condition' that he be transferred from a club in a different Member State;

(b) that requirement or condition has a materially disproportionate effect on British players as, quite obviously, a significantly greater proportion of foreign players than British players play for clubs outside the United Kingdom;

(c) any British based player cannot satisfy the requirement or condition;

(d) the requirement or condition is therefore unlawful, unless it can be justified on objective grounds.

It is further suggested that justification of the differential treatment would be likely to prove very difficult to establish given that, in effect, the European Court of Justice determined in *Bosman* that, admittedly in the context of European principles, the restrictions on a player's right to move clubs at the end of his contract were artificial and without legitimate justification.

The message, therefore, is clear. The provisions of the anti-racial discrimination regime within the United Kingdom are wide-ranging in their potential effect. It follows that the Race Relations Act 1976 provides yet another area of the law to which players, employers, administrators and others who operate in the sports world would be well advised to pay close regard in the conduct of their affairs.

---

19 Another challenge might well be appropriate under the doctrine of restraint of trade. At the time of writing, moves are afoot in English football to reduce the risk of challenge, by lowering the age at which players (*all* players) become 'free agents' upon expiry of their contracts. At present the age is 33.

Chapter 7

Sex discrimination

Introduction

In the previous chapter, we saw how the United Kingdom has introduced a raft of measures designed to outlaw racial discrimination in certain circumstances and how such measures provide a distinct domestic regime extending far beyond the more limited anti-discrimination principles within the rights of free movement under European law. We saw also how the prohibitions against racial discrimination of one form or another have, thus far, had only a limited impact upon the way sport is operated and regulated and how there remains a substantial area within sport where such prohibitions could have an, as yet, largely untapped and unappreciated potential impact. This chapter considers a different type of discrimination, namely sex discrimination, and explains how it is necessary to look beyond the confines of domestic legislation and to embrace the principles of European law in order to gain a full understanding of the general prohibition against discrimination on the grounds of sex as it applies in the United Kingdom. In this instance, the domestic legislation sits alongside the European regime and is intended, in part at least, simply to reflect and implement the general principles laid down by Europe.

Thus, for example, the Sex Discrimination Act 1975 (as amended by the Sex Discrimination Act 1986 and the Employment Act 1989) was introduced in order, in part, to implement the EC Equal Treatment Directive[1]. That Directive cannot itself be enforced directly as between private individuals and has direct effect only against the state and emanations of the state[2]. Article 6 of the Equal Treatment Directive required Member States to introduce into their national legal systems measures designed to afford redress to individuals who establish that they have been wronged by a failure to apply to them the general principle of equal treatment within the Directive. That general principle is reflected in Article 2 which provides:

'... the principle of equal treatment shall mean that there shall be no discrimination whatsoever on grounds of sex either directly or indirectly ...'

---

1 Council Directive No 76/207/EEC of February 1976.
2 *Webb v EMO Air Cargo (UK) Ltd* [1990] ICR 442, in which the principle was reaffirmed that, wherever possible, domestic legislation should be interpreted in such a way as to give effect to the Directive and any interpretations thereof laid down by the European Court of Justice.

Similarly, the Equal Pay Act 1970 is intended to reflect the general principle enshrined in Article 119 of the Treaty of Rome (which is directly enforceable in all cases) as elaborated upon by the Equal Pay Directive[3] (which, like the Equal Treatment Directive, has direct effect only as against the state or emanations of the state). That general principle is simply that men and women should receive equal pay for equal work.

At the heart of all the general principles propounded in the legislation, whether domestic or European, is the generic principle that certain relationships should be conducted without discrimination between the sexes. Further, whereas the European legislation expounds that principle in general terms, the domestic legislation seeks to break it down and provide for its application in specific circumstances which are articulated in some detail. It is therefore the domestic regime which provides the focus for appropriate consideration within the limited context of this book. Any application of the domestic legislation to a particular case, however, should be considered against the background of general principles laid down by Europe, which general principles should be understood to have spawned the more detailed principles laid down by Parliament. Insofar as those detailed principles may appear to have left gaps or to be open to various possible constructions, resort to the general European principles may serve to resolve the problem.

Sex Discrimination Act 1975

The regime laid down by the Sex Discrimination Act 1975, is broadly the same as that applied, in the case of racial discrimination, by the Race Relations Act 1976. For a full discussion of the principles common to both regimes, the reader is referred to the previous chapter.

Thus, like the 1976 Act (racial discrimination), the 1975 Act (sex discrimination) covers[4] both:

– *direct discrimination* (less favourable treatment on the grounds of sex), and
– *indirect discrimination* (the application of a requirement or condition which is gender neutral but which has a disproportionate impact as between the sexes, with which the complainant cannot comply and which is not objectively justifiable irrespective of sex).

The activities within which discrimination is rendered unlawful, are also *broadly* the same as under the Race Relations Act 1976. For example:

(a)   Section 6 targets discrimination in 'employment', whether at the point of recruitment, during its currency or at termination. For this purpose, as with racial discrimination, an extended definition of 'employment' applies so as to cover employment not simply under a contract of service but also under a contract of apprenticeship or *any contract personally to execute any work or labour*[5]. Thus any contract by which a

---

3   Council Directive No 75/117/EEC of 10 February 1975.
4   See s 1.
5   See s 82. Note that a contract is a 'contract personally to execute work or labour' where its *dominant purpose* is the provision of personal service involving work or labour. See *Gunning v Mirror Group Newspapers Ltd* [1986] ICR 145.

sports man or woman is engaged to perform[6] is potentially covered by the Act. To this general principle, however, certain exceptions apply, of which the most important for present purposes are as follows:

- Section 6 does not apply so as to require that contracts should always provide for equal pay as between men and women[7]. This is because (contractual) issues of pay are generally covered by the Equal Pay Act 1970, which is considered below.

- Section 6 does not have the effect of requiring employers not to discriminate in their choice of employees or in the way in which they afford access to opportunities for advancement to their existing employees, if being a particular sex is a genuine occupational qualification for the job in question[8]. But an employer may not plead this 'genuine occupational qualification' defence to defend an allegation of discrimination in relation to the provision of other types of benefit to employees[9] or in relation to dismissal or the imposition of other detriments. Further, the extent of the defence, where it applies, is severely curtailed by the fact that, for present purposes, it applies only[10] where matters of decency or privacy are involved or where the 'essential nature of the job' in question demands a particular sex for reasons of physiology (excluding strength or stamina) or, in the case of 'dramatic performances or other entertainment' for reasons of authenticity. In the context of sport, the exclusion of criteria such as strength and stamina has obvious implications[11]. Whether sport could claim the protection of the defence, as an 'entertainment' where 'authenticity' was required, so as to justify discrimination would depend upon the circumstances. It is thought unlikely that such an argument would prevail in anything other than the most extreme of situations. Certainly, the view of the Equal Opportunities Commission, as expressed in its Code of Practice is that, generally, there are very few instances in which jobs are likely to be subject to a genuine occupational qualification on grounds of sex.

(b)   The Act, by s 12 (which mirrors s 11 of the Race Relations Act 1976), outlaws discrimination by certain members' organisations, being any organisation of workers or employers or any other organisation whose members carry on a particular profession or trade for the purposes of which the organisation exists. It follows that, as with racial discrimina-

---

6   By s 9, the Act applies equally where 'contract workers' are supplied to a principal pursuant to a contract between him and a third party. In such a case, the principal may not discriminate between contract workers of different sexes. For example, a tournament organiser who contracts with a sports agency for the appearance and performance of certain sports stars on the latter's books, is subject to the constraints of the Act, very much as though he were contracting directly with the stars themselves.

7   See s 6(5) and (6).

8   See s 7.

9   In the case of the provision by an employer of benefits to employees in common with (and to the same extent as to) other members of the public, allegations of discrimination will generally fall to be considered not under s 6 but under s 29, which is considered below. See s 6(7).

10   See s 7(2) which lists the circumstances where a genuine occupational qualification may be established, most of which are unlikely to be relevant in the general context of this book.

11   However, see the general exception for sport provided by s 44, which is discussed below.

tion, sporting trade unions and some sporting regulatory authorities and federations are likely to be covered by the prohibition against sex discrimination in relation, in particular, to:

- *access to membership*;
- the *treatment of members*; and
- the *disciplining of members*.

(c)   Section 13 (which corresponds, in part, to s 12 of the Race Relations Act 1976) prohibits discrimination by so called 'qualifying bodies', being those authorities which can confer an authorisation or qualification[12] which is needed for, or facilitates, engagement in a particular profession or trade[13]. It follows that, by this route too, the activities of many sporting authorities are likely to fall within the jurisdiction of the Act and its prohibition against sex discrimination. In *British Judo Association v Petty*[14], it was under s 13 that the British Judo Association was held unlawfully to have discriminated against Ms Petty on grounds of sex when it introduced a policy of not allowing women to referee men's competitions. Ms Petty already held a referee's certificate granted by the BJA and the new policy was held to involve the BJA either in conferring a discriminatory certificate or in unlawfully varying the terms of her existing certificate. Either way, the BJA had contravened the Act, as the grant of a certificate was liable to help Ms Petty in her job as a judo coach, even though it was no part of the BJA's motivation to discriminate. Similarly, in a first instance Industrial Tribunal decision, *Thompson v Professional Pool Players' Organisation*[15], the PPPO was held to have acted unlawfully in refusing membership, and thereby declining to grant professional status, to Ms Thompson in spite of her having played in a number of tournaments and having won an open championship. The point was that membership of the organisation, and the status which such membership conferred, was held to be such as to facilitate engagement in the profession of pool playing[16].

(d)   Sporting authorities may also be caught by the prohibitions in s 29 (corresponding to s 20 of the Race Relations Act 1976) against discrimination by those concerned with the provision of goods, facilities or services to the public or a section of the public[17]. In *Bennett*

---

12 The concept of an authorisation or qualification here embraces 'recognition, registration, enrolment, approval and certification'; further, the word 'confer' includes 'renew' and 'extend' – see s 13(3).

13 Section 13(2) imposes upon any qualifying body which has a statutory duty to satisfy itself as to the 'good character' of an applicant for an 'authorisation or qualification', the additional obligation to take account of any evidence that the latter has himself been responsible for unlawful discrimination in carrying on any profession or trade. This is not mirrored by the Race Relations Act 1976.

14 [1981] ICR 660, EAT.

15 (1991) COIT Case Nos 15898/91 and 47323/91.

16 It is suggested that, even if such membership did not facilitate engagement in the profession, it is likely that the refusal of membership would have been unlawfully discriminatory under s 12 (above) in any event.

17 Exceptions to the general prohibition are provided by s 35. They include situations where restrictions are reasonable for the sake of decency or privacy s 35(1)(c) and situations where physical contact between individuals is likely in circumstances where a member of one sex might reasonably object to such contact with a member of the opposite sex s 35(2).

v The Football Association & the Nottinghamshire Football Association[18] Lord Denning expressed the view that, in providing a system of leagues and membership of individuals in those leagues, the Football Association was thereby concerned with providing facilities to the public so as to bring its activities within the jurisdiction of s 29. It should be noted, however, that s 34 provides that where the body concerned is non profit making and is not established by statute, any rule which restricts its membership (or its provision of benefits) to a single sex, will not contravene s 29. Such an exemption may prove to be of limited comfort to those organisations able to benefit from it, if they may be categorised as an organisation of workers or employers or one whose members carry on a particular profession or trade for the purposes of which it exists. In that event they are likely to be caught in any event by s 12 (above).

(e)   The Act also targets other bodies, such as:

-    local education authorities (s 23) and those in charge of certain educational establishments (s 22)[19];
-    those concerned with the provision of vocational training (s 14);
-    those concerned with the disposal or management of premises (s 30).

The application of the Act to educational and training bodies has obvious importance in the context of sport. Any distinction between the sexes (subject to the permitted exceptions) in offering educational or training places is unlawful. Thus there is effective provision for women to be able to qualify as coaches without being disadvantaged by reason of their sex.

(f)   The Act then goes on to target certain specific acts. In particular:

-    The provisions outlawing indirect discrimination are complemented by s 37 which (like s 58 of the Race Relations Act 1976) targets 'discriminatory practices', namely the application of requirements or conditions which result in acts of indirect discrimination. Section 37 also deals with the operation of practices or other arrangements which are liable to result in the application of discriminatory practices. The effect of the section is to enable the Equal Opportunities Commission (who alone may bring proceedings for its breach) to challenge discriminatory practices[20] even before they have given rise to any example of actual discrimination (perhaps because the nature of the practice is so discriminatory as to deter all female applicants for the benefit in question). In particular, the rules, practices and arrangements of a sporting body could be examined by the Equal Opportunities Commission if they were thought to be potentially indirectly discriminatory.

-    Section 39 (corresponding to s 30 of the Race Relations Act 1976) renders it unlawful for a person with authority over another, or in

18 Court of Appeal, 28 July 1978, CAT No 591.
19 As might be expected, exceptions are permitted, in particular, in the case of single sex establishments (s 26) and in respect of physical training (s 28).
20 The EOC may investigate pursuant to s 58 and, if necessary, issue a non-discrimination notice under s 67.

accordance with whose wishes that other is accustomed to act, to instruct or procure him to act unlawfully under the Act. Again, enforcement is left to the Equal Opportunities Commission. With many sports being structured and controlled in pyramid fashion, with individual sportsmen and women being subject to the regulatory regimes of their 'employing' clubs who are affiliated to one or more national governing bodies who in turn belong to an international federation, it is easy to see the potential for the controlling influence of an international federation to fall within the ambit of s 39. Such a federation would be liable to direct legal action within the United Kingdom in the event that its rules or practices required either its affiliated national governing bodies or the employing clubs to operate in a way which was unlawful under the Sex Discrimination Act 1975.

– Section 40 (which is similar, but not identical, to s 31 of the Race Relations Act 1976) outlaws attempts to induce others to contravene the Act, either by offering benefits or issuing threats. As with ss 37 and 39, it is the Equal Opportunities Commission who deals with alleged breaches. Again, the potential is manifest for s 40 to apply to the world of sport, given the pyramid structure of control and influence which marks the way in which many sports are administered.

– Section 41 (corresponding to s 32 of the Race Relations Act 1976) provides for the vicarious liability of employers for acts done by their employees in the course of their employment[1] and of principals for the (authorised) acts of their agents.

– Section 42 (as with s 33 of the Race Relations Act 1976) makes provision for those who knowingly aid others to act unlawfully under the Act. As under ss 39 and 40 (above), the activities of sports' governing bodies and international federations are liable to come under scrutiny under s 42 insofar as their rules, practices or actions may be seen as encouraging others to act unlawfully under the Sex Discrimination Act 1975.

A LIMITED EXCEPTION FOR SPORT

Section 44 makes special provision in the case of sport, by providing that:

> 'Nothing ... shall, in relation to any sport, game or other activity of a competitive nature where the physical strength, stamina or physique of the average woman puts her at a disadvantage to the average man, render unlawful any act related to the participation of a person as a competitor in events involving that activity which are confined to competitors of one sex.'

It follows that the law does not require events in sports involving competitive physical activity to be open to both sexes. But it should be noted that this is

---

1   For this purpose, whether or not something is done 'in the course of employment' is a question of fact to be decided 'as a layman would decide it' and without reference to the restrictive tests appropriate for determining vicarious liability in other fields – see *Jones v Tower Boot Co Ltd* [1997] ICR 254. It is a defence for the employer to show that he had taken all reasonably practicable steps to prevent either the specific act in question or acts of that description.

as far as this limited exception to the prohibitions under the Act goes. In particular, where the discriminatory act does not relate to *participation as a competitor* in an event, or where the event does not involve a test of physical strength, stamina or physique, the exception has no application.

In *British Judo Association v Petty*[2] the exception did not save the BJA, in that the discrimination which was established lay in the certification of referees, whose contribution to events was otherwise than through strength, stamina or physique. Equally, sports such as snooker, bowls, darts etc, in which women are not at a competitive disadvantage because of their diminished strength, stamina or physique, will not qualify for exemption. Quite how stringently the terms of s 44 would be interpreted in the case of sports such as equestrian events, in which men and women regularly compete on equal terms but in which it might be argued that women are at a physical disadvantage, remains to be seen.

Equal Pay Act 1970

The other limb of the United Kingdom's domestic regime targeted at sex discrimination is provided by the Equal Pay Act 1970, which is an Act designed to eliminate discrimination between men and women as regards terms and conditions of employment. In part, therefore, it reflects the principle, laid down by Article 119 of the Treaty of Rome, namely that:

> 'Men and women should receive equal pay for equal work.'

That principle was elaborated further, by the Equal Pay Directive[3] which provides, by Article 1, that the principle of equal pay means:

> 'For the same work or for work to which equal value is attributed, the elimination of all discrimination on grounds of sex with regard to all aspects of remuneration.'

Thus the principle targets not simply those of different sexes doing identical work, but also those doing work of 'equal value'.

The manner in which the Equal Pay Act 1970 articulates the principle, and expands it so as to cover not simply matters of pay but all contractual[4] terms and conditions of employment, is to provide, by s 1, for the statutory implication into all contracts under which individuals are 'employed' a so called 'equality clause'. Under such a clause, the terms and conditions of employment are automatically modified and upgraded[5] so as to accord with any more favourable terms under which comparable individuals of the

---

2 [1981] ICR 660, EAT supra.
3 Council Directive No 75/117/EEC of 10 February 1975.
4 In this regard, Article 119 is wider than the Equal Pay Act 1970, in that the former applies both to contractual benefits and also to benefits which simply derive, directly or indirectly, from the contractual relationship. Thus payments from, say, an event sponsor rather than directly from the 'employer' might well be covered under Article 119, whereas the Equal Pay Act 1970 confines its attention to the provision of benefits pursuant to the 'employment' contract. This does not mean, however, that there is a lacuna under domestic law. Rather, the issue of non contractual benefits simply falls for consideration under the Sex Discrimination Act 1975 and not the Equal Pay Act 1970.
5 It is to be noted that the statutory remedy requires the disadvantaged sex to be brought up to the level of the preferred sex. An employer may not choose to rectify an *established complaint* by equalising the sexes downwards.

opposite sex are employed. Further, the appropriate comparisons which may be made are between:

- those doing like work, being work *both* which is of a broadly similar nature *and* in which any differences between the things done are of no practical importance to their terms and conditions[6];
- those doing work which has been rated as equivalent work pursuant to a formal job evaluation exercise[7];
- those doing work of equal value[8] in terms of the demands made upon them, for example in respect of such criteria as effort, skill and decision making[9].

It is important to note, further, that, as under the Sex Discrimination Act 1975[10], the Equal Pay Act 1970 is not confined in its application simply to 'employees' in the ordinary sense, but extends to all persons who may be:

'Employed under a contract of service or of apprenticeship or a contract personally to execute any work or labour ...[11]'

It follows that the requirement to accord equal pay and other terms and conditions to comparable men and women in the same employment applies wherever a contract demands that an individual provide his or her own 'work or labour'[12]. As will be seen below, the implications for sport are potentially very significant.

Unlike under the Sex Discrimination Act 1975, a complainant under the Equal Pay Act 1970 has to identify a specific comparator in the same employment. In this regard, the concept of being 'in the same employment' is not always straightforward. By s 1(6), it means employment by the same employer or an 'associated employer' either

- at the same place as the comparator; or
- at a different place, provided that common terms and conditions of employment are applied at the two places.

For this purpose, employers are 'associated' if one is a company of which the other has direct or indirect control or if both companies are under the direct or indirect control of a third person. In this regard, the concept of indirect control raises all kinds of potential uncertainties. For example, might it be said that the constituent clubs of a sporting federation were under the common control of the federation itself? The answer would have to depend upon the degree of stringency of the particular terms of membership of the federation. It is thought unlikely that the degree of control effected by, say, the football authorities is such as to qualify individual member clubs as 'associated employers', although the theoretical prospect and implications

---

6 See s 1(2)(a) and s 1(4). The latter section requires, further, that the frequency in the occurrence of any differences, as well as their nature and extent, should be taken into account in determining whether 'like work' is being carried out.
7 See s 1(2)(b) and s 1(5).
8 This important form of comparison was introduced, by amendment made by the Equal Pay (Amendment) Regulations 1983 (SI 1983/1794), so as to bring the Equal Pay Act 1970 into line with the requirements of European law.
9 See s 1(2)(c).
10 And also the Race Relations Act 1976.
11 See s 1(6).
12 As under the Race Relations Act 1976 and the Sex Discrimination Act 1975, however, the 'dominant purpose' test determines whether or not a contract is one 'personally to execute any work or labour'. See *Gunning v Mirror Group Newspapers Ltd* [1986] ICR 145.

of such being the case in relation to other sports, particularly where the constituent clubs 'employ' both men and women sporting performers, is intriguing.

It can immediately be seen that the Equal Pay Act 1970 has potential implications for the conduct of sport in that, wherever individuals are contracted to perform[13], then, subject to permitted exceptions, their terms and conditions must not discriminate between the sexes insofar as individuals of each sex are being required to do 'like work' or 'work of equal value'[14].

Where men and women are in professional sporting competition against each other, as for example in many equestrian events, the terms upon which they are engaged (and in particular any prize money) must be the same, save to the extent that the employer can bring the difference within the exception (discussed below) afforded to differentials which are genuinely attributable to a material factor other than the difference in sex.

Equally, it may be open to a woman competing in a women only competition to argue that she should receive equal pay and other benefits to those afforded to a man engaged (by the same 'employer') in a comparable competition exclusively for men. In such a case, there might be considerable scope for argument as to whether, in the circumstances, she could properly compare herself with a man and, if so, as to the proper basis of that comparison. In particular, it can be foreseen that there might be considerable debate as to whether she was performing 'like work' or 'work of equal value' in comparison with the man. On whichever basis it might be put (and there is no reason why a claim should not be advanced on alternative bases), such an argument might be the tool used, for example, by women tennis players in their perennial claims at Wimbledon and other tennis tournaments to equal prize money to that afforded to the men. Could a woman tennis player sensibly assert that she does 'like work' to that of a male tennis player? In particular, is her work the same as or of a *broadly similar nature* to that of a comparable man? Do the extra exertions arguably required of a male tennis player amount to differences between what she does and what he does and, if so, can she claim that such differences are of no practical importance in relation to her terms and conditions? Such questions are easy to pose, but difficult to answer with any degree of confidence. The author certainly does not suggest any obvious and clear answer appropriate to all such cases[15]. What is perhaps more clear is that, were such a female tennis player to fail to establish that she performs 'like work', she would be hard pressed to establish an alternative claim that she did work of 'equal value' to that of a comparable male tennis player, on the basis that, in any event (it is tentatively suggested) she would be unlikely to show that the demands made of her (in relation to such criteria as effort, skill, strength and stamina etc)

13 See in particular the broad definition of 'employment' in s 1(6), (above).

14 It is not thought that, under current circumstances, there is any immediate likelihood of claims being advanced in sporting contexts where a comparison could be made of performers doing work 'rated as equivalent' under a job evaluation scheme.

15 See *Capper Pass Ltd v Lawton* [1977] QB 852, where a female cook doing 'cooking on a domestic scale' for a directors' dining room was held to be performing work of a broadly similar nature to that done by a male cook in a works canteen. The comparison did not ultimately amount to 'like work,' because, under the next limb of the test, there were in fact significant differences in the things which they did. Equally, in *Noble v David Gold & Son Ltd* [1980] IRLR 252 the fact that women, by comparison with their male comparators, were generally doing lighter work and that accordingly less physical effort was required of them was used as the basis for a decision that they were not employed on work which was broadly similar to that of the men.

were equal in value to those made of her comparator. In the case of different sports, however, such as snooker, shooting, archery and darts, and even perhaps certain other sports of physical exertion such as athletics, skiing and swimming, the arguments might well be more finely balanced.

Of course, the very nature of an equal pay claim based on a comparison which asserts 'work of equal value' is such that comparisons may be made between 'employees' exercising different disciplines. This means that a sports performer in one sport may seek to compare herself (or himself) with a comparator operating in a different sport completely (or even with a non sporting comparator). Further, the breadth of the potential comparisons which may be made as a result of the criterion of 'equal value' is of particular significance now that the business world is increasing its interest in sport. Indeed, it is already far from unusual to find individual companies or groups of companies[16] with a controlling stake in such operations across a broad range of different activities. The potential for unexpected equal pay claims in such circumstances is manifest. Employers in such circumstances need to beware!

THE 'GENUINE MATERIAL FACTOR' DEFENCE

The final plea of an 'employer' accused of 'employing' individuals of one sex on terms less favourable than those under which he employs members of the other sex, is to assert, in effect, that the differential treatment is justifiable regardless of sex. He may do so by praying in aid the provisions of s 1(3) which provide that:

> 'An equality clause shall not operate in relation to a variation between the woman's contract and the man's contract if the employer proves that the variation is genuinely due to a *material factor which is not the difference of sex ...*'

This 'genuine material factor' defence is often of crucial importance in defeating an equal pay claim but has provoked a considerable amount of case law as to its proper ambit. A full analysis of the cases must be left to the specialist works on the subject but, for present purposes, three important features of the exception should be noted:

– First, the factor relied upon must be both 'material' and 'genuine'. In other words, it must be the actual reason for the differential in question and it must be significant and relevant.

– Secondly, and as the statutory words themselves make clear, a 'material factor' must not itself be the difference between the sexes. This almost goes without saying, given that the Act is part of a regime designed to eliminate sex discrimination.

– Finally, and as a necessary elaboration of the previous point, where the defence involves reliance upon particular criteria (for example, in relation to selection or qualification), then, to the extent that such criteria have a disproportionate effect on one sex so as to be indirectly discriminatory, they must be *objectively* justified. In this context, there-

16 It will be recalled [see s 1(6) above] that the permissible comparison is not confined to a comparator employed by the same employer. An associated employer will suffice.

fore, the broad principles applicable to indirect discrimination under the Sex Discrimination Act 1975 have corresponding application[17].

In the sporting field, the significance of the 'genuine material factor' defence may prove often to be fundamental. This is one result of the House of Lords' decision in *Rainey v Greater Glasgow Health Board*[18] which determined finally that 'market forces' could be cited as a genuine material factor justifying a differential in terms between 'employed' men and women. However, this is not to say that an event or tournament organiser will necessarily be able to defeat equal pay claims simply by asserting that the appearance and prize money offered to the disadvantaged sex (usually women) is 'the going rate' or is sufficient to attract an appropriate number and level of entries. In particular, any such argument will fail if the asserted justification is shown itself to be discriminatory. Thus, an argument (however it may be dressed up) that women simply command a lower fee in the market place than men is one which, whilst being an invocation of market forces, advances a material factor which is itself obviously gender based. Such an argument will therefore fail by reference to that part of the permitted defence which requires that the differential be founded upon a material factor *which is not the difference of sex*.

On the other hand, if an event or tournament is only able to attract men of the highest calibre by offering inflated sums, perhaps because of a proliferation of events competing for their appearance, then it is suggested that the genuine material factor defence may be appropriate if, in comparison, top women competitors are readily attracted without such difficulty because, in their case, there is no such proliferation of competitive events.

Equally, if the paying public is more attracted to watch one sex in competition than another, it would perhaps be arguable that the more popular sex was liable to provide a greater proportion of the event's goodwill so as to justify a greater proportion of the return. Against this would be an argument that the public's view was itself inherently discriminatory and that, accordingly, the asserted 'genuine material factor' was again itself founded upon the difference between the sexes and was therefore incapable of providing appropriate justification under the exception. In reality, of course, the factors leading in such a case to the increased popularity of one sex over the other are likely in any event to be determinative of the initial question, namely whether the comparators were performing 'like work' or 'work of equal value'.

In conclusion, it should be noted that the principle of equal pay has proved, in certain circumstances, to be extraordinarily difficult to apply even in the more run of the mill employment contexts. Where 'employment' is conducted in a context which requires some form of sporting performance, it is suggested that particular difficulties are liable to arise. At present, such a context provides virtually uncharted waters for any consideration of the issues involved, sports cases not having figured to any significant extent in the developing jurisprudence. The scope for future argument is undoubtedly substantial. Various hypothetical issues may be posed:

17 By way of example, see *Enderby v Frenchay Health Authority* [1994] ICR 112. No objective justification is required other than in cases of indirect discrimination – see *Tyldesley v TML Plastics* [1996] ICR 356, *Strathclyde Regional Council v Wallace* [1996] IRLR 670.
18 [1987] ICR 129.

- How, for example, would an Industrial Tribunal approach a claim, say by Laura Davies, the immensely talented, successful and popular woman golfer, to pay equal to that afforded to a journeyman male golfer of moderate repute? Conundrums with similar ingredients may be identified in virtually all sports.

- Are male and female participants in individual sports, in which competition is ordinarily organised on a single sex basis, nevertheless performing 'like work'? Are different relative standards, whether perhaps of skill or strength, sufficient to render the work of the two sexes not 'broadly similar'? Are any such relative differences of sufficient practical importance to their terms and conditions as to mean that they are not performing 'like work'?

- In what circumstances may a sportswoman in one sport claim to be performing 'work of equal value' to a sportsman in either the same or a different sport?

- To what extent and in what circumstances may market forces be relied upon by an employer of sportsmen and women to justify a differential in pay between employees of different sexes (in the same or different sports) under the genuine material factor defence?

These and many other issues face the unsuspecting 'employer' of sporting performers. The extent to which such theoretical claims are simply fanciful remains to be seen. What is clear is that such issues are of sufficient complexity that no plain and obvious answers may sensibly be suggested which will be capable of application in each case. Indeed, it is suggested that the particular implications of 'employment' in a *sporting* context were far from the draughtsman's mind when the Equal Pay Act 1970 went through Parliament.

It therefore follows that the precise circumstances of each individual case should be examined with care.

The role of the Equal Opportunities Commission

Quite apart from an individual's rights of recourse[19] on the occasion of any infringement of the principles enshrined in the above legislation, The Equal Opportunities Commission, established under the Sex Discrimination Act 1975, fulfils general functions similar to those fulfilled, in the case of racial discrimination, by the Commission for Racial Equality. Its specific role is laid down by the Sex Discrimination Act 1975. Its general duties are[20], in particular, to work towards the elimination of sex discrimination, to promote equality of opportunity and generally to review the workings of the Sex Discrimination Act 1975 and the Equal Pay Act 1970. It may conduct investigations[1], require the production of information[2], make reports and

19 Such rights are generally exercised before an Industrial Tribunal. In certain circumstances, however, the legislation requires a complaint to proceed before a County Court.
20 See s 53 of the Sex Discrimination Act 1975.
1 See ss 57 and 58 of the 1975 Act.
2 See s 59.

recommendations[3] and serve non-discrimination notices[4] requiring the persons served to abide by the legislation and, where appropriate, to take certain steps to secure such compliance. In addition it may assist aggrieved individuals in dealing with and presenting their claims[5].

3   See s 60.
4   See s 67. Section 70 provides for a public register of non-discrimination notices. In addition, certain follow-up enforcement powers are accorded to the EOC under s 71.
5   See s 75.

Chapter 8

The employment of sports performers

Introduction

We have already seen, in earlier chapters, how the embodiment of different relationships in a contract of one form or another gives rise to a framework of rights and obligations which serves to regulate the conduct of such relationships and provides avenues for redress in the event of breach or threatened breach of obligations or infringement (or threatened infringement) of rights identified by the contract. With the embrace of professionalism by sport proving to be an ever increasing feature of our times, the role of contracts in sport and the application of the law relating to such contracts are subjects deserving of particular attention by those involved in the business of sport. This chapter is concerned specifically with the contractual and other implications of the employment of sports men and women. In particular, it considers certain features of the employment of athletes and other sports performers which merit particular attention.

In this connection, it should be noted that sports men and women, like anyone else, may be 'employed' under an ordinary contract of service, as where a football club retains the services of its players and the club and the players enjoy the relationship of employer/employees in the ordinary sense of such terms. Equally, the services of individual performers may be 'employed', perhaps for an individual event or a series of events, in circumstances where they retain their 'self employed' capacity, but contract themselves out to perform as independent contractors under a 'contract for services'. The particular terms included in this latter type of contract will be fashioned very much by the circumstances in which the performer's services are required or offered and by the nature of the event or events to which he or she is thereby contracted. Many such circumstances, and the kind of rights and obligations to which they may be likely to give rise, have been addressed in other chapters, and in this chapter the focus is very much on 'employment' in the sense used to describe the ordinary relationship between an employer and his employees. That is not to say that the rights and obligations which are considered in this chapter have no relevance to those wider forms of employment relationship embodied in contracts for services. On the contrary, many of the terms to be subjected to scrutiny may well be appropriate of application to different types of 'employment' relationship. In some cases, such application may require a certain modification of the terms to take account of the differing nature of the relationships in question.

In others, the type of constraints involved in the application of such terms may indeed be inappropriate in the particular circumstances. It goes without saying that each situation which presents itself needs to be carefully considered in the light of its own particular circumstances. Even when considering that type of contract which has been referred to above as reflecting the 'ordinary' employment relationship, namely a 'contract of service', standard terms and conditions are unlikely to suit every situation.

Contracts of service

The first thing to note about the law relating to the employment of sports 'performers' is that there is no set of 'bespoke' legal principles designed to regulate a contract of employment where the service provided by the employee happens to be his or her sporting prowess. Such a contract is governed by the ordinary principles of employment law. Thus, as has already been seen in previous chapters, the raft of domestic measures designed to outlaw different types of discrimination in employment has application, subject to the terms of the legislation, to the employment of sportspersons[1]. Equally, such individuals are entitled to the benefits and protections afforded to employees, and are subject to the obligations imposed upon them, in each case both collectively and individually, under the provisions of the general employment legislation. Such general provisions, a full examination of which must be left to the specialist works on employment law, include the following:

(a)   The Trade Union and Labour Relations (Consolidation) Act 1992 makes provision for the administration and control of trade unions. A 'trade union' is defined, by s 1, in terms wide enough[2] to embrace many of the players' organisations such as the Professional Footballers Association. The Act grants limited rights and imposes particular requirements directly on a trade union itself (for example, by Part I, Chapters III & IV, as to its administration and the conduct of its elections; by Part IV, Chapters I & II, as to collective bargaining and the handling of redundancies and, by Part IV, Chapter V, as to the conduct and effect of industrial action). In addition, the Act accords particular rights to individuals (for example, by Part III, in relation to union membership and activities[3]).

(b)   By s 237, the Trade Union and Labour Relations (Consolidation) Act 1992 also removes from an employee the right to complain of unfair

---

1   Further, as pointed out in the chapters on racial and sex discrimination, such measures apply not simply to employment under contracts of service, but extend to any contracts requiring the personal execution of work or labour (see s 82(1) of the Sex Discrimination Act 1975 and s 78(1) of the Race Relations Act 1976).

2   Under the Act, an organisation qualifies as a 'trade union', in particular, if its membership comprises mainly workers of one or more descriptions and its principal purposes include the regulation of relations between workers of such descriptions and employers or associations of employers.

3   In particular, by ss 146 and 152, an individual has the right not to be disciplined or dismissed for reasons relating to union membership or legitimate union activities. The Act also contains provisions in ss 64 and 174 designed to protect individuals from unjustified disciplinary action by and unjustified exclusion or expulsion from their union.

dismissal[4] if, at the time of his dismissal, he was taking part in 'unofficial'[5] industrial action. In the case of official industrial action, such right is effectively denied him, by s 238, only if all other relevant participants have been treated in a similar fashion. Thus, were the players contracted to a particular team to go on strike, the team could dismiss them, safe in the knowledge that it would be free of any liability for unfair dismissal, provided that it did not 'cherry pick' and choose to keep on (or re-employ within three months) particular favoured players.

(c) The Employment Rights Act 1996 is a consolidating Act designed to bring together the majority of the statutory requirements regulating the terms and operation of contracts of employment. In particular:

  – Part I requires employers to set out in writing for their employees certain basic particulars of their employment. Reference should be made to the terms of the Act itself for the full particulars referred to, but included amongst them are[6] particulars relating to pay, hours of work, holidays, sickness or injury (including any provision for sick pay), pensions, notice, the term of the contract, and[7] a note as to any applicable disciplinary or grievance rules and procedures.

  – Part II reproduces parts of the repealed Wages Act 1986 and, before it, the old Truck Acts. Essentially, it requires employers to pay their employees their wages[8] without any unauthorised or other unlawful deduction and, correspondingly, it prohibits the making of unauthorised payments by employees to their employer. The Act, in particular by ss 13 to 16, carefully defines the circumstances in which a deduction or payment is properly to be regarded as authorised and/or otherwise[9] lawful for this purpose. In principle, the prohibition is intended mainly to inhibit employers from acting unilaterally and without some prior express agreement in the form either of an incorporated contractual term (in writing) or some independent agreement (in writing). Thus, any team/club which wishes to reserve the right in certain circumstances to fine players for disciplinary reasons, should be astute to ensure that such a right is expressly reserved in writing by the contract and that a copy of the contract, or the relevant term, is in the hands of the player in question prior to any attempt to exercise the right.

  – Part VIII lays down detailed provisions, the effect of which is to entitle female employees to take leave of absence from their

4 This right is considered briefly at p 170 below.
5 Because of the cumbersome and virtually unworkable rules laid down by ss 237(2), 20(2) and 21 for distinguishing unofficial action from official action, it will be rare indeed that industrial action will be properly deemed to be unofficial for this purpose.
6 See s 1.
7 See s 3.
8 For this purpose, by s 27, 'wages' include any sums payable in connection with the employee's employment, whether payable under his contract or otherwise. Thus, for example, a *discretionary* bonus (to receipt of which the employee has no contractual right) is included.
9 For example, ss 14(1) and 16(1) exempt deductions and payments respectively where their purpose is simply to reimburse the employer in respect of an earlier overpayment of wages or expenses.

employment for a defined period[10] in order to have children. The right, if duly exercised, entitles the employee to return to work after her period of leave, on terms no less favourable than would have been applicable had she not been away.

- Part IX entitles employees to minimum periods of notice of termination depending upon their accrued length of service[11] and, in the event of termination, to a written statement of the reasons for dismissal[12].

- Part X accords to most employees a most important right, namely (by s 94) the right not to be 'unfairly' dismissed. Certain employees, however, are denied the right. In particular, only employees with at least two years continuous service qualify[13]. Further, and importantly in the present context, s 197 excludes the right in respect of dismissals which take the form simply of the expiry of a fixed term contract[14] (of one year or more) provided that, prior to such expiry, the employee has agreed in writing to exclude a claim in respect of unfair dismissal. Where the right not to be unfairly dismissed does apply, it should be noted that the simple (but vague) concept of 'unfairness' is not actually the criterion for determining whether or not it has been infringed. It follows that the description of 'unfair dismissal' is something of a misnomer, used to describe a dismissal which is simply contrary to the provisions in this part of the Act. The scheme of the relevant provisions is that in each case, for a dismissal to be adjudged 'fair', two criteria require to be satisfied:

  - First, the dismissal must be shown to be for a legitimate reason. By s 98, permissible reasons include, *in particular*, those which relate to capability, qualifications, conduct or redundancy[15]. Alternatively, the reason must involve 'some other substantial reason' of a kind capable of justifying the dismissal. For example, the dismissal of an athlete whose levels of performance had declined to an unacceptable level for one reason or another (perhaps through a persistent injury) would involve a dismissal for a permissible reason, namely one which related to capability (or possibly conduct). In *Gray v Grimsby Town Football Club*[16], the manager's belief that his football team required strengthening in particular areas in order to avoid relegation, was held to be a legitimate reason for dismissing Mr Gray, even though he had played adequately for the team in a similar position for some time.

    On the other hand, certain reasons render a dismissal automatically unfair. These include reasons relating to preg-

---

10 Generally, the period runs for all employees for 14 weeks but may continue in the case of employees with two years service for 29 weeks from the birth.
11 See s 86.
12 See s 92.
13 See s 108.
14 Generally, the expiry of a fixed term contract is treated for the purposes of unfair dismissal as a 'dismissal'. See s 95.
15 It is also permissible to dismiss in circumstances where continuation of the employment would contravene some statutory duty.
16 [1979] ICR 364.

nancy and childbirth (s 99) or to health and safety activities (s 100). In addition, as has been outlined above, the Trade Union and Labour Relations (Consolidation) Act 1992, by s 152, renders unfair any dismissal on grounds related to union membership or activities. It follows that the dismissal of a player by reason of his membership of a players' organisation properly categorised as a trade union would be automatically unfair.

– Once a legitimate reason has been established, s 98(4) provides that the question of whether or not the dismissal is fair or unfair

'(a) depends upon whether in the circumstances (including the size and administrative resources of the employer's undertaking) the employer acted reasonably or unreasonably in treating [the reason] as a sufficient reason for dismissing the employee; and

(b) shall be determined in accordance with equity and the substantial merits of the case.'

It is this second part of the test which is at the heart of the law on unfair dismissal. Further, the test makes it clear that the touchstone is 'reasonableness' rather than 'fairness' or 'justice'. In particular, it is the reasonableness of the employer's decision to dismiss which is required to be scrutinised rather than (directly at least) the impact of that decision upon the employee[17]. Thus, the thrust of the case law is that, provided that the employer has considered all the relevant evidence[18] and has adopted a fair and appropriate procedure in compliance with the essential rules of natural justice, his decision to dismiss will not be impugned if it is thought to fall within the range of reasonable responses open to an employer in such circumstances.

The remedies for unfair dismissal include either:

– re-instatement[19] (by which the dismissal is effectively annulled, back pay is awarded and the employee is required to be restored to his original position);

– re-engagement[20] (which is similar to re-instatement save that the employee is required to be restored to comparable employment); or

– compensation[1] (by which the employee is awarded damages, up to the statutory maximum[2], in respect of his loss[3] resulting from the fact of his dismissal, together with a

---

17 See for example *W Devis & Sons Ltd v Atkins* [1977] AC 931, which also makes it clear, as logic would suggest, that the reasonableness of the employer's decision to dismiss is judged by reference to the information which was available to him at the time of his decision. After acquired information may not be brought into account (save only when considering questions of remedy).

18 One particular question which may arise, particularly in a case which questions the employee's conduct, is as to whether or not the employer has conducted sufficient investigations in order to unearth all material facts.

19 See s 114.

20 See s 115.

1 See ss 122 and 123.

2 Currently, the maximum stands at only £11,300 (SI 1995/1953).

'basic award' which is a formal statutory award akin to a redundancy payment, designed to compensate the employee for his lost accrued years of service).

In relation to such remedies, it should be noted that, save in respect of back pay, orders for re-instatement and re-engagement are incapable of being enforced and in the event of non compliance[4], the Industrial Tribunal (which has exclusive jurisdiction to deal with complaints of unfair dismissal) may award compensation together with an additional (penal) award[5].

– Part XI sets out employees' rights in the event of redundancy and provides for redundancy payments[6] for employees with two years continuous service[7] in the event of their dismissal by reason of redundancy[8].

CONTRACTUAL OBLIGATIONS

Save for the limited extent to which they are subject to statutory regulation, the general flavour of which has been briefly outlined above, contracts of employment, whether relating to sportsmen and women or other employees, are the product simply of an agreement between the parties. Further, quite apart from the parties' express agreement, certain terms are generally implied into such contracts from the very nature of the employment relationship. Thus, an employee is obliged faithfully to serve his employer, to obey reasonable orders, to work with reasonable skill and care, honestly and in good faith and not to abuse his employer's confidential information; the employer, for his part, is, above all, obliged to pay his employee his salary or wages. Moreover, because the relationship between an employer and his employees is a personal one, the courts have in recent times been prepared to imply a general obligation on both parties not to act in such a way as to be likely to undermine the underlying 'relationship of trust and confidence' between them[9].

As with all contracts of employment, it is the context within which a player's contract is agreed which will fashion the practical content, not simply of the general implied terms such as those just referred to, but also of the other specifically agreed terms of the contract. There are, after all,

3   There is provision for his loss to be reduced, however, where his actions contributed to the dismissal (s 123(6)).
4   See s 117.
5   The amount of the additional award is in the discretion of the Tribunal, but in an ordinary case, must fall within the range of between 13 and 26 weeks pay (see s 117(5)).
6   See s 135. The amount of the payment, is calculated, pursuant to s 162 and subject to statutory limits, by reference to the employee's age, rate of pay and length of service.
7   See s 155.
8   For this purpose, by s 139, redundancy occurs where the employer ceases business (or a particular type of business) either absolutely or in a particular location, or where the requirements of such business for employees to carry out work of a particular kind cease or diminish.
9   The tribunals and courts have wrestled with this concept over a number of years and its precise ambit remains unclear. The existence of some such general implied term, however, is beyond argument. See, for example *Woods v M Car Services (Peterborough) Ltd* [1982] ICR 693, CA, *Bliss v South East Thames Regional Health Authority* [1987] ICR 700 and *Imperial Group Pension Trust Ltd v Imperial Tobacco Ltd* [1991] ICR 524.

certain particular features of sport which are likely to affect the expectations held by an employer of his employed players or athletes and the aspirations of the performers themselves. It goes without saying that, wherever possible, the parties to such contracts should give careful thought at the outset of their relationship to the terms upon which they are intent upon binding themselves to each other.

THE PLAYER'S OBLIGATIONS

The general nature of an employee's obligation to his employer has already been described. He binds himself, primarily, to serve his employer. Further, this obligation of service brings with it a certain amount of 'baggage' which may be described in the form of particular duties, namely those of:

- loyalty;
- honesty;
- obedience;
- good faith; and
- reasonable skill and care.

It is suggested that, although the courts will readily imply such terms in any event, they should be expressly spelled out in the contract. Further, they should be elaborated so as to highlight any particular practical content thereof which the parties wish to identify in the light of the circumstances within which they are choosing to contract. For example:

(a) The general duty of good faith and honesty usually imports certain subsidiary obligations which are of particular significance in the context of sporting employment, namely obligations to disclose all conflicts of interest and, in particular, not to take 'secret profits'[10]. The importance of such obligations is such that consideration should be given to elaborating them by requiring a player[11] expressly to covenant:

   - not (without the express sanction of the employer, such sanction not unreasonably to be withheld[12]) to seek or accept payments from third parties in connection either with the operations contemplated by the contract, with the conduct or administration of the sport in question itself or with the employer's business operations generally;

10 *Boston Deep Sea Fishing and Ice Co v Ansell* (1888) 39 Ch D 339. In the event of breach, the employee is bound to account to his employer for such profits – see *Reading v A-G* [1951] AC 507.
11 It is not simply the players of whom such obligations should be expected. Others who would qualify would include managers, coaches and indeed all those seeking employment in a competitive sporting environment. Similar considerations also apply in the context of the engagement *by* a player of an agent or manager.
12 This qualification of the employer's right to object to payments is necessary, given the breadth of the general prohibition which is such as to cover not simply 'bungs' and similar payments but is apt to embrace payments, for example, for media and other comparable activity. The employer has a legitimate interest in wishing to control such activity, but ought not to be allowed carte blanche to prohibit it in all circumstances. The employer will be particularly concerned to monitor his players' endorsements. This is the root cause of the 'sponsor wars', for example where a player accepts money for endorsing a kit manufacturer, different from his team's kit sponsor.

- forthwith to inform the employer of any situation liable to subject either the player or the employer to a conflict of interest;

- to play or perform in the sport in question exclusively for the employer or only with the employer's express permission. It may be that it would be appropriate to modify the stringency of this undertaking, either by stipulating that the employer's permission will not unreasonably be withheld or, perhaps, by expressly recognising the player's right to play for others in certain categories of match or event, such as in the case of international (or other representative) selection. Usually, of course, the rules of the relevant governing body will make express provision for the selection of representative teams, designed to secure the release of all chosen players. In that event, it might be thought appropriate for the contract expressly to recognise the primacy of such rules[13]. Certainly, in one form or another, the contract should be quite clear as to how it deals with the 'club v country' and other representative conundrums[14];

- not to gamble (whether for financial or any other reward) and not to provide information in connection with gambling on the outcome (or general course) of matches/events or on individual performances;

- forthwith to disclose to the employer any information which comes to him, whether concerning his own circumstances or otherwise, which is liable to be of concern or of sporting or commercial interest to the employer[15];

- not to act in such a way as to be liable to undermine the employer's sporting and commercial interests.

(b)   The implied duty of obedience which every employee owes to his employer requires particular consideration in terms of its application in a sporting context. Generally, the duty is not absolute and an employee has to do as he is told only to the extent that what he is told is both lawful and reasonable in the circumstances[16]. A player, however, is expected to perform. Further, his performance is likely to be expected both in competitive situations (for example, in the case of a footballer or rugby player, in matches) and on occasions preparatory to such situations (for example in training.) Moreover, he may be expected to participate in certain overseas tours and other training

---

13 As will be seen below, there may be good reason for the contract to recognise this primacy generally in any event.

14 Such conflicts are becoming more and more frequent. They are most acute where the player is required for representative duty by a governing body to which the employer is not affiliated. In all cases, the employer will want to be satisfied that the player's insurance cover during representative duty is adequate and that his non-availability for representative reasons is not of over-extended duration.

15 One particular example where a player would be obliged to share information with his employer under such a clause, would be where the player, unbeknown to his employer, developed some illness, injury or chronic condition liable to affect his immediate or future ability. Equally, a player who received an approach from another club would have to notify his existing employer.

16 See, for example, *Ottoman Bank v Chakarian* [1930] AC 277.

exercises. It is therefore suggested that an appropriate elaboration of the general duty of obedience would see the player undertaking:

- to attend and perform in such matches or on such other competitive occasions as the employer may reasonably require;

- to attend at such places within the United Kingdom and elsewhere from time to time and participate on such other occasions for the purposes of training or otherwise[17], as the employer may reasonably demand;

- generally to comply with the employer's reasonable instructions.

(c) Of course mere attendance and performance will not necessarily suffice. What the employer requires is that the player or other performer should give of his best. The implied duty to exercise reasonable skill and care alone may not be thought sufficient for this purpose. In that event, the player could not object to a requirement that he agree:

- to play or perform at all times to the best of his ability;
- at all times to use his best endeavours to preserve, develop and enhance his skills, ability and levels of fitness;
- not to act in such a way as to jeopardise his ability to develop and exercise his skills to the best of his ability.

(d) A particular feature of the employment of athletes and other sporting performers, is that the nature of their work, and the environment within which many of them are expected to perform, are such that they are thereby exposed to the risk of injury. Certain implications of this particular feature of sporting employment will be considered further below, but it has some particular significance in the context of an employee's general duties of obedience and reasonable care. The question must arise as to the proper extent to which the employer of a sports performer can intrude into those traditionally private and confidential areas of an individual's life, so as to be entitled, for example, to full access to the employee's medical history and records and even to be free to make stipulations as to appropriate treatment. It is suggested that such issues should not be dealt with by purporting to accord carte blanche to the employer and that a balanced approach is advisable, governed wherever appropriate by broad concepts of reasonableness. It might suffice, for example, if (perhaps in return for a confidentiality undertaking on the part of the employer and his advisers) the player were to agree:

- to submit to any such examination by a consultant or other medical practitioner as the employer may reasonably and from time to time require, whether for the purposes of identifying the player's condition and/or any relevant prognosis or for suggesting appropriate treatment;

17 It may be for example, that a player on suspension or otherwise unable (or not selected) to play, will nevertheless be expected to attend matches. Injured players may still be expected to attend for treatment, rehabilitation or light training.

- to authorise any consultant or other medical practitioner instructed by the employer, upon request, to be afforded access to his medical history and other medical records[18];
- to undergo any treatment which may both (a) be recommended by a consultant or other medical practitioner advising the employer and (b) reasonably be required by the employer.

Quite apart from such particular elaborations upon generally implied terms, the sporting context to a contract under which a sportsperson is employed is such that consideration should be given to including a number of additional and specific player obligations, some of which may overlap or dovetail with those already considered. Particular obligations will now be considered under individual headings.

EXCLUSIVITY AND THE PROHIBITION AGAINST CERTAIN ACTIVITY

As we have already seen, the general duty of good faith and honesty generally imports an obligation not to work in a competitive field for anyone other than the employer and it has been suggested above that employed sportsmen and women should undertake generally not to play or otherwise to perform for anyone other than the club or team which employs them.

But it must be recognised that a successful sports performer often now has available to him or her a substantial number of money making (and other) opportunities which do not involve the actual playing of his/her chosen sport itself and which, to that extent, would not bring the sportsperson into direct competition with his/her employer. Examples include media activity and appearances, endorsements, merchandising, licensing and indeed any other form of commercial activity which seeks to cash in on the substantial levels of goodwill which may be generated by a popular sports star. An employer of such an individual will not sensibly attempt or be able lawfully[19] to prohibit all such activity by his employed players. He does, however, have a legitimate interest in seeking to regulate and control the extent of it. Quite apart from any other considerations, he will wish to ensure that his players are not diverted from their primary function of being able to perform in their sport to their highest attainable standard. Equally, he is entitled to guard against his employees engaging in any activity which is incompatible with or potentially damaging to his own commercial activities. Thus, an employer may seek undertakings from an employed sports performer not to engage in any commercial activities or enter into any commercial contracts which are not compatible with his obligations to his employer or which are liable to damage or threaten the employer's business interests. Such a covenant, whilst it would serve as a general statement of intent, suffers from the defect that it is expressed in such general terms as to be likely to give rise to significant difficulties of application in different sets of circumstances. For example, such a covenant might preclude any form of fundraising on behalf of a 'players' pool'. A more appropriate formulation, therefore, would see the player agreeing:

---

18 Provided that the employer's medical advisers have such access, it is not thought necessary that the employer himself should be afforded similar access.
19 It is suggested that a blanket ban would not be capable of being justified and would, accordingly, be held to be void as being in restraint of trade.

- not to engage or assist (directly or indirectly) in any other trade, profession, business or other commercial activity, without first obtaining the express consent of his employer (such consent not to be unreasonably refused);

- not to agree to allow any third party to use his name, likeness or association for publicity or other commercial purposes, without first obtaining the express consent of his employer (such consent not to be unreasonably refused).

Specifically, the player may be required to undertake:

- not to agree to any endorsement, advertising, merchandising or sponsorship arrangements without first obtaining the express consent of his employer to such arrangements and their terms (such consent not to be unreasonably refused);

- to wear such items of kit and to use such items of equipment as the employer may on occasion reasonably require, and not otherwise to wear or use any kit or equipment which carries any visible logo or brand marking (save with the consent of the employer, such consent not to be unreasonably withheld); and/or

- not to write or publish, or cause to be written or published, any material (for example newspaper articles, including 'ghosted' pieces), nor to participate in any radio or television interview or broadcast, without first obtaining the express consent of his employer to such material (such consent not to be unreasonably refused).

It is not simply commercial activity which the employer may wish to see constrained in his employees. Where the employer's return depends upon his sporting employee's ability to perform to a high standard, he will have a legitimate interest in ensuring that his employee does not unnecessarily or gratuitously expose himself to undue risks of injury. He may do this by extracting a simple covenant from the employee:

- not unnecessarily to engage in leisure or other activities which expose him to an appreciable risk of injury; or

- not, without the consent of the employer, to engage in 'dangerous' activities [including in particular certain named sports and other pastimes].

Finally, the employer will wish to ensure that his employed players understand that they must conduct themselves in an appropriate fashion at all times. It is suggested that, to this end, each employee should be required to agree:

- not to act (or omit to act) in such a way as to bring either himself, his employer (or his employer's business associates, such as team sponsors etc), the relevant regulatory authorities or the sport itself into disrepute.

One elaboration upon this latter undertaking which the parties may in certain circumstances wish to consider, is an express prohibition against the consumption of particular substances including, in particular of course, any performance enhancing or other listed drugs.

PARTICIPATION IN THE EMPLOYER'S GENERAL COMMERCIAL ACTIVITIES

We can see in other chapters how 'the business of sport' has led to sporting organisations looking beyond sport itself for the generation of the kind of revenue which, increasingly, is required to maintain a presence in the higher echelons of sporting achievement. Most successful teams, clubs and other organisations seek to generate income not simply from the gate but also from sponsorship, merchandising, corporate entertainment and other similar sources. The birth and maintenance of individual such sources tends to require substantial amounts of effort and it is likely that the individual sports stars, whose prime task obviously relates to 'the business' on the field of play itself, will be expected to lend their support to their employer's efforts in this direction too. It is suggested that this might be reflected in the contract terms by both passive and active obligations. The player's passive obligation might require him:

-   to license[20] his employer to use his name, likeness, image, voice and other particular features of his identity for the latter's own marketing and other promotional or commercial initiatives[1].

His active obligations might see him agreeing:

-   to make himself available to the employer and the employer's associates [perhaps for a fixed or maximum number of hours each week or month or simply for reasonable periods or even at defined times] for the purposes of participating (as the employer may reasonably direct) in promotional, media or commercial events and initiatives;

-   to submit himself to media interviews in accordance with the employer's reasonable directions and requirements.

Insofar as the employer's arrangements with sponsors (or other commercial partners) impose obligations on the employer to afford the sponsors etc particular access to the players (for example after matches, as part of a club's corporate and other entertainment packages), such obligations should be reflected either in corresponding clauses in the player contracts or by clauses which enable the employer to fulfil his wider obligations in such circumstances.

THE EMPLOYER'S OBLIGATIONS

As has already been mentioned, the primary obligation of the employer is to pay for his employee's services. Whilst such an obligation is plain and obvious in general terms, its application in the context of sporting employees needs to be carefully considered. It goes without saying that the

---

20 It has already been suggested above that the player might be required not, without permission, to engage in commercial activity on his own or another's behalf and also to agree not to licence others to use his name etc for commercial purposes. Obviously the required balance between an exclusive grant to the employer (which seeks to prevent any commercial activity by the player and third parties) on the one hand and a general free for all on the other will require to be carefully considered in each case and provided for in appropriate terms.
1   It may be thought prudent, further, to make express provision as to the ownership of all intellectual property rights arising from the employer's exercise of such licence.

contract needs to be clear as to both the amount payable and the date or occasion of payment. Where the sporting employee is entitled simply to a regular wage, little difficulty is likely to arise. Very often, however, such an employee's entitlement will be structured according to his appearances, his performance or the performance of his team. Any such structure of payment should be manifest in the contractual terms. The kind of issues which should be addressed, as appropriate, include the following:

(a) The flat rate basic wage or salary should be identified. Insofar as such rate is dependent upon particular conditions (such as, for example, the team retaining its position in a particular league) any such 'conditions subsequent' should be spelled out, together with the revised rate of pay to be applied in the event of such conditions occurring.

(b) Insofar as it is intended that the player's rate of pay should be affected in the event of him being disabled from playing, whether through injury[2] or suspension[3], such conditions should also be made clear[4].

(c) Some arrangements will involve an initial 'signing on' fee, whether payable in a single lumpsum or by instalments. Others may include provision for additional payments, for example, after a certain number of (first team) appearances. Equally, it is not unheard of for the contracts of certain professional sportspersons to include a provision which requires the employer to share with the player any future profit on the 'sale' of the player or his registration with the relevant authorities.

(d) Where the sport concerned involves selection from a pool of players, the contract should make clear any additional sums payable in respect of each occasion of selection.

(e) Often a contract will make special provision for the payment of bonuses in the event of certain occurrences. The potential number and type of events which could be made to trigger a bonus entitlement are legion, depending upon the fertility of the negotiators' imagination. In the case of a footballing striker, a fixed payment for each goal scored or for each goal over a certain number scored in a season or competition would not be unusual. Equally, for a goalkeeper, bonuses might be structured in relation to 'clean sheets' and, in the case of a cricketer, to wickets taken or runs scored. Further, teams or individuals may be

---

2 Ordinarily, where an employee's obligation is simply to serve his employer, incapacity through illness or injury will not (in the absence of some contra-indication in the contractual terms) deprive him of his right to be paid. See *Warburton v Co-operative Wholesale Society Ltd* [1917] 1 KB 663 and *Mears v Safecar Security Ltd* [1982] ICR 626. Of course, in relation to sports carrying an appreciable risk of injury, any employer who seeks generally to make the payment of wages conditional on his players staying free from injury, will be unlikely to attract players in sufficient numbers and of sufficient quality to remain much of a force, at least at the higher levels.

3 Such suspension may be the result of particular disciplinary proceedings conducted by the employer, or it may be the product of the rules laid down by the sport's regulatory authority. In each case, the player's contract of employment should specify any effect on his right to receive pay.

4 It will be recalled that any attempt to withhold payment of wages (or to require the payment of a 'fine' by the employee) will be unlawful under Pt II of the Employment Rights Act 1996 (see ss 13(1) and (2) and 15(1) and (2)) unless the employer is thereby acting pursuant to an express term (in writing) contained in the contract.

entitled to specific bonuses in the event of different levels of achievement in their respective leagues and other competitions.

(f)   In the event that the basic rate of pay is designed simply to provide remuneration for the employee's essential obligation, namely to play his particular sport, the parties should consider whether or not to include any extra entitlement in respect of those additional obligations considered above, including the player's obligations in relation to participation in the employer's commercial activities. It would perhaps be unusual for the pay structure to be split in such a way, but there is no reason in principle why the sporting employee's participation in commercial activities should not entitle him to additional remuneration, perhaps even calculated by reference to the success of such activities where such success is capable of being accurately measured (as in the case of a specific merchandising initiative).

(g)   A feature of certain contracts of employment by which sportspersons are rewarded for remaining with their employer for an extended period, is the benefit match (or, in the case of cricket, the benefit year). Any such benefit, and the conditions which trigger it, should obviously be provided for expressly in clear and comprehensive terms[5].

(h)   It is likely that it will prove necessary, in order to facilitate players to perform their obligations to the best of their ability, that certain expenses will be incurred from time to time in the course of doing so. Such expenses, where necessarily incurred, should generally be for the employer's account. The employer ought therefore to agree:

–   to make all necessary arrangements for the provision of transport, accommodation and appropriate subsistence for his employed player in the case of his/her being required to travel, whether to 'away' fixtures or otherwise;

–   to reimburse the player (upon production of appropriate receipts or other similar evidence of payment) in respect of all such additional reasonable expenses as he/she may properly incur wholly and exclusively in the discharge of his/her duties.

(i)   An employee's total 'pay' package often comprises more than simple remuneration in the form of monetary payment. Other benefits are often included and should be expressly dealt with. Such benefits and associated provisions may include the following:

–   *Kit and equipment*: most sports require participants to wear particular kinds of kit and to use particular types of equipment, all of varying degrees of sophistication. Such items are simply the tools of the trade, and it would be usual for the employer to agree to fit out his players with all such items of kit and equipment (perhaps also a uniform for use on appropriate occasions when not actually

5   It may be that the 'right' is not accorded absolutely, but is intended to remain within the discretion of the employer. Such a 'right' might be expressed in terms which simply oblige the employer to consider according to the player the testimonial in question. In that event, the employer would have to exercise his discretion in a bona fide manner (see *Clark v BET plc* [1997] IRLR 348) but could properly refuse the testimonial on cogent grounds. Such a clause would also give the employer some leeway as to the precise nature of any testimonial to which he might duly agree.

playing or training) as they may reasonably require in order to fulfil their obligations.

– *Cars*: in relation to any company car provided to the player, the contract should specify whether or not (as is likely) the employee may enjoy its use for his own private purposes. Equally, the full extent of the benefit should be identified – for example, who is to be liable for insurance, petrol and other running/maintenance costs?

– *Pensions*: it is obviously good practice in relation to individual sportsmen and women to have money put aside for their retirement (whether simply from competitive sporting activity, which in many sports is liable to arrive relatively early, or from work generally). Because of the transient nature of most playing contracts, however, it is likely that some sporting employment contracts will not provide pensionable employment as such. It follows that, in such cases, prudent provision will remain the responsibility of the employee himself who will have to pay for it out of his general remuneration, although some employers may see fit to attribute a particular portion of the remuneration to pension contribution, perhaps even making payment directly into the player's own personal policy.

– *Insurance*: the sporting world is littered with ex-players in straitened circumstances as a result of having been forced to retire early through injury, in circumstances where they were not adequately covered by insurance against just such an eventuality. It is suggested that appropriate insurance cover ought to be a fundamental incident of a sports performer's professional life and that his or her contract of employment should clearly designate the responsibility for procuring such cover. Either the employer should take on such responsibility, or the remuneration offered should, wherever practicable, be such as to permit the individual employee to retain his own personal cover (in which event, the possible interest of the employer ought to be notified to the insurer). The employer in any event has certain statutory obligations under the Employers' Liability (Compulsory Insurance) Act 1969. As the name of the Act suggests, however, such obligations are limited to providing cover in respect of an employer's *liability* in respect of injury sustained by his employees in the course of their employment. The more important requirement, for which special provision needs to be made, arises in respect of insurance cover in the event of injury in circumstances where the employer has no liability. In this regard, there is undoubted force in the comments of Lord Bingham LCJ in the case involving a (successful) claim by an injured young rugby player brought against a referee, *Smoldon v Whitworth*[6], when he remarked:

> 'We are caused to wonder whether it would not be beneficial if all players were, as a matter of general practice, to be insured not against negligence but against the risk of catastrophic injury ...'

Such comments were of general application, albeit in the context of a claim arising from the conduct of amateur sport. In professional sport, it is suggested that the need for appropriate insurance cover is all the more marked.

– *Medical expenses*:   we have already seen how, usually, the employer of athletes and other sports' performers will need to reserve to himself certain rights in relation to the medical examination and treatment of his employees. Moreover, it is manifestly in the employer's best interests to ensure that his players have access to appropriate medical attention, some of which may prove to be specialist, intensive and expensive, particularly where the aim is to restore optimum fitness in the shortest possible time. It is only common sense that, if the employer is to justify the levels of intrusion into his employee's personal life which he seeks to reserve, he will expect to have to pay for the privilege. Insofar as the employer requires his players to submit to particular examinations or treatment, the contract should make it clear that such medical attendance and attention will be at the employer's expense.

– *Holidays*:   the primary obligations of employed sportsmen or women are likely to require their full time attendance and attention during the period of any relevant playing season, together with an appropriate period devoted to pre-season training. Equally, their employer may require their presence for out of season tours and other training exercises. At some stage, however, they must be allowed time away, and their contract should specify their holiday entitlement and should make clear when they should arrange their holidays or, perhaps, the fact that they should agree with their employer convenient and appropriate times to accommodate holiday absences. An appropriate formula might accord to the employees the right to a minimum of [four] weeks paid holiday in each [calendar] year, to be taken [during the close season and in any event] at times agreed in advance by the employer, taking account of the employer's reasonable requirements [such agreement not to be unreasonably withheld].

OTHER TERMS

Primacy of regulatory authorities:

Good order generally requires that all sports are conducted within a general framework of rules and regulations applicable to all engaged and interested in the same sport. Such frameworks are provided by the regulatory authorities which exercise practical control over each sport. Individual sports tend to be structured in a pyramid formation, with an international federation at the apex, from which extend affiliated relationships, first with national bodies (who themselves often oversee important leagues and other competitions each with their own separately constituted regulatory authorities) and on through, perhaps, regional organisations to individual clubs and, often through them, to the foundations of the pyramids, namely the individual sportsmen and women[7]. Participation in such pyramids generally requires an acceptance of certain constraints and disciplines[8] necessarily required of all fellow members. It has already been suggested above that the contracts by which individual sportspersons are employed might expressly recognise the primacy of any rules within the structural pyramid which relate to the release and availability of players for international and other representative matches or events. It is also suggested that it will often be appropriate that such recognition should extend further. In that event, each party to the contract should agree generally to abide by the constitution, bye laws, rules and regulations of the relevant regulatory authority or authorities for their sport. In such cases also, the contract should perhaps make it clear that, in the event of any conflict between its express terms and the constitution etc of such regulatory authorities, the latter should prevail.

Discipline and dissatisfaction:
As has already been seen, it is a requirement under s 3 of the Employment Rights Act 1996 that, included amongst the particulars which employers are required to set out in writing for their employees, is a note of any applicable disciplinary/grievance rules and procedures. Further, because professional sport is necessarily conducted largely in the public eye and disciplinary sanctions are sometimes capable of having a significant impact, both directly and indirectly, upon the earnings of individual sports performers, it is essential that the employer establish a process for dealing with disciplinary matters (and airing grievances) which is both clear and fair. In an interlocutory decision in *Jones v Welsh Rugby Football Union*[9], Ebsworth J expressly recognised the implications of the commercialisation and professionalisation of sport and issued a timely reminder that, when it comes to disciplinary procedures and processes, sport can no longer necessarily be conducted in the same manner as it used to be in years gone by.

What is appropriate, in terms of procedure, will often depend upon the circumstances of the employment and, in particular, the requirements (if any) of any relevant regulatory authority, but certain basic principles may be asserted for application in respect of a disciplinary process. In particular:

– It should identify specific sanctions and the circumstances in which they might be applied. Thus relatively minor infractions might result in, say, a written warning, whereas 'gross misconduct' or persistent breaches of discipline might lead to dismissal, with a graded series of sanctions in between.

– Insofar as the employer wishes to retain amongst the potential disciplinary sanctions available to him a right to fine or suspend his players, the disciplinary rules should obviously make this clear. Moreover, it is

7 Many governing bodies require that each individual player be 'registered' with it and that the subsistence of his/her contract of employment should be pre conditioned upon the employer 'holding' his/her registration.
8 Such constraints will, however, always be subject to the doctrine of restraint of trade, together with any other applicable legal principles, for example as to freedom of movement and freedom of competition under European law, which impinge upon the otherwise unfettered rights of authoritarian bodies to impose restrictions upon individuals' rights to ply their trade. Such bodies are having to become increasingly aware that their restrictive rules and regulations have to be capable of being justified by reference to the requirements of such doctrines. These requirements are considered in earlier chapters.
9 (1991) Times, 6 March.

suggested that such rules should sensibly be incorporated within the contract of employment itself. In relation to fines, of course, (or the withholding of bonuses or other elements of the player's pay package) any attempt by the employer to impose such a penalty in circumstances where his right to do so is not set out in the written contract is likely to prove unlawful under Part II of the Employment Rights Act 1996[10].

– The right to impose sanctions should also identify the person with authority to exercise it.

– The employer may well require some 'breathing space' in which to investigate particular allegations, in circumstances where the player's continued and active presence would be obstructive or otherwise inappropriate. He should therefore consider whether his disciplinary procedure should include a power to place the player on precautionary suspension and, if so, whether such power should extend so far as to entitle the employer to withhold pay for the period of suspension[11].

– Insofar as an individual may be aggrieved at the imposition of a disciplinary sanction, he should wherever possible be afforded an effective right of appeal. In *Wilander and Novacek v Tobin and Jude*[12], Lightman J held that it was *arguable* that the absence of an effective right of appeal by two well known tennis players against their suspension (by the sport's governing body) for drug offences was unreasonable so as, inter alia, to render the application of the disciplinary process in question an unlawful restraint of trade[13].

– Further, the process should identify both the person (or body) to whom and the process by which an appeal should be presented[14]. Whilst there is no legal obligation to afford a right of appeal (or further appeal) to an outside body, such as a nominated body within a League or regulatory authority (or perhaps some other nominated independent arbiter), such a right is likely to go some way towards giving the appearance of absolute fairness. Provision for such appeals is made within the rules of certain

10 See generally above.
11 It is suggested that, if included, a power to suspend without pay should only be exercisable in the most extreme of circumstances, and there should be a clear limit on the maximum length of time during which pay could be withheld. Equally, the procedure should make clear the criteria (if any, beyond the employer's absolute discretion) by which decisions would be taken as to whether or not subsequently to restore pay in respect of any such period of suspension.
12 [1997] 1 Lloyd's Rep 195.
13 The matter was considered by the Court of Appeal [1997] 2 CMLR 346, and it is open to question as to the extent to which Lightman J's reasoning can stand. The Court of Appeal allowed the ITF's appeal and struck out this claim, but did so on the primary basis that the rules in question *did* afford the tennis players an appropriate right of appeal. In addition, the Court of Appeal ventured the surprising view that their right to challenge the suspension by court action itself afforded the players a sufficient right of appeal in any event. It is suggested that any assumption that Lightman J's approach has thereby been dissapproved for all circumstances would be dangerous. Quite apart from anything else, the case under consideration concerned the regulation of drugs in sport, a subject of considerable public interest which, as the courts have recognised, sometimes requires the application of draconian measures for the greater public good.
14 The nature of any such appeal should also be made clear. The essential options are either a complete reconsideration of the matter (the most effective and satisfactory form of appeal) or simply a check that the disciplinary processes at first instance operated fairly and properly and that the disciplinary sanction was an appropriate one in the circumstances. In either case is fresh evidence admissible?

sporting regulatory authorities[15]. Such governing bodies have no doubt recognised the potential for embarrassment, both actual and apparent, which is inherent in the duality of their role both as 'prosecutor' and 'judge' and have seen the sense in the introduction of an external/ independent/objective element into their procedures.

– For the imposition of a significant disciplinary sanction to be recognised as fair in the circumstances, certain safeguards need to be built into the processes. In particular, the procedure needs to guarantee adherence to the relevant rules of natural justice. The nature and effect of such rules have already been considered in Chapter 2. Whilst the minutiae of such rules[16] cannot be identified as appropriate of application in every case[17], their general thrust requires that the process should be *fair* and, to that end, that:

   (i) the player should be given notice of the allegations against him and afforded an opportunity to answer them as best he can;

   (ii) he should be provided with any relevant information which is before the disciplinary (or appeal) authority;

   (iii) his hearing[18] should be such as to enable him effectively to challenge any important evidence laid against him[19];

   (iv) he should not be required to deal with the allegations or attend any hearing alone, but should be accorded some right of effective representation[20];

15 By way of example, the standard form FA Premier League and Football League contract provides for appeals against dismissal for serious or persistent misconduct or breach of duty to be presented to the Board of the FA Premier League or the Football League (depending upon the league of which the employing club is a member) and thereafter to the Football League Appeals Committee, a body established for the purpose.

16 The two essential principles are *'nemo judex in re sua'* (no man may be judge in his own cause, or the rule against bias) and *'audi alteram partem'* (hear the other side).

17 See, for example, *Russell v Duke of Norfolk* [1949] 1 All ER 109, in particular per Tucker LJ at 118.

18 It is suggested that an oral hearing is generally preferable to a process which is confined to written representations.

19 It is impossible to legislate for every situation as to how far this requirement should be taken. The rules of natural justice do not require that, in every case, there should be a form of trial, involving cross examination of witnesses. Arguably, however, it would be wrong to operate a blanket prohibition against such oral evidence, to be applied as a matter of routine in every case. Some limited flexibility to the process should sensibly be accommodated so as to enable exceptions to be allowed in compelling cases. See *Jones v Welsh Rugby Football Union* (1997) Times, 6 March (Ebsworth J).

20 The level of appropriate representation is currently the subject of some controversy. Plainly, there could be no sensible objection to representation by a fellow player or a representative from the relevant players' 'trade union'. Many employers are understandably resistant to any idea that other outsiders, notably lawyers, should be given representative access. It has been recognised as arguable, however, that, where the decision of a domestic tribunal (at least of a licensing or regulatory authority) is liable to have serious consequences for an individual's reputation and livelihood, he should be allowed such representation as he chooses – see *Pett v Greyhound Racing Association Ltd* [1969] 1 QB 125. (In the event the argument failed on the facts – see *Pett v Greyhound Racing Association Ltd (No 2)* [1970] 1 QB 46.) In *Enderby Town Football Club Ltd v Football Association Ltd* [1971] Ch 591, the Court of Appeal decided that the FA's rules denying legal representation before its in house tribunal were, on the facts, not unlawful. Lord Denning MR alone, however, cautiously expressed doubt as to the validity of a rule which prohibits legal representation before a domestic tribunal *in all circumstances*. Once again, therefore, prudence would suggest that, if the general rule is to be that legal representation will not be permitted, some limited degree of flexibility should be retained to cater for exceptional cases which are liable to have serious

(v) any disciplinary decisions should be conveyed or confirmed to the player in writing, in terms which not only identify the sanction imposed but also enable him to understand the essential factual basis upon which the decision has been taken to impose it[1].

The procedure for dealing with grievances is likely broadly to follow a similar process, particularly in relation to hearings and appeals, as the disciplinary procedure[2]. One important difference is that its use is likely to be triggered by the player rather than his or her employer. It follows that the procedure should clearly identify the level of authority within the employer's organisation to which (and the means by which) the player should present his complaint.

Term and termination:

There is no reason in principle why a contract of employment needs to be for a fixed term, although an employer may incorporate a limited protection from claims of unfair dismissal in the case of a fixed term contract (of more than a year), by including an express written waiver by the employee in respect of any 'dismissal' which comprises only the expiry of the term[3]. An alternative form of contract is one which is unlimited in time, but is terminable by notice. The contract should specify either the date when it will expire, or the length of notice required of each party respectively to bring it to an end.

Quite apart from termination by effluxion of time or by notice, the parties will wish to make provision for termination upon the occurrence of certain events or situations. At common law it is always open to a party to bring a contract summarily to an end in the event of a repudiatory breach of contract by the other party[4], but the position should be made clear by providing expressly, perhaps, that

– if either party is guilty of a serious breach of contract, the other party may terminate the contract by giving (14 days) notice in writing to the defaulting party.

There may be other events apart from a serious breach of contract which may entitle one or other party to terminate the contract. So far as the player

consequences for the player's reputation and career. See *Jones v Welsh Rugby Football Union* (1997) Times, 6 March (Ebsworth J).

1 If this requirement is not adhered to, the player is liable to be disadvantaged in the presentation of any appeal.

2 It may be thought that the need for particular safeguards (such as any right to legal representation or of appeal to outside bodies) is generally less pressing under a grievance procedure than in the case of a disciplinary procedure where penal sanctions are liable to be involved.

3 See s 197 of the Employment Rights Act 1996.

4 A repudiatory breach of contract occurs where the breach is sufficiently serious to 'go to the root' of the contract and to signify that the defaulting party is not prepared to abide by his obligations. See eg *London Transport Executive v Clarke* [1981] ICR 355. The other party may 'accept' the repudiation, thereby bringing the contract to an end. To exercise such a right effectively, however, the innocent party should not delay, otherwise he is liable to be regarded as having affirmed the contract and to have lost his right of immediate termination. It should be noted, further, that for the purposes of the unfair dismissal legislation (Part X of the Employment Rights Act 1996) the acceptance by an employer of his employee's repudiation will constitute a dismissal so as to require justification under s 98(4).

is concerned, he may wish to include a right of early termination in the event of relegation of his team from a particular league or level of competition[5]. Alternatively he may wish to reserve the right to leave in the event of his team failing to qualify for a particular competition or if a team in a higher league should seek (lawfully) to secure his transfer and to employ him on acceptable terms. Any such triggers for termination should make it clear whether the contemplated early termination is automatic upon the happening of the event in question or whether exercise of the right requires some positive action by the player himself in the form of the service of notice.

As for the employer, he will often require inclusion of a right of early termination in the event that the player should succumb to significant injury[6]. Any such right, and the precise circumstances giving rise to its exercise, should be articulated with care. In particular, the contract should identify the period of notice to be given in the event of exercise of the right. Further, it should address the criteria for determining whether or not the player is suffering from any 'incapacity' appropriate to trigger the right. In this regard, there are various levels of incapacity. At one extreme there are injuries which are permanently disabling. On the other hand, an employer may wish to reserve the right of early termination where it is clear only that the player will be incapacitated and unable to perform in some shorter term, whether it be six months, a year, a certain number of (league or other) matches, in a particular competition or event or perhaps for the balance of a complete season. Alternatively, and with greater certainty, the clause might be structured so as to trigger the employer's entitlement to terminate in the event that the player proves to be unable to perform in accordance with the contract for a set period etc[7]. In all these cases, the procedure should identify the mechanism for determining whether or not the identified criteria are satisfied. As the determinative issue is liable in such cases to be or to depend upon a matter of medical opinion, it is suggested that the clause might sensibly require exercise of the right of early termination to depend upon:

– the employer's reasonable decision as to [the defined level of incapacity] in accordance with the opinion of a suitably qualified medical consultant.

Because of the career threatening implications of any decision to terminate on the grounds of incapacity, it would be appropriate to include certain safeguards to protect the player's interests. At the very least, it is suggested that he should have the right to a second (medical) opinion. Indeed, it might be thought appropriate to permit the issue to be taken to some form of independent arbitration, in which case the contract should specify the nature and form which any such arbitration should take.

5 It is also possible that the employer will wish to reserve to himself a similar right, in particular where he foresees his ability to maintain a player's wages to be dependent upon the maintenance of his team's position in the higher levels of competition.

6 In an extreme case, where the injury sustained quite obviously precludes any possibility of the player ever performing his principal (playing) obligations, it may be arguable that the contract is thereby terminated by operation of law, pursuant to the doctrine of frustration. The precise application of that doctrine, however, is far from straightforward in employment cases and employers are strongly advised to incorporate and rely upon express provision instead.

7 Employers should be aware, however, that exercise of their right in accordance with such a clause might give rise to a powerful unfair dismissal claim in the event that, at the date of its exercise, either the prognosis for a return to fitness was encouraging or no clear prognosis had been sought.

Chapter 9

Introduction to intellectual property rights

by Malcolm Chapple

A. INTRODUCTION TO INTELLECTUAL PROPERTY RIGHTS

The background

This chapter deals with intellectual property rights. It tries to explain in clear terms how the respective rights are created, how they can be used to the benefit of their owners and how unlawful conduct can be avoided. In the available space it is impossible to give more than the briefest of sketches of the appropriate law. However, this should be sufficient to give enough information to allow those involved in sport to be alert to their potential rights and liabilities. If a particular problem is identified, the first port of call can be one of the standard practitioners' text books on the respective subject and, if the right is based on a statute, that statute. A conscious effort has therefore been made below to keep explanations straightforward and to avoid excessive legal analysis. This section thus seeks primarily to satisfy a very important requirement, namely the actual identification by a sportsman or businessman of any potential problems so that effective investigative or preventative steps can be taken at the appropriate time.

Whilst the general effect of the law relating to every intellectual property right is as summarised below, it is important to emphasise that such law is naturally subject to many and varied exceptions and some unexpected peculiarities. Therefore, in order to be sure of one's rights or liabilities in intellectual property matters, a detailed analysis of the law is almost always necessary. This is the case both in respect of the position of an owner of a right who wishes to preserve or enforce the same, or from the position of someone who is alleged to have infringed the right and has a wide range of potential defences.

APPLICATION OF INTELLECTUAL PROPERTY TO THE BUSINESS OF SPORT

Intellectual property rights are very valuable to those involved in sport for their livelihood. Indeed for a succesful participant in the sports' industry, his intellectual property rights will almost always be, at one stage or another, his prime asset other than human resources. Such rights are the means by which the owner can protect and expand his market and magnify earnings.

In order to succeed in a market, a person needs to acquire, amongst other things, a distinctiveness which the competition cannot copy – something which makes his products different from those of his competitors. There must be some element, or elements, which attract the buying public to that supplier as opposed to other suppliers. The requisite distinctiveness or identity can be based on either the particular way in which the product or service is marketed, say a trade mark or trading style, or even an unusually low price, or the actual product or service itself, ie relying upon a unique innovation which sets the product and service apart. But in order to build up this distinctiveness, and generate appropriate proprietary interests in it, the elements associated with the product or service must be capable of being protected from copying by competitors. If such protection is not available, then the market will almost inevitably ensure that no distinctiveness results. As soon as other traders or service suppliers observe the success which a particular element is giving, they will seek to share in that success and eliminate the advantage of the pioneer trader.

Intellectual property rights are one of the ways, and probably the most profitable and important way, in which a trader can retain a distinctiveness and separate identity for his product or service. However in order to acquire the *right* to protect the respective element of distinction, it is developed public policy that such element should be *capable* of being distinctive and should, for the greater public good, be granted protection. Not everything qualifies for protection by intellectual property rights. Hence an unusually low price is in itself not something which is protectable. Whereas, for example, a particular trade mark (which is not descriptive of the product or service) or a novel design of the product are each capable of being protected from competition, within the law of intellectual property rights.

In essence, intellectual property rights are the means by which a sportsman or sportswoman, or a supplier of sporting goods or services, can project and magnify the profitability of his or her expertise. For example a world class professional tennis player will be paid to play tennis, but even at the highest level, there is a limit to the income which can be generated purely from playing the game. There are inevitable constraints which will make it extremely difficult to earn more than a certain amount from the 'core' activity of actually playing tennis matches – not the least of such constraints will be the practice, recovery and travelling times which are a necessary part of a professional sportsman's life. However by the endorsement of clothing and equipment and other goods or services, the player can greatly enhance earnings. The substantial benefit to the tennis player of such activities is that he or she continues to earn money even when not present and not applying themselves to the tasks associated with the core activity.

Intellectual property rights are the means by which such a sport's star can prevent other people from using his or her name or other distinctive characteristics without permission. Some of those rights protect the player's commercial identity, and thus enable other people to be prevented from using the distinctive features which make the endorsements of that player or athlete so valuable. What happens in the process of endorsement is that the person has allowed his or her name and reputation to be used as part of the means by which customers are lured to buying a particular product or service – ie the sportsman allows the trader to use some of the sportsman's intellectual property rights for a price.

WHAT IS INTELLECTUAL PROPERTY?

All human endeavour has its origin in an idea. Whatever the nature of the endeavour, be it the production of a revolutionary military machine, or the launch of a new name for a computer service, or the use of an innovative sporting technique or piece of equipment, it necessarily starts its existence as an idea in the mind of its original creator. That idea is then refined by the original creator or his collaborators until it eventually reaches a truly workable state. In the course of such refinement it is almost inevitable that the people developing the idea will need to describe the idea, and they will usually prepare a physical manifestation of that idea, by, for example, the drawing of sketches, the writing of a prose description, or the manufacture of a prototype. Then the developers of the idea will probably also wish to discuss it with other people who might be interested in investing in the idea, or, for a range of reasons, contributing in some other way to the success of the end result.

Each original idea can give to its creator a range of rights, which can then be used to protect that idea from certain unauthorised conduct of other people. These rights are known as intellectual property rights. As their name suggests, they all stem from the creativity of the human mind and have intangible roots. However, for the purposes of policing the use of such ideas, it is naturally a requirement that these ideas are capable of being precisely expressed and defined. Indeed for most intellectual property rights, it is a necessary requirement that the idea is recorded in a permanent and physical form, for example as one or more of, amongst others, a drawing, a computer record, a written description or a prototype.

In the present day with the relatively easy movement of capital and ideas, and the ease with which sophisticated production facilities can now be set up in almost any location, it has become even more important to try to harmonise the intellectual property laws of each state, and to grant rights which are trans-national. This process is well advanced so that in certain circumstances someone who has intellectual property rights in, say, the United States of America, can exercise them in the United Kingdom, and vice versa, or an intellectual property right elsewhere can give support to an application for a similar right in the UK. However in essence intellectual property rights are still dealt with on a territorial basis, with each state applying only its own national laws but granting to the citizens of other states rights equivalent to those which would be granted to its own residents.

THE REASON FOR INTELLECTUAL PROPERTY RIGHTS

It may be questioned why intellectual property rights are allowed to continue when world attention is upon breaking down trade barriers, with the goal of ensuring truly free movement of goods and services between countries. They remain, and indeed are being reinforced, because governments throughout the world believe that the best way of encouraging the development of industry and commerce, is to give to inventors and entrepeneurs a sufficient incentive to take the risk and to make the investment in developing new ideas for doing or making things. The only practical incentive in these circumstances is a limited form of protection against plagiarism by others who are seeking a cheap and quick way around a problem. For example, if pharmaceutical companies cannot prevent other people selling generic medicines (ie medicines which copy the respective formula) which have been manufactured without conducting the necessary research, making the appropriate investment and taking the relevant risk, the worldwide research effort would be seriously curtailed and many new and life-preserving medicines would never reach the market place. It can, therefore, be readily appreciated that it is only by granting a restricted protection against unauthorised use of original ideas, that it becomes worthwhile for people to develop those ideas to the benefit of society in general, and themselves in particular.

THE IMPORTANCE OF PROTECTING THE IDEAS

The briefest of studies of the natural world shows that the birth and early development of something is usually crucial for its success in maturity. What is true for the living world is equally true for the success of ideas. Unless an idea is adequately protected and nurtured in its childhood and adolescent phases, it is most unlikely that it will be as successful in maturity for its originator, or subsequent owner, as it would otherwise be. Accordingly, the importance of full and proper protection at the outset for any potentially worthwhile idea cannot be over emphasised. The fruits of too many excellent ideas have been lost by their creators because of a failure to take at an early stage basic and simple steps to protect those ideas.

OWNERSHIP OF INTELLECTUAL PROPERTY RIGHTS

The owner of the right for the time being may not be the person who created the subject matter of that right. Obvious examples of this are when an employee of a company makes an invention in the course of his or her employement, or when a partner in a partnership draws a sketch for the partnership business. In those cases all the intellectual property rights are owned by the company or the partnership repectively. Other examples are when intellectual property rights pass from one person to another by purchase or gift. It is also important to distinguish those rights which require written documents to transfer the right properly in order to give entitlement to sue for infringement (for example registered trade mark, patent, registered design, copyright and design right), from those assets whose ownership can be fully transferred orally (goodwill for passing off and confidential information).

LICENCES

The owner of the right can give a licence to someone else to use or exploit that intellectual property (an athlete's endorsement is an example of this). A licensee in such circumstances usually pays a royalty for the privilege of using the intellectual property. The terms of the licence depend upon what the parties agreed with each other when it was granted. Thus, the relationship of the parties is then governed by the law of contract.

It should be noted that there are three main species of licence for intellectual property rights:

(a)   a non-exclusive licence where the licensor retains the power (1) to grant licences to other people for that relevant right, and (2) to exploit the relevant right himself – ie potentially unlimited number of users; and

(b)   a sole licence where the licensor agrees not to grant licences to any other people, but retains the power to exploit the relevant right himself – ie two users only; and

(c)   an exclusive licence where the licensor agrees not to grant licences, and not to exploit the relevant right himself – ie one user only.

Licences can be granted by written contracts, by oral contracts or by implied contracts or sometimes by operation of statute – some intellectual property rights come with statutory provisions which allow competitors to take a non-exclusive licence to exploit the relevant intellectual property for a period towards the end of its term of protection.

THE GENERAL EFFECT OF INTELLECTUAL PROPERTY RIGHTS

The rights of an intellectual property owner are different in respect of each species of intellectual property right. However there are certain types of court order which are general to all such species. Thus if a right has been infringed or breached, the courts will generally:

(a)   grant an injunction to restrain any future infringement or breach of that right by the defendant – if the defendant does continue to infringe the right in breach of an injunction then he is in contempt of court and is liable to be sent to prison and fined (if the contemnor is a company, it is liable to be fined, to have its assets taken out of its control and to be managed by court appointed managers); and

(b)   award sums of money to compensate the owner of the right for any losses suffered by past infringements – the plaintiff usually has to decide whether he wants his compensation calculated by (1) the damage suffered by the plaintiff ('an enquiry as to damages' which is usually the loss of profit suffered by the plaintiff, and often calculated by reference to a royalty which the defendant would have paid if a licence had been granted), or (2) the profits made by the defendant in exploiting the right ('an account of profits'); and

(c)   award interest on the sums found due upon such enquiry or account from the date upon which the respective loss was suffered or the respective profit was made; and

(d)   award costs to the plaintiff for the expense incurred by the plaintiff in suing the defendant – but intellectual property litigation is no different to other litigation in this respect since the sums recovered by way of costs very rarely reflect the full expenditure by the successful litigant in proving his case.

For a fuller explanation of the fruits which are on offer to a victorious party in intellectual property litigation, reference should certainly be made to the general law on such questions and to the respective statutes which govern the relevant rights. For example there are certain restrictions on the availability of damages in cases where the infringer does not know and has no reason to believe that a respective intellectual property right exists, and in certain circumstances there are additional rights such as the delivery up of infringing goods.

WHAT A PLAINTIFF NEEDS TO PROVE

In general terms a plaintiff in an intellectual property action needs to show ownership, subsistence and infringement of the relevant right. He must therefore prove, on the balance of probabilities, ie that the contended case is *probably* correct, and not merely possibly correct, that:

(a)   the right actually subsists – all the relevant requirements of any particular right must be satisfied, for example as to originality, novelty or distinctiveness, and the subject matter must not come within any exclusions which prohibit the grant of the right, such as on the grounds of morality; and that

(b)   he has ownership of the right – in order to sue for infringement of a right the plaintiff should ensure that all the necessary formalities associated with the right have been satisfied, for example if written assignment is required, then such has taken place; and that

(c)   the respective test of infringement of the right is satisfied – each right has its essential characteristics or distinctive features, and, in practical terms, for infringement to be proved the infringer must be shown to have reproduced such characteristics or features.

PROCEEDINGS WHERE UNLAWFUL CONDUCT IS MERELY THREATENED

With all intellectual property rights, a potential victim of unlawful conduct does not have to wait until there is actual infringement or breach. A threat of unlawful conduct is sufficient to give rise to a cause of action to the owner of the right. Thus, even if someone has not yet done anything wrong, but is merely threatening to do so, the courts can grant an injunction to prevent the threatened action and award the costs of pursuing the action. In those circumstances, naturally, an enquiry as to damages or an account of profits are not ordered, since no loss has yet been actually suffered by the plaintiff.

SPONSORSHIP

Sponsorship is dealt with in detail elsewhere in this book. However it is worth observing in the context of intellectual property rights, that sponsorship is a species of endorsement and gains its value also by reason of intellectual property rights. In the above mentioned example a tennis player is paid to use his reputation to help market other people's goods or services. Sponsorship, on the other hand, is where a trader (whose business probably has nothing directly to do with sport, and may not be as well known as the person or thing being sponsored) seeks to widen and increase his own reputation by paying for his name to be closely associated with a particular sporting event or player.

An overview of intellectual property rights

For the purposes of this book, the most efficient way of explaining the nature of the various intellectual property rights, is probably to tell a fictional story (with a happy ending) of the development and exploitation of a business arising from an original idea for a piece of sports' equipment. Unusually, however, in this example all those rights have relevance – in the real world this would rarely happen.

Claire is a keen and competitive wind-surfer. One evening after an unsatisfactory day's racing, she reflects on what went wrong, and tries to analyse a particular problem which she had experienced that day. The harness which she was then using, was too restrictive and failed to allow her sufficient freedom so that she was unable to use her weight to the best effect. As a result of her dissatisfaction, she decides to buy another harness.

THE IDEA

The following day she telephones various manufacturers around the world who supply the best harnesses, and asks them to send brochures to her about their most advanced products. A couple of weekends later she spends a Sunday morning studying carefully what is on offer. She is disappointed. None of the harnesses seem to be able to overcome the problem which she is encountering. So she gets out her old harness and starts to experiment with its design and load points. After a while, it dawns upon her that she herself might have found an answer to her problem, which the world's manufacturers could not solve. She thinks about it for a while longer, and then decides that if the idea actually worked in practice, it could greatly improve her speed in races, and would be likely to be of great interest to her competitors. Accordingly she decides to develop the idea further.

Claire is an intelligent woman with common sense and much practical ability. She knows a great deal about wind-surfing, but she has no expert knowledge about the materials and fastening equipment which would be suitable for use in the harsh conditions of sea wind-surfing. Therefore she realises that she must seek the advice of an expert on harness webbing. So she contacts a local webbing manufacturer in order to explain her idea to a representative of the company and to investigate the possibilities of pursuing the idea. She has not told anyone else about her idea, and, with her knowledge of windsurfing and having researched the question, she believes that her idea is original.

CONFIDENTIAL INFORMATION

At the beginning of her meeting with a representative of the harness manufacturer, Claire explains how she developed her idea, and how she has not told anyone else about it. She then reveals her idea to the manufacturer 'in circumstances which import an obligation of confidence', so that the explanation of the idea is confidential information which the manufacturer is not allowed to use without Claire's permission. If the manufacturer does try to use the information without her permission and before it has come into the 'public domain', ie it is common knowledge, she can take court proceedings for an injunction to prevent the manufacturer from doing so. The grounds of such proceedings are known as 'breach of confidence'.

In this case Claire is fortunately dealing with honourable people who have no intention of acting unlawfully or treating her unfairly. Furthermore, due to spare design and production capacity, the manufacturer is interested in helping Claire to develop and exploit the idea, possibly even in a joint venture. Accordingly Claire is advised to think about its detail and then to come to another meeting at which the manufacturer's marketing director will be present. She is also asked to prepare a rough drawing of her proposed harness and a detailed written explanation of the idea and its benefits. This she does, and she also makes a mock up of the harness using a sewing machine.

COPYRIGHT AND DESIGN RIGHT

The sketch and the mock up have design right protection, and the written explanation has copyright protection. If anyone copies the design which is set out in the sketch or the mock up, or copies the prose of the written explanation, then she can take Court proceedings for 'design right infringement' and 'copyright infringement' respectively, and obtain an appropriate injunction.

Claire returns to the manufacturer to discuss the position with the marketing director. The manufacturer then agrees to carry out certain development work on the proposed harness for payment at an hourly rate – the manufacturer decides not to get more involved in the project, because the marketing director does not believe that the idea is worth exploiting, but is willing to take on this research work in order to use the spare capacity. Claire sensibly confirms their agreement in writing and emphasises that it was agreed that all intellectual property rights in the developed version of the harness will be owned by her.

A few months later, a prototype harness has been produced. Claire tries it out on a quiet stretch of water when no-one else is around to watch – she realises both from a commercial point of view and an intellectual property point of view it is best to keep the idea a secret until it is fully crystallised and in a marketable state and therefore more easily protected. The trials are a great success, and she is encouraged by the commercial potential of her design. If Claire does exploit it fully, this means that other people will have the advantage of using the improved harness, and Claire will have to share its racing benefits, but she is prepared to allow this in order to ensure that she gains the best return upon her investment of time and money into the project.

PATENT

Claire then makes an application for a patent for the invention which is represented by new harness. Sometime later the patent is granted. Thereafter for the life of the patent, if anyone else uses the invention described in the patent, Claire can sue them for 'patent infringement', and obtain an injunction to prevent the infringers using the invention described in the patent. Patent protection gives a true monopoly, and does not merely protect against copying, and so it is irrelevant that the infringer may also have made the invention by an entirely independent route which did not involve any copying of the information disclosed in the patent. This patent protection is in addition to the design right protection, and is useful in cases where someone tries to use the principle of the invention but not the actual way in which Claire has put it into practice, as set out in the original sketch which she drew or the model harness which she produced.

REGISTERED TRADE MARK

When it is safe for the invention of the patent to be disclosed to the world, which is at the stage of its publication and usually before its grant, Claire starts the process of marketing it. She adopts a good trade mark for the new harness, and advertises it under that brand name. She decides also to register the trade mark, so it becomes a trade mark registered for harnesses for wind-surfers. After its registration, and whilst it remains registered, Claire can prevent by an injunction any other person from using that same trade mark, or any trade mark confusingly similar to it, on windsurfing harnesses and similar products. The grounds of such proceedings are known as 'infringement of registered trade mark'.

Claire's idea is a huge success. Every windsurfer appreciates the improvement which her harness gives to their enjoyment of the sport. Accordingly she sells a large number of the new harnesses. Naturally this leads to other people trying to copy her harness and to take some of her market. However she is alert to the pitfalls of failing to take prompt action to prevent this, and so she retains her intellectual property rights and overcomes the plagiarists. In this she has been assisted by the courts, adopting the maxim 'what is worth copying is worth protecting', provided, of course, that the appropriate legal requirements are satisfied.

PASSING OFF

It happens that the harness is sold in a particular sort of packaging, which whilst not innovative, is very attractive and highly distinctive, and has probably even contributed in some way to the commercial success of the harness. Potential customers have come to know Claire's harnesses by the sight of the packaging alone, and so she has acquired a 'goodwill' in that 'get up'. Then Claire discovers that another harness manufacturer is trying to sell its harnesses in a package which is very similar to her own packaging, ie its get up is confusingly similar, and that potential buyers of her harness are buying the competitor's harness believing that it is Claire's product. She therefore decides to take court proceedings against this other manufacturer for passing off, and obtains an injunction to prevent the use of any packaging which is confusingly similar to her own.

REGISTERED DESIGN

Whilst all this is happening, Claire has turned her attention to the buckles which she has been using on the new harness. They do their job perfectly well, but Claire does not believe that they look as good as they could do. She therefore designs a buckle arrangement which does not have any particular technical advantage, but is much more pleasing to the eye, and is thus likely to improve the sales of the new harness, or indeed of a range of safety harnesses. So Claire applies for, and is granted, a registered design for this buckle. This means that for the period of such registration, which is up to twenty five years, Claire can prevent by an injunction anyone else from copying the design of her buckle on the grounds of 'infringement of registered design'.

Registered design offers in certain circumstances a better protection than any design right which she might have enjoyed, since a registered design grants a true monopoly of use, rather than a protection only against copying. Thus if someone else had independently and previously built an exact copy of Claire's buckle (but had not used it before the date of registration), they would still not be able to exploit it because of Claire's relevant registered design. Truly independent design is a defence to an action for infringement of any copyright or design right, but not to an action for infringement of registered design.

Claire was very lucky in the development of her new harness. She had enough money, expertise and common sense not to have to involve many other people. Hence she minimised the risk of plagiarism before the idea had reached maturity. She was also lucky in realising that she needed professional advice about the best ways of realising the full potential of her intellectual property rights, and ensuring that they were fully and properly protected.

After a while Claire realises that her windsurfing business, whilst being lucrative and interesting, is starting to interfere with her career, and that one of the two has to give. She decides to sell most of her intellectual property rights referred to above, and all her associated commercial interests, to the highest bidder. She then no longer has any right to sue for relevant infringements or breaches, but in her opinion she is amply compensated. In order properly to transfer the rights, Claire signs a number of formal written assignments.

SERVICES

As a result of her commercial and racing successes using the new harness, Claire had also set up a training school for windsurfing. In order to feed off the reputation which she had built up in the trade mark and packaging design for the new harness, Claire had used the same trade mark and a variation of the packaging design for the advertising and promotional material for her training school. This too had proved highly successful, and so she had registered the trade mark also for training services for sailing and windsurfing. Although at this time she had not offered training for general sailing, she had envisaged that if the training school proved successful, it was likely that further schools would open, and that the schools would not restrict themselves merely to the training of windsurfers, but would wish to diversify into general sailing tuition.

Inevitably other organisations had tried to copy the, by then, very well known trade mark and get up for Claire's training schools. However by prompt action, she had obtained injunctions to prevent such further use, and the exclusivity of her trade mark and that get up had been maintained and protected.

Finally when she sold the intellectual property rights in the new harness, Claire decided that she would keep her interest in the training schools, and seek to expand the same, but without day to day involvement. To this end she set up a franchised operation whereby each training school was taken over by a franchisee who obtained from Claire, the franchisor, the rights to carry on the training business under Claire's trade mark and get up and using Claire's know how, subject, amongst other terms, to her right to maintain quality control over the services offered by the schools. Thus Claire ended up with seven large franchisees spread around the coast of the south of England and Wales, which she supervised from a small office in her garden.

PERFORMERS' RIGHTS

It should be noted that Claire did not have any 'performers' rights' in any of her sporting achievements. Performers' rights are rights which are actionable as a breach of a statutory duty under s 194 of the Copyright, Designs and Patents Act 1988. However they only apply to or in respect of performances of a theatrical variety (for example performances of dance, mime, music, or recitation of literary work[1]), and do not apply to sports' performances, however elegant or dramatic!

B. PASSING OFF

What is passing off?

The law of passing off is conveniently summarised in the report of the judgment of Lord Oliver in *Reckitt & Colman Products Ltd v Borden Inc*[2]:

> '... [passing off] may be expressed in terms of the elements which the plaintiff ... has to prove in order to succeed. ... First, he must establish a goodwill or reputation attached to the goods or services which he supplies in the mind of the purchasing public by association with the identifying get up ... under which his particular goods or services are offered ... such that the get up is recognised by the public as distinctive of the plaintiff's goods or services. Secondly he must demonstrate a misrepresentation by the defendant to the public (whether or not intentional) leading or likely to lead the public to believe that goods or services offered by him are the goods or services of the plaintiff ... Thirdly he must demonstrate that he suffers ... damage by reason of the erroneous belief engendered by the defendant's misrepresentation that the source of the defendant's goods or services is the same as the source of those offered by the plaintiff.'

At the outset two important points should be mentioned. First it must be noted that mere confusion between two competitors in the minds of

1 Section 180(2) of the 1988 Act.
2 [1990] RPC 341 at 406.

consumers, does not automatically grant to one a right to restrain the other from using the offending trading style[3]. Second it should be emphasised that there is no requirement of any intention to pass off or otherwise to act unfairly to the complainant – ie innocence is no defence[4].

A concise definition of passing off

There are thus three key elements ('the classical trinity'[5]) to an action for passing off:

(a) a sufficient goodwill owned by the plaintiff amongst potential consumers; and

(b) a misrepresentation by the defendant, in the use of the plaintiff's goodwill resulting in confusion that the defendant's goods are those of the plaintiff; and

(c) the likelihood of damage to the plaintiff arising from such confusion.

The law of passing off applies equally to physical products and to intangible services.

Goodwill

The first hurdle for a plaintiff in a passing off action, is to prove that there is a sufficient goodwill in the particular get up or trading style which is being misrepresented. Goodwill has been defined as the *'attractive force which brings in custom'*[6]. It is an asset of the business, and is directly related to the future trade which a business might be expected to do. Goodwill is, strictly, not the same as a business's reputation – a business may be hugely well known, but its goodwill in a particular trading style may be insufficient for a passing off action to be founded upon it. In general terms, a goodwill abroad, in say the USA, is insufficient for a plaintiff to pursue a passing off action in the United Kingdom[7].

Goodwill is a convenient label for the value which a trader has in the intangible asset of the desire of his consumers to make repeat purchases of his products or services, rather than those of another trader. Accordingly goodwill must be capable of being directly linked with a particular trading style or get up. For example all the major manufacturers of shoes and clothing for sports have highly distinctive designs on their products. Usually they have acquired this distinctiveness by reason of a combination of large scale advertising and large scale sales. It is possible, although rare, for goodwill to arise from *either* advertising *or* sales, and not both. However there must be *either* advertising *or* sales – it is impossible for a trader to acquire goodwill in a trading style or get up until after there has been sufficient exposure of the trading style or get up to potential consumers.

3   *Hall of Arts and Sciences Corpn v Hall* (1934) 51 RPC 398.
4   *Parker-Knoll v Knoll International Ltd* [1962] RPC 265.
5   *Consorzio del Prosciutto di Parma v Marks and Spencer plc* [1991] RPC 351 at 368.
6   *IRC v Muller & Co's Margarine Ltd* [1901] AC 217.
7   *Anheuser-Busch Inc v Budejovicky Budvar* [1984] FSR 413.

A trader's goodwill in a particular trading style is not necessarily restricted to the goods or products to which the style has been applied in the past. Merely because, for example, a trading style of three parallel bands has been previously applied only to sports shoes, does not mean that the goodwill in that get up would not extend to, say, more formal shoes or leisure clothes. The full extent and effect of the goodwill will depend upon the nature and extent of its prior use. Accordingly there is an ill defined 'no man's land' which surrounds the principal activity or product and which is also capable of being protected[8].

It is possible for two traders to acquire goodwill in the same or a very similar distinctive trading style, which neither can prevent the other from using, despite the fact that there is confusion in the minds of consumers. This arises usually as a result of the traders starting the use of the particular style within a short while of each other, so that the court cannot properly decide which of the two first acquired a sufficiently pre-emptive goodwill[9]. Such situation can also arise where there has been co-existence in the market place for a number of years, but one trader has acquiesced in the other trader's use of the trading style, and then in the eyes of the law, has lost his ownership of the goodwill in that trading style. An example of how a trader can lose goodwill is where the trading style becomes so well known that it acquires a generic meaning, and the trader fails to take adequate steps to police its use by others. For example, a manufacturer of a golf tee could allow its trade name, inadvertently or otherwise, to be used for all golf tees, or a supplier of a particular type of services could allow its distinctively designed promotional material and trade mark to be copied by other suppliers. In both examples the get up which could have been protected and could have retained its exclusivity, becomes the norm in the particular sector of the market and the original user's rights are lost.

The requirement of the ownership of the goodwill by the plaintiff would appear to be obvious, but in the case of passing off goodwill, as opposed to other forms of intellectual property, a plaintiff can acquire such rights jointly with others without any agreement or joint venture between them[10]. For example, a number of bottlers of water from a particular spa with alleged health giving properties, could have used a specific trading style which is associated with that spa. The bottlers need not all have come to an agreement to use the trading style, it may just have happened. Then, after a sufficient exposure to consumers of these words when applied to mineral water from that spa, the bottlers would each have built up a collective goodwill in the trading style. Afterwards, if a bottler of mineral water from another spa also applied the same trading style to its own products, any one of the original bottlers would have a cause of action against the invaders, and would be able to prevent the use of the collective trading style.

Passing off goodwill does not have any set time period. It continues for as long as the particular goodwill continues, which is usually for the length of time which the trading style is used, plus a reasonable time thereafter during which the relevant goodwill is slowly lost from the public's collective memory. Goodwill is like a petrol engine. It needs refuelling by use of the particular trading style, in either or both of advertising and sales, but after

8 *Lego Systems A/S v Lego M Lemelstritch* [1983] FSR 155.
9 *Compatibility Research Ltd v Computer Psyche Co Ltd* [1967] RPC 201, cf *Stannard v Reay* [1967] RPC 589.
10 *HP Bulmer Ltd v Bollinger* [1978] RPC 79.

such refuelling, it can only continue for as long as its fuel reserves last. Thus a very well known trade mark is likely to have residual goodwill for longer than a not so well known trade mark.

Misrepresentation

The second element of a passing off action is the requirement of a misrepresentation. This is often the most difficult element to identify. In order to be proved the plaintiff must show, on the balance of probabilities, that a significant proportion of potential consumers would be confused by the defendant's trading style into believing that the products or services to which the defendant's trading style is linked, are in fact the products of the plaintiff, or somehow connected in the course of trade to the plaintiff. Thus if a manufacturer of equipment for racing bicyclists uses a highly distinctive colour scheme on its products and packaging, and thus acquires a goodwill in those 'house colours', another trader which starts to supply repair services for racing bicycles using the same colour scheme, could, in certain circumstances, be prevented from using those same house colours.

Such merchandising of goodwill is used very profitably by some of the leading sports' organisations around the world. Each team has its house colours, known as its 'home strip' ie the strip in which its members play at home games and where there is not a confusing clash of colours with the opposition at away games. In football it will also have a first and sometimes a second alternative strip for when there is such a clash of colours at away matches. An apparently profitable source of revenue for the clubs and the national associations has been the sale of replica shirts, shorts and socks. These garments will be manufactured and sold only with the permission of the respective club or national association. In these circumstances the legal position is that the club or national association owns the goodwill in the get up of their respective garments, and that a supply of a garment without the authorisation of the owner is passing off. It is worth observing that such goodwill is associated with the particular design and colouring of the home strip itself of the club or association, and not necessarily with that design and those colours when applied *only* to shirts, shorts and socks – ie the goodwill *may* cross the product boundaries and can extend to other items to which that design and colouring would not normally be applied by the club or association other than for merchandising purposes. Therefore a trader could be prevented from the unauthorised supply of products incorporating those house colours (provided that they were sufficiently distinctive) even when such products were, for example, coffee mugs, toiletry bags, pens or hats.

If the trading style in question is a trade mark which is descriptive of the goods to which it is applied, or merely lacking in distinction, then it becomes harder for the plaintiff to show the requisite misrepresentation. For example the use on a running shoe of the trade name FAST RUNNERS may not be a misrepresention when put against the use on another running shoe by a different trader of an established trade name SWIFT RUNNERS. Although, to the contrary, there may be passing off if the two respective trade names were FAST LIGHTNING and SWIFT LIGHTNING because the two trading styles are not directly descriptive of a running shoe. Another example is the need for a proprietor of goodwill to have a distinctive get up on which the misrepresentation can act – this accounts in part for the trend for team shirts of the top sports' teams to become more complicated in their schemes. A plain white shirt with a small rose motif would be much more difficult for the English Rugby Football Union to protect from copying, than a white shirt with a specifically coloured collar and three specifically coloured and dimensioned bands on both sleeves.

It is impossible to define rules as to what does or does not amount to a misrepresentation. Each case will depend upon the facts of the actual nature and extent of the plaintiff's goodwill, and the actual nature and extent of the use by the defendant of the trading style about which complaint is made. The best advice which can be given is to look at all the surrounding circumstances, and then to decide for the particular case in question whether or not the buying public is moved to buy because of the plaintiff's source of the product or service, and whether the defendant is appearing to be that source by reason of the defendant's get up or trading style[11]. Unless that test is satisfied, there can be no passing off.

Finally in respect of the second element of passing off, it is most important to remember, and worth repetition, that innocence is no defence to an action for passing off. An actual example of this was when the Danish manufacturer of the well known plastic toy bricks which are sold under the trade mark LEGO, obtained an injunction in the English Courts to stop an Israeli company continuing to launch in the UK a range of garden irrigation products manufactured in brightly coloured plastics and sold under the trade mark LEGO. The Israeli company had used the LEGO trade mark in a number of other countries throughout the world continuously for many years, and had, in fact, been using LEGO for longer than the Danish company – the Israeli company's trade mark having been derived from the names of its original founders, a Mr Lemelstrich and a Mr Goldberg[12].

Damage

The third element of passing off is the requirement for there to be actual or likely damage caused to the plaintiff by the misrepresentation. If the plaintiff will suffer no damage resulting from the conduct of the defendant, however confusing it may be to potential consumers, the plaintiff cannot succeed in a passing off action. However, in practice, the courts are not reluctant to decide that there is damage, or a likelihood of the same, where there is a clear misrepresentation, particularly if the same is intentional.

C. REGISTERED TRADE MARKS

What is a registered trade mark?

The law relating to registered trade marks is governed by the Trade Marks Act 1994. A trade mark is, for example, a colour scheme or a word or a logo which is applied to goods or services. A Register of Trade Marks is kept by Her Majesty's Registrar of Trade Marks at the Patent Office, situated in

---

11 *Hodgkinson and Corby Ltd v Wards Mobility Services Ltd* [1994] 1 WLR 1564 at 1574.
12 *Lego Systems A/S v Lego M Lemelstrich* [1983] FSR 155.

Cardiff. An applicant can apply for a registered trade mark by filling in the appropriate forms which specify the goods or services for which registration is required, providing appropriate examples of the mark, and paying the relevant fees. The Registrar considers the application, and can then advertise it in the Trade Marks Journal. If the applicant overcomes all objections, if any, to the respective application, the trade mark application is granted, and then entered on the Register, for which it is given a seven figure serial number. The proprietor of a registered trade mark can exercise the relevant intellectual property rights only after registration, although he then acquires rights which go back to the date of application. Thus it is only after registration that a proprietor can sue for trade mark infringement and can obtain an injunction against future infringements. The process of registration does not impinge upon the right of the proprietor of the registered trade mark, or the applicant for a registered trade mark, to use the trade mark between the date of application and the date of registration.

The rights granted by registration

For this brief explanation of the law, of particular note are the following provisions of the Trade Marks Act 1994:

(a) section 1(1) – a trade mark is defined as being any sign capable of being represented graphically and distinguishing between the goods or services of one trader to another; and

(b) section 9(1) – the proprietor of a registered trade mark has the exclusive rights in the trade mark which are infringed by use of the trade mark in the United Kingdom without his consent; and

(c) section 10 – infringement occurs if, without the consent of the registered proprietor of a trade mark, another trader uses in the course of trade:

  (i) a sign which is identical to that trade mark and in relation to goods which are identical to those for which it is registered; or

  (ii) a sign which is either identical or similar to that trade mark in relation to goods which are similar to those for which it is registered, and there exists a likelihood of confusion on the part of the public; and

(d) section 11 – a registered trade mark is not infringed by the use by a person:

  (iii) of his own name, provided that such use is in accordance with honest practices or commercial matters; or

  (iv) an earlier right, such as an unregistered trade mark which has been continuously used since before the earlier of registration or the use by the registered proprietor.

Advantages of registered trade marks over passing off

In essence, the law relating to rights and privileges attaching to a registered trade mark is similar to that relating to a passing off goodwill, as defined in the first element of Lord Oliver's speech quoted at the beginning of the section above entitled 'Passing off'. Both of these species of intellectual property rights seek to protect trading arrangements and rely upon the consumers' perception for their effect, and the philosophy behind the two rights is the same. Indeed, in litigation plaintiffs frequently allege both passing off and trade mark infringement against defendants who are using an offending trading style. There are important differences between the two which cannot be ignored, but the immediate practical effect is that the first and last elements of passing off (the subsistence and ownership of relevant goodwill and the likelihood of damage) need not be proved in an action for infringement of a trade mark. The fact of registration of a trade mark, subject to important reservations, gives to the registered proprietor thereof the requisite goodwill and avoids the need for proving damage. Thus, in an action for infringement of a registered trade mark there is no requirement to produce evidence of advertising expenditure or sales, and instead it is sufficient merely to produce a certified copy of the registration certificate. Accordingly there are practical advantages in obtaining a registered trade mark when the costs of litigation are considered – if a litigant does not have to prove as much, there is usually less expense to be incurred.

A further advantage of a registration of a trade mark over reliance upon passing off goodwill is that in appropriate circumstances there is no necessity for a trader to have used the relevant trade mark in respect of any goods or services before applying for registration. A trade mark can be registered by an applicant even before it has been used, thus giving a protection which would not have been available in passing off before the requisite goodwill had been generated.

Disadvantages of registered trade marks

Naturally, however, there are also disadvantages of trade mark registration as against passing off goodwill. In summary the three main disadvantages are:

(a)   in order to obtain the protection of a registered trade mark, the trader must choose a trade mark which does not reflect the nature, quality or geographic origin of the goods or services – thus, for example, the following trade marks could not be registered (1) ATHLETE (for spiked running shoes), and (2) PERFECTION (for anything)[13]; and

(b)   registration will only be granted to cover certain specified goods or services in particular internationally recognised categories, and when registering his trade mark a trader must decide at the outset with reasonable precision with what goods or services he intends to use the trade mark, and any material extension or difference in such products will require a further application for a registered trade mark, albeit for exactly the same form of words or design – thus, for example, a supplier of sports' clothing cannot use a trade mark registration for such clothing to prevent use by another trader of the same trade mark in relation to tennis racquets or weight training services; and

(c)   the formality of registration usually takes over a year and costs significant sums of money, at a stage in the life and development of an idea when financial and temporal resources are both frequently at a

13 'Treat' – *British Sugar plc v Robertson & Sons Ltd* [1996] RPC 281.

premium – on the other hand a trader can rely upon passing off goodwill without spending any additional sums on registration, and without specifying in advance the type of goods or services to which the trade mark will be applied. Thus passing off goodwill can be used to restrain conduct in areas of trade which are not necessarily the same as those in which the goodwill has actually been built up.

The use by others in appropriate circumstances of the same or a confusingly similar trade mark will prevent registration[14]. The effect is the same in passing off where, say, two traders have built up a goodwill in the same trading style, with the result that neither of them has rights which pre-empt the other.

Period of registration

The life of a registered trade mark is the length of time during which it remains registered. Upon registration a trade mark will remain registered for ten years, and thereafter it can be renewed for further periods of ten years for as long as the registered proprietor desires or other interested parties allow[15]. The most common of the circumstances in which another party can force the removal of a trade mark from the Register, are where[16]:

(a)   the other trader proves use of a confusingly similar trade mark which predates the date of application for registration; or

(b)   the registered proprietor has not used the registered trade mark for a period of five years and does not have a proper reason for such non-use; or

(c)   the registered proprietor has failed to police his rights under the registered trade mark, and so the same has become deceptive through its use by others.

D. PATENTS

What is a patent?

The law relating to patents is governed by the Patents Act 1977. A patent is a comprehensive definition and description of its respective invention. A record of patents is kept by Her Majesty's Comptroller General of Patents at the Patent Office, situated in Cardiff. An applicant can apply for a patent by filling in the appropriate forms, by providing a suitable description of the invention which defines the scope of the monopoly which is sought, and by paying the relevant fees. The Comptroller General considers the application and if the applicant overcomes all objections, if any, to the respective application, the patent is granted and then entered on the records of the Comptroller General, for which it is given a unique serial number. The proprietor of a patent can exercise the relevant intellectual property rights only after the patent has been granted, although such proprietor then acquires rights which go back to the date of first publication by the patentee

14 Section 5(4) of the 1994 Act.
15 Section 42 of the 1994 Act.
16 Section 46 of the 1994 Act.

of the essential elements of the invention. Thus, it is only after grant of the patent that a proprietor can sue for patent infringement and can obtain an injunction against future infringements and damages for past infringements from the date of such first publication or the date of commencement of infringement, whichever is the later.

A patent (pronounced with a short 'a' – only formal black leather shoes have a long 'a'!) usually has four main parts – (1) a written description of the invention, (2) drawings showing how the invention works or is applied, (3) a list of the 'claims' of the patent, and (4) a classification section which sets out various pieces of administrative information relating to the patent, including, for example, the name and address of the inventor and proprietor of the patent, the categorisation of the patent, its date of application and date of grant. The claims section describes in as precise form as possible each of the elements which form the particular invention. These elements or integers set out the width of the invention for which protection is being claimed, and for which a monopoly is sought. So when applying for a patent, it is very important to ensure that the claims, and the supporting prose in the body of the written description, explain exactly what has been invented and thus what is being sought to be protected. If the claims are drafted too widely, ie they purport to claim more than what was actually invented by including pre-existing material, there is a risk that the patent will not be granted, or after grant it will be revoked; if they purport to claim less than what was actually invented, the patentee is at risk of giving away part of his invention to the world at large.

The effect of a patent

In essence the grant of a patent gives to the proprietor of that patent a monopoly for the period of up to twenty years from the date of filing of the application therefor[17], for the exploitation of the invention described in the patent. Such invention is the intellectual property 'idea' which the originator formulated, and which for the purpose of the grant of a patent is distilled and precisely defined in the specification of the patent. In this context there is an important difference between patent protection and design right protection. The former gives rights over the idea which is described in the patent, whereas the latter gives rights over the physical representation of the idea in its form as a design as presented in, say, a drawing.

What inventions can be patented?

A patent can only be granted if the invention disclosed in it[18]:

(a) is new, insofar as the invention has not been revealed anywhere else in the world before the date of publication of the patent[19]; and

17 Section 25 of the 1977 Act.
18 Section 1 of the 1977 Act.
19 Section 2 of the 1977 Act.

(b)   involves an inventive step in technology, which means that it is not obvious having regard to all that is already known from the state of worldwide knowledge about the particular technology (ie the 'state of the art')[20]; and

(c)   is capable of industrial application, ie it is of possible use in any type of industry, which usually means that it must have a significant sale value[1]; and

(d)   does not come within certain defined categories of developed ideas which are excluded from being capable of acquiring patent protection.

It bears emphasising that the above conditions are cumulative, and must all be satisfied before a patent application is granted.

The excluded categories of ideas[2] include a discovery, a scientific theory or mathematical method, any aesthetic creation such as a literary, dramatic, musical or artistic work, a scheme, rule or method for playing a game, the presentation of information, and any invention which is offensive, immoral or anti-social. Aesthetic creations, game rules or laws, game tactics or methods and information presentation are all matters for which copyright can provide protection. Computer programs come within the category of ideas excluded from patent protection.

What is new for an invention?

The state of the art at the time of application for a patent includes all knowledge in that area of technology at that time. Accordingly, it is important for an applicant for a patent to ensure that the subject matter of the invention remains confidential until such time as the patent specification is first published, so that the invention itself is not deemed to be a part of the state of the art – which would thus make the invention not new. There are certain allowable statutory exceptions to this rule[3], but for all practical purposes it is necessary for an applicant for a patent to take all reasonable steps to prevent any disclosure of a relevant invention, unless the relevant disclosure is covered by clear and enforceable obligations of secrecy or confidence.

Inventive step

The law relating to inventive step, sometimes also referred to as 'obviousness', was explained in a case which involved the invention of a coupling between the mast and the board of a windsurfer – *Windsurfing International Inc v Tabur Marine (Great Britain) Ltd*[4]. Since it is this characteristic of an invention which is often the most difficulty to analyse, it is worthwhile to set out a summary of the explanation of inventive step. There are four steps

20 Section 3 of the 1977 Act.
1   Section 4 of the 1977 Act.
2   Sections 1(2), 1(3) and 1(4) of the 1977 Act.
3   Section 2(4) of the 1977 Act.
4   [1985] RPC 59.

which need to be followed when assessing the obviousness of an alleged invention:

(a) first, the inventive concept in the patent must be precisely identified; and then

(b) second, the common general knowledge of the art (being that general knowledge commonly known by people skilled in the art) at the date of application for the patent is assumed for a normally skilled but unimaginative reader of the patent; then

(c) third, the differences, if any, are identified between the above inventive concept and the above mentioned common general knowledge; then

(d) fourth, it is decided objectively whether those differences, as referred to in (c) above, constituted steps which either (1) would have been obvious to a man skilled in the art, or (2) would have required any degree of invention.

An invention is not obvious, and is potentially patentable only if the answer to the test in paragraph (d) above is the second limb, ie a degree of invention was required. The size of the 'differences' which amounted to a 'degree of invention' are not relevant. Even the smallest (albeit significant) inventive step will be sufficient for the grant of a patent, if all other requirements are satisfied[5]. Whether a small inventive step results in a patent which is commercially worthwhile to pursue, is, of course, another matter.

Priority date

A patent priority date is not necessarily the same as the date of the same patent's application. Some patents have priority dates which are earlier than the date of the application due to the priority date being carried over from another patent or patent application, either in the UK or in one of the other legal jurisdictions with which the UK is bound by an international treaty[6]. The advantage of an earlier priority date is that it requires the questions of whether the patent was new and not obvious to be assessed at the earlier date, when the common general knowledge of the art was inevitably less advanced. Accordingly, in general terms it should be easier to make an application for a patent with an earlier priority date.

Infringement

The use, and value, of a patent is in giving to its proprietor the right to prevent a competitor from using the invention detailed in the patent. If a competitor does so, he is infringing the patent. The question of infringement is a two stage assessment:

(a) first whether the *conduct* complained of falls within the scope of the monopoly granted by the patent[7] – for example, is the infringer making or dealing in products which are the invention, or is the infringer supplying any equipment relating to an essential element of the

5 *Samuel Parkes & Co Ltd v Cocker Bros Ltd* (1929) 46 RPC 241.
6 Section 5 of the 1977 Act.
7 Section 60 of the 1977 Act.

invention where it is obvious to a reasonable person that such equipment is intended to put the invention into effect in the UK?

(b)   second whether the alleged infringing process or product *falls within the meaning of the claims* of the patent, using normal everyday useage of words and allowing technical words to have their normal technical meanings?

If the answer to both questions is yes, then there is infringement of the patent.

Meaning of claims

The problem in practice is that only rarely does an alleged infringer do exactly what is meant by a strict and literal meaning of the claim. Accordingly, as a matter of public policy, the second limb of the infringement test referred to just above requires that the claims of the patent should be interpreted in a manner which combines a fair protection for the patentee with a reasonable certainty for third parties. Thus claims should be read with a 'purposive construction'[8], as though by a sensible and reasonable man rather than a lawyer who is overinterested in a meticulous verbal analysis! This can itself be further explained by a three stage test where there is a difference between (1) the strict meaning of the patent claim and (2) the respective feature of the alleged infringement[9]:

(a)   does that difference have a material effect upon the way in which the patent invention works; and

(b)   would that lack of material effect have been obscure to a reader skilled in the art at the date of publication of the patent; and

(c)   if it would not have been obscure (ie it would have been obvious), would the skilled reader nevertheless have understood from the language of the claim that the patentee intended that strict compliance with the literal meaning of the claim was an essential requirement of the invention.

Only if the answer to all three questions is no, is infringement proved.

A statutory defence

In the context of sport, the statutory defence provided by s 60(5)(a) of the 1977 Act may be of particular relevance. This says that if an act is done privately 'for a person's own use', and not for commercial purposes, it is not an infringement, even if it would otherwise have been one[10]. However, such private use must be truly and solely private use, and cannot have any element of commercial use. This would appear certainly to rule out, for example, the payment of appearance money in appropriate circumstances where, for example, a sportsman is using a piece of equipment which is patented and for which a licence has not been obtained. It probably even rules out the use

---

8   *Catnic Components Ltd v Hill and Smith* [1982] RPC 183.
9   *Improver Corpn v Remington Consumer Products Ltd* [1990] FSR 181.
10 *Smith Kline & French Laboratories Ltd v Evans Medical Ltd* [1989] FSR 513 at 517.

of such equipment in an organised event for paying spectators, even if the sportsman is not being paid.

Counterclaim for revocation

If a patentee commences proceedings against an alleged infringer for infringement of the relevant patent, the infringer can counterclaim that the patent is invalid and should be revoked on a number of grounds, such as the patent is not new, is obvious, is not capable of industrial application, does not sufficiently describe the invention or has been granted to a person who is not entitled to it[11].

Marking of articles

There is a defence against an action for infringement of patent that the alleged infringer did not know and had no reason to believe that the relevant patent existed. In order to overcome this defence, it is insufficient for the proprietor to stamp merely the word 'patented', or some similar indication, on articles made according to the patent. The innocence defence can only be overcome by stamping articles if the the full number of the patent is included[12].

E. REGISTERED DESIGNS

What is a registered design?

The law relating to patents is governed by the Registered Designs Act 1949 as amended by the Copyright Designs and Patents Act 1988, the complete amended text of the 1949 Act being set out in Schedule 4 to the 1988 Act. A registered design can be a design for almost any sort of article provided that it has eye appeal. A record of registered designs is kept by Her Majesty's Comptroller General of Patents at the Patent Office, situated in Cardiff. An applicant can apply for a registered design by filling in the appropriate forms, providing a suitable description of the design, and paying the relevant fees. The Comptroller General considers the application and if the applicant overcomes all objections, if any, to the respective application, the design is registered, for which it is given a serial number. The proprietor of a registered design can exercise the relevant intellectual property rights only after the design has been registered, although that proprietor then acquires rights which go back to the date of application. Thus it is only after registration of the design that a proprietor can sue for infringement of registered design, and can obtain an injunction against future infringements and damages for past infringements.

11 Section 72 of the 1977 Act.
12 Section 62(1) of the 1977 Act.

It should, however, be noted that if there is a co-existing design right or copyright upon which an application for a registered design is based (and which must at that time be owned by the same person), the applicant for the registered design can take action for infringement of design right or copyright before the design is actually registered.

A registered design has a certificate of registration. This certificate contains a representation of the relevant design, either in drawings or photographs, which are appended to and form part of the certificate. The certificate also contains (1) a statement by the proprietor of the registered design of those features of the design which are claimed to be novel, and (2) the nature of the articles or category of articles to which the design applies.

The effect of a registered design

The registration of a design grants to the proprietor of that registered design a monopoly for the period of up to twenty five years over the copying of the design described in the certificate of registration[13]. Such design is the intellectual property 'idea' which the originator formulated, and which, for the purpose of the grant of a registered design, is precisely defined in the certificate of registration. There is an important difference between patent protection and registered design protection. The former gives monopoly rights over the use of the actual idea which is described in the patent, whereas the latter gives rights over the physical representation of the idea as presented in a drawing or model. It is a strict requirement that there must be no functional *reason* for the design – as opposed to functional *use* for the design, which is allowed.

There is also an important distinction between registered design protection and unregistered design protection. The former grants a monopoly over the design for the period of its registration, whereas the latter grants only a right to prevent others *copying* the design in question. Thus if an allegedly infringing article can be proved to have been designed by entirely independent means and processes, the alleged infringer has a complete defence to an action for infringement of design right, but not to an action for infringement of registered design.

What designs can be registered?

Section 1 of the 1949 Act as amended by the 1988 Act defines a design as:

> 'Features of shape, configuration, pattern or ornament applied to an article by any industrial process, being features which in the finished article appeal to and are judged by the eye, but does not include:
>
> (a) a method or principle of construction; or
> (b) features of shape or configuration of an article:
>
>   (i) which are dictated solely by function which the article has to perform; or

13 Section 8, Sch 4 of the 1988 Act.

(ii) are dependent upon the appearance of another article of which the article is intended by the author of the design to form an integral part.'

In order to achieve registration a design must be new at the date of application for the registration. Such a test of novelty is not satisfied if the design, or any similar design with insignificant differences or with variations which are common to the trade, has been published or registered in the UK before the date of application for registration.

There are certain categories of design which are also excluded from potential registration. The most common exclusions are those relating to:

(a) goods for which questions of aesthetics are not normally taken into account by a person acquiring products made to the design[14] – for example, goods which are hidden from view to the consumer, like an electrical terminal block used within a domestic washing machine; and to

(b) goods which are not sold as separate articles – for example, a design for the wing panel for a well known type of motor car has recently been refused registration because it was not designed for sale on its own, but as part of the body design of a car, whereas a steering wheel or a wing mirror, which are each designed as individual items, are capable of being registered[15].

These exclusions and the wording of the definition of a design which is capable of being registered, reflect the philosophy behind a registered design, namely that registration is intended to protect traders from plagiarism by competitors where a product is sold by reference to eye appeal or aesthetic qualities only.

Shape and configuration

An example of the application of shape and configuration, which are closely related and, in any event, usually considered together, is the drinks' bottles which sportsmen use. Their purpose is to provide a container which safely keeps liquid refreshment near to hand and in a convenient manner. These basic requirements, however, can be satisfied by a very large number of possible designs. The precise shape and configuration of the bottle or container usually will have nothing to do with its purpose, but everything to do with the target of catching the eye of potential consumers. Thus a shape and configuration of such a container, if novel, is capable of being registered as a design. The position would, of course, be different if, for example, the water bottle was designed with eye appeal but in order to fit into a bottle carrier on a racing bicycle.

There is a difference, albeit with a thin and not necessarily clear dividing line, between shape and configuration. An example of such difference is the ribbing on a hot water bottle. The courts have decided that such ribbing is configuration, and is not a question of shape. However in another case the courts have decided that the grooves in the seat of a plastic chair were part of both the shape *and* the configuration of the same.

14 Section 1(3), Sch 4 of the 1988 Act.
15 *Ford Motor Co Ltd's Design Application* [1993] RPC 399.

Pattern and ornament

These two elements are also closely related. Their meaning is that which is to be expected from the two common English words. It is to be noted that words and numerals which do not form part of an overall and integral design, do not qualify for registration, since, of course, the words and numerals cannot be new.

Eye appeal

It is a fundamental requirement of a registered design that the novel features of the same should be judged by eye appeal only. Pure functionality has no place in the assessment of registerability. Furthermore the degree of artistic merit, if any, is also irrelevant – the test is how the design could appeal to the consumer and not to an art critic or design expert.

The condition of eye appeal for registration does not, however, exclude functionality. Those novel parts of the design upon which registration has been based, can have a functional use in addition to their aesthetic appeal. An example of this dual role is the bumps and recesses which lock the toy LEGO bricks together. The bumps and recesses have a functionality insofar as the LEGO bricks would not lock together without them. However their precise layout and dimensions are not determined by function, but purely by aesthetic considerations. Accordingly the Courts have decided that such bricks, with the novel features of the shape and configuration of the bumps and recesses, can be registered as a registered design[16].

Novelty

In order to be capable of registration, a design must be novel at the date of the application for its registration, ie its details must not be in the public domain at that time. The mere fact that there is a novel design need not be secret. The critical requirement is that the details of such design are kept secret. Such secrecy does not preclude the disclosure of the design to other people, provided that when it is disclosed, the persons to whom it is disclosed are under a duty to keep it confidential.

The disclosure of a design before the application for its registration, or the state of the art at the time of such application, will include any oral explanation of relevant designs, provided that they contain clear and unmistakable directions. The prior publication of the design need not be in a written or other physical form. However, given the nature of registered designs, it is, of course, likely that only a physical representation of the design will be able to define it with sufficient precision for anyone else to reproduce the design.

16 *Interlego AG v Tyco Industries Inc* [1989] AC 217.

Must fit must match exclusion

A design of an article which is dependent upon the appearance of another article, cannot be registered as a registered design. This provision of the 1949 Act, as amended, is effectively the same exclusion as is applied to the subsistence of unregistered design right. The effect of these exclusions is that, for example, a supplier of racing bicycles cannot prevent by means of such intellectual property rights the manufacture and supply by other people of spare parts for those bicycles.

Infringement of registered design

In summary, the registration of a design allows the proprietor of the registration to restrain other people from applying the design, or any design not substantially different to that design, in any significant way for commercial purposes. The test as to whether a design is 'not substantially different' from a registered design is an objective one judged through the eye of a consumer, taking into account the prior art. The court compares the representation of the design on the certificate of registration with that on the allegedly infringing article. If the latter has all the novel and striking features of the former there is infringement. It is insufficient for it to have just some, or even a majority, of those novel features.

Inevitably difficulties arise on the question of infringement where the design of the offending article is not exactly the same as the registered design. In such cases the Court assesses the differences in the context of the prior art. If the registered design is a radical departure from the pre-existing art, then even large differences can still amount to infringements. On the other hand, if the registered design is only slightly different in material respects to the prior art, then only small differences in the design of the offending article will prevent a finding of infringement.

Counterclaim for revocation

Similar to the position in patent litigation, if a proprietor of a registered design commences proceedings against an alleged infringer for infringement of the relevant registered design, the infringer can counterclaim that such registered design is invalid and should be revoked on a number of grounds, such as it is not novel or comes within the 'must fit must match' exception.

Marking of articles

As in the case of patent infringements, there is a defence against an action for infringement of registered design that the alleged infringer did not know and had no reason to believe that the relevant design was registered. In order to overcome this defence it is insufficient for the proprietor to stamp merely the word 'registered', or some similar indication, on articles made to the registered design. The innocence defence can only be overcome by stamping articles if the the full number of the registered design is included[17].

17 Section 9 of Sch 4 of the 1988 Act.

F. COPYRIGHTS

What is copyright?

Copyright is the protection given to the owner for the time being of a copyright by the provisions of Part I of the Copyright, Designs and Patents Act 1988. It subsists in the record of an idea, and not in the idea itself, and can take form in one of nine forms, which are divided into three categories, namely as (1) literary, dramatic, musical or artistic works, (b) sound recordings, films, broadcasts or cable programmes, or (c) typographical arrangements[18]. Copyright seeks to protect the skill and hard work of creation and authorship of a copyrightable work, and it is used to restrain other people from copying the work. It is not a monopoly right, and accordingly even if two works are exactly alike, the alleged infringer can avoid a finding of infringement provided that he can show entirely independent creation, ie there was no copying of his work from the other. Such a result is, in theory, possible. However it must be said that in practice, the courts become more unlikely to decide that there was independent creation, the more complex the work and the greater the similarity.

Originality in copyright

It is a fundamental requirement for copyright that the subject matter of the same must be original. This originality is not the same as is required for, say, patents and registered designs. The subject matter of the copyright need not be new, it must merely not have been copied from another source. The end result which is represented by the subject matter of the copyright must be the creation of its author alone. For example three athletes could each write independent explanations of a method of weight training. That method of weight training could have been well known to the public for many years. However each of the three explanations of the same attracts copyright as a literary work, and the respective authors could prevent other people copying the explanation without consent. In essence copyright is not concerned with originality of ideas, but in the originality of expression of ideas.

The element of originality does not have any requirement for a threshold of labour to have been expended on the copyrightable work. Copyright does not reflect merely the number of hours which has been invested in the authorship of the work. Instead it does reflect the skill and judgment which goes into a work[19]. Accordingly a time consuming task like the tracing of a drawing would not attract copyright to the end result, whereas a simple drawing of three concentric circles would attract copyright where the same were of precise dimensions and in a precise spatial arrangement[20].

Similarly in general terms there is no requirement for qualitative merit in the copyrightable work for the same to attract copyright. For example for the three explanations of a weight training regime mentioned above, there is not a requirement that they reach a particular standard of grammar or use of vocabulary before copyright can subsist in them. They merely need to fall

18 Section 1 of the 1988 Act.
19 *Interlego AG v Tyco Industries Inc* [1988] RPC 343.
20 *Solar Thomson Engineering Co Ltd v Barton* [1977] RPC 537.

properly within one of the categories of copyright work, in this example, as literary works.

Finally as to originality, it is obvious that very few, if any, works are original in every single respect. There will almost always be similarities in a work to a previous work and an author will usually be inspired sub-consciously by a range of stimuli in relation to the work. Indeed the author of the second work may even expressly acknowledge the influence which the previous work had on the subsequent work. The use of such building blocks and stimulation does not prevent a work being original. The test is if the embellishment of the pre-existing material is sufficient to attract copyright, when the new work is considered as a whole. Thus translations of books from one language to another are deemed to be original and copyright subsists in the translation as well as the untranslated book – although an unauthorised translation in these circumstances would still be an infringe-ment of the untranslated work, even though the translation had its own copyright.

Authorship and ownership in relation to copyright

There are statutory provisions[1] which define precisely who is the 'author' of a copyright work. In summary the author is the person who creates the work. Where such creation is done by electronic or other means to which the human hand is not directly associated, the author is the person who sets up the arrangements for the creation of the work – for example, in computer generated works the author is the person controlling the computer program at the material time, in sound recordings or film the author is the person who undertakes the necessary technical arrangements, and in the case of a broadcast the author is the person transmitting the same (unless that person has had no responsibility whatsoever for its content) and the person who provides the programme and who makes with the broadcaster the arrange-ments necessary for its transmission[2].

Some copyright works are created in collaboration by one or more persons where the contribution of each author is distinct from the others. In this case there is 'joint authorship'. In the absence of an agreement to the contrary, joint authors usually hold an equal share in the copyright work.

The first owner of a copyright work is the author, or joint authors, except where that author or authors were employees acting in the course of their employment when creating the copyright work, in which case, unless there is agreement to the contrary, the employer is the first owner. One of several joint owners of a copyright cannot grant a licence binding on the other joint owners, but he can sue on his own without joining the other owners as plaintiffs. Finally in this context it is important to note that a joint owner can obtain an injunction against a joint owner to restrain publication of a joint work without consent.

1 Section 9 of the 1988 Act.
2 Section 6(3) of the 1988 Act.

Copyright in literary works

In the context of copyright, a literary work excludes any dramatic or musical work, ie one that is written, spoken, played or sung. However the definition of a literary work[3] expressly includes tables (such as a football pools coupon), compilations (such as a fixture list, a directory or a list of batting averages) and computer programs (but not, it should be noted, in every mere translation of a computer programs).

This last example of copyright in literary works is, of course, becoming increasingly important. As the silicon chip, and the information recorded on it, takes over more and more of our lives, the effect of copyright in computer programs has ever increasing influence in the commercial world. The sports industry is no exception.

Copyright in artistic works

In the context of copyright, an artistic work includes any of a graphic work, photograph, sculpture or collage, a work of architecture being a building or model of a building, or a work of artistic craftsmanship. In the 1988 Act the nature of artistic works is expressly extended[4] in respect of:

(a)   'building' as including any fixed structure or part of a building or fixed structure; and of

(b)   'graphic work' as including any painting, drawing, diagram, map, chart, plan, engraving, etching, lithograph or woodcut; and of

(c)   'photograph' as meaning 'a recording of light or other radiation on any medium on which an image is produced or from which an image may by any means be produced, and which is not part of a film'; and of

(d)   'sculpture' as including a cast or model made for the purposes of sculpture.

Accordingly a still photograph or sculpture of an athlete performing or a chart setting out tactical moves from set pieces in a rugby game are all artistic works, which, so long as they satisfy the test of originality for copyright, would attract copyright protection.

Copyright in films and broadcasts[5]

Sport at its highest levels attracts huge interest from the general public. Accordingly part of the commercial value of sport is its ability for a performance to be recorded, broadcast and replayed, therefore greatly expanding its audience, and thus profitability. Film in this context means a recording on any medium of a moving image which may be reproduced by any means; broadcast means a transmission by wireless telegraphy of, amongst other things, visual images for receipt by members of the public.

3   Section 3 of the 1988 Act.
4   Section 4 of the 1988 Act.
5   Sections 5 and 6 of the 1988 Act.

It must be emphasised that under copyright law the athlete or sportsman who is actually performing on the film or broadcast, does *not* own or have any legal interest in the copyright for the same. For the performer to acquire such rights, there must be an agreement for that purpose with the owner of the relevant copyright, since there is no underlying proprietary right in a sporting performance itself.

Duration of copyright

The copyright in a literary, dramatic, musical or artistic work expires at the end of a period of seventy years from the end of the calendar year in which the author of the work died[6]. If there is joint authorship, then the copyright period expires at the date computed from the death of the last surviving author. There are three exceptions to these general rules:

(a)   if the identity of the author is unknown, copyright expires at the end of a period of seventy years from the end of the calendar year in which the work was first published – even if such identity becomes known after the expiration of that seventy years but before the copyright would otherwise have expired, there is still no extension of the copyright period; and

(b)   if the work was computer generated, in which case the period is fifty years from when the work was made; and

(c)   copyright effectively expires twenty five years from the end of the calendar year in which the relevant article was first marketed, where such copyright is in an artistic work which has been exploited by an industrial process, ie has been reproduced in over fifty separate articles which have been marketed.

Infringement of copyright

A copyright owner acquires by reason of the 1988 Act the exclusive right to do in the UK the following acts in relation to the respective work, namely to copy the work, to issue copies of the work to the public, to perform, to show or play the work in public, to broadcast the work or include it in any cable programme, and to make or do any of these acts in relation to an adaption of the work[7]. Copyright is infringed if a person does, or authorises another person to do, any of these acts, and it is irrelevant whether they are done in relation to the whole or any substantial part of the copyright.

Copying the work is defined in the 1988 Act as meaning a reproduction of the work in any material form, including the storage of the work by electronic means. It also includes in the case of an artistic work, a reproduction of a two dimensional work in three dimensions, or a reproduction of a three dimensional work in two dimensions[8].

---

6   Section 12 of the 1988 Act.
7   Section 16 of the 1988 Act.
8   Section 17 of the 1988 Act.

Secondary infringement of copyright

The acts of infringement referred to above are all categorised as primary infringements. Additionally there are secondary infringements of copyright which relate, in general terms, to the use to which infringing copies are put[9]. For example it is a secondary infringement of copyright to import or possess in the course of business, or to sell or let for hire an infringing copy of the copyright work. It is also a secondary infringement to do these acts in relation to an article which is designed or adapted to make infringing copies. This last mentioned infringement would cover commercial dealings in, for example, casts taken from an original sculpture.

The important difference between primary and secondary infringements is that it is an essential element of secondary infringement for the alleged infringer to have had knowledge, or reason to believe, that the article in which he was dealing was an infringing copy, or to be used to make infringing copies as the case may be.

What is an infringing copy?

It is naturally a necessary requirement for proof of any copyright infringement to show that the offending work has been copied from the copyright work. If there is no copying, there cannot be any infringement, and so a plaintiff in a copyright infringement action must show a causal link between the copyright work and the offending work. The actual copying need not, however, be from the copyright work itself. The infringer can infringe by copying a copy, or even by following oral instructions which describe the copyright work with sufficient detail.

As with the other forms of intellectual property, in practice the most difficult question in relation to infringement is usually the assessment of the degree and nature of similarity between the intellectual property and the offending work, which amounts to infringement. The test in this case is a determination of the amount in the offending work which has been taken from the original parts of the copyright work. In order for infringement to be proved, such amount must represent a substantial part of the work from a qualitative rather than quantitative point of view[10].

Defences

Apart from the obvious defences to a copyright infringement action, such as lack of ownership by the plaintiff or no subsistence of copyright, a defendant has a number of statutory defences. Of particular importance in the context of this book are the defences relating to fair dealing[11]. These allow a person to do acts which would otherwise be infringements of copyright. Those acts include copying of literary or artistic works for research or private study, provided that there is a sufficient acknowledge-

---

9 Sections 22–26 inclusive of the 1988 Act.
10 *Ladbroke (Football) Ltd v Willian Hill Football Ltd* [1964] 1 All ER 465.
11 Sections 29 and 30 of the 1988 Act.

ment, and copying any copyright work for criticism, review and news reporting[12]. There is one exclusion from this last defence insofar as it is not deemed to be fair dealing, and is infringement of the copyright in an artistic work, if a photograph is included in a report of current events, even with a sufficient acknowledgement.

The other important defence which needs mention is that of non-derogation of grant. This principle allows copying of a copyright work and operates on the basis that a copyright owner who has sold or otherwise supplied a reproduction of that copyright work to a customer, cannot act to thwart the licence which is impliedly granted. This is a reflection of and deals with similar mischief as equivalent 'must fit must match' exceptions in the law of registered design[13] and the law of design right[14].

Damages for infringement of copyright

There are two departures from the norm in the way in which copyright damages can be awarded. First no damages are awarded if it is shown that the infringer did not know, and had no reason to believe, that copyright subsisted in the relevant work[15] – this is a reason for including on or in a copyright work an indication that it is subject to protection, by, for example on a drawing adding a note to such effect at the bottom of the work.

Second, in certain cases, a plaintiff in a copyright action can recover 'additional damages', ie more than would otherwise be awarded on an enquiry as to damages or an account of profits[16]. These damages are awarded in cases were the justice of the case demands greater compensation than that otherwise on offer, taking into account all the circumstances and in particular the flagrancy of the infringement and the benefit accruing to the defendant by reason of the infringement. Additional damages are appropriate where, for example, a competitor has achieved a great commercial advantage by reason of the copyright infringement, for which a simple enquiry as to damages or an account of profits would not adequately compensate the plaintiff. Sometimes additional damages are also used as a form of punishment in order to deter other potential infringers.

G. DESIGN RIGHTS

What is design right?

Design right is the protection given to the owner for the time being of a design right by the provisions of Part III of the Copyright, Designs and Patents Act 1988. In many respects the law of design right is closely similar to and an amalgam of the law of copyright and the law of registered designs.

---

12 The 'Sports News Access Code of Practice', which is subscribed to by all mainstream television broadcasters, has its origins in the exception for news reporting and the case of *BBC v British Satellite Broadcasting Ltd* [1992] Ch 141.
13 Section 1(1)(b) of Sch 4 to the 1988 Act.
14 Section 213(3)(b) of the 1988 Act.
15 Section 97(1) of the 1988 Act.
16 Section 97(2) of the 1988 Act.

Indeed until the 1988 Act there was no design right and the protection which it seeks to give to design right owners, was given by a limited form of copyright protection. Accordingly design right cannot apply to any works which were made before 1 August 1989.

Design right subsists in an original design itself, and not in its record[17]. This is different to the position in copyright where the copyright subsists in the actual record of the design. However design right does not come into existence until the design has been recorded in a 'design document' or in an article made to that design[18]. A design document is defined as meaning any record of a design including a drawing, written description, photograph or data held on a computer. Design right seeks to protect the skill and hard work of creation and authorship of a relevant design, and it is used to restrain other people from copying that design. It is not a monopoly right, and accordingly even if two articles are exactly alike, the alleged infringer can avoid a finding of infringement provided that he can show entirely independent creation, ie there was no copying of his article from the design of the design right. Such a result is, in theory, possible. However, again, it must be said that in practice, the courts become more likely to decide that there was not independent creation, the more complex the article and the greater the similarity.

Originality in design right

It is a fundamental requirement for design right that the relevant design must be original. This requirement of originality is more onerous than that for copyright. In particular there is an express statutory provision which disqualifies a design from protection by stating that a design is not original if it was 'commonplace' in the design field in question at the time of its creation[19]. Accordingly this introduces a degree of novelty in order for design right to subsist.

Subject matter of design right

A drawing or model could attract either copyright in the design document or model, or design right in the design recorded in that document or model. However, it should be noted that the owner of the respective rights is prevented by the 1988 Act from relying on both of them where they co-exist[20]. For the purpose of design right, 'design' is defined in the 1988 Act as being the design of any aspect of the shape or configuration (whether internal or external) of the whole or part of an article[1]. Such definition goes on by expressly excluding from protection three classes of design:

(a)   a method or principle of construction; or

17 Section 213(1) of the 1988 Act.
18 Section 213(6) of the 1988 Act.
19 Section 213(4) of the 1988 Act.
20 Section 51 of the 1988.
1   Section 213(3) of the 1988 Act.

(b) features of shape and configuration which enable an article to be fitted to or matched with another article – the 'must fit must match' provision for design right; or

(c) surface decoration.

Infringement of design right

Like copyright, design right has primary infringement and secondary infringement, where the latter requires a plaintiff additionally to prove the requisite knowledge of wrong doing on behalf of the defendant – ie that the defendant knew or had reason to believe that he was dealing in an infringing article. There is no infringement of design right unless the act is done for commercial purposes. The acts of primary infringement are the making of articles to the respective design, or the making of a design document recording the respective design for the purpose of enabling such articles to be made[2]. The acts of secondary infringement include the importation to the UK, possession, sale and letting for hire of an infringing article[3].

A design right is infringed if the offending article is (1) copied from the respective design, and (2) is produced 'exactly or substantially'[4] to that design. The infringer of such design right must either do the act which is prohibited, or authorise another to do such act.

The test for infringement of design right is different from that of copyright[5]. There are three stages of the relevant test[6] which the Court applies:

(a) first the alleged infringing article is compared with the design document or model; and

(b) second it is decided whether copying by the defendant took place – this is the same requirement as in copyright; and

(c) third, if such copying took place, the court decides whether the alleged infringing article is made exactly or substantially to that design – the decision as to whether the offending article is substantially similar is an objective test to be decided through the eyes of the person to whom the design is directed.

Thus, in the third stage of the test for an alleged infringement of a design right in, say, an item of equipment for racing bicycles, the court adopts the position of a reasonable and objective racing cyclist.

Ownership of design right

The first owner of design right is the person who created the design. This is usually the person who also recorded the design in the design document, but it need not necessarily be the same person. Where the design document is

2 Section 226 of the 1988 Act.
3 Section 227 of the 1988 Act.
4 Section 226(2) of the 1988 Act.
5 *C and H Engineering v Klucznik & Sons Ltd* [1992] FSR 421.
6 *C and H Engineering v Klucznik & Sons Ltd* [1992] FSR 421 at 428.

computer generated, the first owner is the person who set up the computer to do the task.

There is an express provision in the 1988 Act to the effect that the first owner of a design right where it is created under a commission, is the person who does the commissioning[7]. There is no such express provision for copyright.

Duration of design right[8]

Design right expires fifteen years after the end of the calendar year in which the design was first recorded in a design document or article; except if articles made to that design are made available for sale or hire anywhere in the world within five years of the end of the calendar year in which it was recorded, then the design right expires ten years from the end of the calendar year in which the first sale or hire was made. Accordingly design right could last for just over ten years, or just under sixteen years depending upon its exploitation and when it was first recorded.

Damages for infringement of design right

The provisions as to damages are similar to those of copyright infringement. There are thus two departures from the norm in the way in which design right damages can be awarded. First no damages are awarded if it is shown that the infringer did not know and had no reason to believe that design right subsisted in the relevant design[9]. Second in certain cases a plaintiff in a design right action can recover 'additional damages'[10], ie more than would otherwise be awarded on an enquiry as to damages or an account of profits. These damages are awarded in cases where the justice of the case demands greater compensation than that otherwise on offer, taking into account all the circumstances and in particular the flagrancy of the infringement and the benefit accruing to the defendant by reason of the infringement. Additional damages are appropriate where, for example, a competitor has achieved a great commercial advantage by reason of the design right infringement, for which a simple enquiry as to damages or account of profits would not adequately compensate the plaintiff.

H. CONFIDENTIAL INFORMATION

What is confidential information?

Confidential information can be very valuable intellectual property for two reasons other than from the point of view of its subject matter. First the grant of protection does not necessarily require as much formal preparation

---

7 Section 215(2) of the 1988 Act.
8 Section 216 of the 1988 Act.
9 Section 233 of the 1988 Act.
10 Section 229 of the 1988 Act.

as the other forms of intellectual property. The idea which forms the basis of any confidential information must still be capable of reasonably precise definition, but the idea can be at a much earlier stage of development and does not require the permanent record necessary for copyright and design right protection, or the detailed written explanation necessary for the grant of a patent. Second, there are certain situations where it may be better to forgo the monopoly protection of a patent, which requires full disclosure of the relevant invention and is limited to twenty years, and thus maintain the monopoly of use of the confidential information for a longer period whilst keeping that information a secret. The latter advantage is, of course, only useful where 'reverse engineering' does not assist the plagiarist – ie the confidential information cannot be discovered by a careful analysis of the end product.

This intellectual property right should not be confused with a right to privacy, which does not currently exist in English law. The law of confidence should also be distinguished from the duties of confidentiality which can be imposed on employees under express or implied terms in contracts of employment.

A concise definition of the law of confidence

The law of confidence is a broad doctrine to the effect that if someone receives information in confidence, that person is not allowed to make a profit from the use or disclosure of the information without the consent of the person imparting the information ('the owner', who may or may not have been the originator of the idea which is crystallised in the confidential information). If the recipient of confidential information does somehow use or disclose it without the owner's consent, then the recipient is guilty of an infringement of the owner's rights. Thus, the necessary elements to an action for breach of confidence can be defined in the following way[11]:

(a) the information imparted must be of a confidential nature; and
(b) the plaintiff in the action must be the owner of the confidential information; and
(c) that information must have been communicated to the recipient in circumstances which import an obligation of confidence on the recipient; and
(d) there has been unauthorised use or disclosure of that information by the recipient, or someone who has received that information from the recipient, to the detriment of the owner.

Information must not be in the public domain

It is a natural prerequisite of an entitlement to protect confidential information, that the relevant information must be truly confidential and capable of reasonably precise definition. Accordingly, even if an athlete has an original idea for a novel way in which to train for an event, that idea does

11 *Fraser v Thames Television Ltd* [1984] QB 44, [1983] 2 All ER 101.

not acquire the protection of the law of confidence when imparted to someone else until it has been adequately defined. For example the athlete can explain to her coach that she has developed a method to exercise more efficiently a set of muscles 'by the use of weights'. Since it is well known that the use of weights exercises muscles, the coach is not in receipt of confidential information until the athlete explains how the particular use of weights is significantly different to any other use which has been previously known. It is only when an original idea acquires sufficient definition to be clearly identifiable and to be capable of being realised in the real world, that it can be protected under the law of confidence.

Ownership of confidential information

There is no requirement for the person imparting the confidential information to be the owner of the same, or even the person who thought up the original idea. In the normal course of commerce, ideas can be passed from one person to another as they develop, each owner for the time being adding value to the idea and then selling on the idea when a new area of expertise or exploitation is required. Thus, in circumstances of the transfer of confidential information the owner for the time being could be someone who has purchased the idea from the originator or a subsequent owner, or even merely someone who has been given the idea by the originator or a subsequent owner.

If a person imparts confidential information to someone who has already had the same idea, and so is already aware of that confidential information, the imparting person is not able to stop the other party from dealing with the information in any way in which he chooses. The reason for this is, of course, that the latter person is merely dealing with his own information, and not with that of the other person. In reality, the problem for the latter party in this case would be to prove to the Court's satisfaction that he was actually fully aware of the confidential information before it was told to him by the other party.

Transmission of confidential information

The way in which confidential information is imparted is also obviously a vital factor in the assessment of whether it truly remains confidential, and there are two important consequences from this element of the law of confidence. First, it is not necessary for the confidential information to be written down – it can be imparted orally, in writing, or in some other concrete form such as a computer record. Naturally there are reasons why it is desirable for the confidential information to be recorded in a concrete form, for example as best evidence of what information was actually communicated, but it is not a necessary requirement for protection. This is the characteristic of confidential information which can make it such a valuable intellectual property right, because the person who originates the idea is thus able to discuss it and seek advice about it, without having to go through any detailed formalities.

Second, it is not necessary for there to have been an express requirement on behalf of the person imparting the information, for the recipient to keep it confidential. The law can imply this requirement in appropriate circumstances. So in the case of the athlete with a new weight training regime, if she takes her coach to the side after training one day and explains the idea, it is possible that the information will satisfy the requirement of element (c) above of the law of confidence (the 'obligation of confidence'), even if she did not expressly say words to the effect: 'This is a secret. I tell it to you in confidence and you must not tell anyone else'. The test as to whether there is an obligation of confidence in a particular case can be summarised in these terms – in all the circumstances would a reasonable man standing in the shoes of the recipient of the information have realised upon reasonable grounds that the information was being given to him in confidence[12]?

An implication of confidence is not automatic, and so wherever possible (and there are very few occasions where it would not be possible) the person communicating the confidential information should ensure that it is so communicated expressly under an obligation of confidence. This can be a simple expression of the confidentiality of the discussion, and does not need to follow any particular formula of words. All that is needed is to make it reasonably clear to the recipient that the future use of the information is subject to the owner's approval.

Detriment to the owner

The fourth element of the law of confidence, element (d) above ('detriment to the owner'), required for an action for breach of confidence is the unauthorised use of the information to the owner's detriment. Such use can be authorised by the owner either expressly or by implication, and can be restricted to a certain field of interest. For example, if an athlete develops a novel training regime and then explains it in confidence to a rower, a footballer and a skier, all of whom would benefit from the use of that regime, the athlete can prevent each of the recipients from using it for purposes other than that specified, say for their own particular sport. Thus each of the recipients could be prevented from using it for any other purpose, or as is more likely, could be prevented from exploiting the idea to a wider extent by, for example a restriction on applying it to the writing of a skiers' training book which contains an explanation of the training method. When granting any such licences, the owner of confidential information should be alert to the risk that the information will thereby seep into the public domain, and there is nothing which the owner can do to recover the confidentiality of information once it has been lost.

Third parties

The obligation of confidence rests not only upon the original recipient, but also upon all persons who receive the information from the recipient, and who at the same time or some time thereafter become aware that the

12 *Coco v AN Clark (Engineers) Ltd* [1969] RPC 41.

information was confidential. But that obligation terminates when the confidential information ceases to be truly confidential, and when it is thus in the public domain and part of public knowledge. Accordingly in the example of the athlete's novel weight training regime, if the athlete had herself published an article in a sports' magazine about her method, she can no longer claim that the relevant information is confidential, and so her legal case would fail at the first hurdle.

Obligation of confidentiality under the law of contract

Sometimes the imparting of confidential information is also subject to the law of contract, and it is almost always better, if possible, to ensure that there is an express contract covering the disclosure of information. The reason for this is that, importantly, a clear and expressed contract, preferably in writing, ensures that there is less likelihood of misunderstandings about the nature of the obligations upon the recipient. All too often litigation arises in these circumstances not because the recipient has decided intentionally to act unlawfully, but because either the owner or the recipient has misunderstood the true nature of their relationship. The law of contract applies since the offeror (the orginator) agrees to disclose the confidential information to the offeree (the recipient) in consideration of the undertaking by the offeree not to use or disclose the information.

Period of confidential information

The period of protection for confidential information is for all the time until the information comes into the public domain.

Chapter 10

Sport and marketing

Introduction

Sporting bodies have become increasingly alert to the fact that they are operating in a commercial world, in which, whilst money may not always guarantee success, it is often a pre-requisite of success. As a result, they have been forced to look to areas outside their mainstream sporting activities in order to maintain and enhance the value of their balance sheets. The reality of the world in which many sports now operate is that survival is impossible, at least at the higher levels, through sport alone. This has led to sport seeking out other sources of income and relying proportionately less on money taken at the turnstiles or from sporting performance itself. The popularity of sport generally and the allegiance of members of the public to particular performers on the sporting stage, both individual and collective, have increasingly been recognised as assets which are themselves capable of commercial exploitation. This realisation has led to an influx of revenue from three main sources, namely:

- merchandising (where the sports personality or organisation markets his/its own reputation for profit)
- sponsorship (where the sports personality or organisation sells association with his/its reputation in order to enhance the reputation of the sponsor)
- television

All three such sources pose their own individual difficulties and merit separate attention[1], but at the heart of any respective examination lies a common theme which needs to be underlined. What sport is doing in each case is seeking to draw on a particular feature of its existence to generate revenue. That feature may variously be described as 'identity', 'reputation', 'image' or 'profile' and the attributes which give it marketability are 'distinctiveness' and 'attractiveness'.

It is the distinctiveness (or 'recognisability') and attractiveness (or 'popularity') of the 'identity' of a sporting entity, be it an individual, a team, a competition, an event or even a venue, which gives it the power from which a commercial return may be derived. In commercial and legal terms, this 'pulling power' may be described as 'goodwill' which is a word which has been aptly and succinctly described as an:

1 See the chapters which follow.

'Attractive force which brings in custom.'[2]

Sport has such an attractive force in abundance. In seeking to market itself by the above means, sport is seeking to harness its 'goodwill' or 'attractive force' and to put it to commercial use in order to make it 'bring in custom'.

Thus it is access to sporting goodwill of one form or another which a third party such as a broadcaster, a sponsor or a licensed merchandiser seeks and for which, depending upon the strength of the power or attractive force in the circumstances in question, he may be prepared to pay substantial sums. In each case, the aim is to borrow the goodwill of the particular sporting identity and to put it to use to enhance the commercial prospects of the associated third party.

In the case of the sponsor, he seeks by association to feed off the goodwill of his sponsored subject, by transferring some of its power to his own identity, so as to engender an enhanced goodwill or attractive force of his own.

On the other hand, a licensed merchandiser seeks to exploit the goodwill of his licensor, by establishing a market in which the attraction of the goods sold derives directly from that very goodwill.

A television broadcaster taps his subject's popularity indirectly, by getting his programme before as great a number of viewers as possible (or viewers of a discreet category) in order, for example, the better to exploit the commercial opportunities available to him through his medium.

Of course it is not only through third party activity that the commercial value of sporting goodwill may be exploited across diverse fields of activity. A sporting body may choose, for example, to operate its own merchandising activity directly rather than by the grant of licences to third parties. For example, Manchester United and many other sporting organisations themselves sell a wide catalogue of goods, many without any particular sporting connection other than an obvious and visual association with the identity of the club etc.

Further, if carefully managed, a marketing initiative through any of the means mentioned, whether directly or via third parties, may itself serve to increase and enhance sport's goodwill by, for example, giving the identity of the particular sporting entity a wider currency and thereby increasing its distinctiveness and recognisability. Thus the goodwill of sport both provides the fuel for the marketing drive and is also a product of it. This section and the following three chapters are therefore concerned, at one and the same time, with both 'sports marketing' and the 'marketing of sport'.

Of course, as with any money spinning asset, the trick is not simply to exploit the profitability of sport to its maximum effect, but also to prevent others from cashing in on its ability to bring in custom, by using it in an unauthorised or uncontrolled way for their own purposes. 'Bootlegging', 'piracy', 'plagiarism' and 'ambush marketing' are all well known phenomena which provide testimony to the power of sport's goodwill, but which are liable, if allowed to go unchecked, to dilute its pulling power. Such activities tend to diminish the exploitable value of such goodwill and of individual rights of access legitimately granted to it.

Marketing imperatives

Any official marketing drive, whether through merchandising, sponsorship or the sale of broadcasting rights, is liable to raise certain generic issues which, if

2   *IRC v Muller & Co's Margarine Ltd* [1901] AC 217 at 223.

not addressed, are likely to lead to legal difficulty. Such issues can usefully be expressed in the form of two imperatives of broad ranging significance to the person or other body conducting the marketing drive. These imperatives require the 'marketer' (wherever and to the extent possible):

1. to establish a specific 'identity' giving rise to a definable goodwill which is immediately identifiable as being 'owned' by him (viz: define the boundaries of the asset); and
2. to take steps to guard against the unauthorised 'abuse' of that same goodwill by third parties (viz: set up legal fortifications along those boundaries).

The importance of the above imperatives in many different contexts will be seen in the chapters which follow, in which the legal implications of the three types of marketing initiative referred to above are discussed. In general, however, the imperatives derive from the very nature of the asset which such marketing initiatives seek to exploit. Unlike many other assets, you cannot see, feel or package goodwill, which, as already mentioned, means simply 'commercial pulling power'. Its etherial character is such that its legal ownership cannot be suggested, let alone established, by any concept simply of its 'possession'. Further, it is not only a legal 'person' which may generate goodwill. Thus it has been appropriate, above, to describe sport itself as having goodwill, in the sense of an 'attractive force' which may be utilised to bring in trade. More particularly, goodwill may attach not simply to a football team or a particular sports star, but also to a particular competition, event, occasion or location. Additionally, in a particular sporting competition or on a particular sporting occasion, different strands of goodwill may be discerned, attaching variously to the individual participants and the organisers, but coming together to produce a combined goodwill which may be greater than the sum of its constituent parts. What is more, the very ephemeral nature of goodwill may, in certain circumstances, make it especially difficult to identify any recognisable proprietary interest therein and, correspondingly, make it impossible to use legal action to deny third party access to it. Sport may indeed have a commercial pulling power in the form of an attractive force which may be used to bring in custom, but the question needs sometimes to be posed:

'By whom may such custom legitimately be brought in?'

In any particular instance, adherence to the above imperatives may assist in providing an answer to this question.

Contracts

Marketing, of course, is but one form of business. In the context of sport, marketing involves a partnership between sport itself and the business interests seeking to derive some commercial benefit from an association with sport. The kind of marketing initiative with which this book is concerned, inevitably involves contractual arrangements of one form or another. As with any contractual arrangement, however, certain disciplines and understandings are required if the relationships within the arrangement are to prosper and develop harmoniously and without conflict. In particular, a systematic approach is advised to the agreement of contractual terms. Contracts are simply negotiated agreements. They are designed to identify particular rights, obligations and constraints. They do not require to be in writing and the process of reducing an agreement to writing may sometimes be regarded as an unnecessary intrusion into time which could otherwise be used for other more directly profitable tasks. However, there can be no doubt that many potential problems will be avoided by the sort of conscious and disciplined process which is likely to be involved in any attempt to reduce to writing all the terms agreed between the parties. Equally, such a process may well itself identify particular points which demand specific agreement. Unless an attempt is made, expressly and specifically, to articulate all agreed terms, such points might otherwise be allowed to pass without comment and, therefore, without agreement, leaving the parties to argue over them (each perhaps having to assert conflicting implied terms) only when problems subsequently arise. It is no more than common sense to suggest that, in any form of marketing arrangement, the parties should identify at the outset exactly what they intend to achieve by their arrangement and how best they should go about seeking to achieve it. They should identify what specific terms require to be agreed and, in doing so, they should have regard to the marketing imperatives referred to above. The process of reducing agreed terms into writing is important, not simply because such process concentrates the mind and is liable to identify exactly what terms require to be agreed. In addition, a written contract will lend certainty to what has been agreed and will provide an important and authoritative reference point in the event of argument or difficulty in the future. Finally, it is of fundamental importance that, for it to fulfil its proper function, the written contract should be *clear* and *comprehensive*.

The essential aim of the contract should be to identify and clarify certain basic provisions so that the nature and extent of the rights and obligations of each side are clear. In addition, there are many potential questions which may arise in relation to the performance of a contract and answers to many such questions may readily be provided by addressing them in express written terms during the negotiation of the contract at the outset.

Marketing contracts come in different shapes and sizes and it is impossible to legislate for every eventuality, but it is suggested that in each case the aim in articulating the terms of the contract (in accordance with the marketing imperatives previously referred to) should be to provide for the orderly delivery of maximised benefits to each party without associated injury to other parties.

The contract will identify specific rights and obligations and will provide limitations and other safeguards. Further, whilst the precise terms of individual contracts will vary according to the nature and circumstances of the particular arrangement, the process leading up to the agreement and articulation of such terms may well be broadly the same in each case. This is because in all bar the most simple of marketing arrangements there are likely to be similar generic problems which will need to be addressed if they are effectively to achieve their full potential.

Such problems may usefully be confronted during the negotiation process by posing a series of questions:

(a)   What are the aims of the contract?
(b)   What are the potential third party interests which may result in activity liable to thwart the parties in their efforts to achieve such aims?
(c)   What terms need to be agreed in order

  –   to deliver those aims to maximum effect;
  –   to prevent conflict with any other interests of the parties;

    – to provide sensible boundaries to the rights of the parties;
    – to inhibit third parties in the performance of their activities to the detriment of the parties?

Furthermore, whereas certain contractual relationships might properly be categorised as adversarial in their nature, the kind of marketing arrangements referred to in this chapter involve a partnership in which, broadly speaking, the parties will or ought to be working to the same agenda. They will each wish to see the sporting element of the arrangement succeed and flourish, thereby enhancing the goodwill from which each seeks to benefit. Within limits, what is good for one party is likely to be good for the other. But because there are indeed limits to such a proposition, the identification of the parties' respective rights and obligations in clear written terms at the outset ought to be afforded a high degree of priority. This is particularly so in circumstances where there may be different means of measuring and achieving the 'success' of the arrangement and where, as is likely, the particular contractual relationship has to exist in the midst of a web of other relationships in which all kinds of other interests may impinge upon the otherwise narrow relationship between the parties to the particular marketing contract itself. The very fact that the parties are contemplating a relationship in the nature of a partnership, designed to secure broad common objectives, however, ought to enable the process of negotiation to proceed in a sensible and constructive fashion, provided that the potential for difficulties of one form or another is recognised, identified and sensibly addressed.

Practical measures

Adherence to the above marketing imperatives should not stop with the agreement and articulation of contractual terms. The parties' objectives will not be achieved unless due thought is given to the imposition of particular practical measures as much as to the identification and enforcement of strict legal rights as such. The point is that, in certain circumstances, the law alone simply will not be apt either:

(a)   to permit the identification of any specific proprietary rights of 'ownership' in particular goodwill; or

(b)   to prevent intrusion by third parties into any asserted exclusive access thereto.

In such circumstances, the purity of the marketing drive will be in danger of adulteration unless sensible practical steps are taken to inhibit such third party intrusions wherever possible.

The limitations of the law

For example, the law does not immediately recognise any general idea of property simply in a person's features or image[3]. For example, in *Palmer v*

---

3 Note, however, Laws J's statement, obiter, of a 'principle' that the disclosure of a photograph taken without authority would be actionable as a 'breach of confidence', in *Hellewell v Chief Constable of Derbyshire* [1995] 1 WLR 804 at 807. This is one instance of the court appearing to be concerned at the law's failure to recognise a right of privacy. The court came close to recognising such a right in *R v Khan* [1996] 3 WLR 162. *See also*

National Sporting Club Ltd[4], a pugilist was unable to prevent photographs of his fight being exhibited on public display or his name being shown in relation thereto[5].

Similarly, in *Sports and General Press Agency Ltd v 'Our Dogs' Publishing Co Ltd*[6] the purchaser of 'exclusive photographic rights' at a dog show was unable to prevent others from taking and publishing their own photographs[7].

Again, in an Australian case, *Victoria Park Racing and Recreation Grounds v Taylor*[8], a racecourse owner was not able to object when a third party erected a platform outside the racecourse itself and proceeded to film and broadcast from his vantage point.

In certain circumstances, of course, the use of a photograph or other image of a sporting personality may infringe a contractual right[9] or it may convey a particular message or innuendo which tends to bring the individual in question into disrepute or ridicule such as to give rise to a cause of action in defamation. Thus, for example in *Tolley v JS Fry & Sons*[10] , a cartoon depiction of a well known amateur sportsman in an advertisement was held to convey an implied message that the sportsman had been paid to endorse the advertised product and accordingly to give rise to a claim in defamation[11]. Similarly, in *Ettingshausen v Australian Consolidated Press Ltd*[12] a well known Australian rugby league player was held entitled to complain about the publication in a magazine of a photograph taken of him naked in the changing room, on the basis either that it suggested that he had allowed such

'Should There be a Law to Protect Rights of Personal Privacy' (Bingham LCJ) [1996] 5 EHRLR 450. Depending upon how it is effected, it seems likely that the introduction of the European Convention on Human Rights into United Kingdom law will result in limited rights to privacy being recognised by the law. Article 8 of the Convention recognises, inter alia, that 'everyone has the right to respect for his private and family life, his home and his correspondence'.

4   1905–10 MacG CC 55.
5   See also *Dockrell v Dougall* (1899) 80 LT 556 and *Merchandising Corpn of America Inc v Harpbond Inc* [1983] FSR 32.
6   [1916] 2 KB 880; affd [1917] 2 KB 125, CA.
7   Compare the position in the United States of America, where the courts recognise 'rights of publicity' in celebrities' names, likenesses and performances which will sometimes enable them to prevent the use of their profiles without their consent – *Uhlaender v Henricksen* 316 F Supp 1277 (1970) and *Dzurenko v Jordach, Inc* 464 NYS 2d 730 (1983). The American courts also recognise a principle that the unauthorised 'misappropriation' of the fruits of another's labour is unlawful – see, for example, *International News Service v Associated Press* 248 US 215 (1918); see also *Pittsburgh Athletic Co v KQV Broadcasting Co* 24 F Supp 490 (WD Pa 1938) in which an unauthorised radio broadcast describing baseball games from information supplied by observers from outside the grounds was held to infringe the organiser's proprietary rights derived from its 'creation of the game, its control of the park and its restriction on the dissemination of news therefrom'; see also *National Exhibition Co v Fass* 133 NYS 2d 767 (Sup Ct 1954).
8   (1938) 58 CLR 479.
9   See, for example, *Stackemann v Paton* [1906] 1 Ch 774.
10   [1931] AC 333.
11   Where false statements are made maliciously (without justification or excuse) there may be a claim in malicious falsehood. Moreover, where such statements are published in writing or other permanent form and are calculated to damage the sporting personality in his professional capacity, such an action does not require proof of special damage – see s 3 of the Defamation Act 1952.
12   (1991) 23 NSWLR 443.

a publication or that it exposed him to ridicule as someone 'whose genitals had been exposed to public view'[13].

In addition, some protection may be available where a particular 'nom de plume' or other specific badge of identity (eg 'Gazza' or, believe it or not, 'Giggsy') is registered as a trade mark[14] and is then utilised by a third party. In all such cases where protection may be available, the law intervenes not in recognition of a general right of property in the Plaintiff's personal identity as such, but to support other established rights. Thus in the case of defamation, the law accepts that an individual is entitled to protection from false statements calculated to sully his reputation. In the case of a trade mark, the law recognises a right of exclusive ownership in the mark itself[15]. In the latter case, of course, such recognition derives from express statutory provision.

Where such independent causes of action are not available, the common law has generally struggled to find any infringement of rights where someone has simply sought to 'cash in' on the attractive features of another's identity, personality or operation in order to further his own ends. Difficulties may arise in a number of different guises. For example:

- A manufacturer of goods (or a purveyor of services) may seek (without permission) to use another's image simply to help boost his own sales.
- The organisers of an event or competition may seek to exploit the marketablity of its profile (and thereby to increase such profile and its marketability even further) by granting exclusive broadcasting rights. Such 'exclusivity' may be challenged either by another broadcaster able to gain access for his cameras to the site where the sporting action takes place or, perhaps, by a participant (whether an individual or a team) who asserts an entitlement to strike his own broadcasting deal in respect of his own particular involvement in the event or competition (perhaps to specific matches).
- Equally, the organisers may fall prey to 'ambush marketers' whose activities they would wish to curtail so as to preserve their exclusive access to the profile of 'their' event etc.

In each such case, any attempt to prevent the encroachment in question, involves an assertion by the claimant, be he the organiser of a sporting contest, a sports star or any other person with a marketable involvement in sporting activity, that he has a *proprietary right* over his recognisable identity which, being marketable, gives rise to goodwill (commercial pulling power) worthy of protection. The process by which the courts, especially in the United Kingdom, have been willing to identify and recognise such a proprietary right and/or to recognise any relevant goodwill derived therefrom, however, has been (and to some extent remains) slow.

Problems of the kind described are addressed in greater detail in Chapter 11, but it is worth making the general point at this stage that they may be significantly reduced in practice, by a conscientious adherence to the marketing 'imperatives' previously referred to.

13 See also *Williams v Reason* [1988] 1 WLR 96n where John Williams, the Welsh and British Lions rugby union star brought a libel action against John Reason, the Daily Telegraph sports correspondent for suggestions that he had infringed his amateur status. This was a more traditional allegation of defamation, in that the publication complained of took the form of specific assertions in written articles.

14 It remains to be seen whether Eric Cantona succeeds in his attempt to register as a trade mark the phrase '*Ooh aah Cantona*'!

15 The same may, broadly, be said in the case of copyright actions and other claims recognised by the law of intellectual property.

One example where a failure to address such imperatives at the appropriate (earliest) stage gave rise to particular difficulty arose during 1996, when the English Rugby Football Union (RFU) felt able (initially) to seek to go its own way in securing a broadcasting contract for Five Nations and other matches played at its ground at Twickenham. In doing so, it no doubt took the view that, whilst 'the Five Nations Championship' had its own recognisable identity and profile, which in turn had a significant value through the pulling power of the competition, there were no contractual or other arrangements between the five participating governing bodies in place such as to identify and allocate 'ownership' of that pulling power. In such circumstances, not altogether surprisingly, the RFU proceeded on the footing that the only proprietary right available to be exploited when it came to granting broadcasting rights was the right of entry to particular venues where Five Nations' matches were to be played. The RFU's argument would surely have been that, in the absence of specific agreement on the point[16], the mere fact that such matches were part of a competition between national teams of five countries did not serve to endow the competition as a whole with any proprietary rights which the RFU's independent stance infringed. In the event, the ructions caused by the RFU's unilateral initiative were resolved without court proceedings, to the great relief of the sport itself and all those involved or interested in the Five Nations Championship. Resolution appears to have been achieved, however, by pragmatic and commercial means rather than by any persuasion as to the rights or wrongs of the RFU's argument. The other Unions simply indicated that, unless the RFU altered its stance, they would change the competition and not play England at all. The view advanced by such other Unions (that the goodwill of the competition belonged to the five governing bodies jointly[17]) was accordingly never put to the test[18]. Even if the majority argument had been established as correct, it is suggested that it is nevertheless far from clear that, in the absence of contractual provision, the RFU could have been prevented (by legal action) from providing access to Twickenham to particular broadcasters on such terms as it felt fit.

Whatever the relative merits of the legal arguments raised, the RFU case illustrates perfectly how the organisation of a competition such as the Five Nations is inextricably bound up with the exploitation of the commercial rights therein and what chaos is liable to result if such rights are not appropriately addressed by clear contractual provision and one of the constituent elements attempts to 'go it alone'.

A similar problem, albeit in a different context, lies at the heart of the Director General of Fair Trading's decision during 1996 to refer to the Restrictive Practices Court the FA Premier League's broadcasting agree-

---

16 Had the 'imperatives' referred to earlier been addressed at the outset, no doubt the matter would have been covered by express agreement.

17 The concept of joint ownership of goodwill is now well recognised in law, as shown by the cases such as *Bollinger v Costa Brava Wine Co Ltd* [1960] RPC 16 and [1961] RPC 116, in which goodwill in the name 'champagne' was held to be shared by the wine growers and shippers of the 'Champagne' region in France. See also the similar 'sherry' case, *Vine Products Ltd v Mackenzie & Co Ltd* [1969] RPC 1, the 'scotch whisky' case, *John Walker & Sons Ltd v Henry Ost & Co* [1970] RPC 489 and finally the 'advocaat' case, *Warnink BV v Townend & Sons Ltd* [1979] AC 731.

18 For a discussion of similar issues in an American context, as they arose between a League of baseball clubs and individual players (who were employees of the clubs) see *Baltimore Orioles Inc v Major League Baseball Players Association* 805 F 2d 663 (7th CIR 1986), from which, however, no clear statements of principle of general application emerged.

ments with BSkyB and the BBC. The reference raises competition issues and suggests that the League operates as a cartel by requiring, in its rules, the centralised negotiation of such agreements on behalf of all clubs from time to time within the Premier League. Such issues are discussed elsewhere in this book, but the rules which were the subject of such reference, themselves raise the question as to who owns the goodwill to which any broadcasting rights are designed to provide access. The FA Premier League would no doubt provide an answer different from that profferred by the RFU in the case of the Five Nations Championship above, and would argue that it was they who constructed and organised the competition and that, accordingly, it was they who owned at least that part of the goodwill which was apt for the grant of broadcasting rights thereto. It was no doubt partly a recognition of the potential difficulties involved that prompted the Premier League rules, sensibly and in accordance with the 'imperatives' identified above, to incorporate express provision on the point, in an attempt to bind its member clubs by contract, although the validity and effectiveness of such an approach will be determined according to competition law in the proceedings before the Restrictive Practices Court.

The problems of protecting goodwill from unauthorised encroachment have led, as will be seen below[19], to the courts in various jurisdictions flirting with the idea of recognising a general tort of 'unfair competition' under which, in broad terms, it would generally be unlawful for a third party to make unauthorised use of the fruits of another's endeavours. Such a tort, if adopted in the United Kingdom, would undoubtedly render the marketing efforts of individuals and other sporting bodies far more secure, although its precise ambit would require to be clearly identified. No longer would access to and ownership of goodwill be as crucial as it currently is and the activities of the bootleggers and ambush marketers would more easily be inhibited and controlled. As yet, however, the United Kingdom courts have emphatically declined to embrace the existence of such a tort[20]. Further, with the influence of European law moving ever further towards a so called 'free market' with prohibitions of increasing stringency against barriers to competition, it is suggested that the adoption of a new tort of any such general application is unlikely. It is more likely that any additional judicial protection will come from an increased readiness in the courts to recognise the prevalence and importance of (and value in) the kind of marketing opportunities described above and an increased willingness to adapt existing causes of action, such as, particularly, passing off, to modern commercial circumstances. As will be seen below, there are some indications[1] that the courts (or at least some judges) are now moving in such a direction.

---

19 See Chapter 11.
20 See *Warnink BV v Townend & Sons Ltd* [1979] AC 731. See also generally below.
1   See for example, the Australian authorities referred to in Chapter 11 and *Mirage Studios v Counter Feat Clothing Co Ltd* [1991] FSR 145, also discussed in that chapter. But it should not be thought that such cases signal a 'sea change' in the courts' approach. See for example *Re Applications by Elvis Presley Enterprise Inc*, Chancery Division 18 March 1997 (Laddie J) reported briefly in: (1997) Times, 25 March.

Chapter 11

Merchandising

Introduction

In the previous chapter we saw how a sporting entity with an established 'identity', 'profile' or 'reputation' is likely to have a money making asset in the form of a commercial pulling power or 'goodwill' derived from such identity. This section examines the process by which that pulling power may be used to deliver a commercial return through the harnessing of the identity in question and by its use to promote the sale of products by association with it. This process is often referred to as 'character' 'personality' 'reputation' or 'image' merchandising or licensing.

The scope for the marketing of merchandise through a particular sporting association or affiliation has been shown to be such that it can generate substantial profits. Further, such profits may derive from the sale of goods which have no clear and obvious relation to sport at at all, let alone to the particular sport, individual, team, club or location in question. With Newcastle United Football Club having had to spend over £15 million to bring Alan Shearer to St James's Park, breaking the then world transfer fee record in the process, it is little wonder that football clubs in particular have been forced increasingly to look to maximise their revenue by unleashing the potential sums available from a product sales drive so as thereby to exploit their commercial pulling power or 'goodwill'. Virtually all major football clubs in the United Kingdom now have an established merchandising operation which targets their (active and passive) fans and generates sales of goods containing some visual signification of affiliation. Such operations may be conducted through retail outlets sited at the clubs' own grounds or elsewhere, through other licensed retail outlets, through wholesalers who supply yet further retail outlets and through mail order catalogues. Manchester United Football Club, for example, is now a public limited company with diverse interests, many of which have little to do with football, save that they derive much of their attraction in the market place from the name, image and general 'cachet' derived from the club's football team. Indeed, the Club's merchandising turnover, which peaked in 1995 at in excess of £23 million has outstripped revenue taken at the gate (less than £20 million). Whilst these commercial operations have been launched on the back of Manchester United's sporting successes over the years, it will increasingly be the case that clubs will have to look to such commercial successes themselves to provide the financial foundations for the achievement of sporting success in the future.

Further, by a focussed approach to such merchandising activity, sport seeks in turn to enhance the very profile which it is seeking to exploit. In this way, its profile is both the fuel for such marketing efforts and, to some extent, the product of them.

Sporting allegiance is often tribal and needs itself to be nurtured and developed in order to increase its commercial pulling power, from which product sales may be derived. The followers of a particular team or individual recognise something in its/his identity to which they feel an attraction. It is this attractive and recognisable identity, with which they wish to be associated, which endows the team or individual with a particular image, profile or 'brand', which in turn builds a 'pulling power' or 'attractive force' which further generates allegiance and which may be exploited to bring in custom.

Even individual events, competitions and locations may have a sufficient identity of their own to generate the kind of pulling power which may be exploited by a carefully constructed and marketed merchandising campaign.

The building of a recognisable 'identity'

Remembering the two particular 'imperatives' identified in the previous chapter[1], sporting bodies and individuals and organisers of events and competitions will therefore seek consciously to build an individual and recognisable identity and thus to develop and strengthen the commercial pulling power attached thereto. This may be done in part by pursuing success on the field of play and by other means of generating 'popularity', such as through sensible ticketing arrangements, by organising promotional events, by participation in charitable or community events, by establishing and supporting fan clubs and their operations and so on. One particularly important method of developing and protecting an exploitable identity is through actively seeking to create specific and recognisable 'badges' of identity in the form of particular items of intellectual property such as trade marks (in the form of logos, names and the like) designs, and specific copyright material.

The identification and creation of such items of intellectual property serves two distinct purposes, each reflecting one of the 'imperatives' already mentioned:

–   First, such items themselves serve to *promote* and cement the identity of the sporting body or individual concerned, thus assisting to make such identity instantly recognisable by that section of the public at which the marketing drive is aimed and, subject to the other ingredients of 'popularity', making the products on sale attractive to it.

–   Further, the rights which attach to such items of intellectual property help enable their owner to *protect* his identity and prevent third parties from damaging his marketing drive by 'borrowing' his image or profile and making use of its pulling power to bring in custom for themselves. By definition, specific items of intellectual property belong to their owners, whose proprietary rights are recognised and will be enforced by the courts. It follows that third parties make use of another's trade marks etc at their peril.

1   Such imperatives are, essentially, to *develop* and *protect* a recognisable identity.

A PROPRIETARY RIGHT IN 'IDENTITY'?

In the absence of specifically identifiable items of intellectual property, it may be difficult to identify any sufficient proprietary right capable of supporting a cause of action intended to curtail the encroaching activities of third party operators. The extent to which a sporting event, personality or other entity attracts proprietary rights recognisable by the law is a developing subject of some difficulty.

One problem is that, without established intellectual property rights, it may be difficult to establish a sufficient public identity or 'profile' with a proprietary 'pulling power' or 'goodwill' of the kind which the courts will readily recognise as being capable of protection from unauthorised third party intrusion, for example by means of a passing off action. This may pose fewer difficulties for a sports star or other person, such as a football team, either of whom is readily able to build a profile through his/its performances on the field of play, or for a business which is devoted to the production of goods in relation to which there is liable to be 'identity', and therefore value, in the name and physical attributes of the goods produced themselves. The more acute difficulties arise, however, in the case of, say, a sporting event, competition or occasion which does not represent any immediately recognisable form of legal 'person' or 'property' and in relation to which any 'profile' is altogether more ephemeral and less easily identified as giving rise to any proprietary rights or interests beyond those of its consituent parts, namely those participating in the sporting contest represented by such event, competition or occasion.

Passing off

In addressing difficulties of the kind described, the courts have not been prepared to accept that *any* unauthorised attempt to make commercial use of things of value created through the endeavours of others should be regarded as unlawful and actionable at the suit of those responsible for their creation[2]. Litigants, therefore, have been left to bring their claims within existing and established causes of action. The most important of such causes of action, in the present context, is passing off. For a general discussion of the law of passing off, reference should be made to Chapter 9. For present purposes, the ingredients of a passing off action have been described as comprising a:

> 'classical trinity of (1) a reputation (or goodwill) acquired by the plaintiff in his goods, name, mark etc, (2) a misrepresentation by the defendant leading to confusion (or deception), causing (3) damage to the plaintiff.[3]'

The particular hurdles for a plaintiff may be described as threefold:

---

2 In the United States of America, such a principle has been succinctly expressed in the proposition that it is 'unfair to reap what another has sown' – see *International News Service v Associated Press* 248 US 215 (1918), *Pittsburgh Athletic Co v KQV Broadcasting Co* 24 F Supp 490 (WD Pa 1938) and *National Exhibition Co v Fass* 133 NYS 2d 767 (Sup Ct 1954).

3 Per Nourse LJ in *Consorzio del Prosciutto di Parma v Marks & Spencer plc* [1991] RPC 351 at 368.

- He has to be able to establish some identifiable 'identity', 'image' or 'profile' with a discernible value for promotional purposes (goodwill or 'commercial pulling power').
- He has to establish some misrepresentation of connection between the defendant and him, which is likely to give rise to confusion (deception) in the market place.
- He has to show that, as a consequence, he has been or is liable to be damaged.

ESTABLISHING A PROMOTIONAL VALUE IN IDENTITY

In reality, the first of the above hurdles is unlikely of itself to prove crucial in itself, although it is worth noting that an 'identity' or 'reputation' without commercial pulling power will not be enough on its own[4]. It is now generally accepted that the operations of those engaged in sporting activity and administration (other than those who can properly be described as amateurs) is 'business' activity. Professional sports performers and organisers of sporting competitions and other events will readily establish that, in so far as they are in the public eye and have a public following (or have a proprietorial right to or interest in an event or competition with a public following) they have a pulling power and, accordingly, own an asset of value for promotional purposes.

THE NEED FOR A MISREPRESENTATION OF CONNECTION LEADING TO CONFUSION

Next, the plaintiff has to be able to show that the public, or some relevant section thereof, is liable to be confused, by some misrepresentation by the defendant, into believing that the plaintiff has some material connection with the defendant or the product or service promoted by him. The position is straightforward where the plaintiff and the defendant are each engaged in similar fields of activity. In such circumstances, any false juxtaposition of the defendant's product and the plaintiff is liable to suggest that the product is indeed in some way associated with the plaintiff and may readily be shown to be actionable because the scope for confusion is patent and there will be little difficulty in establishing likely damage as a result. Thus the manufacturer of a training shoe who 'passes it off' as having been made by another manufacturer will have little difficulty in obtaining appropriate relief. Equally, it is suggested, a well known footballer would have a legitimate and actionable complaint if his identity were borrowed to promote a particular type of football boot.

Particular problems may arise, however, where the parties' primary fields of activity are different. In such circumstances, traditional thinking may make it difficult for a plaintiff to persuade a court that even a clear misrepresentation of connection between the defendant's goods or services is liable to cause confusion in the buying public or is likely to damage the plaintiff in his business activities. For example, the absence of a 'common field of activity' may lead to difficulties where a well known footballing star

---

4   See, for example, *Athletes Foot Marketing Associates Inc v Cobra Sports Ltd* [1980] RPC 343 at 353 to 354.

in order to establish an actionable passing off where a clothes manufacturer chooses to market T-shirts showing a photograph or other picture of him in action on their front. The footballer's recognised business is playing football rather than selling clothing, and so (the defendant would argue) the manufacture of the T-shirts would not suggest any business connection between them and him, would not be liable to cause any confusion in the minds of the public (and, further, would not be likely to cause the footballer any damage in his business).

What this traditional argument fails to acknowledge is that a footballing star has a real potential for commercial earnings, extending far beyond his primary field of activity on the football field, which he is likely to wish to exploit (in so far as he may not already be doing so) by licensing his 'identity' to a third party's sales drive. Furthermore, an unauthorised use of his identity may both (falsely) suggest some legitimate conection (through just such a licensing arrangement) and impair his potential earnings through the exploitation of genuine licensing arrangements.

In recent times, there have been signs which suggest that the tide may have turned and it will be seen below that the assumptions which underpin the traditional arguments just referred to can no longer be regarded as sacrosanct in all circumstances. The signs may be seen as suggesting that the courts are now more ready to recognise that, in the modern world, the potential for commercial activity for those with a pulling power derived from a popular and recognisable identity extends far beyond the limits of the particular activity in which such pulling power was first developed. In particular, it is suggested that the courts are now prepared, more readily than hitherto, to accept that the sports industry has developed to such a degree that those operating within it who have built a significant 'identity', 'profile' or 'reputation' are likely to wish, at some stage, to exploit the commercial pulling power derived therefrom in order to seek a financial return in fields extending far beyond those in which they first made their reputation. As will be seen below, however, such changes as may have taken place in the courts' approach has not diminished the need, in a passing off action, to establish a misrepresentation which is likely to lead to confusion.

DAMAGE

Finally, a plaintiff must establish actual, or a likelihood of, damage. Crucially, a misrepresentation leading merely to confusion is not sufficient for a passing off action. In such circumstances, potential damage to the plaintiff's interests may be found in a number of different ways:

– First, and most obviously, damage may be established in the diversion of custom from the plaintiff. This is the classic passing off situation, where the public is mislead into purchasing the defendant's product, having been misled into thinking that it is in fact the plaintiff's product[5]. In *Adidas Co Ltd v O'Neill Co Ltd*[6] (an Irish decision) the unauthorised use of Adidas's three stripe badge of identity was held not to be passing off

---

5   See, for example, *My Kinda Town v Soll and Grunts Investments* [1983] RPC 15. See also *Spalding v AW Gamage Ltd* [1914] 2 Ch 405 where damage lay in the use of a name, 'Orb Footballs'.

6   [1983] FSR 76, Ir SC.

only because the defendant had sufficiently distinguished his goods by use of his own mark.

- Diversion of custom will only be likely to arise where the plaintiff is already operating in the market exploited by the defendant. The plaintiff may, of course, be engaged in the business of endorsement and licensing in addition to his primary field of activity. If so, he may be able to claim that the defendant's activities have deprived him of income from potential licensees etc. Where that is not the case, damage may derive from evidence that the plaintiff had designs on entering that particular market[7] and that the defendant's activities have reduced his opportunity to do so.

- In some circumstances, damage may be shown to have been caused to the plaintiff's reputation. This may arise, for example, where the plaintiff would not wish to be associated with the kind of products promoted by the defendant[8].

- In other cases, an implied connection with the plaintiff has been found to involve a suggestion that he had some kind of business responsiblity for the product in question (for example by endorsement or by licensing) and that, accordingly, he might thereby be exposed to the risk of litigation[9]. Such a case may also involve damage to the plaintiff's reputation where, for example, the products in question are of inferior quality. Generally in such a case, the implied connection between the plaintiff and the defendant requires a suggestion that the plaintiff has some insight into or control over the quality of the product being promoted. Thus this kind of connection and potential damage is all the more likely to be found where the product in question bears some relation to an area of expertise in which the plaintiff has qualification, for example where, in the case of a sports personality, the product being promoted is an item of sportswear or equipment.

- Finally, in some cases, involving the unauthorised use of an identity with very particular distinctiveness and exclusivity, the courts have been prepared to infer damage simply from a tendency to impair or dilute that distinctiveness[10].

A TORT OF 'UNFAIR COMPETITION'?

In the United States of America, the courts have gone furthest in recognising a principle of commercial misappropriation which, as part of a

---

7 See for example *Eastman Photographic Materials Co Ltd v John Griffiths Cycle Corpn Ltd* (1898) 15 RPC 105 and *LRC v Lilla Edets* [1973] RPC 560 and *Lego System A/S v Lego M Lemelstrich Ltd* [1983] FSR 155.

8 See, for example, *Annabel's (Berkeley Square) v Schock* [1972] FSR 261 (nightclub being associated with an escort agency) and *Harrods Ltd v R Harrod Ltd* (1923) 41 RPC 74 (department store and moneylending). See also the example, albeit in relation to a defamation claim, of *Tolley v JS Fry & Sons* [1931] AC 333.

9 See, for example, *Walter v Ashton* [1902] 2 Ch 282, *Warnink BV v Townend & Sons Ltd* [1979] AC 731 and *Reckitt & Colman Products Ltd v Borden Inc* [1990] 1 WLR 491.

10 See, in New Zealand, *Taylor Bros Ltd v Taylors Group Ltd* [1991] 1 NZLR 91 and *Wineworths Group Ltd v Comite Interprofessionel du Vin de Champagne* [1992] 2 NZLR 327 (NZ CA); and in the United Kingdom, *Taittinger v Allbev Ltd* [1993] FSR 641 and *Harrods Ltd v Harrodian School* [1996] RPC 697. In the latter case, the Court of Appeal emphasised that even under this head of damage, the law was not protecting the value of the name or identity as such but only the goodwill which it generated.

wider tort of 'unfair competition', prohibits the unauthorised commercial exploitation of the fruits of another's labour[11]. This is now partially provided for (in the USA) by statute, in that s 43(a) of the Lanham Trade Mark Act 1946 prohibits a person from making

'... any false designation of origin, false or misleading description of fact or false or misleading representation of facts which ... is likely to cause confusion, or to cause mistake, or to deceive as to the affiliation, connection or association of such person ...'

In addition, the American courts are willing to recognise certain proprietary 'rights of publicity' in celebrities' names, likenesses and performances which will sometimes enable them to prevent the use of their profiles without their consent[12].

The common law continues to insist, however, upon proof that some form of public confusion has been induced by a positive misrepresentation of connection between the defendant's goods or services and the plaintiff's business. The courts in common law jurisdictions do not go so far as to recognise any proprietary right in the 'fruits of a person's labour' or in his 'persona' per se. To put it another way, the common law does not regard the *use* of another's identity or goodwill but only its *abuse* (by misrepresenting such a connection so as to cause public confusion) as actionable.

In order to try to get round the limitations of a passing off action, litigants have frequently argued in favour of widening the ambit of available relief, by borrowing from American jurisprudence and suggesting some kind of recognition of an actionable infringement of proprietary rights wherever some intangible value achieved through the efforts of one individual is tapped by another for unauthorised commercial purposes. The conundrum was recognised by Dixon J in *Victoria Park Racing and Recreation Grounds v Taylor*[13], where he said[14]:

'If English law had followed the course of development that has recently taken place in the United States, the 'broadcasting rights' [the subject of dispute] might have been protected as part of the quasi-property created by the enterprise, organisation and labour of the plaintiff in establishing and equipping a racecourse and doing all that is necessary to conduct race meetings. But courts of equity have not in British jurisdiction thrown the protection of an injunction around all intangible elements of value, that is, value in exchange, which may flow from the exercise by an individual of his powers or resources whether in the organisation of a business or the use of ingenuity, knowledge, skill or labour. This is sufficiently evidenced by the history of the law of copyright and by the fact that the exclusive right to invention, trade marks, designs, trade name and reputation are dealt with within English law as special heads of protected interests and not under a wider generalisation ... [It] is not because the individual has by his efforts put himself in a position to obtain value for what he can give that his right to give it becomes protected by law and so assumes the exclusiveness of

11 See for example *International News Service v Associated Press* 248 US 215, 63 L Ed 211, 39 S Ct 68 (1918); *Pittsburgh Athletic Co v KQV Broadcasting Co* 24 F Supp 490 (WD Pa 1938) and *National Exhibition Co v Fass* 133 NYS 2d 767 (Sup Ct 1954).
12 See, for example, *Uhlaender v Henricksen* 316 F Supp 1277 (1970) and *Dzurenko v Jordache Inc* 464 NYS 2d 730 (1983). See also *Onassis v Christian Dior New York Inc* 472 NYS 2d 254 (Sup Ct 1984) and 488 NYS 943 (1st Dep't 1985) and *Midler v Ford Motor Co* 849 F 2d 460 (9th Cir, 1988).
13 (1938) 58 CLR 479 (Aust HC).
14 At 508.

property, but because the intangible or incorporeal right he claims falls within a recognised category to which legal or equitable protection attaches.'

It has been suggested in Australia[15] that the 'champagne' 'sherry' and 'scotch whisky' cases[16] did involve the creation of a new tort of 'unfair trading', in which, for example, a misrepresentation of connection was not a necessary ingredient. Such suggestion has not survived subsequent scrutiny and the position remains that no such tort exists and litigants are required to satisfy the requirements of the established tort of passing off[17].

However, it appears that the courts may increasingly be prepared to relax the historically rigorous *approach* to such requirements and, in particular, to be less stringent as to what will suffice for an actionable wrong to have been committed. In particular, there are indications that the courts are prepared to allow for damage to goodwill to be more readily established than hitherto has been the case. Thus, for example, 'personality marketing' is now recognised as an important area of a well known person's potential sources of income. Such marketing involves the advertising of goods or services in association with the identity and profile of a celebrity, who may or may not be an individual. As already indicated, where such advertising is unauthorised by the celebrity, the common law has readily recognised it as unlawful where the celebrity himself operates in the same field as the goods or services advertised; but has traditionally been reluctant to recognise any actual or potential confusion or damage for the purposes of a passing off action in circumstances where the celebrity's field of activity is quite different from that involved in the actions complained of[18].

THE COMMONWEALTH APPROACH

The Commonwealth courts have increasingly been prepared to challenge the traditional approach, by recognising that, in the modern world, sports stars and other celebrities are often to be found endorsing or licensing the manufacture of different products across a wide spectrum and that their profile may well give rise to a commercial pulling power capable of bringing in custom from fields outside the sporting fields in which they first acquired their celebrity status. In such decisions, the endorsement or licensing of products has itself been recognised as one of the celebrity's fields of activity.

In this regard, Australia has led the way. In *Henderson v Radio Corpn Pty Ltd*[19], for example, some professional ballroom dancers succeeded in an

---

15 See, for example, *Hexagon Pty v Australian Broadcasting Commission* [1976] RPC 628.
16 *Bollinger v Costa Brava Wine Co Ltd* [1960] Ch 262 and [1961] 1 All ER 561; *Vine Products Ltd v Mackenzie & Co Ltd* [1969] RPC 1 and *John Walker & Sons Ltd v Henry Ost & Co Ltd* [1970] RPC 489.
17 See, in Australia, *Cadbury Schweppes Pty Ltd v Pub Squash Pty Ltd* [1981] 1 WLR 193 and *Moorgate Tobacco Co Ltd v Philip Morris Ltd* (1984) 156 CLR 414 and [1985] RPC 219. The authorities are even clearer in the United Kingdom: see *Mogul SS Co v McGregor Gow & Co* [1892] AC 25; *Warnink BV v Townend & Sons Ltd* [1979] AC 731; *Harrods Ltd v Schwartz-Sackin & Co Ltd* [1986] FSR 490; revsd [1991] FSR 209, CA; *Associated Newspapers v Insert Media* [1988] 2 All ER 420 and *Swedac v Magnet & Southerns* [1989] FSR 243.
18 See, for example, *McCulloch v Lewis A May (Produce Distributors) Ltd* [1947] 2 All ER 845; *Tavener Rutledge Ltd v Trexapalm Ltd* [1975] FSR 479; *Lyngstad v Anabas Products Ltd* [1977] FSR 62; *Wombles Ltd v Wombles Skips Ltd* [1975] FSR 488 and *Stringfellow v McCain Foods (GB) Ltd* [1984] RPC 501.
19 [1969] RPC 218. See also *Totalizator Agency Board v Turf News Pty Ltd* [1967] VR 605.

action against defendants who had used a photograph of them on a record cover, the court holding that the defendants had thereby misappropriated their professional/business reputation. Although the court recognised that there could be said to be a common field of activity in a broad sense, in that the plaintiffs did have an interest in records which were for dancing or dance teaching, the mere fact that there was an implied (false) representation of connection with the plaintiffs was sufficient for the actionable wrong to be complete. This was because it was to be inferred that the target customers would be liable to believe that the plaintiffs' picture was an indication of their recommendation for or approval of the record.

Equally, in the sporting world, in *Paracidal Pty Ltd v Herctum Pty Ltd*[20] a professional horse rider was entitled to prevent the unauthorised use of his picture in a riding school's advertisements.

In *Hutchence v South Sea Bubble Co Pty Ltd*[1], pirate T-shirts depicting references to the pop group 'INXS' gave rise to passing off relief, on the footing that many members of the public would assume that the group had given their approval to such goods in return for some kind of financial benefit. This was in spite of the fact that the garments were sold as 'Bootleg T-shirts' with labels disclaiming any association with the group. The court felt that no sufficiently clear disclaimer had been given to dispel the potential for confusion.

In *Pacific Dunlop v Hogan*[2], the actor who played 'Crocodile Dundee', Paul Hogan, persuaded the court that an advertisement for shoes in which the main actor had been dressed like the character in the film was actionable, on the basis of an implicit misrepresentation that Mr Hogan had some kind of commercial arrangement with the shoe manufacturers[3].

Even in Australia, however, the courts' consideration of whether or not an actionable wrong has been committed is conducted within the confines of the established principles of passing off. Thus, relief is granted only where there is established a misrepresentation suggestive of some business connection between plaintiff and defendant which is both liable to cause confusion and likely to damage the plaintiff's business interests. In *Honey v Australian Airlines Ltd*[4], the mere use by an airline of the name and photograph of a well known athlete in a poster reccommending sport to schools was held not to be actionable, on the basis that, as the airline was found not to have been advertising as such, there was no implicit representation of any business connection between it and the athlete[5].

The Australian courts have even been prepared to adopt a liberal view in the case of fictional characters. Where cartoon or other similar characters

20 (1983) 4 IPR 201.
1 (1986) 64 ALR 330.
2 (1989) 87 ALR 14. See also *Shoshana Pty v 10th Cantanae Pty Ltd* (1987) 18 FCR 285.
3 Interestingly, in an earlier 'Crocodile Dundee' case, the court appeared to be prepared to recognise a cause of action even in the absence of any misrepresentation. See *Hogan v Koala Dundee Pty Ltd* (1988) 83 ALR 187, which should not, however, be relied upon. A further 'Crocodile Dundee' case arose in Canada – in *Paramount Picture Corpn v Howley* (1992) 39 CPR (3d) 419n, an injunction was granted in respect of unlicensed T-shirts, on the basis that trade customers would assume that the official Canadian distributors had licensed them and thereby given an assurance of quality.
4 (1989) 14 IPR 264.
5 See also *Shoshana Pty Ltd v 10th Cantanae Pty Ltd* (1987) 79 ALR 279 in which the (inadvertent) use of the name of a well known television personality (Sue Smith) in an advertisement for video recorders was held on the facts *not* to be liable to mislead the public into thinking that she had endorsed the product.

have achieved a certain public prominence, their creators have been able to restrain their use in third party 'character marketing' drives, on the basis that the court has been willing to infer that such pirate marketing gave rise to a likely assumption amongst members of the public that, as with 'personality marketing' in the case of celebrities, the creators of the characters would have had some kind of commercial association with the marketing in question. Thus in *Children's Television Workshop Inc v Woolworths (NSW) Ltd*[6] the sale of unauthorised 'Muppets' was held to be an actionable wrong at the suit of the creators of the television show, Sesame Street.

The same applied in the case of the creators of a cartoon character known as 'Fido Dido' in *Fido Dido Inc v Venture Stores (Retailers) Pty Ltd*[7].

In each case, the court was prepared to infer confusion (and, therefore, relevant misrepresentation) in the field of merchandising/licensing in order to found the basis for passing off relief.

A similar approach has been adopted elsewhere. In Canada, for example, in *Athans v Canadian Adventure Camps Ltd*[8], a world champion water skier failed to establish that an unauthorised use of a photograph (which he used for commercial purposes) in a brochure advertising a summer camp for children amounted to an actionable passing off only because, as the court found, the plaintiff would not have been obviously recognisable from the photograph by the segment of the public to whom the brochure was addressed. The scope for confusion, therefore, was absent or minimal. Interestingly, the court nevertheless granted the plaintiff relief under a wider tort apparently recognised in Canada of 'appropriating the plaintiff's personality'. Such a tort recognised a proprietary right in the exclusive marketing for gain of a personality, image and name[9]. Such a tort, even in Canada, is of uncertain ambit[10] and generally the grant of relief is considered by reference to established passing off principles.

In *National Hockey League v Pepsi-Cola Canada Ltd*[11], the NHL, the governing body in Canada for professional ice hockey, sought passing off injunctions in respect of Pepsi's advertising, inter alia during broadcasts of NHL Stanley Cup play off matches, and of its scratch card and bottle top contest known as the 'Diet Pepsi $4,000,000 Pro-Hockey Play-Offs Pool'[12]. Although denying the NHL relief on the facts, the court at first instance[13],

---

6　[1981] RPC 187.

7　(1988) 16 IPR 365 (Australia).

8　(1977) 80 DLR (3d) 583.

9　See also *Mazatti v Acme Products Ltd* [1930] 4 DLR 601 and *Krouse v Chrysler Canada Ltd* (1973) 40 DLR (3d) 15. In the latter case, the court found that there was no passing off in the case of the use of a photograph of a professional football player because of a lack of confusion. The court recognised the existence of a tort of misappropriation of personality, albeit no such tort was held to have been committed on the facts. Compare the English case of *Kaye v Robertson* [1991] FSR 62 in which the Sunday Sport newspaper was held entitled to publish a revealing and unsavoury 'interview' with the actor, Gordon Kaye, from his hospital bed, together with photographs, in circumstances where he had suffered brain damage rendering him incapable of giving his consent.

10　See *Heath v Weist-Barron School of Television Canada Ltd* (1981) 62 CPR (2d) 92 and *Joseph v Daniels* (1986) 11 CPR (3d) 544.

11　(1993) 102 DLR (4th) 80; affirming (1992) 92 DLR (4th) 349.

12　The issue was particularly sensitive, as Coca Cola had secured sponsorship of the play-offs themselves and had secured the right to be called the 'official soft drink' thereof and yet Pepsi had secured exclusive advertising rights during broadcasts, via Molson who had purchased the broadcasting rights.

13　At 359.

whose judgment was upheld on appeal, expressly recognised a species of passing off where there was no common field of activity but where:

> 'A defendant has promoted his product or business in such a way as to create the false impression that his product or business is in some way approved, authorised or endorsed by the plaintiff or that there is some business connection between the defendant and the plaintiff. By this means a defendant may hope to 'cash in' on the goodwill of the plaintiff.'[14]

In South Africa, the courts have shown that they are equally ready to grant relief, recognising a general tort, derived in part from American jurisprudence[15], of 'unlawful competition' based upon a 'general sense of justice of the community'[16].

Similarly, in Hong Kong, the courts have been prepared to grant relief to preserve character merchandising rights[17].

Finally, in New Zealand, the courts appear, confusingly, to have issued different signals of intent at different times. In *Tot Toys Ltd v Mitchell*[18], for example, the court rejected a 'character merchandising' complaint, emphasising that a passing off claim requires proof not only that the plaintiff has developed an image of value for promotional purposes and that the defendant has made promotional use of that image in a manner liable to confuse the public into thinking that he or his product has some association with the plaintiff or his product, but also that the plaintiff has suffered damage beyond simply an impairment to his licensed merchandising potential.

On the other hand, in *New Zealand Olympic and Commonwealth Games Association Inc v Telecom New Zealand Ltd*[19], the court recognised that the defendant's unauthorised play, for promotional purposes, on the plaintiff's Olympic symbol[20] could amount to an actionable passing off upon evidence of confusion of the public into believing that the defendant was a sponsor of the plaintiff. Further, in such a case, the court recognised as a sufficient head of damage the impairment of the defendant's own prospects of exploiting the sponsorship market.

THE POSITION IN THE UNITED KINGDOM

The United Kingdom courts have generally lagged behind the more radical developments elsewhere, although some recent developments suggest that they too may now be prepared to adopt a more liberal approach. The problem has not been that the United Kingdom courts have insisted upon applying different principles to cases of passing off (although they have not been prepared to embrace a general tort of wider application). Indeed, in

---

14 See also *Visa International Service Association v Visa Motel* (1984) 1 CPR (3d) 109.
15 See, for example, *Wyatt Earp Enterprises Inc v Sackman Inc* 157 F Supp 621 (SDNY 1958) and *Charles Chaplin v Charles Amador* 93 Cal App 358 (1928).
16 See *Atlas Organic Fertilizers Pty Ltd v Pikkewyn Ghwano Pty Ltd* 1981 (2) SA 173 and *Lorimar Productions Inc v Sterling Clothing Manufacturers* [1982] RPC 395.
17 See *Shaw Bros (Hong Kong) Ltd v Golden Harvest (HK) Ltd* [1972] RPC 559.
18 [1993] 1 NZLR 325.
19 [1996] FSR 757.
20 The symbol comprised the Olympic rings, access to which the plaintiff had licensed to certain of its sponsors and which were found to have attracted valuable goodwill. The defendant had not used the rings themselves, but rather a verbal depiction of them (the word 'ring' repeated three times in a line and again twice in a line underneath).

Lego Systems A/S v Lego M Lemelstrich Ltd[1] relief was granted where an Israeli company began marketing its brightly coloured plastic irrigation equipment in the United Kingdom under the mark 'Lego', the name used by the plaintiff for its brightly coloured plastic miniature building blocks for children. In particular, the fact that the plaintiff operated in a different field of activity from that in which the defendant was involved was not fatal to the claim, as the court found that there was a sufficient recognisable identity (and goodwill) in the plaintiff's name (which was very well known) to give rise to a real risk that the public would be deceived into believing that there was a business connection between the two companies[2].

It can be seen that even in the United Kingdom, there have been decisions which provide support for a plaintiff who complains of unauthorised use of his identity to assist the marketing of products, even where such products are unrelated to his established field of activity. But it must be recognised that the British courts have generally appeared more reluctant than their Commonwealth counterparts to find that the *evidence* is sufficient to establish an actionable passing off, whether in relation to an appropriate *misrepresentation of connection* or as to likely consequent *confusion* or as to the probabilty of *damage*. In particular, they have tended to show a reluctance to find as a fact that the use of the name of a celebrity or fictional character for marketing purposes carries with it an inference that such use has been sanctioned for reward (so as, potentially, to give rise to a misrepresentation of connection liable to confuse the public) or even that such sanctioning is indeed an important feature of the potential earning capacity both of celebrities and the creators of fictional characters etc. (so as, in certain circumstances, to give rise to potential damage to the plaintiff's commercial interests).

The United Kingdom courts' traditional approach can be seen in a number of cases. In *McCulloch v Lewis A May (Produce Distributors) Ltd*[3], a children's entertainer who went by the name of 'Uncle Mac' was unable to prevent use of such a name in connection with a breakfast cereal, such a product existing in a different field of activity from that practised by the plaintiff.

In *Conan Doyle v London Mystery Magazine Ltd*[4], there was held to be no goodwill capable of protection in the name 'Sherlock Holmes'[5].

In *Wombles Ltd v Wombles Skips Ltd*[6], *Tavener Rutledge Ltd v Trexapalm Ltd*[7], and *Lyngstad v Anabas Products*[8], relief was refused in the cases, respectively, of the use of the name 'Wombles' (a well known television cartoon family) in association with rubbish skips, the marketing of a lollipop under the title 'Kojakpops' evoking the lollipop-sucking television policeman 'Kojak', and the sale of pirate T-shirts and other memorabilia depicting the name and image of the pop group 'ABBA'. In each case, the activities in question were

---

1   [1983] FSR 155. The point here was that the name 'Lego' was extremely well known and there was therefore real scope for confusion. See also *LRC International Ltd v Lilla Edets Sales Co Ltd* [1973] RPC 560 ('Marigold' rubber gloves were sufficiently well known to justify an injunction in respect of toilet tissues) and *John Walker & Sons v Rothmans International* [1978] FSR 357 ('Red Label' whisky as against cigarettes).
2   See also, *Annabel's (Berkeley Square) v Schock* [1972] FSR 261.
3   [1947] 2 All ER 845.
4   (1949) 66 RPC 312.
5   Compare the American case of *Lone Ranger Inc v Cox* 124 F 2d 650 (4th Cir 1942).
6   [1975] FSR 488.
7   [1975] FSR 479.
8   [1977] FSR 62.

held not to be actionable, on the grounds that there were insufficient grounds for finding a misrepresentation leading to the kind of confusion necessary for an actionable passing off.

In the later of the above cases, although relief was refused, the need for a common field of activity was not regarded by the courts as a necessary *requirement* for a passing off action. On the other hand, so it was reasoned, the absence of a common field of activity rendered the scope for confusion less likely. To that extent and as a matter of jurisprudence, the courts' approach is not dissimilar to that of some of the Commonwealth courts referred to above.

Where the United Kingdom courts have often diverged from their Commonwealth counterparts is in failing readily to find sufficient *evidence* of any misrepresentation leading to confusion. This may derive from a reluctance to acknowledge that, in the modern age, endorsement and merchandising, or licensing a name or image for merchandising purposes, has become an increasingly important additional source of revenue for sporting celebrities and others with a marketable profile. In *Tavener Rutledge*, Walton J felt able to say[9] that there was no basis yet (in 1974/5) for an assertion that, because of the growth in merchandising business, the creators or other owners of a fictional character should be assumed to have an association with any advertised products which utilised the profile of such fictional character either by licensing or by endorsement.

Equally, in *Lyngstad*, it was remarked that there was no evidence which supported the suggestion that it was customary for pop stars to grant licences for merchandising purposes[10].

Such reasoning sounds less plausible now than perhaps it did at the dates of the decisions in question although it is true that, even in *Tavener Rutledge*, a case concerned with (fictional) 'character marketing', it was recognised that it should more readily be assumed that there might be the requisite confusion in relation to '*personality* marketing', where the name or profile of a real-life individual is concerned. In such a case, it was thought, that members of the public would more readily be likely to assume that the individual had given his sanction to the particular marketing initiative.

It is suggested that, at least in the case of individual celebrities and in appropriate cases even in the case of events and competitions with a high public profile[11], the market has now developed to such an extent that any *clear and unauthorised use*[12] of the name or identity of the person (or event etc) concerned to derive commercial 'pulling power' for third party marketing purposes now *should* be recognised as an actional abuse of goodwill, on the basis that it imports a connection through licensing, endorsement or some

---

9 At 484.
10 [1977] FSR 62. Compare the later Australian case of *Hutchence v South Sea Bubble Co* (1986) 64 ALR 330, above.
11 For example, events such as the Olympic Games, the World, European and FA Cups, the Open Golf Championship, Wimbledon, a Lord's Test Match, the Five Nations Championships, the London Marathon, to name but a few.
12 This kind of use is to be distinguished from the commercial exploitation of opportunities to access a particular market made available by the fact that an event or competition is taking place. This latter type of exploitation does not, of itself, involve any obvious representation of connection.

other form of commercial connection[13]. This is particularly likely to be the case where the celebrity has himself already widened his field of activity to embrace merchandising, licensing or endorsement[14]. In such a case, it might be thought that the scope for confusion should often be presumed. Further, the celebrity (or the owner of the event etc) might expect little difficulty in showing damage to his goodwill or 'pulling power' on the basis that, in the modern world, he may be thought to have endorsed the quality of the 'bootleg' or other goods[15] or that sales thereof might divert customers away from goods with which he does have a commercial association. Even where the celebrity etc has yet to branch out into diverse fields, he may be able legitimately to claim that the activities of the 'bootleggers' nevertheless cause confusion and, importantly, damage to his business interests in that they may diminish his opportunities for expansion into new fields[16].

The position of unauthorised marketing by association with the profile of someone who is fictional[17] is more problematic, as the person seeking to enforce the right to goodwill is inevitably at one stage removed from the profile itself and may have no marketable profile of his own. This was the particular problem addressed in *Tavener Rutledge*. The problem came before the court again, however, in the 'Teenage Mutant Ninja Turtles case', *Mirage Studios v Counter Feat Clothing Co Ltd*[18], in which Browne-Wilkinson VC adopted and approved of much of the reasoning in the Australian cases, *Children's Television Workshop* and *Fido Dido* referred to above. In a significant judgment (albeit only an interlocutory judgment), he recognised in particular the importance of licensed marketing in today's commercial world, when he said:

> 'In my judgment the law as developed in Australia is sound. There is no reason why a remedy in passing off should be limited to those who market or sell the goods themselves. If the public is mislead in a relevant way ... that is sufficient to found a cause of action in passing off brought by those people with whom the public associate that feature or that quality which has been misrepresented.[19]'

CONCLUSION

It might have been thought that Browne-Wilkinson VC's judgment (in *Mirage Studios v Counter Feat Clothing Co Ltd*[20]) was a sign of things to come.

---

13 Although see *Stringfellow v McCain Foods (GB) Ltd* [1984] RPC 501, in which, admittedly still in 1984, the court maintained a reluctance to make the necessary finding of confusion. See also *Merchandising Corpn of America v Harpbond Inc* [1983] FSR 32 and the case of 'The Beatles', *Harrison and Starkey v Polydor Ltd* [1977] FSR 1. In particular, see the 'Elvis Presley' case, *Re Applications by Elvis Presley Enterprises Inc* (1997) Times, 25 March, Laddie J, discussed below.
14 See for example, *News Group Newspapers v Rocket Record Co* [1981] FSR 89.
15 This was the assumption drawn, in the context of a defamation claim, as long ago as 1931, when, in *Tolley v JS Fry & Sons* [1931] AC 333 an advertisement for chocolate featuring a caricature of a well known amateur sportsman was held to carry an implicit suggestion that he had been paid to endorse the advertised product (thereby compromising his amateur status).
16 See, for example, *IPC Magazines Ltd v Black and White Music Corpn* [1983] FSR 348 and *News Group Newspapers v Rocket Record Co* [1981] FSR 89.
17 In the sporting context, this may apply to a mascot or other character generally associated with a particular event (eg 'World Cup Willy').
18 [1991] FSR 145.
19 See also *IPC Magazines Ltd v Black and White Music Corpn* [1983] FSR 348.
20 [1991] FSR 145.

In that event, the United Kingdom courts' traditional reluctance to recognise the true ambit of the marketing potential of the identity of sports and other celebrities might now be expected to give way to an increasing recognition that such an identity is indeed an asset capable of commercial exploitation across a wide range of different fields, extending well beyond the particular field in which the identity first secured its particular profile or reputation. In particular, one would have expected the courts more readily to recognise the importance of *licensing* and *endorsement* when asked to constrain the unauthorised activities of third parties intent upon cashing in on the profiles of such celebrities.

The Australian cases and their approval by Browne-Wilkinson VC certainly do provide some suggestion that well known sporting figures (and the proprietors of sporting events and competitions) with a distinct profile and a particular commercial 'pulling power', may now find it easier than hitherto to deter and constrain the activities of third party operators who seek to cash in on such pulling power by suggesting some connection which does not in fact exist. But it is clear that *Mirage Studios v Counter Feat Clothing Co Ltd*[1] should not be regarded as having, at one stroke, swept away the principles established by earlier cases and to have introduced a new form of passing off. This much was made quite clear in another interlocutory decision, *Nice and Safe Attitude Ltd v Piers Flook (trading as 'Slaam! Clothing Company')*[2], in which Robert Walker J re-emphasised that the three ingredients of passing off remained *goodwill*[3], a *misrepresentation leading to deception* and *damage*. Further, in analysing those ingredients, he made it clear that cases such as *Lego System A/S v Lego M Lemelstrich Ltd*[4], whilst they may have relaxed the importance of the concept of a 'common field of activity', had not consigned it to history. As he said:

'It must still be very relevant to the likelihood of deception'.

Finally, in *Re Applications by Elvis Presley Enterprises* [5], a case primarily concerned with the effect of registered trade marks in the names 'Elvis' and 'Elvis Presley' and in a signature 'Elvis A Presley', Laddie J took the opportunity briefly to review the position in English law of character/personality merchandising. In a decision in which the court appears to have taken a step back from the position presaged by the 'Teenage Mutant Ninja Turtles case', he firmly rejected the notion that people who purchased Elvis Presley memorabilia did so upon the assumption that it came from an 'official' source. In his view, the court should generally assume that, in the absence of special circumstances, the public are unconcerned as to whether or not personality memorabilia derives from a source with the authorised imprimatur of the personality in question and that a name attached to particular goods is generally seen simply as an indication of subject matter rather than of source.

1 [1991] FSR 145.
2 [1997] FSR 14.
3 He preferred the use of the word 'goodwill' over the word 'reputation', making the point that a reputation which is devoid of commercial pulling power will not suffice. See, for example, *Athletes Foot Marketing Associates Inc v Cobra Sports Ltd* [1980] RPC 343.
4 [1983] FSR 155.
5 Chancery Division, reported briefly in: (1997) Times, 25 March.

Merchandising by licence

Most sporting personalities and other entities will not be equipped to mount their own merchandising operations themselves. Equally, many will not wish to be diverted from their mainstream sporting activity. In such cases, any exploitation of their commercial pulling power in the field of merchandising is likely to come through the grant of specific licences to third parties, permitting them to 'borrow' the identity and pulling power of the sporting celebrity in order to promote their own commercial activities. In launching such an initiative and in particular when entering into contractual licensing arrangements, there are various potential pitfalls which should be addressed. These may be considered by reference to particular terms which may be included in the contract:

- *Intellectual property*[6]:
  As has already been mentioned, items of intellectual property are the most important means of establishing and cementing identity. They also serve to provide recognisable proprietary rights which may be enforced by the courts. They are likely to play an important role in any merchandising operation. It follows that, where the celebrity or other sporting body owns particular items of intellectual property, the licence should certainly identify them, specify the rights of access thereto which are granted to the licensee, and require the licensee (and licensor) to preserve and protect them.

- *The nature of the licensee's rights and obligations*:
  The contract should make it clear whether it purports simply to grant to the licensor a *right* to use the licensor's profile in his merchandising operation or whether it extends an *obligation* upon him to do so. In so far as a specific obligation is imposed to produce and market goods, then the extent of that obligation should be clearly defined. In particular the range of goods covered by the licence should be spelt out. In any event, the licensor will wish to insert terms designed to procure an acceptable level of quality for all goods marketed, whether pursuant to an obligation or simply in accordance with a right. In particular the licensee should specifically undertake that all goods will be of satisfactory quality and fit for their intended purpose(s), and that he will ensure compliance with all relevant legislation relating to design, quality and safety. It may be that, in certain circumstances, a particular specification will be laid down. In other circumstances, a process for securing the licensor's approval of samples (including any packaging etc) may be appropriate before the licensee may release any particular goods onto the market.

- *Ownership and protection of goodwill*:
  In the absence of clear contractual provision, problems may well arise as to the true ownership of any goodwill generated by the merchandising efforts of the licensee in accordance with his licence. As the merchandising effort is intended to be launched on the back of the profile of the licensor, it is suggested that the contract should specify that any goodwill generated thereby (and any intellectual property which might be created in the process) should be regarded as belonging to the licensor and as being subject to the terms of the licence. In this way, the merchandising

6 For a summary of what is meant by 'intellectual property', see Chapter 9 above.

drive will at the same time serve the purposes both of feeding off and itself feeding the profile of the licensor.

– *Protection from third party activity*:
With the licensor retaining 'ownership' of his own goodwill or commercial 'pulling power', including that generated by the licensed merchandising operation itself, any legal action in respect of third party encroachment will need to be taken by the licensor. He should therefore require that the licensee should co-operate with him by, in particular, bringing to his attention any suspect or threatened activity and otherwise as the licensor might reasonably require. In the case of an exclusive licence in particular, the licensee may need to agree to lend his name to any legal action.

– *Exclusivity and incompatible activity*:
Manifestly any licensee will seek to secure either total exclusivity of access to the licensor's profile or, at the very least, exclusivity within his identified market, whether such market be identified by geographical sectors or by categorisation of products. The extent of any intended exclusivity (or the absence thereof) should be clearly spelled out. Exclusivity may operate both ways, however. It may be, for example, that the licensor will wish to constrain his licensees' activities in feeding the image of other sporting celebrities etc. If so, again, the contract should so specify. What is more, the licensor may wish to impose wider constraints of more general application, perhaps by procuring an undertaking that the licensee will not engage in any activity liable to damage the business or image of the licensor or to render him liable to disciplinary or contractual action at the suit of any relevant sporting authority or, in the case of an individual sports star, his employers. Further, particularly in the case of an individual celebrity licensor, the licensee's interests may require that the licensor should not contravene the rules of appropriate governing bodies and should not act in a manner liable to damage the image of the licensee. Equally, if it is intended that the licence should be personal to the licensee and that he should not be able to grant sub-licences to others, express provision to that effect should be made.

– *Methods of sale*:
If the licensor wishes to ensure that the goods to be marketed under the licence are sold through specific retail outlets[7], the contract should say so. Equally, it may be that, for example in the case of a football or other sports club, the licensor will have its own outlets (at its ground and elsewhere and perhaps even by mail order) from which it will wish to offer licensed merchandise for sale. In such a case the contract should include provision appropriate to secure supplies in such quantities and at such prices as may be appropriate.

– *Prices and quality control*:
The extent to which the licensor is involved in the setting or sanctioning of prices and quality control needs to be specified.

---

7 Conversely, the licensor may wish the goods not to be marketed by certain means, such as through street vendors etc.

– *Payment*:
A licensor may stipulate any number of methods for payment of the consideration for the grant of the licence. One method may be a once and for all lump sum payment, with or without provision for royalties. Alternatively, royalties alone may be payable, in which case it might be thought appropriate to include a provision for a guaranteed minimum payment or 'floor' in respect of a defined period or periods. Any contract which makes provision for royalty payments or payments according to quantities of sales achieved will require to include a mechanism for monitoring sales and triggering payments. In addition, provision for some form of audit procedure would generally be prudent.

– *Allocation of risk and insurance*:
Traditionally, the licensor will seek to obtain an indemnity from the licensee in respect of all liabilities arising from the nature use or quality of any goods produced pursuant to the licence and indeed from any failures to comply with obligations imposed by law or the terms of the licence itself. In particular, the licensor will wish to pass on to the licensee any liability which he might incur to third parties for example, in the case of sales by the licensor, under the Sale of Goods Act 1979[8], the Consumer Protection Act 1987[9] or through an argument that his 'endorsement' of the product gives rise to a liability at least in respect of specific attributes covered by the endorsement[10]. It is suggested that the contract should accordingly include provisions which:

(a)   allocate all such risks of liability to the licensee;
(b)   require the licensee to take out appropriate insurance cover;
(c)   give to the licensor an express indemnity from the licensor in respect of all such liability.

– *Recognition of licence*:
In order that, in the minds of the public, the merchandising operation serves to cement and increase the profile of the licensor, the contract should make provision that all goods manufactured should display some acknowledgment of the fact that they are made under licence from the licensor. In this way, in the event of any unauthorised third party activity in the form of 'bootlegging' etc, the task of establishing the licensor's proprietary rights, and especially the necessary confusion leading to potential damage will be made easier. Equally, a clear signal to purchasers that the licensor is not himself the manufacturer may assist in resisting any liability under the Consumer Protection Act 1987.

– *Duration and termination*:
The contract will normally be for a specific period. Alternatively it may be terminable by notice, in which case the length of the notice should be

8   Under this Act, a contract for the sale of goods imports certain terms, the most important of which is (by s 14) that the goods are of merchantable quality, namely that they are reasonably fit for their intended purpose.
9   Under this Act, liability for a defective product may attach to anyone who holds himself out as a 'producer', by putting his name on a product or by using a trade mark or other distinguishing mark in relation to the product.
10   The argument might be founded upon a form of collateral contract or warranty. See, for example, *Shanklin Pier Ltd v Detel Products Ltd* [1951] 2 KB 854, *Andrews v Hopkinson* [1957] 1 QB 229, *Wells (Merstham) Ltd v Buckland Sand and Silica Co Ltd* [1965] 2 QB 170 and *Lexmead v Lewis* [1982] AC 225.

specified together with the means of giving it. In addition, there will normally need to be provision for early termination in the event of particular breaches of contract. Certain breaches may be regarded as sufficiently serious as to bring the contract automatically to an end. In other, less serious situations, it might be thought sensible to provide for the licensor to serve a default notice which would bring the contract to an end only if such notice were not complied with (by remedying the breach) within a specified period. Other events which might trigger immediate termination would include the licensee becoming insolvent or ceding control to some third party or third parties.

– *Post termination obligations and restrictions*:
  In the event of termination, whether for cause or upon expiry, provision may need to be made for the sensible disposal (eg by continuing sales by the licensee) or the handing over to the licensor of surplus stocks, together with the taking of any final accounts. Further, the licensee should undertake not to use the licensor's name, profile or identity after the license has come to an end and to hand over to him any items of property belonging to him and all copyright material or other material produced in the course and for the purposes of the merchandising operations under the licence.

COMPETITION LAW

Finally, as with all commercial contracts, the implications of competition law should be considered when entering into a merchandise licensing agreement. For an outline of relevant provisions of competition law, reference should be made to Chapter 4, but for present purposes the following particular points should be noted:

– Under the Restrictive Trade Practices Act 1976, where two or more parties to the agreement carry on business in the United Kingdom either in the manufacture of goods (the licensee) or the supply of goods (the licensor and the licensee) or in the provision of services (the licensor and, possibly, the licensee), then the agreement ought to be registered if it includes relevant restrictions accepted by at least two parties. The relevant restrictions are set out in sections 6 (goods) and 11 (services) and are wide ranging. They include broad restrictions as to prices, terms and conditions, quantities, manufacturing processes and particular markets. By sections 9 and 18, however, no account is taken of restrictions which relate solely to the goods or services the subject of the agreement itself so that it may be said that the Act is concerned with restrictions on the parties' general freedom to trade rather than the manner in which their own trading relationship is conducted. The same sections also exclude restrictions designed to secure compliance with approved standards of quality or design. Further, Schedule 3 provides a list of exemptions which includes agreements for exclusive dealing, trade mark registered user agreements, patent and registered design licences and assignments, licences and assignments of unregistered design rights and copyright licences and assignments (ie intellectual property licences). The effect of falling within any such exemption is that the agreement will not be registrable provided that it only contains the limited restrictions identified in the Schedule and no other relevant restriction. Although many ordinary licence agreements will not be caught by the Act or will be subject to an exemption, the Act should not be ignored, because any failure to register a registrable agreement has the effect of rendering all relevant restrictions therein void.

– The Competition Act 1980 is unlikely to affect most merchandising licence agreements as it is not concerned with businesses with a turnover of less than £10 million or with a market share of less than 25%[11]. In the case of a business which does qualify, the Act is concerned with 'anti competitive practices', namely a *course of conduct* liable to *restrict, distort or prevent competition*[12]. The regime laid down by the Act is unwieldy. It does not render particular agreements unlawful or void, but simply provides for them to be investigated by the Director General of Fair Trading and for possible referral to the Monopolies and Mergers Commission for a determination as to the public interest, as a result of which the Secretary of State may order the 'course of conduct' to cease, or impose terms.

– In European law, under the Treaty of Rome, agreements or practices which are liable either:

(a)   to *prevent, restrict or distort competition* (Article 85); or
(b)   to amount to an *abuse of a dominant position* (Article 86)

are unlawful in so far as they may *affect trade between member states*. Most merchandising licence agreements will not be likely significantly to affect such trade (or will come within the de minimis provisions). The Commission has determined, however, that individual celebrities who seek to exploit their popularity and profiles internationally are potentially subject to the regime of European competition law[13]. Further, any merchandising operation which sets up a web of separate production or distribution contracts, each with exclusivity within a particular area within the European Community and with corresponding prohibitions against straying further afield, may well give rise to a sufficient insulation of individual markets as to fall foul of Article 85[14]. Similarly, the use of logos and other marks or items of intellectual property in order to support a partitioning of the European market[15], or the designation of goods as 'official' so as to suggest endorsement and, therefore, superior quality[16], have all been identified as practices which may, in appropriate circumstances, give rise to potential breaches of European competition law.

For a more detailed examination of the requirements and implications of European law, see the Chapter 4.

---

11 See the Anti-Competitive Practices (Exclusions)(Amendment) Order 1994, SI 1994/1557.
12 See s 2(1).
13 Re *RAI/UNITEL* [1978] 3 CMLR 306.
14 See, for example, *Re Davidson Rubber Co Agreements* [1972] CMLR D52 and *Re Vaessen/Moris* [1979] 1 CMLR 511.
15 See, for example, *Dunlop Slazenger International Ltd v EC Commission*: T-43/92 [1994] ECR II-441.
16 See, for example, the 'tennis ball' cases, *Tretorn* 1994 OJ L 378/45, *Danish Tennis Federation* [1996] OJ C138/7 and *Dunlop Slazenger International Ltd v EC Commission*: T-43/92 [1994] ECR II-441.

Chapter 12

Sponsorship

The partnership between sport and commerce

Sponsorship of sport has for some time been on the increase. Commercial opportunities for the sponsorship of sport have increased in recent times to the point that such sponsorship has now become big business. In 1996 it has been estimated that the total sports sponsorship market in the United Kingdom was in the region of £350 million. The Barcelona Olympics of 1992 are said to have been sponsored to the tune of about $700 million. In the United States of America, Michael Jordan's earnings from promotional activities have been estimated at approximately $40 million per annum. Of course, sponsorship or patronage schemes may always exist where the object of the 'sponsor' is genuinely philanthropic and where the sponsor seeks to derive no particular benefit for himself and is motivated simply by a desire to procure success for his particular beneficiary. Such sponsors are inevitably rare and, without question, most sponsors expect a return of some kind for their money and see the relationships created by their sponsorship as business relationships.

That sponsorship is now big business is true both for sport itself, to which substantial revenue may be available from its sponsors[1], and also for the sponsors, to whom substantial and valuable marketing opportunites are available through their chosen association with sport. For example, a sponsor may benefit directly, simply by means of that association. Equally, sponsors increasingly recognise the extent of the potential benefits available to them indirectly, through television and other media exposure and through access to and exploitation of intellectual property rights connected with the sport, event, competition or competitors concerned.

In addition to the interests of the parties involved in a sponsorship relationship, the general public also has an interest in seeing that the sponsorship 'industry' flourishes because, realistically, the partnership between sport and commerce which is at the heart of such industry is an essential feature of the drive to maximise the development of sporting achievement in the United Kingdom. The power of sport to engender a 'feel-good factor', for example through the success of national teams or competitors in international competition, and the importance of that power,

---

1 The importance of sponsorship is well illustrated by the financial difficulties being experienced at the time of writing by the British Athletic Federation due, in part, to a substantial drop in its annual sponsorship revenue.

should not be under estimated. It is a matter of record, for example, that the rate of industrial production in Britain immediately after England won the World Cup in 1966 rose dramatically.

Tobacco sponsorship

Certain sectors of industry have been especially attracted to the benefits of sponsorship, few more so than tobacco companies, who currently provide in excess of £9 million each year across a wide range of activities from the mainstream sports such as cricket, rugby league, tennis and football to minority and other 'fringe' sports such as gliding, lacrosse, bobsleighing and even shove-halfpenny. The tobacco industry recognised the concerns expressed by particular sections of government and certain pressure groups which, in some countries, resulted in sponsorship and other promotional activities by tobacco companies being banned. As a result, for some years the tobacco industry, acting through the Tobacco Manufacturers' Association, have agreed to accept certain voluntary retraints on its sponsorship and related activities. Those restraints and guidelines are currently contained in a voluntary agreement between the Association and the Minister for Sport, dated 31 January 1995. They include restrictions on the use of promotional material, a cap on expenditure on the promotion of sponsored events away from the venue, a general cap on expenditure to keep company expenditure to 1985 levels (indexed for inflation) and prohibitions on sponsoring youth sports or sports whose audience is predominantly under 18. The operation of the agreement is monitored by COMATAS, the Committee for Monitoring Agreements on Tobacco Advertising and Sponsorship, which reports annually to the Secretary of State for Health.

Sponsorship of television programmes by tobacco companies is effectively already banned, as a result of the regulatory regime established by the Broadcasting Acts 1990 and 1996 and the Independent Television Commission's Code of Programme Sponsorship to which all relevant broadcasters are obliged to adhere[2]. Such a ban is, in any event, required by 19 December 1998 pursuant to the Television without Frontiers Directive[3]. In addition, at the time of writing, the Labour government has announced its intention to ban all advertising and sponsorship by tobacco companies. Whilst it is likely that any such ban will be phased in over an extended period and that time will be afforded to the recipients of tobacco sponsorship to enable them to target alternative sources of sponsorship, it is inevitable that certain sports will be hard hit. In particular, sports such as snooker, cricket, darts, angling and motor sport are currently particularly well served for sponsorship by the tobacco industry and it is hard to predict how the sudden loss of such an important revenue source will easily be replaced. A number of sports may well find the transition a turbulent experience. The more mobile sports, such as motor sport, have spoken of substantially relocating away from Europe in response to this announcement and similar developments elsewhere.

---

2   The regulatory regime, the ITC's role within it and the contents of this and other Codes of Practice issued by the ITC are discussed in detail in Chapter 13.
3   Council Directive 89/552/EEC, amended by 97/39/EC. See in particular Articles 17(2) and 27(1).

The nature of sponsorship

As with any business arrangement, certain disciplines and understandings are required if the partnership between sport and commerce is to prosper. Much of this discipline and understanding may be facilitated by a proper identification and definition of the contractual relationship or relationships involved in and affected by the particular sponsorship arrangement. As there is no established jurisprudence attaching specifically to the field of sponsorship, the legal issues are determined by the application of ordinary contractual principles. This work does not attempt to identify and examine the whole range of such principles, there being a range of other treatises on the subject, to which the reader is referred as necessary. This section is more concerned with practical matters and seeks to examine the nature and implications of a sponsorship relationship and to highlight the processes which need to be addressed in order to make such a relationship succeed.

Of course, there are many types of sports sponsorship. The list of persons, events, occasions, competitions or locations which are or might be amenable to sponsorship is potentially endless. They are referred to herein generally as 'sponsored subjects'. In addition to individual sports stars, other categories of sponsored subject range from a one off event such as a marathon or a boxing promotion, to a competition or league extending over a period of time and comprising a number of individual events or matches, or to an individual team or a particular stadium, venue or piece of equipment. The different varieties of sponsored subject are beyond enumeration or definition because, wherever sport (whatever that may mean) is played, there is the potential for sponsorship in one guise or another. Further, each variety of sponsored subject, and often each example within each variety, is liable to throw up its own particular quirks and problems. For example, the sponsorship of an event which takes place exclusively within a private stadium is likely to be more easily controlled than one which uses, say, the public highway (such as the London Marathon or the Tour de France) or the open seas (such as a round the world yacht race or a more modest regatta).

Common to virtually all sponsorship contracts is the provision of money by the sponsor to be used to further a sporting purpose. Further, the precise nature of any particular arrangement will depend in part upon the basic needs of the sponsor and the spondee (viz: the sponsored subject or the owner thereof) and the size of the fund which the sponsor is prepared to make available. In general terms, most sponsorship deals may be categorised broadly as arrangements which grant money:

(a) to an individual or individuals in order to further that individual's or those individuals' sporting ambitions, either generally for a period or in relation to a particular championship or event; or

(b) to promote or facilitate a particular sporting event, competition or venue; or

(c) to an organisation such as a sporting body or club to help fund its activities, whether through the provision of specific assets or equipment, the financing of the recruitment and remuneration of players and other staff or simply generally; or

(d) to a local authority, school or other organisation in order to provide or maintain facilities for the community or part of it; or (in recent times)

(e) to a broadcaster or production company, to assist in funding the televising/filming of particular sports events.

Whatever the category of sponsorship, the obligations and rights of the parties, together with any appropriate safeguards, will be determined by the terms of their agreement. It is no more than common sense, to say that the parties to a sponsorship arrangement ought sensibly to focus at the outset upon precisely what the arrangement is intended to achieve and how best they wish to seek to achieve it. This will involve identifying particular rights and obligations. It may also require particular limitations and other safeguards to be provided for.

It should be remembered that sponsorship is but one form of marketing and seeks, in common with other marketing initiatives, to harness the 'identity' 'image' or 'profile' of a sporting individual, event or competition and to borrow his/its goodwill or 'commercial pulling power' in order to generate sales of the sponsor's products, which may comprise goods or services and may have little to do with the sporting context of the sponsorship arrangement itself. In setting up a sponsorship arrangement, the terms agreed ought sensibly to address the two 'marketing imperatives' identified above in Chapter 10 above. Thus many of the contract terms will be determined by the need to:

(a) establish a specific 'identity' giving rise to a definable goodwill ('pulling power') which is immediately identifiable as attaching to the sponsored subject;

(b) make provision to guard against the unauthorised 'abuse' of that same goodwill by third parties.

The sponsorship contract

Any sponsorship arrangement (other than, perhaps, one which is genuinely and entirely philanthropic and which would more probably be described as 'patronage') will involve a contractual relationship. For present purposes, a contract may be regarded as arising where two or more persons take on reciprocal obligations for good consideration with the intention that such obligations should be legally binding. Whilst no particular formality is required for a sponsorship contract, its implications and potential complications are such that a formal written contract is advised wherever possible. After all, the rights and obligations of the parties will be both identified and limited by the terms agreed between them and it makes sense for such terms to be clearly articulated in a written document. The more complicated the sponsorship relationship, the more important it is that the terms are carefully thought out and defined at the outset.

The aims of sponsorship

The power of particular sporting activities to attract substantial sums in the form of sponsorship has increased dramatically in recent years. Sponsorship involves marketing by association and, after a slow start, major companies have fast come to appreciate the marketing power for their products of a publicised and sensibly exploited association with sport. Similarly, it is only recently that sport itself has come to appreciate the strength of its goodwill or 'commercial pulling power'. The British public loves its sport and spends significant amounts of its leisure time participating in, watching and otherwise following sport in one form or another. Sport has been recognised as providing ready access to attentive audiences of different descriptions varying only according to the profiles of those most interested in either sport in general or specific sports, competitions or tournaments in particular. Sports sponsorship involves using sport as a vehicle for corporate or 'brand' advertising, by making use of such captive audiences in order to boost the public's awareness of the sponsor's corporate identity and, in particular, its brand(s). Furthermore, the proliferation and increasing quality of television coverage of sporting events has served to assist the acceleration in the influx of sponsorship monies, particularly into the more popular sports and their flagship events and competitions. It has been estimated that between 1989 and 1996, money spent on sports sponsorship of one form or another in the United Kingdom increased by over 45% to reach a figure of about £350 million. Even this figure pales into insignificance by comparison with the market in the United States of America where sports sponsorship spending is said to have approached $2.5 billion in 1993 alone.

For all types of commercial sponsorship, the general aims of sponsor and spondee are likely to be similar. For the sponsor, the ultimate aim is usually to provide (good) publicity by association with the sponsored subject, with a view to using such publicity to boost his profile and thereby to increase his sales. For the spondee, his aims may be more complex. In the case of an individual sponsored sports star, the aim may often simply be to provide an extra source of income to supplement that derived from competing. In the case of other types of sponsored subject, such as a competition, event or location, the aim will often be to use the sponsor's money to help ensure the 'success' of the sponsored subject by whatever means such 'success' may be measured. These days many sporting events are simply not viable without sponsorship money. As already indicated, the aims of both sponsor and spondee ought to be able broadly to co-exist and to complement each other. It follows that achievement of the spondee's aim will often itself assist the pursuit of the commercial aims of the sponsor. Further, this harmony of interest as between sponsor and spondee is unlikely to be threatened in the more parochial of sponsorship relationships, involving simply the two parties with little significant potential for incompatible or conflicting third party activity. In such a case, the negotiations ought to be straightforward and to focus simply upon the obvious interests of the two parties.

Conflicts of interest – regulating the web

A sporting event or competition is often likely to involve a large number of relationships, including perhaps many different, often competing, interests. It is this web of relationships and interests which gives rise to the greatest potential for disharmony and conflict. It is important therefore to identify the extent of such web at the outset. Only then (if at all) will it be possible to take steps towards regulating this web of diverse interests by seeking, where possible, to put in place sensible and clear contractual arrangements in order to reduce the potential for conflict by restricting the opportunities for the unnecessary introduction of undesirable interests and/or by accommodating such interests in a controlled and regulated manner where (as, to some extent, will almost invariably be the case) their introduction cannot be avoided.

The extent of the web

In seeking to identify the true extent of this web of relationships and diverse interests in any particular sporting event, competition, team or individual sports star, the starting point should be the structure or 'pyramid' of organisation within the sport and/or event etc itself. Such an organisational pyramid may itself embrace many different bodies, each with its own particular function and interests at different levels within it. For example, an international sports federation may organise a particular competition, but may delegate responsibility for running an individual event to an organising committee which might be, for example, an affiliated national body. In such an example, both the international federation and the national body are likely to have an interest in the package of benefits associated with the event or competition, in which potential sponsors are likely also to be interested. Further, the pyramid of a sport with mass appeal, such as football or athletics, may involve any number of bodies, many or all of which may have some involvement in a particular tournament or competition looking for sponsorship and most of which will themselves be looking to maximise not simply their sporting, but also their financial, return from their participation. The pyramid of many such sports builds from foundations comprising the individual players/competitors themselves and moves upwards through clubs, leagues (of which there may be different tiers, each with its own rules and interests) and other competition organisers and on to one or more levels of regional associations and thence onwards to national and/or continental organisations, leading finally to one (or more – boxing is a good example) world international federation. Each individual or other body thus involved in or linked to the organisation of or participation in a particular sport or sponsored subject is likely to have his/its own commercial interests and may even have or seek his/its own individual sponsor. Each such individual or body, therefore, provides potential for conflict with the interests of the sponsored subject itself and its sponsor. Further, this may apply at whichever level within the pyramid of organisation the particular sponsorship is directed. Thus, the sponsor of an individual sportsperson will be as concerned with the potential for conflict from others elsewhere in the pyramid as will the sponsor of, say, an international championship organised by or through a world federation. The nature of the problem for each level within the pyramid is the same, although the perspectives for viewing such problem may vary from level to level.

Of course, it is not simply within such pyramids of organisation where parties with an interest in the sponsored subject are liable to be found and where, accordingly, potential for conflict may exist. Individuals or other bodies within the pyramid may, in pursuit of their own commercial interests, introduce outsiders to the pyramid and confer on such outsiders an interest in a particular sponsored subject, very much in the same way that the sponsor himself is introduced and gains his interest. It is this combination between (a) bodies within the pyramid and (b) third parties with outside interests which comprises the overall web of relationships and interests referred to above, and which it is important to identify, regulate and control to the extent practicable, if the orderly conduct of a sponsorship relationship is to be achieved. Indeed, it is through the introduction to the sport's organisational pyramid of outside commercial interests (such as sponsorship itself) that the greatest scope for conflict between competing interests is unleashed. For example, where one sponsor fails to secure exclusive sponsorship rights to a sponsored subject, opportunities for conflict may arise directly via additional sponsorship of the very same subject, although the avoidance of any potential for quite such obvious conflict will surely and readily be capable of negotiation. Equally, there may often be different sponsorship opportunities arising at different levels within the pyramid – different individuals or other bodies involved in organising or competing in an event may seek to introduce to the pyramid their own separate sponsorships, not all of which will necessarily happily co-exist. Thus the interests of the sponsor of an FA Premier League football club may be challenged when one of its players secures or seeks to secure his own personal sponsorship deal. Alternatively, different clubs within the League may secure sponsorship from competing companies or from companies in competition with the sponsor of the League itself, or of the competitions organised by the FA, UEFA or FIFA. In cricket, for example, there has existed in recent times the enticing possibility of England (Tetley Bitter) playing the West Indies (Red Stripe) at the (Fosters) Oval. Hypothetically, such a match might itself attract sponsorship from, say, Courage as might the television broadcasts from Bass. In addition, other connected events or facilities, such as the provision of catering, stands, large screens or other spectator facilities to enhance a particular subject may also each attract their own sponsorships. The potential for such conflicts simply through sponsorship deals alone, if allowed to go unchecked, is endless.

But it is not only through the introduction to a sport's organisational pyramid of individually negotiated sponsorship deals that potential for conflict arises. There are many other examples of third party outside interests being introduced to the pyramid and thereby giving rise to potential conflicts with particular sponsorship interests. The potential for such conflict through broadcast sponsorship has already been mentioned. Broadcasting provides an important opening for third party interests to access the goodwill of a sporting event. Most broadcasters are themselves in a position to introduce conflicting interests, for example through the sale of advertising slots both during and adjacent to the broadcast coverage itself. Such slots may well be deliberately targeted by an event sponsor's competitors or may coincidentally be purchased by incompatible interests. One example of just such a clash of interests arose in Canada when Coca-Cola sponsored the National Hockey League's Stanley Cup Play-Off matches (arguably the most popular event in Canada's sporting calendar) and thereby also became the 'official soft drink' of the competition, whereas Pepsi Cola was able to secure exclusive soft drink advertising during broadcasts of the matches, through an arrangement with Molson who had secured the broadcasting rights[4].

Other advertising opportunities may be made available to outsiders, through the letting of space on perimeter boards, hoardings or screens at particular stadia or other competition venues or on adjacent sites.

Equally, the organisers of an event may appoint particular companies as 'official suppliers' to the event, whether of kit or equipment which is used in the event itself or even of other items not obviously associated with the sport (as where there is, say, an 'official' soft drink, film, credit card, computer or other product which is marketed by association with the sponsored subject.)

4   See *National Hockey League v Pepsi-Cola Canada* (1993) 102 DLR (4th) 80 affirming (1992) 92 DLR (4th) 349.

Other levels within the pyramid, may also seek to appoint their own official suppliers, thereby widening the web yet further and increasing the potential for conflict.

It follows that the web of interested parties who may introduce conflicting interests may extend far beyond the pyramids of organisation within the sport itself, and include all kinds of outside bodies attracted to the goodwill or 'commercial pulling power' of the sport or the sponsored subject in order to exploit their own commercial interests.

Unless carefully thought out and controlled wherever possible at the outset, the sort of conflicts described above can have implications beyond simply impairing the impact of the message intended by the sponsor's association with the sponsored subject and, perhaps, causing confusion. In addition, for example, such conflicts may result in damage to the sponsored subject and also to the sport itself and the other entities within its pyramid. Thus, for example, it was just such conflict which initially prevented the appearance of a Pepsi Cola sponsored basketball superstar, Shaquille O'Neal, in the 1994 World Championships in Toronto because his team was sponsored by Coca Cola. This led to the kind of publicity which is unlikely to have been welcomed by any of the parties involved. Many of the same parties were involved in 1996, when Coca Cola withdrew its $1 million per annum sponsorship of the Los Angeles Lakers basketball team because of its star player's continued promotion of Pepsi Cola.

The message must surely be that where there is scope for a potential sponsor's interests to be damaged by the exploitation of opportunities associated with his own particular sponsored subject, he would be especially well advised to try to curtail the availability of such opportunities or at least to preclude or inhibit their exploitation by his competitors. Further, the potential for and consequences of intrusion by conflicting third party interests should be addressed and provided for to the extent possible at the very outset in order to prevent the need for subsequent 'fire fighting' when problems arise which had not been addressed in the relevant contractual terms.

How to regulate the web

Wherever practicable, and to the extent possible, it makes sense to address such difficulties compendiously so that the web of interested parties is regulated so far as possible by a series of interconnecting contracts, each providing for rights and obligations which correspond with and accommodate each other and which, taken together, form a hierarchical structure in which the positions in the hierarchy of the parties involved, in terms of the relative primacy of their particular rights and obligations, is clearly understood[5]. It must be recognised, however, that most sponsorship deals are struck at a time when individual bodies within the sporting pyramid to which the sponsor is being introduced already have their commercial arrangements in place and that, accordingly, certain types of potential conflict are likely to be unavoidable. The extent to which this may be so still

5   As discussed below, a weather eye needs to be kept open on the rigours of those aspects of competition law and the restraint of trade doctrine, which are designed to prohibit measures calculated to inhibit fair competition.

requires to be identified and examined so that, for example, particular damage limitation measures may be put into place as appropriate.

The avoidance or mitigation of conflict may sometimes be capable of being achieved to a greater or lesser extent by ensuring that the more important parties with a legitimate association with the sponsored subject are bound together by an umbrella contract to which they are all party. Where this is not practicable, individual contracts may usefully incorporate express terms which require their parties to make the grant of other rights to third parties subject to particular stipulations designed to give appropriate protection to relevant interests. By such means, incompatible or undesirable activity by parties within the web is more easily curtailed. In addition, the opportunities for bodies with no contractual link to the organisational pyramid, and thus who remain outside the web, to seek nevertheless to use the sponsored subject(s) in an unauthorised and gratuitous manner to secure therefrom a marketing or other advantage may be restricted.

Particular terms of a sponsorship agreement

Ultimately, the terms of a sponsorship agreement, as with any contract, are a matter for negotiation and agreement between the contracting parties. Further, the course of the negotiations will depend in part upon the respective bargaining power of the parties, both as between themselves and within the web of all the other interested parties. The circumstances of particular sponsorship opportunities are so diverse that it would be quite impossible for any work to provide for every situation. There are, however, a number of general issues which may well require to be covered, depending upon the nature of the sponsorship involved. Some of them will be considered in the following paragraphs.

A. THE PARTIES

As has been seen above, many sponsorship contracts exist in the middle of a web of other relationships. Any number of other parties may have a relationship with the sponsored subject, from broadcasters to providers of particular facilities or services, or to merchandisers and other companies with a particular accreditation. The involvement of many of such other parties with the sponsored subject may, actually or potentially, be via a contractual relationship with the sponsor's own spondee and yet may nevertheless introduce interests which, unless carefully regulated, may conflict with those of the sponsor.

Under the doctrine of privity of contract, only the parties to a contract may sue or be sued under its terms. Careful consideration should therefore be given at the outset to the persons who appropriately should be party to the sponsorship contract.

Where it is not possible to bring all interested parties under the one umbrella contract, consideration should be given to requiring the contracting parties, in one form or another, to do all they can to secure that the sponsorship the subject of the contract is able peacefully to co-exist with the interests and activities of other interested parties. This may be achieved in large part by requiring the spondee, in his contract with the sponsor, to undertake only to award rights to third parties upon particular terms, which terms would themselves need to be designed to preserve and, to some extent, promote the integrity of the package of rights granted to the sponsor.

Further, where the circumstances are such that the spondee finds it necessary to negotiate contractual arrangements with other bodies before his sponsorship arrangements are themselves in place, he would be well advised, in the course of such negotiations, to seek to protect the interests of his potential future sponsors. Otherwise he may find that the value of any sponsorship package is severely diminished.

In the case of a sponsored event such as a golf tournament or athletics meeting, the sponsor's desire to enhance and preserve the value of his investment might prompt him to seek to bind any especially important player or athlete by seeking to make him a contracting party to the sponsorship contract itself. This may be the more easily achieved where part of the sponsorship monies is earmarked for appearance money or prize money. Equally, where a team or club is offered sponsorship, it would be wise for the individual members of the team or employees of the club themselves to be contractually bound to the sponsor.

B. THE NATURE AND PRESERVATION OF THE 'RIGHTS' GRANTED TO A SPONSOR – THE BUILDING AND PROTECTION OF 'IDENTITY'

We have already seen how any marketing initiative mounted in connection with sport seeks to tap sport's goodwill or 'pulling power'. The value in sponsorship terms of any particular sponsored subject derives from the strength of that pulling power. The more powerful the goodwill, the more a sponsor will be expected to pay for access to it. Further, the very nature of such power demands that the sponsored subject have an 'identity' which is *distinctive, recognisable* and *attractive*. The exploitation of sport for commercial purposes is liable to repay the concerted building of such identity.

It follows that, at the heart of any sponsorship contract will be a desire to establish and preserve the identity of the sponsored subject and to ensure that it maximises its distinctiveness, its recognisability and its ability to attract custom. This is as true in the case of sponsorship of an individual sports star as it is in the case of an event, competition or location.

In this context, the establishing of identity is important not simply to maximise the commercial returns from the sponsorship. In addition, it may assist in the all important process of warding off undesirable and unauthorised encroachments from bootleggers, ambush marketers and the like. This is because the limitations of the law are such that the absence of a distinctive and recognisable identity will prove fatal when it comes to any attempt to identify a proprietary right which the courts will protect in the face of such encroachments. Thus, and as has been discussed in Chapter 11 above, in spite of occasional flirtations with a broad principle of 'unfair competition' which, broadly, would see legal protection (against encroachment) afforded to the fruits of a person's labour in all circumstances[6], the United Kingdom courts will only intervene to provide protection where clearly identifiable and traditional proprietary rights can be established. Further the limitations

---

6   Such a tort would borrow from the American approach – see *International News Service v Associated Press* 248 US 215 (1918), *Pittsburgh Athletic Co v KQV Broadcasting Co* 24 F Supp 490 (WD Pa 1938) and *National Exhibition Co v Fass* 133 NYS 2d 767 (Sup Ct 1954).

of the established causes of action provide particular boundaries beyond which the law will provide no assistance.

A sponsor will of course be interested in maximising the commercial return from his sponsorship. He will wish to see the identity of his sponsored subject cemented and enhanced wherever possible. It is axiomatic that the more distinctive, recognisable and attractive its 'identity' and the greater the sponsor's potential commercial return, the greater is likely to be the risk of unauthorised third party encroachment into the areas for access to which he has paid his sponsorship monies. He will therefore also be interested in curtailing such third party encroachment.

The most effective way of both building or cementing identity and also developing specific proprietary rights capable of legal recognition and enforcement lies through the creation of specific intellectual property rights. The parties to a sponsorship relationship, therefore, ought to give thought to the identification and creation of such rights where appropriate. This may involve the creation and, where necessary, registration of particular trade marks in the form of names, logos, symbols, 'get up' and the like. A particular example, in an extreme form, is that of the Olympic Rings which are the subject of their own Act of Parliament, the Olympic Symbol etc (Protection) Act 1995, which has the effect of preventing the unauthorised use of the Rings for commercial purposes. Equally, the specific creation of particular trade marks and other distinct items of intellectual property are liable to deter certain types of unlawful encroachment and, where such encroachment occurs or is threatened, to provide an established route for preventing or terminating it by legal process.

The creation of specific items of intellectual property is liable to serve the wider purpose of cementing a distinctive and recognisable identity generally and thereby, in so far as such identity provides commercial pulling power, putting into place one fundamental feature of perhaps the most important cause of action which may be utilised to ward off unauthorised encroachment, namely passing off.

An actionable passing off occurs where damage is caused to a person's goodwill or business due to an unauthorised third party 'borrowing' his identity by falsely misrepresenting, either expressly or impliedly, that it is his or that it is connected with his goods or services, thereby giving rise to confusion amongst the public or a section thereof. The limitations of a passing off action, however, should not be underestimated[7] and are perhaps what give rise to the greatest difficulty when it comes to maximising the value of a potential sponsorship package in the marketplace. For example, no grant of exclusive sponsorship rights, however well defined, can prevent third parties from conducting their own marketing drive and, in doing so, seeking to derive some form of benefit from, say, a subliminal (as opposed to a specifically suggested) association of some kind, either with the sponsored subject itself or simply with the sport therein being performed. At the time of the Winter Olympics, for example, advertisements utilising particular winter-sports images and conveying messages which have some connection with the fact that the Games are in progress are not necessarily, of themselves, an infringement of any proprietary right held by either the organisers of the Games or their official sponsors, and yet may nevertheless be seen as diluting the value of such rights.

7   See generally above, in Chapter 11.

In assessing any potential sponsorship package, therefore, the potential sponsor will wish to satisfy himself as to the extent to which and the means by which the integrity of his package can be guaranteed and the value of his association with the sponsored event may be preserved and enhanced. This will involve a number of practical measures to be taken both by him and by the spondee. For example, he will be interested in the arrangements for controlling access by others to the site or sites concerned and he will wish the rights and obligations of those with an authorised interest in the sponsored subject to be well and carefully defined and constrained. In addition, he will wish actively to promote his own association with the sponsored subject in order to derive maximum public appreciation thereof. The spondee, for his part, will want to ensure that the sponsor exercises such rights as are granted him personally and does not delegate or license them to another. By all these methods, undesirable activity may be inhibited and/or damage thereby restricted. In particular, and as suggested above, an additional and more sophisticated method of control is through the careful building and cementing of identity with the aid of specifically created items of intellectual property in connection with the sponsored subject, thereby constructing specific, and legally recognisable, proprietary rights.

Of course, the sponsor will himself require permission to 'borrow' the identity of the sponsored subject for his own legitimate commercial purposes and will expect licensed access to any specific items of intellectual property associated with it. The identification and delineation of his rights will provide the basic framework on which the relationship between the parties will be built. In addition, upon that framework may be constructed other associated rights and obligations, in particular the sponsor's general rights of public association and connection with the whole range of identifying features related to the sponsored subject. In the circumstances, a number of issues should be addressed, in relation both to intellectual property rights and, more generally, to the extent and nature of the right of the sponsor to 'borrow' the sponsored subject's identity and goodwill by publicising his association with the sponsored subject. For example:

(a)   What specific items of intellectual property are involved and/or should be created?

(b)   In particular, should the sponsor be accorded naming rights, incorporating his name within the title of the sponsored subject (no doubt to the consternation of subsequent sponsors, many cricket followers still identify one particular competition as 'the Gillette Cup') and/or within the logo or other mark? Should individual prizes or trophies be named by/after the sponsor?

(c)   Is it clear that the spondee owns/controls and is able to grant rights in respect of the identified items of intellectual property?

(d)   What rights of access to and use of the identified items of intellectual property should the sponsor be given? For example:

   –   to what extent should he be entitled to use them for his own promotional material?
   –   to what extent are his rights exclusive – should the spondee undertake not to grant rights to others, and to use his best endeavours to prevent and/or stop any abuses by others?
   –   should the sponsor's use of such rights have any territorial restriction?

- for how long should his rights extend – what use, if any, might he make of them after the end of the event in question, after expiry of the term of the sponsorship contract and/or upon termination otherwise of such contract?

(e) What should be the 'make up' of any livery used in terms of size, colour etc?

(f) Should the spondee himself be constrained in the extent and nature of any exploitation of the intellectual property rights or in his use of the sponsor's name and association with the sponsored subject? For example, it might be appropriate to require the spondee only to use the sponsor's name and association with the sponsored event for and in accordance with the proper purposes of the sponsorship agreement itself and not to do so after its termination or expiry.

(g) To what extext should the rights be personal to the sponsor and non-assignable?

C. EXCLUSIVITY

One of the most obvious but crucial considerations which will require to be addressed is the extent to which the sponsor is accorded exclusive access to the sponsorship rights granted by the spondee. If he is not accorded absolute exclusivity, he will almost certainly require that he be the only sponsor from within his sector of the market, in order to prevent the dilution of his message to that part of the public which he particularly wishes to attract. Thus, amongst multiple sponsors, there might, for example, be one car manufacturer, one brewer, one financial institution, one credit/charge card and so on. Thus far, the decision for the parties is likely to be a relatively straightforward one which ought not to give rise to great difficulty. An additional concern for the sponsor, and therefore also for the spondee, however, will be to ensure that the total or market exclusivity intended for the sponsor is not diluted in practice by the activities of others. Such activities are often 'unauthorised' in the sense that they simply involve a third party using the opportunity afforded by the fact that an event with which he has no connection is taking place to cash in on its profile. He does this by targeting its audience and/or suggesting some association with it which in truth he does not enjoy. This kind of dilution of an official sponsor's exclusivity is sometimes referred to as 'ambush marketing' and is dealt with separately below.

In addition to the unauthorised activities of the ambush marketers, sponsors need to keep a weather eye open for potential incompatible or damaging activities by or through other parties with a legitimate interest in and connection with the sponsored subject. Reference has already been made to the web of different interests which may envelope one particular event or competition. As will readily be appreciated, the potential for mayhem is considerable unless the ambit of that web is identified and each strand put into place according to a carefully prepared, well understood and expressly articulated central plan. As has been mentioned, the aim should be to require the contracting parties, in one form or another, to do all they can to secure that the sponsorship the subject of the contract is able peacefully to co-exist with the interests and activities of other interested parties. The interrelation of the sponsor's interests with those of other parties may usefully be addressed under certain specific subject headings:

– *Co-sponsors*:   It goes without saying that any sponsor, if he is to share the sponsorship role in relation to a particular sponsored subject, will be anxious to ensure that none of his competitors are included, that the number of co-sponsors is not excessive, and that the interests of his co-sponsors are compatible with his own. He will also wish to agree measures designed to ensure that the prominence given to his role corresponds to his share of the sponsorship pot and that his image is not dwarfed by that of one or more of his co-sponsors.

– *Site advertising*: Many venues for sporting events themselves offer opportunities for advertising on perimeter boards and elsewhere. The sponsor of the event or match taking place will obviously wish to ensure that, wherever possible, his name is prominent amongst such advertising and that the name of his competitors is not. In addition, he will wish to ensure that the purity and strength of his message is not unduly diluted by a proliferation of advertising opportunities afforded to others, or by disadvantageous placement, particularly out of the view of any television cameras. The number and extent of such opportunities will need to be the subject of specific control.

– *Broadcasting*:   Television broadcasts very often represent the jewel in the crown when it comes to increasing public awareness of the sponsor's corporate identity through his sponsorship of the sponsored subject. The sponsor therefore has a real interest in seeing that his exposure to television is maximised. This, together with his general interest in seeing his sponsored event or competition flourish, will prompt him to seek specific guarantees wherever possible as to the nature and quality of the coverage. In addition, he will wish to ensure, so far as is legitimately possible, that the very television broadcasts from which he seeks to benefit are not used by others unduly to dilute the impact of his sponsorship or even to inflict damage on his particular interests[8]. He will be interested in the relationship between the sponsored subject and the broadcasters and will wish to ensure that such relationship is operated in a manner which does not undermine the essentials of his own sponsorship relationship. In relation to the broadcaster's relationship, his interests may, where possible, require the pursuit of certain specific aims, namely:

  – to maximise his own exposure to the highest quality of extended coverage, preferably on one of the most popular channels and at peak viewing time;
  – to veto any incompatible sponsorship of the broadcast itself;
  – to restrict the purchase by his competitors of opportunities for inclusion of commercial messages (eg sponsored replays or 'man-of-the-match' awards) within, or advertising slots alongside, any relevant broadcast.

8   See for example, *National Hockey League v Pepsi-Cola Canada* (1993) 102 DLR (4th) 80 affirming (1992) 92 DLR (4th) 349, where Coca Cola was the sponsor of the Stanley Cup ice hockey play-offs and Pepsi Cola secured an exclusive right to advertise soft drinks during broadcasts of the matches. Thus, although Coca Cola was the 'official soft drink' of the competition, the only advertisements during the broadcasts were for a rival product.

In other words, the sponsor of a competition or event will be interested in the whole contractual arrangement with the broadcaster. For example, he will be concerned as to the number and location of the cameras, to the quality of the pictures, the commentary and generally the production as a whole and to the scheduling of both live and recorded coverage. He may also be interested in securing access to archive material, as to which his rights will require to be specifically provided for.

Ideally, the sponsor will wish himself to be a party to the negotiations and the contract with the host broadcaster in order to influence the agreement of broadcasting terms and to be able himself to take appropriate action to enforce them. If that proves not to be possible, he ought to be able, in his contract with his spondee (assuming it is the spondee selling the broadcasting rights), to require him to adopt a particular approach to the sale of broadcasting rights and to ensure that any broadcasting contract contains provisions designed so far as possible to secure the sponsor's aims and protect his interests.

Particular clauses will require to be tailored to the circumstances in question, but a word of caution needs to be sounded. By definition, the sponsor's aims will include the inhibition of activity on the part of his competitors and it follows that care should be taken to reduce the risk of infringing the competition laws of the European Community, the United Kingdom and, where appropriate, other individual countries. In this regard, direct constraints on the broadcaster, simply prohibiting him from affording promotional opportunities to the sponsor's competitors, whether via programme sponsorship, sponsorship of replays or 'man-of-the-match' awards, or straight advertising, are likely to be at risk. It would be safer to avoid blatant blanket prohibitions in favour of specific grants to the sponsor himself and/or partial restrictions. Thus, for example, the sponsor might himself offer to sponsor the broadcast as well as the event itself, or seek a right of first refusal in respect of such sponsorship. Equally, the broadcaster might sensibly be required to ensure that advertising carried on behalf of third parties should not claim, either expressly or by implication, any association or connection with the sponsored subject. In addition, the broadcaster should be required to ensure, so far as practicable, that the coverage should avoid any unofficial or unauthorised advertising by, for example, unnecessarily drawing attention to the activities of anyone obviously seeking to make use of the occasion to publicise particular commercial interests unrelated to the event, its organisers and official sponsors. Finally, if the broadcast has a different sponsor from the event itself, the broadcaster should be required to undertake that the broadcast and commentary should clearly distinguish between the roles of the different sponsors – it will, of course, assist the avoidance of confusion if the sponsor of the sponsored subject is able to secure the right to incorporate his name or other identifying feature in the title of the event itself, in which case the broadcaster's contract could properly include a term requiring the full title of the event to be used at all times.

One particular problem soon to be upon us is that posed by new technology, whereby the advertising at a particular venue, say around the perimeter, may by read by a computer and replaced in the broadcast picture with a different message. Such 'virtual advertising' technology may provide great opportunities for broadcasts to be tailored, for example to suit different audiences in different parts of the country or world. The sponsor and spondee should be alive, however, to the increased opportunities which may be caused thereby for unwelcome advertising to be carried within the broadcast. It may be that, in any event, the spondee will require that broadcast images are not tampered with in any way. On the other hand, the ability to change such images may provide him with an increased capacity to earn revenue from sale of the broadcasting rights, in which case he and his sponsor should ensure that appropriate protective conditions are written into the broadcasting contract.

– *Merchandising*:   Both sponsor and spondee will wish to restrict opportunities for pirate merchandising. As already mentioned in relation to unauthorised third party encroachment generally, this aim may be aided by the concerted building and cementing of 'identity', both by the creation of specific intellectual property rights and otherwise, so as to ease the establishment in appropriate circumstances of either a passing off action or, in the case of specific items of intellectual property, such rights of action as are apt to enforce and protect them. In addition, the parties will need clearly to identify and allocate any official merchandising rights both as between themselves and, through licences or other contractual arrangements, to be exercised by third parties. The sponsor may wish himself to be able to produce clothing or other articles to publicise his involvement in the sponsored subject and his rights to do so together with any limits to such rights, for example on his use of any logos or other marks, should be spelt out. Equally, he may legitimately wish to ensure that any merchandise manufactured or sold by third parties is tasteful, of appropriate quality and compatible with and, ideally, promotional of his own image. The extent to which he will be in a position to insist on an ability to control any merchandising initiative will depend on the circumstances. He will wish to consider a number of possibilities:

- – Initial agreement as to the means by which the merchandising initiative will be conducted; for example, how many manufacturers, distributors and other contractors will be used? For what period will contracts be awarded? On what terms will they be awarded?
- – A right to participate in the appointment of manufacturers or licensees, perhaps through a veto on the grant of licences or other contractual terms.
- – A right to vet and approve individual products and their make-up, alternatively a requirement that all items conform to particular standards of quality etc.
- – A right to have particular logos, other marks or identifying features incorporated in individual products.
- – A right to be a party to any licences or other contracts awarded, with the licence holder or other contracting party acknowledging the sponsor's interests and being required to give specific undertakings designed to protect or prevent harm to the sponsor's image.

In addition, the sponsor and spondee will want an embargo upon either of them carrying out their own independent merchandising initiatives. Alternatively, in so far as such initiatives are contemplated and are not prohibited, their nature and extent ought to be clearly identified.

- *Official suppliers*:   As ever, the sponsor (and any sensible spondee) will wish to ensure that his interests are not harmed by an insensitive grant of rights to others to describe themselves as having some official seal of approval from the sponsored event. For example, if American Express provide sponsorship for an event, they will not wish to find Visa, Mastercard or Diners Club being accorded the right to call themselves the 'official' credit/charge card of that same event. The parties may wish to approach this issue very much in a similar way to that raised by the question of merchandising, which is discussed in the previous chapter.

- *Participating individuals/teams etc*:   As has already been pointed out, the scope for difficulty is increasingly acute when it comes to regulating the potentially conflicting interests of the competitors and other parties actually participating or wishing to participate in a particular event. Many such individuals, teams and other parties will already have their own sponsorship and promotional contracts in place, some of which will have been put into place for a fixed term and without reference specifically to the event. Some of them are liable to be with competitors of the sponsor of the event itself. In other words, the occasion of the event itself may well be too late to influence the negotiation of such contracts. Nevertheless the rules of entry to the event may be constructed in such a way as to control the exploitation of individual interests by participation therein. The interests of sponsor and spondee should here be regarded as one. Each will want the purity of identity inherent in the sponsorship arrangement, and perhaps in the name of the event itself, to be maintained and preserved. It may be that the rules of entry are published before a sponsor has been appointed, in which case the spondee will enhance his prospects of maximising his opportunities for attracting substantial sponsorship interest by paying close attention to prescribing tight controls within such rules. Specific terms should be included, as necessary, as to the clothing and equipment worn or used by individuals, as to the livery of individual teams, and as to the extent generally to which such participants are to remain at liberty to use the event to publicise the interests of their own sponsors and other third parties not officially associated with the event itself. The rules of entry may be used to provide important protections for the sponsor. In addition, they provide an opportunity, where appropriate, for requiring the participants to provide positive assistance in the active promotion of the sponsor's image. Thus, with certain events such as an athletics meeting, it may be appropriate within limits for prescribed clothing to be worn, in which case such clothing might bear the name of the sponsor. Equally, rules might lay down particular stipulations under which participants must make themselves available in certain circumstances for media or other interviews, in which case the location and backdrop of any interview may be designed with particular image enhancing features.

- *Film and video makers*:   In addition to television and other broadcasting arrangements, some events will give rise to other filming, video and photographic attractions. Such attractions and their potential for both legitimate and unauthorised exploitation should be considered. The sponsor himself may wish to make use of such attractions, in which case his contract should identify any specific rights granted, together with any limitations attached thereto, for example as to how such rights may physically be exercised, and the period and territory within which any films, videos or photographs might be used. The potential problems of 'virtual advertising', to which reference has been made, at page 273, may also need to be specifically provided for and/or guarded against by express provision. The issues are largely the same as in the case of a live television broadcast save that, in this instance, the image manipulation processes would take place in the edit suite rather than in the course of the filming itself.

In addition, the parties will wish to be vigilant to ensure that no unauthorised filming, recording or photography takes place which might subsequently be exploited to the disadvantage of either sponsor or spondee. The difficulty is that, as has previously been explained, a sporting event does not necessarily attract or give rise to any relevant proprietary rights in itself. In particular, there is no copyright in the event itself. This means, for example, that filming cannot be prevented unless such filming is carried out in breach of some specific contractual or other right such as might be the case where specific restrictions are stipulated as conditions of entry (whether in a contract for the sale of a ticket or otherwise) to a particular venue. It follows that careful thought needs to go into the terms and conditions to be applied to any such rights of access (in particular via tickets or other accreditation means such as the grant of hospitality packages). Such terms and conditions might sensibly prohibit the use of any film video photographic or other recording equipment save where expressly authorised. In many circumstances, such terms might be subject to a further exception in the case of photography etc for purely private or non commercial use.

–   *Corporate hospitality*:   Most sporting events of any consequence have long since recognised that they provide significant opportunities not simply for the entertainment of ordinary spectators but for businesses to entertain their customers. Facilities for such business entertainment often command substantial fees and increasingly are seen by purchasing companies as a powerful tool for assisting in the process of cementing important business relationships. A sponsor will be concerned to ensure that the grant of such facilities is controlled and that their use is not abused to his detriment. Whilst a prohibition against grants to his competitors might be inappropriate and even unlawful, particular con-straints on the purchasers should be considered. Prominent displays of their own corporate image might sensibly be prohibited. Equally, they might be required to agree not to publicise their association with the event otherwise than through ordinary invitations to their guests and to ensure that even such invitations should not convey a suggestion of any closer association than simply that the company has purchased the facilities in question. Other terms governing the grant of facilities should oblige the purchaser to control the activities and behaviour of his guests, and make express provision for the distribution of tickets (no resale etc). As with other parties having potentially conflicting interests, the sponsor's inter-ests may be protected and advanced either by his being party to the contracts with such third parties or by the incorporation into his sponsor-ship contract of specific obligations on the spondee to secure particular obligations from the third parties. In the latter event, the spondee should be required also to accept a policing role, undertaking to take all reasonable steps to enforce the obligations imposed on the third parties.

D. AMBUSH MARKETING

Much of the benefit to a sponsor of his sponsorship arrangement derives, in one form or another, from his association with the sponsored event, competition, individual or programme and the opportunites to which such association exposes him. He will therefore wish to include in any relevant contract, provisions to prevent, so far as may be practicable, any dilution of the strength and effectiveness of the message intended by that association by incompatible or inappropriate activity on the part of others. This may not be straightforward in some circumstances and it should be recognised that it may simply be impossible to achieve satisfactory protection. Indeed there may be practical, commercial or even legal reasons which will frustrate a sponsor in his attempt to secure protection. As has already been seen, with the potential for a large number of parties to have different roles and interests in the same sporting event or competition, the 'owner' of the event or competition itself may be able to impose specific contractual restraints upon those individuals, teams and others with a direct interest, through active participation or otherwise, in the sponsored subject. But the unauthorised activities of others with no direct interest in the sponsored subject but intent upon cashing in on its profile to enhance their own image and otherwise to advance their own aims by suggesting some association with the subject which does not in truth exist, may prove altogether more difficult. Where such association is clearly suggested, a passing off action is likely now to be held to be available to provide some protection, on the basis that the United Kingdom courts appear increasingly to recognise that the ability to license the right to use the established profile of an individual or other prominent business entity for merchandising and endorsement activities outside the particular fields in which they established such profile is itself an important business asset[9]. Further, where such unauthorised activities occur, the courts may well be prepared to infer a (false) representation that the individual or business whose profile has been used has participated therein either directly or by endorsement or licence, and may thereby find the ingredients necessary for relief in passing off.

The position is different where no visual or other clear connection is displayed or otherwise represented between the advertised goods or services and the sponsored subject. An advertiser may, legitimately, simply seek to use the opportunity afforded by the sponsored subject's existence to target the section of the public which the sponsored subject has conveniently caused to be identified and/or gathered together and/or which, the advertiser believes, is likely to be interested in the products which he wishes to advertise. In such circumstances, no action for passing off will lie even where the advertiser seeks to draw on a subliminal association between his products and the sponsored subject. Where such (lawful or unlawful) activity is planned as part of a concerted campaign (which may be designed for promotional purposes, or as a defensive measure to damage the official sponsor's own campaign by diluting his message) it may be described as 'ambush marketing' or 'parasitic marketing'. As such, it is regarded by some as a dubious or illegitimate marketing practice (it is almost invariably so

---

9 See the discussion of this topic in Chapter 11 above, and see in particular *Lego System A/S v Lego M Lemelstrich Ltd* [1983] FSR 155 and *Mirage Studios v Counter Feat Clothing Co Ltd* [1991] FSR 145.

regarded by those who have an official association with the sponsored subject, who will have paid substantial sums therefor!)

The reaction of Kodak, official sponsors of the 1988 Seoul Olympics, can well be imagined when the Fuji airship floated into view over the stadium and was caught by the broadcasting cameras. It may be that Fuji felt that such activity was both legitimate and appropriate, in circumstances where, at the 1984 Olympic Games, it had been an official sponsor and Kodak had secured appointment as the 'official film', not of the Games themselves, but of the United States track team. Other examples are legion:

- At the 1990 Football World Cup, Coca Cola were official sponsors, but Pepsi Cola sponsored the Brazilian team[10].
- VISA sponsored the Winter Olympic Games at Lillehammer in Norway in 1994. Its rival, American Express, chose to take television advertising which promoted the wide acceptance of its cards in Norway, supported by the clever message that American visitors to Norway did not require a visa[11].
- Also at the time of the Winter Olympics of 1994, the fast food retailer Wendys, derived considerable impact with their advertising campaign featuring a champion figure skater, to the detriment of McDonalds who held official sponsorship rights.
- At the time of the 1988 Seoul Olympic Games, American Express ran advertisements which depicted the main stadium, thereby conveying a suggestion of some official connection.
- At the 1984 Olympic Games at Los Angeles, Nike chose to rent advertising hoardings in the vicinity of the venues, whereas Converse, a rival shoe manufacturer was an official sponsor.
- At the culmination of the 1994 British Open Championship in golf, the television cameras lingered on the banner being pulled by a light aircraft containing a congratulatory message to the winner from a small, but enterprising, golf related advertising business.
- At the Atlanta Olympics in 1996, the well known hamburger fast-food chain, McDonalds, were an official sponsor. Their rival, Burger King provided sponsorship to the British team.
- At the time of football's European Championships ('Euro 96') in England in the summer of 1996, Nike put significant resources into their campaign featuring particular players and slogans impliedly suggestive of a connection with the championships which they did not have.

The extent to which such activity, at least where lawful, should nevertheless be regarded as 'illegitimate' is perhaps a matter for a debate which is beyond the scope of this work. To some, it represents nothing more than a wholly appropriate method of securing cheap publicity. In some circumstances, however, whilst not unlawful, it can be very damaging to official sponsors. Where it occurs, it is always extremely aggravating to both the organisers (who may feel they missed an opportunity for securing additional revenue, from the 'culprits') and to the official sponsors (who see a dilution in the

10 The clashes between the two companies have been intense. See, for example, *National Hockey League v Pepsi-Cola Canada* (1993) 102 DLR (4th) 80 and (1992) 92 DLR (4th) 349.
11 In fairness, it should be pointed out that American Express have justified this and similar campaigns as being no more than a legitimate response to VISA's own campaigns which, they claim, have used its association with the Olympic Games to attack American Express.

strength and purity of their own publicised message). Whilst it will be beyond the powers of the parties to guarantee the absence of any form of 'ambush marketing' careful thought at the outset may enable express provision to be made in order to limit the opportunities.

It may be, for example, that the sponsor would first seek a general undertaking from the spondee to use his best endeavours to prevent the sponsored subject (or any of its constituent elements eg competitors) from being used by unauthorised third parties for publicity purposes. Beyond that, it has to be said that money tends to talk and the extent to which a sponsor is able to secure effective protection from competitive activity is liable to depend, in part, upon the depth of his pocket. For the larger and more popular sporting events, it may be that the sums required would prove to be beyond the budgets of most companies. Equally, for many events, the organisers will be looking for more than one sponsor, although in that case each sponsor will no doubt seek an entitlement to vet and veto his fellow sponsors, or will demand that the organiser promise not to appoint any of his competitors or any company whose image may be incompatible with or damaging to his.

In seeking to deal with potential 'ambush marketing' opportunities, the contract terms will, as always, need to be tailored to suit the circumstances of the occasion. However, there are a number of general points which can be made, most of which will repay careful consideration in each individual case. For example:

– *Legal difficulties*: One of the difficulties when it comes to attempting to prevent competitive activity is that there are clearly defined legal regimes, both in Europe and the United Kingdom and also in other countries, the aim of which is to outlaw or regulate contract terms and other practices whose object or effect is unduly to stifle legitimate competition. The impact of such regimes within the United Kingdom is considered generally elsewhere in this work and, in the present context, all that needs to be said is that any measures adopted by the parties to inhibit the activities of others should be carefully weighed against the requirements of such regimes. In the case of the larger sponsorship opportunities, as in relation to the Olympic Games, the football, cricket or rugby World Cups and other events of mass appeal, or in the case of long term sponsorship contracts, it is perfectly possible that restrictions may be suggested which would prevent, restrict or distort competition within the European Community and affect trade between Member States and so be at risk under Article 85 of the Treaty of Rome. Equally, a monopolistic organisation with control over a particular sport, may conceivably be regarded as abusing its dominant position in relation to the imposition of restrictions and, if doing so in such a way as to affect cross border trade, breaching Article 86. Further, particular agreements containing anti-competitive provisions may be void and unenforceable unless registered under the Restrictive Trade Practices Acts of 1976 and 1977, and in extreme circumstances there may even be some theoretical scope for investigation by the Office of Fair Trading and by the Monopolies and Mergers Commission under the Fair Trading Act 1973 (in the case of a 'monopoly situation') or the Competition Act 1980 (in the case of 'anti-competitive practices'). In addition, stringent restrictions may fall foul of the doctrine of restraint of trade, depending upon their reasonableness in the circumstances in the light of the respective interests of the affected parties and the general public.

Such matters should therefore be kept well in mind when negotiating particular terms designed to secure some protection from competitive activity. For example, blanket prohibitions against all kinds of competitive activity are manifestly more likely to be at risk than those which seek simply to preserve a sensible balance between the need to safeguard the value of the rights purchased by the sponsor on the one hand and the rights of third parties legitimately and freely to market their goods or services as they may see fit. Futher, restrictions which are placed directly upon the rights of the sponsor or spondee (as where, for example, the spondee agrees not to carry competitive advertising on perimeter boards) are less likely to be open to challenge than attempts to impose restrictions on third parties (as where, for example, an attempt is made to prevent a broadcaster from carrying any advertisements for the goods or services of the competitors of the event's sponsor).

– *'Clean' stadium*:   Many venues will have scope for advertising, either on perimeter boards or other hoardings or screens. As one of the main benefits being purchased by the sponsor is likely to be advertising, both on such very boards etc and through their being caught on camera by the broadcast coverage of the sponsored subject, it is not unreasonable that he would wish to secure some restrictions, and in this case probably a total ban, on the spondee's right to sell such advertising space to his competitors or those with whom he reasonably would not wish to be associated. In addition, he will wish to ensure that appropriate measures are in place to prevent unofficial and unauthorised advertising material being displayed elsewhere within the stadium or other venue. As has already been discussed, such measures may be addressed in the terms and conditions giving rights of entry/access to the competition itself, to the venue or to particular facilities.

– *'Clean' environs*:   Because 'unofficial' advertising can readily be controlled within the venue itself, some companies target hoardings and other advertising sites outside, but in close proximity to, the venue. One such example is that referred to at page 278 above involving Nike at the 1984 Olympic Games. It may be that the best solution here is for the organiser of the sponsored subject and/or his official sponsors themselves to seek to purchase the rights to such advertising sites, be it from the local authority or other owners as the case may be. Such advertising opportunities could then be exploited by the official sponsors or their letting could be brought under the same kind of control as those within the venue itself. Equally, it may be appropriate to seek, as (so it is understood) the London Marathon manages to achieve, an air exclusion zone, thereby preventing any ambushers from operating in the manner of the small advertising company at the 1994 Open Golf Championship referred to at page 278 above.

– *Corporate hospitality*:   As has been discussed above, most sponsors will seek constraints on the spondee's ability to grant corporate hospitality and other facilities to their competitors so as not to dilute the competitive advantage which they seek to draw from their association with the sponsored subject. In addition, he will be concerned to ensure that others, to whom facilities are properly granted, are not thereby afforded undue opportunities for promotional activity. He will be likely to seek safeguards in his sponsorship contract which make provision for the terms upon which such facilities should be let or otherwise provided.

They might sensibly provide, for example, for restrictions on the extent to which the purchaser of such facilities should advertise his presence at or connection with the sponsored subject, either at the location of the facilities or indeed otherwise.

- *Merchandising*:   The subject of pirate merchandising has already been discussed above, under the heading 'Exclusivity'.

E. INDIVIDUALS AS SPONSORED SUBJECTS

An individual may receive sponsorship income in many different circumstances. He may be sponsored by a clothing or equipment manufacturer, in which case he will be required to wear his sponsor's clothing or use his sponsor's equipment during competition. Most manufacturers are anxious to 'sign up' the more popular sporting stars ahead of their competitors. Equally, some companies with no direct sporting connections of their own are anxious to tap the publicity opportunities provided by an association with one or more sporting stars. In every case, what the individual requires is money and what the sponsor seeks is publicity. Further, the value derived by the sponsor from the arrangement is dependent in large part upon the success of the individual concerned and his ability to generate good publicity through his profile. For this reason, a number of specific terms may need to be considered:

- *Quality of performance*:   Where a competitor, whether in the form of an individual or a team, seeks sponsorship, the sponsor may feel it appropriate to require the competitor to use his/its best endeavours to achieve successful results; alternatively, it may be thought sufficient for the amount of sponsorship available to be dependent upon results, whether measured by reference to performance in specific tournaments or competitions or to, say, positioning in a league or by reference to any system of world or other ranking. Specific bonus payments may be made available on the attainment of specified targets such as the winning of particular tournaments, selection for particular representative teams or qualification for particular championships etc. Equally, a drop in the measured quality of performance may be provided for by a corresponding reduction in the rate of sponsorship remuneration or, in extreme circumstances, by early termination.

- *Quantity of performance*:   Provision may be made for a competitor (again, whether an individual or team) to engage in particular sporting activity to a particular schedule. The competitor may be required to play in particular competitions/tournaments or to play in a specified number of matches, competitions, exhibitions, tournaments and so on. Again, individual circumstances will mould the appropriateness of particular provisions and, as with terms designed to procure the highest quality of performance, terms may be framed so as to impose specific obligations upon the competitor, or alternatively the quantitative level of his/their performance may be a criterion in the calculation of any sums due from the sponsor.

- *Injury, suspension etc*:   Commercial sponsors are likely to regard even a sponsored sportsperson of star quality who is 'out of the game' as a diminishing asset. They are likely to require 'their' stars to be performing and, through their performances, to be enhancing their own and their sponsors' profiles. Inevitably, many sponsors will wish to make specific provision to reduce or extinguish their obligation to continue making payments in the event that the sponsored star is prevented by one reason or another from performing. Such terms will require to be tailored to the specific circumstances and requirements of the particular parties involved and are likely to be regarded as of particular importance in the case of longer term contracts.

– *Good behaviour.*   Commercial sponsors are unlikely to embrace the adage that there is no such thing as bad publicity and are likely to be particularly concerned with the image of their sponsored stars. Their nightmare is that such stars should be convicted of a serious criminal offence or, perhaps worst of all, found to have failed a drugs test. In the case of sponsored teams, sponsors may have in mind damaging publicity through the activities of the team itself (or the club[12]) or perhaps even its supporters. Provision for suspension or termination of the sponsorship contract on the happening of particular events (which may not all be possible to define with great precision) may therefore be appropriate. On a wider front, a sponsor may insist that the sponder should agree to conduct himself in a proper and lawful fashion. Equally, it will often be appropriate to require the individual spondee (or each member of a sponsored team) to conduct his affairs in an appropriate fashion and, in particular, that:

– he should adhere to the requirements of the law;
– he should comply with the rules and principles laid down by the ruling body of the sport in question and/or the organisers of particular competitions etc[13]; and
– he should refrain from gratuitously indulging in certain activities which might put him unnecessarily at risk of injury.

Finally, the sponsor will no doubt require a general undertaking that the spondee will not act in any way which is liable to damage the sponsor's interests.

– *Accessibility:*   A sponsor who provides a sponsored star (or team) with substantial sums of money is liable to expect the star (or members of the team) to make himself/themselves available for the sponsor's own promotional occasions, either by personal appearances and involvement or simply by use of his/their name(s) and/or likeness in promotional material. In the case of other types of sponsored subject, the sponsor may still seek from his spondee particular rights of access to particular stars who may be competing in or otherwise associated with the sponsored subject. The nature and extent of any demands of access which may be made by a sponsor, either directly of sponsored competitors or indirectly in the case of other types of spondees, will obviously depend upon the circumstances. Much may depend, in the case of a sponsored event or competition for

12 Examples may include nefarious activity in the transfer market, the payment of 'bungs' and the evasion of tax.
13 The primacy of the rules and requirements of the relevant authorities should generally be recognised. Thus, it may be that the rules of entry to a particular competition prohibit the display of an individual's or a team's sponsorship on clothing or equipment, or even that such rules require participants to display the name or logo of the competition sponsors. In such circumstances, it should be recognised that the interests of the personal sponsors may simply have to give way to those of the authorities in question.

example, on the position of the sponsor and spondee within the web of relationships and interests associated therewith and the extent to which interrelated contracts are already in place or may still be put into place. The circumstances of each case will inform the extent to which the sponsor's aspirations may be achieved.

F. PROMOTIONAL OBLIGATIONS

The name of the game for a sponsor is publicity. He will wish to exploit to the full his association with his sponsored subject and will seek to procure particular obligations requiring his spondee himself or itself actively to promote his name and association. He may require the spondee actively to promote his name and profile by using all reasonable endeavours to publicise his association with and sponsorship of the sponsored subject. In addition, he may seek certain more specific undertakings. As already mentioned above, a sponsor of an individual or team, for example, may require that his clothing or equipment be worn or used or that any clothing or equipment used should be adorned with his name and/or logo. A sponsor may require either his own sponsored competitors, or individuals participating in his sponsored competition or event, to be available for press and other interviews and he will wish to ensure that, where possible, the facilities for the conduct of media interviews are suitably adorned with his name, logo or other identifying features. Again, the circumstances of the particular contract will themselves inform the degree to which the parties feel it appropriate, or even possible, to make express provision in this regard. It should be noted again that the extent to which opportunities may exist for the advertising of particular competitor's sponsors' names may often be constrained by the rules of the particular competitions or tournaments in which the sponsored competitor will be expected to compete or, in the case of a sponsored individual in a team sport, the obligations owed by the individual to his team (and/or his team's sponsor). Any sponsorship contract should therefore be drawn in such a way as to recognise, where appropriate, the primacy of any such constraints, at least to the extent that they simply cannot be avoided.

G. ORGANISATION AND LIABILITY

The various topics already discussed show that the sponsor's interests are likely to pervade virtually all aspects of the sponsored subject. In particular, he is liable to be interested in many, if not all, the other contracts entered into by his spondee. As has been pointed out above, he may seek to be made a party to such contracts or he may legitimately wish to be allowed some influence over the fixing of the terms of such contracts. Further, we have seen that a sponsor may seek to have his association with the sponsored subject formally acknowledged by the incorporation of his name into the name of the sporting competition the subject of his sponsorship. Where the sponsor seeks and is permitted to maximise his sphere of influence over the conduct of such competition, it is possible that he may thereby unwittingly expose himself to potential liabilities as well. It may be, for example, that he would be seen as an 'occupier' of particular venues or parts thereof, depending upon the degree to which he had control of them[14]. Equally, to the extent that he seeks to influence the spondee in the latter's enforcement of third party contracts, he may, in appropriate circumstances, expose himself to actions for inducing breach of contract or unlawful interference with business.

Where the spondee is a limited company, the influence of the sponsor may be such as to endow him with the obligations of a director. Section 741(2) of the Companies Act 1985 defines a 'shadow director' as a person in accordance with whose directions or instructions the (formal) directors are accustomed to act. The potential for such liabilities may cause the parties to consider the extent to which the sponsor should be permitted and entitled to take a formal role in the organisation of the event or competition the subject of his sponsorship. Where his association with the sponsored subject is to be of particular prominence and importance, it is likely that the degree of his anticipated influence across the whole web of relationships involved will be similarly significant and, in such cases, good order suggests that his general organisational role and entitlements ought to be given careful consideration at the outset. The clear delineation of the limits of his authority will assist in averting conflict during the currency of the sponsorship contract.

H. RISK ALLOCATION AND INSURANCE

With the best ordered relationships, there always remains scope for things to go wrong. This should be recognised and provided for in the contractual terms agreed. This can be done in three ways. First, the risk of particular eventualities may be expressly allocated between the parties. Thus, for example, the risk of third party claims may be allocated to the spondee.

Secondly, particular risks may be covered by insurance and the responsibility for effecting appropriate cover should be expressly allotted to one party or the other (usually the one to whom the particular risk is allocated) together with an obligation, where appropriate, to ensure that the other party's relevant interest is noted on the policy, either as an additional insured or as a loss payee. It would be appropriate, in particular, to seek public liability cover. In addition, in relation to a sponsored individual, it would be prudent to seek cover in respect of injury or sickness. In relation to sporting events and other competitions, cover should be considered in respect of the risks, for example, of cancellation, postponement or curtailment, the absence through injury or sickness of particular competitors, the weather, the failure or interruption of any broadcast coverage (whether, for example, through the broadcaster pulling out, as in the case of the European club rugby competition sponsored by Heineken in 1996, through a communication/satellite breakdown, or otherwise) and so on.

Thirdly, the parties may make provision for indemnities and exclusions or limitations of liability in particular circumstances. However, it should be noted that, in certain circumstances, the Unfair Contract Terms Act 1977 renders invalid clauses designed to exclude or limit liability. For example, in

---

14 See, for example, *Creed v McGeoch & Sons Ltd* [1955] 1 WLR 1005, *Bunker v Charles Brand & Son Ltd* [1969] 2 QB 480 and *Fisher v CHT Ltd (No 2)* [1966] 2 QB 475.

the case of liability for negligence[15], liability for death or personal injury may not be excluded or restricted. Other types of liability may be excluded or restricted[16] only in so far as the term satisfies the requirement of reasonableness, defined[17] as a requirement that:

> 'The term shall have been a fair and reasonable one to be included having regard to the circumstances which were or ought reasonably to have been known to or in the contemplation of the parties when the contract was made.'

I. TERM AND QUANTIFICATION

It goes without saying that the extent of the sponsorship arrangement needs to be clearly defined. This will usually mean that the sponsor will agree to provide a certain amount of money or that he will provide money at a particular rate over a period. In each case, the amount or rate of money involved (or a formula for calculating the same) and (where appropriate) the period in question (and/or the mechanism for bringing the period to an end) should be identified. When specific payments are to be made and the timings of such payments should also be agreed and any circumstances triggering a right of repayment, if any, of sums previously paid should be articulated.

J. ENDS WHICH CANNOT BE GUARANTEED

As will already be clear, it will often be the case that the achievement of particular ends, on which the commercial success of a sponsorship contract may ultimately depend, cannot be guaranteed by either party. In such circumstances, obligations may nevertheless be framed in such a way as to improve the chances of achieving the ends in question. For example:

- *Best endeavours*: It may be appropriate for the relevant party to undertake to use his best endeavours to achieve the end in question[18]. The organiser of a sponsored competition might be expected to promise to use such endeavours to secure the best available field of competitors, or to procure particular terms (favourable to the sponsor) from other contractors such as broadcasters etc. Equally, a sponsored individual may have obligations to others, such as his team or employers, the organisers of the events or competitions in which he is likely to compete and so forth – his ability to perform for his sponsor free of all restrictions may in practice be (or become) severely curtailed by such obligations, in which case the best he may be able to do in terms of giving a positive

15 Defined by s 1(1) so as to embrace breach of any obligation, contractual or otherwise, to take reasonable care or exercise reasonable skill and including breach of the common duty of care under the Occupiers' Liability Act 1957.

16 By s 4, indemnity clauses are regulated only to the extent that the party giving the indemnity is acting as a consumer (as defined by s 12). As the sponsorship under consideration is, by definition, commercial and not philanthropic, it follows that it is unlikely that the spondee would ever be able to challenge an indemnity clause under the Act.

17 See s 11.

18 An obligation to use 'best endeavours' means simply an obligation to take all available steps which are capable of producing the desired result. See *IBM United Kingdom Ltd v Rockware Glass Ltd* [1980] FSR 335 and *Sheffield District Rly Co v Great Central Rly Co* (1911) 27 TLR 451.

covenant to dance to his sponsor's tune is to undertake to use his 'best endeavours'. An alternative, and less stringent, obligation may be expressed by an obligation to use 'reasonable' endeavours.

– *Conditions precedent/subsequent*: A condition precedent is a stipulation which must be satisfied before a contractual obligation arises. A condition subsequent is a stipulation which, if satisfied, extinguishes an existing contractual obligation. Both forms of condition may be found apt to define or constrain particular obligations or to encourage a particular level of performance. For example, the amount of financial assistance to be provided by the sponsor may be made conditional upon any number of different eventualities. In the case of a particular event or competition, the depth of a sponsor's pocket may depend on factors such as the strength of the field, the success/failure of a particular competitor/ team, the extent and nature of any media coverage which might be secured and even the weather.

K. FORCE MAJEURE

Particular events and competitions have a habit of being cancelled, postponed or disrupted for various reasons such as the weather, contractual disputes, civil unrest and political inteference. Equally, individual competitors get sick or injured. Thought should be given, and appropriate provision made, as to what should happen on any such occasions. Again, the use of some form of condition precedent or subsequent might be appropriate.

L. SPONSOR'S OBLIGATION AND CONSTRAINTS

The sponsor's primary obligation is almost invariably to provide money. A kit, clothing or equipment manufacturer, may take on additional obligations to supply his wares in specific quantities. In each case, the amounts involved, or a formula for calculating them, will manifestly require specific agreement, as will a schedule (or formula) of payment/supply.

In addition, there may well be other obligations or constraints which it is necessary to impose upon the sponsor. For example:

– The nature extent and duration of any use which a sponsor may make of his spondee or his association with his spondee should ideally be spelt out. In particular, it is likely that most spondees, especially the established stars or other businesses with a marketable profile, would wish to secure a specific covenant designed to preclude the sponsor from seeking to exploit any association after the expiry of the particular sponsorship contract.

– There may be occasions when a potential sponsor might reasonably be expected to agree not to grant other sponsorships, or to do so only subject to particular conditions.

– Prudence would sometimes suggest that the spondee should secure an undertaking from his sponsor, either in the form of a positive obligation or through some form of 'best endeavours' covenant, not to act in any way which is liable to damage the spondee's interests, the sponsored subject itself or the sport in question or to frustrate the aims or breach the rules of any appropriate governing body or bodies thereof.

M. MONITORING

In some instances it will be appropriate to introduce into the contract a formal process for monitoring its performance. This may be especially appropriate where the contract incorporates conditions precedent or subsequent, in which case the process of monitoring may provide a means of clearly identifying when, if or to what extent the conditional stipulations have occurred. Equally, monitoring may lead to early identification of problems or defects in performance which can then be addressed at the earliest stage. The precise method of monitoring which is appropriate will depend upon all the circumstances. It may be that, in most cases, the process need not be agreed formally as part of the contract itself but should take place simply as a matter of good commercial husbandry[19]. Formal provision for monitoring may simply involve an agreed procedure to be applied by the parties themselves, perhaps according to a particular timetable, or it may involve third parties in carrying out the process so as to assess particular standards of performance.

N. OPTIONS

The sponsor may wish to include in the contract an option to extend his involvement whether, for example, by increasing the period of sponsorship or repeating the sponsorship on another occasion (say, in relation to the same event the following year) or in some other respect. Any such options will require careful thought so as to define their precise nature and ambit.

O. SPONSORS' PERKS

Most sponsors will wish to make use of their association with the sporting subject to further their aims beyond simply increasing public awareness of their corporate identity. Internally, such association may provide a means of engendering a particular 'feel-good' factor amongst their own employees. Equally, it may enable them to provide their favoured customers or suppliers with privileged 'inside' access to the event in question which they might otherwise find it impossible to secure. The facilities to be afforded to a sponsor should be the subject of clear definition and agreement at the outset. Rights of access to the venue itself, a prescribed number of available tickets and their location, the site and extent of the sponsor's own 'private' facilities for association and entertainment, and any rights or restriction in the use of such facilities are all likely to be subjects which will require to be addressed.

P. PROPER LAW, JURISDICTION AND DISPUTE RESOLUTION

Many sponsorship contracts will relate to international events and/or involve parties from different countries. It makes sense, therefore, to make express provision for the proper law of the contract, namely the law by which the

---

19 In any event the sponsor will be concerned to have access to all data made available to the spondee, for example by broadcasters.

contract is to be interpreted. In addition, it may be felt sensible to provide that the courts of a particular country should have exclusive jurisdiction to adjudicate in the event of dispute. Alternatively, provision may be made for arbitration, in which case an arbitrator or arbitrators should be nominated or the mechanism for appointing the arbitrator(s) expressly agreed.

Chapter 13

Television

Introduction

Television reaches out to virtually every home in the country. Indeed, watching the television is Britain's most popular leisure activity, with 97% of households containing a television set (77% have a video recorder), and over 80% of the population tuning in at some stage every day (94% do so every week). The effect of television on our daily lives is considerable, and is well illustrated by the extraordinary statistic that the average time spent by an individual watching the television each day is a staggering four hours. Moreover, the ever increasing popularity of sport has meant that major sporting events now receive extensive televison coverage[1] and thereby reach audiences which would only have been dreamed of in days gone by. The largest televison audience for a sporting event shown on one channel in the United Kingdom was Torvill and Dean's performance in the ice dance championship at the Winter Olympics of 1994, which was watched by some 23 million viewers. Football's Euro '96 achieved huge audiences over an extended period, reaching a peak at one point, albeit across two channels, of about 26 million. Furthermore, the dramatic changes which have taken place over the last ten years in the delivery of broadcasts to the home, in particular with the introduction of cable and satellite services, has meant that the extent of sporting coverage has been the subject of a corresponding and dramatic increase. The televised coverage of sporting events of one form or another has more than quadrupled since 1988 and now stands at over 12,000 hours per year. This means that an avid fan would fail in any attempt to watch every sports programme in the course of a year, even with the aid and maximum use of his video recorder and even were he to be able to stay awake for an uninterrupted period of 12 months!

It must follow that this marriage between sport and televison is one made in heaven, not simply for sporting authorities, bodies and individuals, all of whom desire the kind of public exposure which television can give them, but also for the marketing industry which surrounds sport and which has been discussed in the preceding chapters. Televison provides the most potent vehicle, not just for the marketing of sport itself, but also for 'sports marketing', namely the marketing of goods and services via a publicised association with sport.

---

1 The sports which attract the the most coverage, at least on terrestrial television, are football, horse racing, snooker and cricket.

The rise in televised sports coverage is likely to continue and even accelerate further, with the move towards digital broadcasting systems. Such systems involve (through a process known as multiplexing) the transmission, on single frequencies, of multiple signals (which mean multiple channels), which are then decoded for viewing at the point of delivery, by receivers in or next to individual television sets. Currently, the statutory structure within the United Kingdom contemplates the licensing of at least 18 digital terrestrial channels, which will transmit on six multiplex frequencies and serve, in the medium term, between 60 and over 90 per cent of the population. It will immediately be apparent that this new digital technology is likely to result in the delivery of a greatly increased and widened diet of, amongst other things, both live and delayed coverage of sporting action.

We have already seen how the goodwill (commercial pulling power) of sport may be harnessed and exploited through sponsorship and merchandising. The sale of broadcasting rights is but one further means (probably the most potent and important of all) of milking such goodwill. It is axiomatic that the commercial return from, say, a marketing initiative involving sponsorship will often depend in large part upon the extent of any television coverage. Thus, when it comes to the commercial exploitation of, or via, a sporting event or competition (or indeed a team or individual competing within it), the question of television coverage is likely to be the key ingredient. Further, with the ever increasing coverage of sporting events on television, it can be said with confidence that the commercial industries of marketing sport and sports marketing, which have already seen something of an explosion in recent years, are set for a further period of steady, if not dramatic, acceleration.

For example, it is understood that the television rights to the Sydney Olympic Games in the year 2000 have already been sold for $705 million and $350 million in the United States of America and Europe respectively. Further, the exclusive rights to broadcast international and domestic rugby union in South Africa, New Zealand and Australia have recently been acquired by News Corporation for $550 million.

The nature and extent of the change in the market over recent years can readily be seen by an examination of the position in relation to professional football in England. In the 1987–1988 season, the broadcasting rights in respect of live League football were sold for £3.1 million. The following year saw the introduction to the market place of satellite television, whereupon such rights were sold for £11 million per season (exclusively to ITV for a period of four years). In 1992, the price had risen to £214 million for a five year deal (involving BSkyB and the BBC). In June 1996, BSkyB and the BBC signed deals worth £743 million for a period of four years.

The regulation of sports broadcasting

The immediacy of television and its potential for exerting influence over human behaviour require that programmes should be delivered in a structured and regulated way. In addition, regulation is demanded in order to prevent exploitation and to guarantee certain minimum standards, not only as to the quality of broadcasts, but also as to their content in relation, for example, to taste and decency. The scheme of regulation in the United Kingdom is delivered in the case of commercial or independent television by, principally, the Broadcasting Acts 1990 and 1996[2]. In the case of the BBC, a Royal Charter and an Agreement with the (erstwhile) Secretary of State for National Heritage provide a looser framework of regulation. Both the Royal Charter and the Agreement were renewed and revised in 1996. The Agreement (dated 25 January 1996) requires the BBC, as a public service, to remain independent at all times both in relation to programme content and scheduling and in relation to its own management. It also sets general standards for its programmes, both as to their nature and their content. In particular, by paragraph 3, it obliges the BBC to provide a wide ranging coverage of sporting and other leisure interests.

Sport's relationship with television manifests itself in different forms. Most directly, sport attracts, and often actively seeks, broadcast coverage of specific events. Further, broadcasts (other than by the BBC) may themselves now be sponsored and there are sponsors who are liable to be particularly attracted to programme sponsorship where the programme in question involves sporting coverage. In addition, event sponsors (and many others involved in the event in question) will be anxious to secure maximum broadcast exposure for their names and their association with the event being broadcast and may seek to purchase advertising slots in the course of such coverage.

All such relationships require to be established and conducted with due regard for the statutory environment within which they fall to be regulated and it is necessary for those bodies who are party to such relationships to have a general appreciation of the regulatory scheme established by, primarily, the Broadcasting Acts 1990 and 1996.

In broad terms, that regulatory scheme (for commercial television) is maintained and policed by the Independent Television Commission[3], which is a body established by s 1 of the 1990 Act primarily to regulate:

- the provision of television programme services provided from places within the United Kingdom otherwise than by the BBC and the Welsh Authority; and
- the provision of cable and other similar television services within the United Kingdom[4].

In the discharge of its duties, the Commission has the statutory objectives[5] of trying to ensure:

- fair and effective competition in the provision of such services[6];
- that a wide range of services is made available throughout the United Kingdom; and

2 Both Acts need to be seen against a background of, and are intended as a specific application of, the general principles laid down by the European Community in the Television without Frontiers Directive (1989/552/EEC as amended by 1997/36/EC), to which reference is made below.
3 The BBC is required, on a day to day basis, effectively to regulate itself, but is subject to annual audit by reference to the standards and requirements laid down by the Royal Charter and the Agreement.
4 See Part II of the 1990 Act.
5 See s 2(2) of the 1990 Act. Broadly similar objectives, save as to fair and effective competition, are included amongst those set for the BBC by its Agreement with the Secretary of State.
6 It is to be noted that the articulation and pursuit of this objective of fair competition is not intended to constrain the competition authorities in the exercise of their functions in the same field. The sanction of the Commission will not necessarily provide any protection from the ordinary rigours of competition law.

– that services provided are of high quality and of wide ranging appeal to a variety of tastes and interests.

The primary function of the Independent Television Commission lies in the grant and control of broadcasting licences under Part I of the Act, and is a topic which, in itself, falls outside the subject matter of this book. For present purposes, the Act lays down various requirements as to the services which are licensed by the Commission, which requirements need to be born in mind by those who seek directly to use the services of licensed broadcasters, whether for advertising or for broadcasting their activities.

In particular, the Commission is charged, by s 6, with the obligation to do all it can to secure that the service complies with specific requirements, included amongst which are that broadcasts should not include material which:

– offends against good taste or decency, is likely to encourage or incite crime, lead to disorder or otherwise be offensive; or
– exploits the possibility of conveying messages or otherwise influencing the minds of persons watching, without their being fully aware of what has occurred.

In addition, the Commission has a general regulatory function and is entitled to impose requirements in pursuit of its 'general responsibility with respect to advertisements and methods of advertising and sponsorship'[7].

Of particular importance amongst the Commission's functions is the drawing up of statutory codes designed to give guidance as to appropriate practice within the broadcasting field. The 1990 Act makes provision for a number of codes of practice and compliance with such codes is generally a condition of any licences granted by the ITC.

For example, the Commission publishes a general 'Programme Code' which both explains the rules applicable to ensure impartiality in respect of matters of political or industrial controversy or relating to public policy[8] and gives guidance as to expected standards relating to matters such as sex and violence[9].

In addition, and perhaps most importantly in the context of this book, the Commission publishes and enforces two codes of practice, both produced pursuant to s 9, relating respectively to advertising and sponsorship[10]. In particular, such codes

– govern standards and practice in advertising and in the sponsorship of programmes; and
– proscribe advertisements and methods of advertising or sponsorship which are prohibited.

Other ITC Codes include a Technical Performance Code and the ITC Rules on Advertising Breaks. In addition, the Commission has recently issued a Code on Sports and other 'Listed' events, to which reference is made below.

7 See s 9(5) of the 1990 Act.
8 See s 6(3) of the 1990 Act.
9 See s 7 of the 1990 Act.
10 So far as the BBC is concerned, the position is governed by the Royal Charter and, more particularly, the Agreement, which requires the BBC's mainstream funding to come from the television licence revenue. The prospect of advertising and, in particular, programme sponsorship is not ruled out absolutely and for all time, in that, by para 10.10 of the Agreement, sponsorship of particular programmes is prohibited *without the prior approval of the Secretary of State*.

THE ITC CODE OF PROGRAMME SPONSORSHIP

The ITC first published a Code of Programme Sponsorship in January 1991. Prior to that, sponsorship of terrestrial television services had generally been prohibited by the Broadcasting Act 1990, with a less restrictive regime applying to the fast developing satellite and cable services, which had been subject to a separate regulatory regime under the former Cable Authority. The ITC's first code was amended and republished in January 1994 and, after a period of consultation and review, the current code was issued in March 1997.

The code applies to all television services licensed by the ITC and seeks to give effect to the requirements imposed in relation to television sponsorship by Chapter IV of the EC Directive on Television Broadcasting, 'Television without Frontiers'[11], and the 1989 Council of Europe Convention on Transfrontier Television. In some respects, it goes further than simply to regulate programme sponsorship itself and it is important to note that licences granted by the ITC make compliance with the code a condition and require the licensee to make its contents generally known to employees and programme-makers.

The ITC has described its general aim in regulating the sponsorship of programmes as being:

'To ensure that the development of this source of revenue and programme finance does not alter the character of programme services in such a way that they become adversely influenced by commercial considerations ... [both as to] the content of individual programmes and the range of programmes and programme types on offer ...'

Particular objectives include:

- the preservation of editorial and creative independence and integrity;
- the achievement of a satisfactory and integrated quantitative balance between commercial communication and programme material;
- the achievement of an appropriate degree of transparency to viewers of both the sponsor's role and the distinction between that role and the programme content.

In seeking its objectives, the ITC has recognised that its regulatory role now has to be fulfilled in the context of a considerably changed commercial environment. In particular, the ITC recognised that the nature and pace of technological change, and the increasing choice of channels and methods of programme delivery engendered thereby, has meant that in certain respects the first versions of the code were out of date. In some instances, the current code represents a limited relaxation of previous restrictions, where they were identified as having been disproportionate in relation to the mischiefs at which they had been aimed.

Core requirements of the code which are of particular relevance for present purposes may be identified as follows:

- The distinction between sponsorship and advertising (and, therefore, between advertisers and sponsors) must generally be made clear (for example in the case of sponsors' credits)[12]. Thus advertising which refers

---

11 89/552/EEC as amended by 97/39/EC.
12 See para 2.

to the sponsorship of a specific programme may not be transmitted in advertising breaks within or immediately adjacent to that programme.

– Certain categories of sponsor are prohibited or restricted[13]. Prohibited sponsors include those whose objects are political, those engaged in the manufacture or supply of tobacco products or prescriptive pharmaceuticals and (subject to the previous approval of the ITC) those who are prohibited from advertising under the ITC Code of Advertising Standards and Practice. Suppliers of betting or gaming services may not sponsor childrens' programmes and, for example, bookmakers may not sponsor programmes containing coverage of horse or greyhound racing (or the results of such racing).

– Certain categories of programme may not be sponsored[14]. Further, the code contains restrictions on the use in sponsored programmes of the presenters of unsponsorable programmes[15]. Such programmes include, in particular, news and current affairs programmes. Specific exceptions include specialist sports reports presented outside the context of a general news programme.

– The code imposes strict requirements and prohibitions on the nature and extent of sponsorship credits[16]. The general aim is to prohibit so called 'surreptitious sponsorship' and to require that any sponsorship should be clearly identified at the beginning and/or end of the programme. Other ('bumper') credits may appear at the beginning or end of commercial breaks but not otherwise within programmes themselves. The length and content of all such credits are strictly regulated. Further, the sponsor's name may not be incorporated in the programme title, save where the title is itself that of a sponsored event (eg the Coca Cola Cup Final)[17].

– The code contains general prohibitions[18] against references to the sponsor within the programme itself (including generic references to the sponsor's unbranded product, service or business). Any such references are likely to be seen as being promotional[19] and without justification. Similarly, there is a general prohibition against the practice of 'product placement'[20].

– One area where the rules have seen some limited relaxation, is in the case of any 'single interest channels' (such as, for example, a channel devoted to sport or even to one particular sport), which are likely to afford a wide range of advertising/sponsorship opportunities of various kinds. In relation to such channels, it is recognised that the potential viewers are liable to have a higher than average commitment to the subject matter of

13 See para 4.
14 See para 6.
15 See para 6.5.
16 See para 8.
17 This only applies in the case of terrestrial channels 3, 4 and 5. In the case of, for example, satellite services, the requirement is simply that the distinction between the event sponsor and the programme sponsor must be made clear.
18 See para 10.
19 The code provides an express reminder, in para 10.1, of the prohibition contained within the ITC Programme Code against 'undue prominence for commercial goods and services in programmes of any kind (whether sponsored or not)'.
20 See para 12.

the channels concerned and to be generally (perhaps even discerningly) receptive to an increased availability of information. Such availability might be curtailed by undue regulation aimed at restricting certain types of promotional activity. Thus, paragraph 10.3 of the code now provides:

> 'The ITC is prepared to apply a less stringent test ... to advertiser-supplied programmes broadcast on single interest channels provided the identity of the advertiser supplier is made transparent to viewers at the beginning of the programme. For example, travel programmes funded by a tourist authority would be acceptable on a themed travel channel. Such programmes must not, however, contain material which directly encourages the purchase or rental of the sponsor's product or service eg by providing information on prices, exhortations to purchase or contact details.'

– Specific provisions are designed to preserve 'programme integrity' and to prevent the distortion of programme agendas for commercial purposes[1]. To that end, sponsors are expressly prohibited from exerting influence on either the content or the scheduling of sponsored programes, at least in such a way as to affect the editorial independence and responsibility of the broadcaster. The position is underlined by a specific requirement[2], in the case of commissioned programmes, that the broadcasters should themselves, by contract, secure their right to editorial control.

– The code also legislates as to appropriate coverage of 'Events'[3]. In particular, whilst it recognises that the coverage of events or locations which are themselves sponsored may itself be sponsored, any visual or aural references to advertising, signage or branding must be limited to what can clearly be justified by the editorial needs of the programme itself[4]. Equally, references in the programme coverage to the event sponsors should identify accurately the sponsors' role (for example, stating which elements within the event are subject to the sponsorship in question) and should provide 'appropriate' recognition for the event sponsor (in particular, end credits are permitted), subject again to all such references being clearly justified by the editorial needs of the programme itself. Where events are sponsored by tobacco companies, or where there is branding, signage or advertising for any tobacco company, the coverage must be consistent with the requirements of the Voluntary Agreement between the Minister for Sport and the Tobacco Manufacturers' Association[5].

---

1 See para 9.
2 Paragraph 9.2.
3 See para 13. The BBC has its own code which lays down similar restrictions.
4 By para 13.2, such advertising or branding will not be regarded as acceptable, unless (a) the event is organised by a body independent of television, advertising and promotional interests (b) television coverage is not the principal purpose of the event and (c) the event is open to members of the public irrespective of whether or not it is televised.
5 The current Voluntary Agreement is that dated 31 January 1995 and is due to run until 1 June 1999. Its general aims are to restrict the extent and nature of any use of a sponsored event to promote smoking, to limit and regulate the display of tobacco advertising at sponsored events and to require the inclusion in any promotional/advertising material of appropriate health warnings. At the time of writing, the Government has just announced that it intends to take appropriate steps to outlaw all future tobacco advertising and sponsorship. It remains to be seen exactly how this declaration of intent will be brought into practice.

– One area of developing technology in which the ITC has shown a particular interest is in electronic imaging or 'virtual advertising' systems. Systems such as 'EPSIS' or 'Imadgine' permit the alteration of a received broadcast image, so as, for example, to permit different markets to be separately targeted by apparently showing different advertising signage at a broadcast event (on, say, perimeter or other fixed boards) in different regions or countries. The systems work by altering the broadcast signal itself. Such systems, if unchecked, are liable to provide considerable scope for programme makers to lose editorial control. The ITC has, therefore, issued a Sponsorship Guidance Note on 'Virtual Advertising'. It should be regarded as being, in effect, part of the code, as it is a requirement of the code itself[6] that any use of electronic imaging systems during coverage of an event should comply with such Guidance Note. The Guidance Note provides, in particular, that:

(a) electronic imaging systems must be 'transparent', in that explanatory credits should explain that such systems are in use;
(b) such systems should not impair picture quality;
(c) they should only be used to replace (and not add to) existing advertising signage which itself complies with the code;
(d) the broadcaster must retain the contractual right to refuse to carry an altered signal and must not gain any financial benefit from the use of such systems nor be involved in the sale of 'virtual advertising' to advertisers or their agents.

THE ITC CODE OF ADVERTISING STANDARDS AND PRACTICE

The advertising code, like the sponsorship code (with which it should be read as providing an all embracing code of practice in relation to advertising[7] and sponsorship) applies to all services regulated by the ITC and is mandatory under the terms of all licences issued by the ITC. The current code was issued in the middle of 1997. The general principle of the code is that advertising (namely *all* publicity material inserted in breaks in or between programmes) should be legal, decent, honest and truthful. Further, the code requires that advertisements should be clearly distinguishable as such and lays down a raft of measures concerning the nature and content of permissible advertisements.

It should be noted in this regard that the Television without Frontiers Directive[8] also contains restrictions on, amongst other things, advertising on and sponsorship of television programmes. Broadly, such restrictions are reflected by the relevant ITC codes which were drawn up with the provisions of the Directive in mind. But one particular measure in the Directive is worthy of specific mention. Such measure, which is required to be introduced by law by 19 December 1998[9], is that:

6 See para 13.5.
7 In addition, the ITC Rules on Advertising Breaks make provision as to the length, number and scheduling of commercial breaks.
8 Council Directive 89/552/EEC, as amended by 97/36/EC.
9 See Article 27(1).

'[In] sports programmes and similarly structured events and performances containing intervals, advertising and teleshopping slots shall only be inserted between the parts or in the intervals'[10].

'LISTED' EVENTS

So far as the broadcast coverage of sporting events is concerned, there is limited restriction provided in the regulatory scheme itself, and such coverage is simply subject to the general disciplines of the law applicable to all areas of human activity, such as those discussed elsewhere in this book like competition law and the law relating to freedom of movement.

The advent of satellite and other forms of subscription television has lead to increased concern that many of the public's favourite sporting events may cease to be generally accessible through free-to-air broadcast coverage and that televised pictures of such events may increasingly become the preserve of the relative few who are willing and able to afford the subscriptions and other expenses required to access satellite and other forms of encoded signal. Such concern is reflected, for example, in the Council of Europe Convention on Transfrontier Television which underlined the basic principle, of general application, that televised coverage of events of high public interest should have the widest accessibility. In particular, Article 9 bound the signatories to:

'avoid the right of the public to information being undermined due to the exercise by a broadcaster of exclusive rights for the transmission or retransmission of an event of high public interest and which has the effect of depriving a large part of the public in one or more other parties of the opportunity to follow that event on television ...'

More recently, on 22 May 1996, the European Parliament passed a general resolution on the broadcasting of sports events, which comprised a number of important general principles. In particular, the European Parliament resolved[11] that it:

'1. Considers it essential for all spectators to have a right of access to major sports events ...

5. considers that exclusive broadcasting rights for certain sports events which are of general interest in one or more Member States must be granted to channels which broadcast in non-encrypted form so that these events remain accessible to the population as a whole ...

9. considers that, to promote competition and maximise public access to sport, different transmission rights to the same event should not be sold to a single broadcaster in one package but unbundled and put on the market separately (eg live television coverage of an event separate from television highlights and radio transmission rights ...)

11. requests that where the broadcasting rights for a sports event are granted to an encrypted channel, this channel should be obliged to make available, in return for a reasonable fee, extracts of this event to other channels which express an interest ...'

10 See Article 11(2).
11 OJ C166, 10/6/96 p 109.

The point was re-emphasised when, on 12 November 1996, the European Parliament proposed[12] specific amendments to the Televison without Frontiers Directive[13]. Such amendments were, initially, not accepted by the Council and the matter was referred for further consideration by the Conciliation Committee. The result was an amending Directive which was eventually approved on 19 June 1997[14]. The Television without Frontiers Directive, as thus amended, introduced a coherent scheme of control, the fundamental elements of which (for present purposes) may be described as follows:

(a) The fundamental principle, enshrined in Article 2, is that jurisdiction to control the activities of a broadcaster is accorded exclusively to the Member State within which that broadcaster is based[15]. Other Member States are generally not permitted to impose restrictions on the broadcasts which come from broadcasters established in another Member State[16].

(b) Member States are required to exercise appropriate control of broadcasters established on their territory[17]. The measures which a Member State may properly take in order to control the activities of broadcasters established within its territory must obviously accord with Community law generally, subject to the derogations provided by the amended Directive itself. Such measures must ensure that such broadcasters comply with the provisions of the Directive (as amended)[18].

(c) The Directive expressly recognises that special provision is or may be required in order to ensure that a substantial proportion of the public is not deprived of the possibility of following certain sporting (or other) events of 'major importance for society'[19] via live coverage or deferred coverage on free television[20]. To this end, express sanction is given[1] for a Member State to impose controls on the broadcasting of

12 OJ C362 2/12/96 p 56.
13 89/552/EEC.
14 97/36/EC. By Article 27, Member States are required to introduce equivalent/compatible domestic laws by no later than 19 December 1998.
15 The Directive uses the word 'established', which is further explained by the detailed provisions of the Article.
16 See Article 2a, which provides a limited exception in the case of matters such as pornography and violence. A further exception is contemplated in the case of broadcasters who establish themselves in one Member State in order to circumvent the controls imposed by another Member State but direct most of their broadcasts to the second Member State. As to this latter exception, see para 14 in the Recitals and *Van Binsbergen v Bestuur van de Bedrijfs-vereniging*: 33/74 [1974] ECR 1299 and *TV10 SA v Commissariaat voor de Media*: C-23/93 [1994] ECR I-4795. Contrast *EC Commission v Belgium*: C-11/95 [1996] ECR I-4115.
17 Article 2(1).
18 Article 3(3).
19 Paragraph 18 in the Recitals to the amended Directive cites, by way of example, the Olympic Games, the football World Cup and the European football Championship.
20 Free television, for this purpose, has a restricted meaning and encompasses broadcasting of programmes accessible to the public without payment in addition to the modes of funding of broadcasting that are widely prevailing in each Member State (such as licence fee and/or the basic tier subscription fee to a cable network). See paragraph 22 in the Recitals. It should be noted, however, that paragraph 44 in the Recitals and Article 3 provide that a Member State may require television broadcasters under its jurisdiction to comply with more detailed or stricter rules in the areas covered by the Directive. Any such more stringent rules must, of course, remain compatible with Community law.
1 Article 3a(1).

designated events which fall within such category. Further, because of the jurisdictional principles referred to above, each Member State is required[2] to take appropriate steps to ensure that broadcasters established within its territory do not exercise any exclusive rights purchased by them[3] in such a way as to circumvent the controls imposed within another Member State in relation to events designated by the other Member State.

(d) The workings of the amended Directive will be the subject of further review before 19 June 2002[4].

Precisely where this concern to preserve important events for free-to-air coverage will ultimately lead, remains to be seen. Within the United Kingdom, Part IV of the Broadcasting Act 1996 already makes special regulatory provision (the nature of which is considered below) for the broadcasting of certain sporting and other events of national interest ('listed' events). The legitimacy of such an approproach now has the sanction of the Television without Frontiers Directive (as amended) referred to above. The provisions of the Broadcasting Act 1996 in this area amplify the restrictions in relation to the televising of listed events which were previously provided by s 182 of the 1990 Act (now repealed). Section 97 of the 1996 Act perpetuates the essential framework of the previous regime by providing for the identification of particular 'listed' events of national interest[5], to be certified by the Secretary of State. Such certification is to be issued only after consultation with particular relevant bodies, namely:

- the BBC;
- the Welsh Authority;
- the Independent Television Commission; and
- (in relation to individual events) the person from whom the broadcasting rights may be acquired.

Currently, the list of such events is strictly limited, if not arbitrary. Moreover, the restrictions in relation to listed events do not apply in relation to agreements relating to particular events which were entered into prior to such events first being listed. This means that, subject to the requirements of competition law discussed elsewhere, there currently remains a 'window of opportunity' for long term broadcasting agreements, free from restriction, to be entered into before the list is revised and additional events added to it. At present, the list comprises only:

- the FIFA World Cup football finals
- the FA Cup Final
- the Scottish FA Cup Final
- the finals weekend of the Wimbledon Tennis Championships
- the Olympic Games
- the Grand National
- the Derby
- Cricket test matches involving England

---

2 See Article 3a(3).
3 The Directive applies, in this respect, to purchases made after the date of publication of the amended Directive – see Article 3a(3).
4 See Article 25a.
5 The term 'national interest' here is used to include interest within England, Scotland, Wales or Northern Ireland.

In a pre-emptive attempt to puncture any enthusiasm in the Secretary of State for extending the list, the Major Spectator Sports Division of the Central Council of Physical Recreation, in consultation with the Sports Council, has drawn up a voluntary code, the aim of which is to ensure that major sporting events generally will be readily available to the public (viz: not simply on subscription terms) in live, recorded and/or highlights programmes. This voluntary code, which was drawn up in 1996, is due to run initially for five years. It is subscribed to by the governing bodies of most of the major sports in the United Kingdom[6] and its major aim is to strike a balance between the objectives both of maximising income from the sale of broadcasting rights on the one hand and achieving the widest possible broadcasting exposure on the other. It seeks to achieve this by requiring governing bodies, when negotiating with broadcasters, to strive to ensure the availability, at a fair market price, of either live, recorded or highlight coverage on a terrestrial channel on the one hand, and on any subscription channel on the other. The code itself contains provisions for the monitoring of its application by an ad hoc Monitoring Committee and, as a final indication of intent, requires its individual subscribers each year to allocate a proportion of broadcasting income (at least 5%) to the development of their particular sport.

The statutory regulatory scheme in relation to listed events is striking, in that it targets broadcasters rather than rights holders and thereby circumvents the potential problems of extra-territorial effect, in the case of events such as the Olympic Games, for which the broadcasting rights are held and controlled by the IOC, an organisation based in Switzerland. The scheme has two main themes. First, it distinguishes between two categories of broadcasts[7], namely those made (by the BBC and independent television) without specific charge for their reception (which may be referred to, for present purposes, as 'category one broadcasts') and those which may be received only upon specific payment, by means of 'pay per view' or subscription (here referred to as 'category two broadcasts'). This latter category obviously currently includes, for example, satellite and cable channels. Secondly, the scheme primarily targets broadcasting *contracts* and renders them void in certain circumstances.

The general aim of the scheme is, by promoting 'unbundling', to ensure that live coverage of listed events should be generally available to all viewers and should not be confined to 'pay per view', satellite or other subscription channels[8]. To that end, the 1996 Act lays down a raft of measures applicable specifically to the broadcasting of listed events:

- section 99 prevents the grant of exclusive[9] live broadcasting rights;
- section 100 requires that each individual broadcasting contract should identify that the right of live broadcasting granted thereby is limited to either what has been referred to above as 'category one' or 'category two'

---

6   The initial subscribers were the British Athletic Federation, the Football Association, the Lawn Tennis Association, the PGA European Tour, the FA Premier League, the Racecourse Association Ltd, the Royal and Ancient Golf Club of St Andrews, the Rugby Football League, the Rugby Football Union and the Test and County Cricket Board.
7   See s 98 of the 1996 Act.
8   To this extent, the Act is generally in line with European policy as described above.
9   The exclusivity referred to is exclusivity of broadcasting within the United Kingdom or any area of the United Kingdom.

broadcasts and that, therefore, the event organiser must deal with the grant of broadcasting rights under the two categories separately;

– section 101 prohibits a broadcaster from delivering live coverage in one of the two above categories unless:

   – another broadcaster has secured the right to deliver equivalent[10] live coverage in the other category, or

   – the consent of the Independent Television Commission is first obtained.

It should be noted, therefore, that the Act is concerned only with providing the best *opportunity* for live coverage to be made widely available. It does not guarantee live coverage, still less does it restrict all live coverage to terrestrial channels, but before the ITC will give its consent to the restriction of coverage to one category, however, it will require to be convinced that broadcasters in each category have been afforded a reasonable opportunity to acquire the rights. In approaching listed events in this way, the Broadcasting Act 1996 represents a dilution of the initial proposals for change. Lord Howell presented the original aim of the legislation to the House of Lords[11] as being that Parliament should:

'Keep faith with the millions who have no access to Sky, who cannot afford the £300 that is necessary to plug into Sky and to receive Sky Sport.'

The point was evidently then regarded as one of principle. Lord Howell went on:

'In that way we shall remain true to the heritage of British sport on television, and to the millions of young people who need the inspiration of sporting excellence to take up and enjoy sport.'

The Independent Television Commission has an important role to play in implementing and policing the regulation of the broadcasting of listed events. In particular:

– it is required[12] to publish and maintain a code for determining when a broadcast is to be considered as 'live' and to give general guidance, for example as to the circumstances in which it will give its consent to restricted coverage under s 101;

– it is required to police the operation of s 101 and, in the event of breach, may impose financial penalties[13] (in the case of commercial broadcasters) or report to the Secretary of State[14] (in the case of the BBC or the Welsh Authority).

In April 1997, the ITC published its Code on Sports and Other Listed events. In it, it laid down criteria for determining when a transmission is deemed to be 'live'. Essentially, any transmission which occurs whilst the event or individual match[15] is in progress will be regarded as live and accordingly subject to restriction. The code also articulates certain matters

10 Equivalent in the sense of live coverage of the same part of the listed event, for delivery to the same area of the United Kingdom.
11 Hansard, column 126, 6/2/96.
12 See s 104 of the 1996 Act.
13 See s 102 of the 1996 Act.
14 See s 103 of the 1996 Act.
15 Where an event or match (eg a cricket test match) is conducted over several days, each day's play will be regarded for these purposes as a separate event.

which the ITC will take into account in giving or revoking its consent to restricted coverage under s 101. In particular, the ITC will wish to be satisfied that all broadcasters (in each category) have had a genuine opportunity to acquire the rights on fair and reasonable terms. In this regard, the ITC will expect to see that:

– invitations to tender were issued to all broadcasters openly, simultaneously, in good time[16] and without favour in terms, particularly, of conditions or costs;
– the package of rights on offer was not more attractive to one category of broadcaster[17];
– the price was fair and reasonable and non discriminatory as between the two categories of broadcaster.

The concept of a 'fair and reasonable price' is a potentially difficult one. What is a fair and reasonable price will depend, no doubt, on all the circumstances. The code merely identifies certain specific criteria, namely:

– any previous price history (in relation to the same event or similar events);
– the time of day for live coverage;
– the revenue/audience potential associated with live transmission of the event;
– the period for which the rights are offered; and
– the competition in the market place.

Broadcasting contracts – general

Before a contract can effectively grant a licence to broadcast coverage of a sporting event, it is necessary that it should first be established that the grantor does indeed have some relevant proprietary right to which he is legitimately able to grant access in the form of the broadcasting rights the subject of the proposed licence. This may appear to be stating the blindingly obvious and, at first blush, it might be thought that there could be no doubt as to the rightful ownership of the rights the subject of a broadcasting licence of the kind here envisaged. Closer analysis reveals, however, that the position may not be entirely straightforward. Problems may derive from the fact that, as we have already seen in Chapter 9, the law does not immediately recognise a proprietary right in the concept of a sporting event itself. It follows that the participants in a sporting event cannot complain when others choose to watch their endeavours, provided that such spectators do not infringe some other proprietary right distinct from the sporting competition itself. Further, in so far as such spectators have a 'right to watch' the event, they surely have a right to capture the event on celluloid, in the form of photographs or moving pictures and the law does not recognise any restriction in their right then to put such pictures on public display. Thus, in

16 What constitutes an appropriate tender period will depend upon the circumstances. In its consultation paper, the ITC had suggested that, in ordinary circumstances, a reasonable time would be no more than half the time between the date of the invitation to tender and the event itself. This rule of thumb was omitted from the published code.
17 The code indicates that, ideally, live or 'as live' rights should be offered separately from other rights such as to highlights, delayed transmission etc.

Palmer v National Sporting Club Ltd[18], a boxer was unable to prevent the public exhibition of photographs taken, without his permission, of one of his fights.

In principle, there is no reason why the position should be any different in relation to the broadcasting of sports events, whether by terrestrial or satellite means. And so it proved, in an Australian case, *Victoria Park Racing and Recreation Grounds Co v Taylor*[19], where a broadcasting company was held not to have infringed any proprietary right when it erected a scaffold outside a racetrack, from which it was able to film the racing on the track itself.

In the circumstances described, and with the law failing to recognise in a sporting event a distinct form of proprietary 'sports right', the question might be posed as to why, nevertheless, 'broadcasting rights' are regularly identified in relation to popular sporting events, as being of such considerable value. Equally, it might be queried why television companies have been prepared in recent years to allow the costs of access to such 'rights' to spiral so spectacularly. The answer is straightforward. Whilst the so called 'right' to broadcast may not reflect any distinct proprietary right in itself, such a 'right', when granted by a contractual licence, is in truth parasitic on the grant of the right of access to some other identifiable right which indeed *is* recognised by the law as proprietary in its content. Thus, in *Victoria Park Racing*, if the racetrack owners had also owned the surrounding land, including that part on which the broadcaster's scaffold had been erected, they could legitimately have prevented the broadcasting of 'their' racing. Any injunction which they might have obtained in those circumstances, however, would have been founded not upon their 'right' not to have 'their' activities filmed without authorisation, but upon the broadcaster's trespass upon their land.

It is not simply the 'owner' or organiser of a sporting event who has an interest in establishing some kind of 'right' capable of supporting a grant of broadcasting rights. A broadcaster who acquires the exclusive right to broadcast an event will be astute in his attempts to prevent others from encroaching upon that grant. But he too will need to find some other recognisable proprietary right to which his grant may be allied, if his grant is to remain the valuable asset which he contemplated when purchasing his licence in the first place. The kind of difficulties which may otherwise arise may be illustrated by *Sports and General Press Agency Ltd v 'Our Dogs' Publishing Co Ltd*[20], where the purchaser of the 'exclusive photographic rights' at a dog show was powerless to prevent others from taking and publishing their own photographs[1].

18 1905-10 MacG CC 55.
19 (1938) 58 CLR 479.
20 [1916] 2 KB 880; affd [1917] 2 KB 125, CA.
1   Compare the position in the United States of America, where the courts recognise 'rights of publicity' in celebrities' names, likenesses and performances which will sometimes enable them to prevent the use of their profiles without their consent – *Uhlaender v Henricksen* 316 F Supp 1277 (1970) and *Dzurenko v Jordache Inc* 59 NYS 2d 788 (1983). The American courts also recognise a principle that the unauthorised 'misappropriation' of the fruits of another's labour is unlawful – see, for example, *Pittsburgh Athletic Co v KQV Broadcasting Co* 24 F Supp 490 (WD Pa 1938) in which an unauthorised radio broadcast describing baseball games from information supplied by observers from outside the grounds was held to infringe the organiser's proprietary rights derived from its 'creation of the game, its control of the park and its restriction on the dissemination of news therefrom'; see also *International*

The message from the cases already cited, must be that 'broadcasting rights' may, *in effect*, be created, but that their creation depends upon the existence, identification and protection of other distinct and recognisable proprietary rights to which they may then be attached. Futher, the nature of the recognisable proprietary rights which can best be nurtured in order to give rise to such consequential 'rights' of broadcasting, are clear from the examples of the two cases cited above, *Victoria Park Racing* and *'Our Dogs'*. The former case shows how the right of physical access to an event is all important. In the latter case, it was the dog show's failure to constrain the activities of others with access to the venue which diluted the value of the exclusive grant of photographic rights to the plaintiff.

Thus it can be said that the effectiveness and value of any grant of exclusive broadcasting rights will generally be determined by the ability effectively to police:

– access by others to the location of the event in question; and
– the behaviour of those to whom such access is granted.

Further, the ability to police such access and behaviour involves both the ability to keep others out (see *Victoria Park Racing*) and the creation of enforceable obligations and restrictions applicable to those others afforded legitimate access to the same event (see *'Our Dogs'*). In this latter respect, for example, the obvious safeguard would be a contractual proviso to the sale of tickets or to the grant of other accreditations, prohibiting (commercial) photography or other filming etc.

Another feature flowing from the law's failure to recognise a proprietary right in a sporting event itself and the consequent need to create such a 'right' by the identification and protection of other, associated but recognisable, proprietary rights, is that it is not always easy to identify precisely who 'owns' the 'rights' which are to be licensed to a broadcaster. The problem may not arise in the case of a discreet individual event held at a privately owned stadium, where the right of access to the venue is likely to determine, in a practical sense, who has the ability to grant licences to broadcast proceedings held within it. The problem becomes altogether more acute where:

(a)   the event is held in a public place, as in the case of, say, a marathon, motor rally or ocean yacht race; or
(b)   the occasion in question is not a one off event but a series of happenings, all occurring at different locations owned by different individuals or bodies, as in the case of a league, championship or other similar competition.

In relation to events conducted in public places, the problem may ultimately prove to be insoluble[2], if a persistent maverick broadcaster is minded to use hand held cameras or to find locations where the siting of cameras and their accoutrements does not give rise to an actionable obstruction, perhaps obtaining access to neighbouring properties for such purpose.

In relation to leagues and other similar championships, the position in practice is that the identification and delineation of relevant proprietary 'rights' is determined either by practical constraints (as where the right to

---

News Sevices v Associated Press 248 US 215 (1918) and *National Exhibition Co v Fass* 133 NYS 2d 767 (Sup Ct 1954).

2   Events on the high seas are especially difficult to defend against 'unauthorised' broadcasting.

licence broadcasting is determined, on a match by match basis, according to who controls the rights of access to each match) or by contract between the participants in the league or championship in question (as where the rules of the governing body, to which all participating clubs or individuals subscribe, stipulate that such body alone has the right to grant broadcasting licences in relation to matches conducted under its umbrella). Indeed, it is suggested that, where events or matches are likely to take place in a number of different locations and involve various different participants, the question of who 'owns' the broadcasting 'rights' to such events or matches is best dealt with expressly at the outset, in the setting up of the league or competition concerned. Such an orderly approach is likely not only to maximise the overall value of any grant of broadcasting rights, but also to avoid the sort of squabbles between participating bodies as, for example, marked the negotiation in 1996/97 of the contracts to broadcast international rugby union matches in the Five Nations Championship from 1997/98 onwards. In the absence of a clear contractual agreement between the participating governing bodies, the (English) Rugby Football Union sought to go its own way and negotiated a contract (with BSkyB) for the live transmission of matches involving England at Twickenham and were only brought into line with the other nations' governing bodies by the latter's retaliation with the practical measure of excluding England from the competition.

It is suggested that the question of 'ownership' of relevant broadcasting 'rights' should be uppermost in the minds of those responsible for setting up any form of sporting league, championship or other competition of significance and that the right to grant licences to such 'rights' (and any prohibitions against doing so) should be the subject of express agreement wherever possible. As to any such agreement, however, a word of warning needs to be sounded, in that, as we have already seen in Chapter 4 above, a concerted approach between participating bodies to the right to grant broadcasting access to particular events has the potential for attracting the interest of the competition authorities. In setting up any constitutional rules, or otherwise negotiating participation agreements, therefore, a weather eye needs to be kept on the requirements of both European and domestic competition law.

Unfortunately, as discussed in Chapter 4, the precise implication of competition law for such rules and agreements is currently uncertain as a result, under European law, of the Court of First Instance decision in the Eurovision case, *Metropole Television SA v EC Commission*[3] and, at common law, of the Director General of Fair Trading's reference to the Restrictive Practices Court of the FA Premier League's rules providing for the centralised collective sale of broadcasting 'rights' in relation to Premier League matches.

Broadcasting contracts – their contents

The precise terms of any grant of broadcasting rights will be determined by the particular circumstances of the contract in question. In each case, however, it is likely that a number of generic issues will need to be addressed. This section seeks to consider some of the more obvious ones.

3 Joined cases T-528/93, T-542/93, T-543/93 and T-546/93, CFI Transcript 11 July 1996.

– *Parties*

Generally, a principal broadcasting contract will be between the 'owner' of the event or competition in question and a broadcaster (or group of broadcasters) known as the 'host' broadcaster, namely the broadcaster to whom is accorded the right to place cameras at the event and to originate the picture signals for transmission. In addition, other contracts may provide other broadcasters with licensed access to the host broadcaster's signal, for example for transmission in foreign territories and/or for delayed (recorded) transmission or where separate arrangements are made for terrestrial and satellite coverage. Careful consideration should be given as to who is the 'owner' of the event or competition in the circumstances and, accordingly, as to who should be party to the contract in that capacity. Further, either all licensed broadcasters should be party to the one umbrella contract, in which the rights and obligations of all concerned are clearly defined or, alternatively, the subsidiary licensed broadcasters' contracts should be 'back to back' with the host broadcaster's contract. In any event, the structure of relationships between the 'owner' of the event in question, the host broadcaster and the other licensed broadcasters should be put into place with care. One alternative is for the 'owner' to contract solely with the host broadcaster(s) (who may comprise a union of broadcasters, such as the European Broadcasting Union), obliging the latter, or according to him the right, to contract with other licensed broadcasters by granting specific sub-licences. In this event, any relevant protections for the 'owner' in relation to the sub-licensing of other broadcasters, will need to be provided for in the definition and proscription of the host broadcaster's right/obligation to grant such sub-licences. Finally, consideration should be given as to whether or not the contract should include amongst its parties certain other interested participants, such as the event or programme sponsors.

– *Rights 'ownership'*

Attention has already been drawn, above, to the potential difficulties in identifying an appropriate proprietary right capable of sustaining an effective grant of a licence to broadcast, and the associated difficulties in establishing rights of 'ownership' to any such right. For these reasons, the 'owner' who purports to grant a broadcasting licence should be required to warrant his 'ownership' and/or his right to enter into the contract in the agreed terms.

– *Exclusivity*

The broadcaster will usually require some form of exclusivity in his right to broadcast a sporting event or competition. Such exclusivity may be defined in terms of the coverage itself (live transmission, terrestrial or satellite coverage etc) and/or it may relate to a defined territory (or territories) for transmission. It is no more than commercial common sense that exclusivity increases the premium which a broadcaster is likely to be prepared to pay for his contract, and it follows that rights 'owners' generally are prepared, where able, to offer some form of exclusivity in the bargaining process. Equally, it should be remembered that exclusivity, particularly when taken to particular extremes (as in the case of contracts extending over a lengthy period), is the lifeblood of the competition regulatory authorities. It follows that the negotiation of a broadcasting contract should balance the desirability of an exclusive grant against such considerations as may be liable to render a contract 'anti-competitive' in the context of the various strands of competition law, both European and domestic. The relevant principles of competition law are discussed in Chapter 4, but for present purposes, it may be said generally that every particular feature of exclusivity should be capable of being shown to be justifiable. Hence the tendency in recent times for broadcasting contracts which grant exclusive live rights to satellite or other subscription channels, to impose parasitic obligations (or grant associated rights) to guarantee some limited delivery of coverage on terrestrial television. In particular, any grant of specific exclusivity should be of a nature and extent as arguably to be, itself, a product of free competition (as with an exclusive short term contract, liable to come up for competitive bidding from time to time) rather than to be unduly inhibitive of competition generally (as with longer term arrangements and, especially, those confined to satellite delivery). In this regard, a resolution of the European Parliament on the broadcasting of sports events, of the 22nd May 1996[4], postulated a conundrum that, whilst a grant of exclusive rights should generally be of limited duration, the current competition situation was such that long-term contracts constituted the best guarantee for free-to-air channels to broadcast major sports events in a manner accessible to the population as a whole. As mentioned previously, the Television without Frontiers Directive[5], as now amended[6], contemplates and sanctions the imposition of specific controls by individual Member States to restrict the exercise by broadcasters of exclusive rights in relation to listed events[7], if such exercise is liable to deprive a substantial proportion of the public of access to the coverage. In the circumstances, any grant of exclusive rights should perhaps be subject to a proviso that they will be exercised in accordance with the requirements of the amended Directive and the Broadcasting Act 1996.

– *Territorial licences*
Where the host broadcaster's rights are confined to transmission within a particular territory, transmission into other territories may also be contemplated[8]. As mentioned above, such 'foreign' transmissions may be licensed directly by the rights 'owner' himself or by sub-licences from the host broadcaster. In one form or another, the rights of such foreign broadcasters need to be defined. In particular, they will require defined rights of access to a clean signal from the host broadcaster. Equally, the extent to which they require access to commentaries, interviews and other material provided by the host broadcaster will need to be considered, as will their rights, if any, of access to the event by their own personnel, cameras and otherwise, although it is not unusual for the host broadcaster to be jealously protective of his camera positions.

4 OJ C166/109, 10/6/96.
5 89/552/EEC.
6 97/36/EC.
7 The concept of 'listed events', as defined by the Broadcasting Act 1996, is discussed in outline earlier in this chapter.
8 It should here be remembered that Article 3a(3) of the amended Television without Frontiers Directive (89/552/EEC amended by 97/36/EC) requires Member States to ensure that exclusive rights are not exercised in one Member State in such a way as to contravene the legitimate controls imposed by another Member State as to the broadcasting of designated events of public importance within that second Member State.

– *Extent of coverage*
Contracts, whether with the host broadcaster or a sub-licensed operator, need to be clear as to the nature of the coverage embraced thereby. Further, in identifying different categories of coverage (live coverage, delayed coverage, recorded highlight coverage etc) the contract should be specific as to any particular *rights* granted on the one hand and as to specific *obligations* imposed on the other. Generally, the event 'owner' will seek to impose obligations on the broadcaster, designed to achieve a particular level and quantity of coverage. He will want to ensure that his event is transmitted to the public in a structured way, at popular times and for sensible periods of time. The broadcaster is likely to have other scheduling pressures and may seek to limit his obligations in favour of a simple grant of a right to broadcast in such manner as he should choose. The negotiation process will be likely to reflect these competing interests of the parties. In relation to scheduling considerations, the contract or contracts will, in all probability, need to provide a balance between the grant of rights and the imposition of obligations.

– *Quality of coverage*
In addition to the amount of coverage required of or afforded to a broadcaster, the 'owner' of the event or competition in question will wish to ensure that the quality of coverage provided is appropriate. Equally, the broadcaster himself will require the kind of facilities necessary in order to deliver pictures of the quality (and diversity) to which he aspires. Manifestly, particular warranties of quality may be required of the broadcaster, both in relation to his signal or picture and in relation to his commentary. This is particularly important where the 'owner' of the event is relying upon the host broadcaster to make these available to foreign broadcasters. Such warranties should seek to guarantee an uninterrupted signal and commentary wherever possible, as well as targeting the quality thereof itself. In addition, the contract may need to provide the broadcaster with the means and facilities to deliver the quality required. For example, specific provision may be appropriate for the number and even type of cameras and other equipment used; the contract may identify particular commentators and techniques to be used; commentary positions may be provided for; access to individual participants may be guaranteed in certain circumstances, for example for interviews at appropriate times; parasitic facilities, for interviews and generally for the broadcasters' other legitimate activities, should be identified and appropriate rights of access to them should be provided for.

– *Legal and other regulatory requirements*
Any broadcasting contract should require adherence to any relevant requirements of the Broadcasting Acts and, where appropriate, the Television without Frontiers Directive[9]. Further and in particular, broadcasters should undertake to comply with any applicable codes of practice, such as those issued by the Independent Television Commission (eg the ITC Programme Code, the ITC Code of Programme Sponsorship, the ITC Code of Advertising Standards and Practice and the ITC Code on Sports and other Listed Events) and the Sports News

9   Council Directive 89/552/EEC as amended by 97/36/EC.

Access Code of Practice[10]. In the case of the BBC, it should be required to adhere to the principles contained in its Charter and its agreements with the Secretary of State. In addition, broadcasters should agree not to contravene (or cause others to contravene) the rules of the event or competition the subject of the broadcasting contract, or the constitutional rules and regulations of the governing body or bodies with jurisdiction over the sport in question.

– *Promotional obligations*
One of the purposes of a broadcasting contract is to give the event being broadcast a wider currency than would be available simply through the turnstiles. Generally, the 'owner' of a sporting event seeks to maximise his audience and to maximise the goodwill of his event and of those with whom his event is legitimately associated, principally the sponsor(s) and 'official suppliers'. The broadcasting contract may be used to further such ends. In particular, the broadcaster may be required to publicise and promote his coverage in advance in a defined and structured manner. Further, such advance promotional coverage or 'trailers', and indeed coverage of the event itself, may be required to include appropriate prominence for the name of the event and, perhaps, its sponsors. Any particular logos, designs and other material associated with the event or its sponsors may also be required to feature in such coverage, and provision may be made for particular credits at the beginning and end of particular transmissions, and also for 'bumper' credits either side of commercial breaks, subject always to the relevant provisions of the applicable Codes and, in the case of tobacco sponsored events, the Voluntary Agreement between the Minister for Sport and the Tobacco Manufacturers' Association. Where appropriate, commentators and others may also be required to make oral mention of the event by its sponsored title.

– *Ambush marketing*
Promotional obligations, however well defined and adhered to, may sometimes be undermined by the activities of others. The opportunity, gratuitously and without legitimate authority, to cash in on the goodwill attaching to a particular sporting event is increased by television coverage of that event. The broadcasting contract should therefore be astute to include appropriate provisions to eliminate or reduce such opportunities. The contract might sensibly impose a general obligation on the broadcaster not to allow his coverage to give any unnecessary prominence to the names or activities of those not legitimately associated with the event the subject of his coverage. Pursuant to such a term, for example, the cameras would not linger on an unauthorised sign or other manifestation designed to publicise the goods or services of someone seeking free publicity for his business. Equally, the broadcasting contract should endeavour to prevent the broadcaster from affording legitimate publicity opportunities to others which would be liable to confuse the public perception of who has a legitimate association with the event in question. Specific obligations in relation to legitimate advertising are considered below, but, in addition, the relationship between sponsorship of (and other legitimate association with) the *event*

10 See p 311 below.

itself and sponsorship of the *broadcast coverage* should be carefully considered. Specific terms should be designed to prevent avoidable conflicts of interest, perhaps by

- affording the event sponsor the right of first refusal in respect of any broadcast sponsorship opportunity;
- requiring that no broadcast sponsorship opportunities should be offered or awarded to particular categories of business;
- providing for a mechanism for the appointment of broadcast sponsors which includes safeguards designed to protect the interests of other pre-existing interests associated with the event.

- *Advertising obligations*

Commercial television generally incorporates advertising slots during sporting coverage. Such interruptions can sometimes become intrusive and objectionable. The broadcasting contract ought to make express provision for such advertising. Specific timetables might be agreed. Alternatively, rules may be laid down both as to the extent and length of any commercial breaks and/or as to the occasions when such breaks may be taken[11]. Subject to issues of competition law, provision may be made as to who should be allowed to take advertising slots during the coverage itself and immediately adjacent to it. In this regard, it might be appropriate to afford the event 'owner', his sponsors and other parties associated with the event itself, some kind of priority in bidding for such advertising slots. Equally, the broadcaster might agree a procedure for vetting potential advertisers and vetoing inappropriate advertisements (for example, advertisements from direct competitors of an event sponsor would no doubt be regarded as inappropriate for inclusion during coverage of the event itself). In addition, in order to protect the event owner's goodwill and that of its sponsors, the broadcaster should be obliged to ensure that no advertisement be allowed to suggest any connection with the event which was not an authorised and legitimate (official) connection. Finally, the 'owner' of the event should consider whether or not the broadcaster should be prohibited from using electronic imaging systems so as to change the advertising appearing on billboards sited at the event itself. Insofar as the broadcaster is permitted to use such systems, careful consideration should be given as to the extent and nature of any permitted 'virtual advertising' changes which he should be allowed to effect. In particular, the broadcasting contract should bring any altered images (if permitted) within the constraints, if any, imposed in relation to advertising generally.

- *Copyright and future use of broadcast material*

Ownership of the copyright in any broadcast material should be expressly provided for. In the event that the 'owner' of the event to be

---

11 Such matters are already provided for under the ITC's regulatory regime, by the ITC Rules on Advertising Breaks, issued in accordance with ss 9(7) and (8) of the Broadcasting Act 1990 to give effect to the requirements of the Council of the European Community Broadcasting Directive (85/552/EEC) of 3 October 1989 and the 1989 Council of Europe Convention on Transfrontier Television. See also Chapter IV of the Television without Frontiers Directive (89/552/EEC as amended by 97/36/EC).

broadcast requires an assignment of such copyright[12], the broadcaster's rights to future use of the material, whether in 'repeat' showings, compilations or otherwise, would need to be provided for, perhaps by express licence. In the event that copyright remains with the broadcaster, the event 'owner' will no doubt wish to retain for himself (and perhaps for his sponsors) some express rights of access to and use of the material, whether simply for promotional purposes or indeed for other commercial ends. For example, rights in relation to videos and/or on-line distribution may sometimes prove to be exploitable assets of substantial potential value. Whoever is designated as the owner of the copyright, however, the provisions of s 30(2) of the Copyright Designs and Patents Act 1988 should not be forgotten. That section provides a defence to a breach of copyright claim in the case of 'fair dealing[13] ... for the purposes of reporting current events'[14]. Furthermore, in *BBC v British Satellite Broadcasting Ltd*[15], it was held that such a defence was not limited to the reporting of current events in general news programmes but extended to items of (genuine) sporting news. In that case, the section protected the broadcast on satellite sports bulletins of short clips (of between 14 and 37 seconds in length) showing highlights of World Cup soccer matches taken from the broadcasts by the BBC of the complete matches. The fallout from that case resulted in the mainstream broadcasters[16] subscribing to a Sports News Access Code of Practice as to the amount of sports material which may be taken off air and used in news programmes[17]. Quite apart from the Code, consideration should be given as to whether or not the broadcasting contract should include an express obligation on the broadcaster to make available to other broadcasters appropriate footage for inclusion in sports, news and other current affairs programmes[18]. In this regard, the policy of the European

---

12 Subject to commercial constraints, this is the arrangement which the event 'owner' is likely to seek, so that he can control the exploitation of any future use of archive footage, for example by the grant of individual licences, particularly to the broadcasters of similar such events in the future.
13 The Act does not define the concept of 'fair dealing', which remains a question of fact to be determined according to the circumstances of each case. See *Hubbard v Vosper* [1972] 2 QB 84.
14 For the defence to be effective, the 'dealing' generally has to be accompanied by an appropriate acknowledgement. By s 30(3), however, this is not so in the case of 'the reporting of current events by means of a sound recording, film, broadcast or cable programme'.
15 [1992] Ch 141.
16 The original subscribers to the Code were the BBC, ITV, ITN, BSkyB, TV-AM and Channel 4.
17 The Code, in particular, limits the secondary broadcaster's use of the primary broadcaster's material to bona fide national or regional *news* programmes (or news slots) and does not permit any use in specialised sports news, sports review or sports 'magazine' programmes. It also defines the nature, length and timing of useable extracts, identifies the number of occasions on which they may be broadcast and requires the display, on each occasion of use, of a visual credit to the primary broadcaster. Compliance with the Code is, by the terms of its preamble, agreed by its subscribers to provide a 'fair dealing' defence to a claim for copyright infringement. At the time of writing, the Code has recently expired, but it is thought likely that it will be re-introduced in similar form, although it is understood that certain broadcasters are concerned as to how the development of 'pay per view' broadcasts should be accomodated in any such code.
18 As indicated in the previous note, the Code does not contemplate use of another broadcaster's material in anything other than a bona fide news programme.

Parliament is clear. In its resolution of 22 May 1996[19] on the broadcasting of sports events, it emphasised:

> 'That the news media have a right to free new gathering and the public a right to adequate and rapid information, and that holders of 'exclusive broadcasting rights' should not therefore prevent other TV broadcasters from showing excerpts from or summaries of events in which there is great public interest by demanding payment beyond that required to cover costs or by making stipulations as to the time of the broadcast ...'

– *Payment*

It goes without saying that a broadcasting contract should identify the price payable for the grant of the broadcasting rights in question. Such provision should either identify any particular sum agreed, or specify the formula for calculating any sums payable. In addition, the dates or events triggering particular payments should be clearly identified, together with any provision for interest in the event that payment should be delayed.

– *Cancellation/curtailment/postponement*

The negotiation of a broadcasting contract should address the possibility of cancellation or postponement. In particular, consideration should be given as to whether or not it is appropriate for the 'owners' of the event or competition in question to give specific undertakings that such event or competition will take place, or will take place on a specified date or dates. In relation to certain sporting events, such as those which are at the mercy of the weather, any undertaking in quite such absolute terms would be inappropriate, but in such a case a modified obligation might nevertheless be fitting. In any event, the prospect of cancellation, curtailment or postponement should be expressly dealt with. Obviously, if the event in question is simply cancelled, there will be nothing to broadcast. If the event is merely postponed, questions will arise as to whether or not the broadcaster should be obliged to cover the postponed event. Equally, in the event of cancellation, curtailment or postponement, the contract should clearly identify on which party the risk should fall. Particularly in the case of curtailment, there should, for example, be no doubt as to whether or not the broadcaster's payment obligations are affected.

– *Insurance*

In so far as either party is liable to sustain loss through the failure or interruption of the anticipated broadcast coverage, whether as a result of the weather, technical breakdown, or otherwise, consideration should be given as to the appropriate allocation of the risks of such failure or interruption. Equally, it might be thought prudent to impose upon one of the parties (normally the one to whom the risk is assigned) an obligation to obtain appropriate insurance cover.

– *Term and termination*

In the case of a specific, one-off event, the period of the broadcasting contract will be determined by the date and length of the event itself. In the case of a continuing or recurring event, or a league or championship, it is likely to be necessary to provide for a fixed term or at least for an indeterminate term terminable by notice. In every case, it is likely that the parties will wish to include express provision for early termination. The events likely to trigger a desire to terminate will depend upon the circumstances of each case, but included amongst them would surely be a significant or continuing breach of an important obligation under the contract itself such as the non payment of an instalment under the broadcaster's payment schedule. In the case of an international competition, the elimination of particular participants (perhaps the British competitors) might provide a legitimate trigger for an early termination. Particularly in the case of such competitions with a high potential political content, such as the Olympic or Commonwealth Games, the broadcaster may require a warranty as to particular levels of participation.

– *Disputes*
The contract should specify both the law by which it is to be governed and the mechanism, if any beyond ordinary court action by which disputes should be determined. In so far as arbitration is to be provided for, the process for identifying an arbitrator or arbitrators and the rules by which such arbitration should be conducted should be clearly identified, and it should be made clear whether the parties agree to arbitration as the *exclusive* means of resolving disputes.

Chapter 14

Insurance

by Colin Wynter

Introduction

Wherever there exists a 'risk' or chance that something may happen which might bring about injury, damage or financial loss, insurance may be available for the benefit of the person or persons having an 'insurable interest'[1] in the person, premises or event at risk. As has been higlighted in other chapters, recent events in the courts have shown the need for sports administrators and others involved in playing, supervising or administering sports events to be alert to the need for and availability of insurance cover. For this, even though the sports person or administrator will seek the guidance of insurance brokers or other intermediaries when considering and arranging their insurance requirements, there should also be some understanding of insurance law and of its general underlying principles.

Once begun, disputes with insurers can be protracted and costly affairs. By understanding from the outset of the insurance the way in which an insured's obligations are likely to be construed by the court, and the potential consequences of any breach of duty/conditions/warranties on their part, insured sports persons/administrators can go a substantial way towards avoiding such disputes by, for example, identifying each of those areas in which the insured has contractually promised (ie warranted) strict compliance, and thereafter ensuring that they and (if applicable), their employees comply with the requirements of the relevant contractual promise. It is hoped that this chapter will provide some assistance in that task.

The law relating to insurance, whilst governed by general principles of contract law, is in several fundamental respects quite different and distinct from the general law of contract. This can prove an unpleasant and costly trap for the unwary. For example, whereas the breach of a 'warranty' in a general commercial contract will allow the innocent party only to sue for damages, but not to terminate the contract itself, the breach of a warranty in an insurance contract will automatically discharge the 'innocent' party (almost always the insurer) from its obligations under the insurance, but will not allow the innocent party to sue for any damages.

It is not possible in a single chapter to do justice to a subject that has spawned a considerable number of specialist texts. Instead, the subject of insurance is dealt with here in terms of (a) a general overview of the most

---

1 *Prudential Insurance Co v IRC* [1904] 2 KB 658 at 663; *Thomas v National Farmers' Union Mutual Insurance Society Ltd* [1961] 1 All ER 363.

fundamental insurance principles, and (b) a commentary on the various types of insurance that are commonly available, and which are particularly suited to the needs of those involved, in whatever capacity, in the playing, supervision or administration of sport.

There is a wide range of readily available insurance protections that can be obtained in pre-packaged form from general insurance brokers and, increasingly, direct from insurance companies. Particular examples include employers' liability, and public (or 'third party') liability insurance. Also available, but usually only with the assistance of specialist brokers, are custom made insurance protections, designed in order to protect those with the necessary insurable interest (see below) against a specific or unusual peril. One example of such bespoke cover is 'key man' insurance, which may be taken out by the owners or major sponsors of, say, a motor racing team or football club, against the risk that its number one driver or star player may, through injury or death, cause loss of income and profit to the owners and/or sponsors. Whilst such insurance will fall into one or other of the general categories of insurance, specialist assistance will be required in order to structure appropriately the precise nature and scope of the protection required.

When considering the type and extent of insurance cover required, the individual or other sporting body will need first to consider the areas in which he/it is exposed to potential injury, damage or loss, and also his/its potential legal liability to pay damages to others in respect of such matters. This exercise, or 'risk assessment', is the necessary first step for anyone wishing to make adequate insurance provision in respect of their potential losses/liabilities. Any risk assessment, if it is to be of any value, must be effected against a background of up to date knowledge of legal developments and trends in the areas of law relevant to the risk sought to be insured.

Insurers will themselves, where certain types of cover are sought, seek to have the risk 'surveyed' by their own surveyor, for the purpose of identifying particular areas of risk in respect of the business being broked. Once in receipt of the survey report, insurers may decide variously to reject the risk outright, to impose specific terms and conditions over and above those that would normally be applied, to rate the risk on a higher basis (ie require greater premium) and/or insert into the contract of insurance specific exclusions in respect of identified loss events and/or circumstances.

Fundamental insurance principles

'UBERRIMAE FIDEI' AND DISCLOSURE

All contracts of insurance are contracts of 'uberrimae fidei' ie of the utmost good faith. This has several important consequences, principal of which are the obligations imposed on the potential insured extra-contractually[2] (a) to disclose to insurers, when in the process of seeking/placing insurance (usually this is done by the completion of a proposal form by the applicant), every circumstance about which he knows and which is 'material' to the risk

---

2   *Banque Financière de la Cité SA v Westgate Insurance Co Ltd* [1989] 2 All ER 952, CA; affd [1990] 2 All ER 947, HL. NB: The significance of the duty being an extra-contractual one is that a breach of the duty cannot give rise to damages.

being considered by the insurer, and (b) not to misrepresent to the insurer any circumstance or matter which is material to the risk.

MATERIALITY AND INDUCEMENT

'Materiality' has, in this context, been defined by the House of Lords as meaning any matter which, if disclosed to the prudent insurer, would have 'an effect on the mind of the insurer in weighing up the risk'[3]. This definition sets a fairly low threshold in order for something to be considered as being 'material' to the risk in question, since it does not require that the misrepresentation or non-disclosure should have been such as to have persuaded the notional prudent underwriter to write the risk, but simply that the misrepresentation or non-disclosure should have had an effect on the mind of the insurer in weighing up the risk in question.

For example, a football player who, when seeking personal accident insurance, fails to disclose to insurers that his hobbies are bungee-jumping, sky-diving and hang-gliding, will have made material non-disclosures, since the fact that the footballer undertook such hazardous activities would almost certainly have had 'an effect on the mind of the insurer in weighing up the risk'.

It is particularly during the period in which the insurance is being placed that the insured must observe this duty. Disclosures to insurers may be made in proposal forms completed by the insured and/or their broker, or may be made in the form of a written presentation (usually by a broker) to insurers; they may even, exceptionally, be made orally. However the information is disclosed to insurers, the duty remains on the proposed insured throughout not to misrepresent material facts and circumstances, and to disclose to insurers all facts and circumstances that are material to the risk.

The consequences of any failure by the insured to observe its duty of good faith are exceptionally severe. Insurers can, should they so wish, and should the court accept that the insurer was 'induced' by the relevant material non-disclosure or misrepresentation into entering into the contract of insurance on the terms that it did, avoid the contract of insurance 'ab initio' ie 'from the start', the effect being that the contract is deemed and declared, in effect, never to have existed. The insured will be entitled to the return of any premium that may have been paid, but it will lose any right that it may have had under the insurance to be paid or indemnified in respect of any claim or claims that would otherwise have fallen to be paid under the insurance. So, for example, the forgetful footballer who fails to disclose, when applying for personal accident insurance, the material circumstance that he had suffered a broken leg several years previously, may find himself without cover when claiming subsequently for loss of earnings as the result of a sports accident.

The remedy for insurers for breach by an insured of its duty of utmost good faith is avoidance of the contract of insurance. It is an all or nothing remedy, and insurers do not have the choice to sue instead for damages, or to repudiate the particular claim whilst allowing the contract of insurance to continue. Should insurers fail to avoid a contract of insurance after having become apprised of material non-disclosures, they may be held to have

---

3   *Pan Atlantic Insurance Co Ltd v Pine Top Insurance Co Ltd* [1994] 3 All ER 581 at 587, per Lord Goff.

waived, and thus lost forever, the right to avoid on the basis of those material non-disclosures.

Insureds must also be aware that the law will always, save in particular and exceptional circumstances (eg where there is a signed agency agreement between the insurer and the broker), consider the broker as the agent of the insured. On a practical level, this means that any breach by the broker of the insured's duty of utmost good faith will be taken as a breach of the duty by the insured himself[4]. If, therefore, an insured informs his broker of particular material circumstances which the broker thereafter forgets or omits to pass on to insurers, insurers will still be able to avoid the contract for material non-disclosure, despite the fact that the insured may himself have done all that he could to make disclosure[5]. In such circumstances, the insured's remedy will be to sue his own brokers for breach of contract/ negligence in their handling of the placing/broking process.

'INSURABLE INTEREST'

It is a principle of insurance law that insurance can only be effected by a person or persons having an 'insurable interest' in the person, object or event being insured. This means that only those persons having a legal or equitable interest in the thing to be insured can properly insure it. Such persons have an 'interest' in the thing to be insured in that they stand to benefit by the thing's continued safety and to suffer loss in the event that the thing were to be damaged, lost or destroyed[6]. The rationale behind the principle is that persons having the requisite 'insurable interest' will, in normal circumstances (save eg where fraud is concerned) have the same interest as insurers in keeping safe and free of harm the thing that has been insured. Also, in terms of obtaining disclosure of matters relevant to the risk, persons having an insurable interest will be better placed to give the requisite disclosure than would persons who are less connected with the thing that is being insured. The requirement that an insured should have an interest in the thing that is to be insured appears to have had its origin in the 18th century at a time when there was a moral drive to eradicate the culture of gambling, which had spread so far into society that newspapers published odds on the chances of survival of ailing personalities, in order to allow wagering to take place![7] So far as the sports person/administrator is concerned, the point to note is that it is important to make certain, when entering into an insurance contract, that the insured does have an 'insurable interest' in the thing that is being insured. If the insured does not have any such interest, the policy of insurance will be invalid and thus unenforceable[8].

A party other than the insured can have his/its interest noted on an insurance policy, with the effect that he/it becomes an additional loss payee in the event of an insured peril taking place. For this, the insured will need to have had the authority of the other party to cover his/its interest. The sponsor of a sports event (eg a cricket test match) may, for example, require

---

4   See eg *Rozanes v Bowen* (1928) 32 Ll L Rep 98 (failure to disclose material facts).
5   See eg *Roche v Roberts* (1921) 9 Ll L Rep 59.
6   *Lucena v Craufurd* (1806) 2 Bos & PNR 269.
7   Welford *Insurance Guide and Handbook* (4th edn, 1901) pp 27 and 28.
8   *Cosford Union v Poor Law and Local Government Officers' Mutual Guarantee Association Ltd* (1910) 103 LT 463, 75 JP 30, 8 LGR 995.

its interest to be noted on a policy of insurance, taken out by the sports body running the event, providing insurance cover, say, against the risk of rainfall and the consequent abandonment of play, and refunds of ticket prices. The sponsor, if his interest were to be noted on the policy, would be interested in the insurance/insurance proceeds, but would not be an actual insured.

POLICY CONDITIONS

The term 'condition' may mean several different things in an insurance contract, depending upon the circumstances in which the words appear and the way in which the 'condition' may have been described by the parties in the policy document(s). A condition may be described variously as:

(a)   a condition precedent to risk;
(b)   a condition precedent to liability;
(c)   a simple condition;
(d)   a warranty.

The consequence of a breach of a condition by an insured will depend upon the type of condition that has been breached. Although the condition may have been described in policy documents as being of this or other type, it is the court which will ultimately determine the nature of the condition;[9] how the condition was described will be only one of the factors taken into account by the court, which will generally be looking to give effect to the intention of the parties, in the context of the commercial purpose of the insurance that was effected.

CONDITIONS PRECEDENT TO RISK

If such a condition is not satisfied by the insured, the insurer is treated as never having come on risk (ie never to have insured) the thing insured. So, for example, where it is a condition precedent to risk that the insurance premium shall have been received from the insured, insurers will be held not to have come on risk until receipt by them of the relevant premium. If an insured peril (say, a fire) were to have occurred before the receipt of the relevant premium, insurers would not be liable to indemnify since they would never have come on risk in the first place. This position may be complicated where the insured has made payment of the premium to his brokers. Even though brokers are almost invariably considered as the agents of the insured for most purposes, including the placement of insurance, they can at the same time, depending upon the precise arrangements existing between the brokers and the insurers, be the agents of insurers for the purpose of collecting and passing on premium.

CONDITIONS PRECEDENT TO LIABILITY

If such a condition is not satisfied by the insured, the insurer will not be required to make payment in respect of any claims/losses occurring

9   See eg *Schuler AG v Wickman Machine Tool Sales Ltd* [1974] AC 235; *Re Coleman's Depositories and Life and Health Assurance Assocaition* [1907] 2 KB 798.

subsequent to the insured's failure/continued failure to satisfy the condition. It might, for example, be a condition precedent to liability of an American football player's personal accident policy that, before playing any game of football, his ankles should each be strapped with protective tape. If the player were to suffer an ankle injury after having failed to strap his ankles, insurers could properly decline to pay in respect of any claim arising out of that accident. Note that the contract of insurance will have been and will remain in force. It is only the claim that is repudiated, and not the insurance contract itself.

SIMPLE CONDITIONS

A failure by an insured to comply with a simple condition merely gives insurers the right to claim for damages for breach of contract against the insured. This is usually an ineffective remedy for insurers and it is thus seldom sought. It may, for example, be a simple condition of an American football player's personal accident policy that he should keep a reasonable supply of ankle strappings available for his use. Unless such a condition could be construed as being a condition precedent to either risk or liability, the insurer's only remedy would be to claim or counterclaim against the insured for damages suffered as the result of the insured's breach of the condition.

WARRANTIES

As we have seen above, a failure by an insured to comply with the provisions of a warranty has the effect of discharging insurers from any liability to the insured as from the date of the breach. A warranty is in effect a contractual promise, variously (i) that certain facts and matters stated by the insured as being true are in fact true, or (ii) that certain specified precautions will be taken by the insured during the period of the insurance. There are several ways in which such a contractual promise can be made by an insured, but the most common are:

– by a statement of facts (usually provided in response to a proposal form questionnaire) given at the same time as a signed declaration by the insured that the statements given are true and accurate, together with an acknowledgment/acceptance by the insured that such statements will form 'the basis of' any contract of insurance entered into between insurers and the insured.

– by an express agreement (only in marine insurance will warranties be implied) by the insured that certain things will be done or observed. Usually the words 'warranty' or 'warranted' will be used in the appropriate clause, in order that the intended purpose of the relevant clause should be apparent, not only to the parties to the insurance, but also to the court, in the event of there being some future dispute on the issue of the insured's compliance with the matters warranted. So, for example, it may be a requirement of a football club's material damage insurance (see below) that it should warrant to have available, in good working order, at its ground, fire extinguishers and a burglar alarm. If a loss were to occur under the policy at a time when the insured was in breach of the warranty (eg no fire extinguishers present), the insured would be held to have broken its warranty (or contractual promise) and insurers would be discharged from any liability as from the date of the breach. This would be the case even if the loss and the breach were unconnected (eg a fire at a time when the burglar alarm was not working). The rationale for this is most clearly stated by Lord Goff in *Bank of Nova Scotia v Hellenic Mutual War Risks Association (Bermuda) Ltd, The Good Luck*[10]:

'... if a promissory warranty is not complied with, the insurer is discharged from liability as from the date of the breach of warranty, for the simple reason that fulfilment of the warranty is a condition precedent to the liability of the insurer. This moreover reflects the rationale of warranties in insurance law is that the insurer only accepts the risk provided that the warranty is fulfilled. This is entirely understandable; and it follows that the immediate effect of a breach of a promissory warranty is to discharge the insurer from liability as from the date of the breach. In the case of conditions precedent, the word 'condition' is being used in its classical sense in English law, under which the coming into existence of (for example) an obligation, is dependent upon the fulfilment of the specified condition. Here, where we are concerned with a promissory warranty ie a promissory condition precedent, contained in an existing contract of insurance, non-fulfilment of the condition does not prevent the contract from coming into existence. What it does ... is to discharge the insurer from liability as from the date of the breach ...'

It should be noted that insurance policy wordings frequently make use of a general clause (eg 'all things to be done, observed or fulfilled by the insured shall be conditions precedent to insurer's liability ...') in order to make what would otherwise read and be construed as simple conditions into conditions precedent, and even warranties. Such clauses are generally honoured by the courts[11], although ambiguity and/or inappropriateness of a particular clause being classed as a condition precedent may persuade the court to disregard the description given by the policy wording to the clause[12].

Types of insurance available

There are four main types of insurance which are likely to be of relevance to sports persons, organisations and administrators. Combined policies, providing cover in respect of some or all of the following heads can be obtained so as to meet the precise requirements of the particular sports person, organisation or administrator:

---

10 [1992] 1 AC 233 at 262F to 263C. See also *Forsikringsaktieselskapet Vesta v Butcher* [1989] 1 All ER 402 at 406 f, per Lord Griffiths.
11 *Roberts v Eagle Star Insurance Co Ltd* [1960] 1 Lloyd's Rep 615 (condition precedent that burglar alarm would be set whilst premises unattended) and *Bennett v Yorkshire Insurance Co Ltd* [1962] 2 Lloyd's Rep 270 (condition precedent that sales ledgers be maintained).
12 Re 'ambiguity', see *London Guarantie Co v Fearnley* (1880) 5 App Cas 911 and *Pioneer Concrete (UK) Ltd v National Employers Mutual General Insurance Association Ltd* [1985] 2 All ER 395. Re 'inappropriateness of classification', see *Re Bradley and Essex and Suffolk Accident Indemnity Society* [1912] 1 KB 415.

(a)   material damage insurance;
(b)   liability insurance;
(c)   benefits insurance;
(d)   contingency insurance.

MATERIAL DAMAGE INSURANCE

This type of insurance is intended to protect the insured in respect of loss of or damage to its own premises or other property. What should be insured will depend upon the nature of the sports person/organisation seeking the insurance. A football club, with its own ground, stands and changing areas will wish, for example, to insure its premises against the risk of damage or destruction, typically by fire or flood, but also, if required, by vandalism or wind. A football club with no ground, stands or changing area of its own may nevertheless have won a number of trophies which it may wish to insure against loss, damage or theft. Each of these insurances, since they relate to a risk of loss or damage to the insured's own property would fall to be included within a material damage policy of insurance.

Also available within material damage insurance are, amongst other things, protections in respect of legal expenses and consequential losses caused by business interruption. This last is important for those organisations whose income is dependent upon the regular occurrence of a sporting event or fixture (eg the owner/operator of a sports hall). Without such cover, the consequence of a fire or other catastrophe may be that the insured would recover the reinstatement cost of the premises damaged in the fire, but nothing at all in respect of the losses that would be suffered during the period in which the premises would be closed whilst being rebuilt.

LIABILITY INSURANCE

As the description suggests, this type of insurance is intended to insure against any legal liability incurred by an insured in respect of claims brought against it by third parties. Employers' liability insurance (which insures in respect of personal injury claims brought against the insured by its own employees) and Public liability insurance (which insures in respect of claims brought by third parties – members of the 'public' – for damages for personal injury or loss of or damage to property) are the most essential for the sports administrator/ organisation.

Also needing to be considered under this head is insurance in respect of coaches, referees, and others in similar positions of responsibility. Recent court cases (see Chapter 1 above) have made it clear that coaches and referees can, in appropriate circumstances, incur legal liability to those in their charge, if their standards of supervision/control are found to have fallen below the standards of a reasonably competent, qualified coach/ referee, and if that fall in standards is found to have resulted in injury to persons under their charge.

Product liability may also constitute a potential risk and one against which insurance may need to be sought, particularly by those involved in producing, selling or marketing sports related merchandise and paraphernalia.

BENEFITS INSURANCE

This type of insurance provides a 'benefit' to the insured in the event of certain specified events occurring. This would include matters such as travel insurance, life insurance, medical expenses insurance and personal accident insurance for the benefit of the individual sports person. The wording of personal accident insurance policies usually provides cover in respect of injuries sustained by the insured by reason of 'violent, accidental, external and visible means'. This will exclude, recovery by the insured in respect of diseases and degenerative weaknesses (eg osteoarthritis) unless such conditions have themselves been caused by some 'violent, accidental, external and visible means'.

The insured may, by his own conduct, expose himself to an increased risk of injury. The reckless lunge of a footballer which results in a career ending injury to himself may be said to have wilfully exposed himself to an increased risk of injury by the choice and timing of his tackle. Whether or not the injured player receives payment under his personal accident policy will depend upon whether his conduct is considered by insurers (or, ultimately, the court) as having been negligent (in which case the player will recover under the policy) or as having constituted a wilful exposure to danger. The term 'wilful exposure' has however been restrictively construed by the courts. In *Morley v United Friendly Insurance plc*[13], the insured jumped onto the bumper of a car that was being driven by his fiancee. He fell from the bumper and was killed. The deceased's accident policy excluded liability for accidents caused by 'wilful exposure to needless peril'. The word 'wilful' was held by the Court of Appeal to refer to the insured's state of mind when carrying out an act, as well as to the deliberate nature of the act. It followed that, unless there was a reckless (as opposed to negligent) assumption of the risk of injury, the policy exclusion did not apply. The deceased's conduct in the Morley case was held to have constituted 'horseplay' which, whilst deliberate, was not accompanied or preceded by any reckless assumption by him of the risk of injury.

Where an injured sportsman does not have personal accident insurance providing him with insurance against the risk of injury, he will need to establish legal liability for the injury on the part of some third party if he is to recover damages in respect of the injury and its financial consequences. Whilst it is also open to the injured sportsman with personal accident insurance to pursue a claim for compensation in the courts against the third party responsible for the injury, litigation may be the only means of compensation for the uninsured, injured sportsman. Where the injury is sufficiently serious to end or curtail the player's playing career, the sums at stake may be large, further encouraging the uninsured, injured sportsman to resort to litigation. As an increasing number of such cases come to court, sports organisations and governing bodies might wish to reflect upon the comments of Lord Bingham in *Smoldon v Whitworth*[14]:

> '...We are caused to wonder whether it would not be beneficial if all players were, as a matter of general practice, to be insured not against negligence, but against the risk of catastrophic injury ...'

---

13 [1993] 1 Lloyd's Rep 490; see also *Marcel Beller Ltd v Hayden* [1978] QB 694.
14 [1997] ELR 249.

CONTINGENCY INSURANCE

This type of insurance insures against the happening (or the non happening) of a particular event or circumstance. Most obviously, this would include matters such as weather insurance in respect of losses suffered following the abandonment of a sporting fixture as the result of excessive rain ('pluvius' insurance). Also available is insurance in respect of losses suffered as the result of other contingencies such as, for example, the non appearance of a visiting football team.

Chapter 15

Aspects of taxation

by Timothy Brennan

Introduction

'The Inland Revenue is not slow – and quite rightly – to take every advantage which is open to it under the taxing statutes for the purpose of depleting the taxpayer's pocket'[1].

It may be no surprise that where sport is run as a business activity with a view to profit, those engaged in the activity are liable to the incidence of taxation on the same principles as other businessmen. Less obviously, the same is true where sport is not run primarily with a view to profit; tax liabilities may arise even where the participation of those involved is seen by them as uncommercial. Not only is there no blanket tax exemption for a sports business, but sports authorities, clubs and other sporting bodies enjoy no particular tax free status by association with sporting activity[2]. They are accordingly exposed to a potential charge to corporation tax, to the responsibilities placed on employers for deduction of income tax and national insurance contributions and to the Value Added Tax regime. Individuals engaged in sport may be liable to tax not only on commercial earnings as competitors and otherwise, but as administrators or even as the officers or officials of unincorporated clubs. Early appreciation of the potential impact of taxation on the activities of sporting organisations and sportsmen and women may enable effective tax planning to avoid otherwise unnecessary and troublesome burdens.

While this chapter identifies some of the areas of potential interest and concern it cannot deal comprehensively with all possibilities and is not a substitute for skilled professional advice.

Taxation of sporting organisations

Most sporting organisations operate either as registered companies (limited by shares or by guarantee), or as unincorporated associations. The definition of 'company' for the purpose of the charge to corporation tax encompasses

---

1 *Ayrshire Pullman Motor Services and DM Ritchie v IRC* (1929) 14 TC 754 at 764 per Lord Clyde.
2 The position may be contrasted with certain other jurisdictions, such as Australia and Canada, where non-profit making sports organisations enjoy certain exemptions.

both (though not a partnership)[3]. In either case they incur potential charges to corporation tax on taxable profits and capital gains.

Income and gains likely to be taxable include income from trading and similar activities (including those such as bar and catering profits), investment income, rents from property and even fund-raising income. Sponsorship income is treated by the Inland Revenue as taxable.

Clubs, societies and associations

TRADING

There is no statutory definition of what amounts to a 'trade'. The term

'is commonly used to denote operations of a commercial character by which the trader provides to customers for reward some kind of goods or services'[4].

The term 'trade' includes every trade, manufacture, adventure or concern in the nature of trade[5]; even a single transaction may amount to an adventure in the nature of trade[6]. The Inland Revenue is likely to take interest in any form of profitable commercial activity by a sporting organisation, regardless of how close a connection such activity may have with sport. Thus, the use of a rugby club's facilities as parking for cars may incur a tax liability. Fine distinctions sometimes have to be drawn. For example, the objects of a company limited by guarantee were to encourage interest in the Olympic Games and to organise and co-ordinate British participation. One of its chief functions was to assist the preparation and fund the sending of a British team to the games. The Inland Revenue contended that the association was carrying on a trade of exploiting its logo and granting the status of sponsor. In the event, the Special Commissioner held that the activities of the association as a whole were non-commercial and therefore it could not be said that it was carrying on a trade[7].

Mutual trading

Subscriptions and contributions made by individual members to the funds of their club are not regarded as taxable income of the club, because the members cannot trade with themselves or make a profit out of themselves[8]. As a corollary to this exemption, the general running expenses of the club are not normally regarded as being allowable against any tax which the club

---

3   Income and Corporation Taxes Act 1988, s 832(1) ('ICTA 1988'). In this context 'unincorporated association' connotes two or more persons bound together for common purposes by mutual undertakings, in an organisation which identifies who controls it and its funds, and which can be joined and left at will: *Conservative and Unionist Central Office v Burrell* [1982] 1 WLR 522, [1980] STC 317.

4   *Ransom (Inspector of Taxes) v Higgs* (1974) 50 TC 1 at 78 per Lord Reid, [1974] 1 WLR 1594, [1974] STC 539.

5   ICTA 1988, s 832(1).

6   *Wisdom v Chamberlain (Inspector of Taxes)* [1969] 1 WLR 275.

7   *British Olympic Association v Winter (Inspector of Taxes)* [1995] STC (SCD) 85. The significance of this first-instance decision, largely on its own facts, should perhaps not be overestimated. It certainly does not decide that national sporting organisations never trade.

8   *National Association of Local Government Officers v Watkins* (1934) 18 TC 499 at 506 per Finlay J. Contrast *IRC v Stonehaven Recreation Ground Trustees* (1929) 15 TC 419.

would be liable to pay on its commercial activity. (This of course does not apply to a proprietary 'club' which, despite its name, is in reality a commercial organisation run by its proprietor for profit.) The mutual trading exemption is likely to apply if income is derived from members, if any surpluses are applied for the benefit of members and distributions and surplus assets on winding-up go to the members. The cardinal requirement is that all the contributors must be entitled to participate in the surplus and that all the participators in the surplus must be contributors to the common fund; in other words, there must be complete identity between the contributors and the participators[9]. Non-voting associate members of a football club who had rights and privileges equal to those of voting members have been held to be members of a mutual organisation[10].

Contributions within the mutual trading exemption would include payments made by members for goods or facilities provided to members by the club. Payments made by members in respect of their personal guests would normally be treated in the same way. This would not, however, extend to charges made to members for private use of club facilities. Receipts from visitors (casual or otherwise) who, in return for payment on a commercial basis, are allowed to use a club's facilities will be receipts from a taxable trade in the club's hands[11].

Dissolution of unincorporated associations

Where an unincorporated association is dissolved, the distribution of its assets constitutes an income distribution[12]. Where substantially the whole of the association's activities have been of a social or recreational nature, it has not carried on an investment business or a trade other than a mutual trade, and the amount distributed to each member is not large, it is given the option of treating the amounts distributed as capital receipts of the members for the purpose of calculating chargeable gains arising to them on disposal of their individual interests in the association[13].

If the relevant billing authority so decides, a club, society or other organisation neither established nor conducted for profit may attract discretionary relief from business rates in respect of its premises used wholly or mainly for the purposes of recreation[14].

Gambling

The winnings of an individual gambler are unlikely to constitute trading receipts, even where he follows his own system for betting and makes his

---

9 *Municipal Mutual Insurance Ltd v Hills (Inspector of Taxes)* (1932) 16 TC 430 at 448 per Lord Macmillan.
10 *Westbourne Supporters of Glentoran Club v Brennan (Inspector of Taxes)* [1995] STC (SCD) 137.
11 *Carlisle and Silloth Golf Club v Smith (Surveyor of Taxes)* [1912] 2 KB 177; affd [1913] 3 KB 75, CA and see Revenue Interpretation RI 84 (August 1984).
12 ICTA 1988, s 209, limited where s 490(1) (mutual trading) applies to the amount distributed out of profits charged to corporation tax or out of franked investment income.
13 Extra Statutory Concession C15.
14 Local Government Finance Act 1988, s 47(2)(c), s 48(3). See also under Charities. Agricultural land is exempt altogether, but land used mainly or exclusively for purposes of sport or recreation or as a racecourse does not so qualify: s 51 and Sch 5, paragraph 2(d), (e).

living from it[15] or bets on his own performances as a sportsman[16]. The position is otherwise where the winnings form part of the regular income of the taxpayer's business[17] or where a betting system is exploited through newspaper articles[18]. A bookmaking (or casino or similar) business is a trade, taxable as such, even though its profits arise from gambling. Winnings from betting, including pool betting, or lotteries, or games with prizes are not chargeable gains for the purposes of capital gains tax, nor does disposal of a right to such winnings give rise to a chargeable gain. Nor do losses in such activities give rise to allowable losses[19].

DEDUCTIBLE EXPENDITURE

Revenue expenditure

To the extent that an organisation or an individual is trading, revenue disbursements and expenses incurred wholly and exclusively for the purposes of the trade may usually be deducted from the gross income of the trade in order to compute the amount of the profits to be charged to tax[20]. 'For the purposes of the trade' means 'for the purposes of earning the profits of the trade'[1] and there is likely to be limited scope for deductions beyond the amount of expenditure directly connected with earning the trading income.

Legal expenses incurred in defending professional disciplinary proceedings wholly and exclusively for the purpose of preserving the taxpayer's trade or profession (for example by avoiding the imposition of a life time ban) may be deductible[2]. Fines and penalties imposed as a result of such disciplinary proceedings are unlikely to be deductible[3].

Sponsorship of sport which is wholly and exclusively for the purpose of the sponsor's trade is likely to be deductible as being in the nature of advertising expenditure[4].

15 *Graham v Green (Inspector of Taxes)* [1925] 2 KB 37.
16 *Down (Inspector of Taxes) v Compston* [1937] 2 All ER 475 (golfer).
17 *Burdge v Pyne (Inspector of Taxes)* [1969] 1 WLR 364 (club proprietor gambling at his own club).
18 *Graham v Arnott (Inspector of Taxes)* (1941) 24 TC 157.
19 Taxation of Chargeable Gains Act 1992, s 51(1).
20 ICTA 1988, s 74(1)(a).
1 *Strong & Co of Romsey Ltd v Woodifield (Surveyor of Taxes)* [1906] AC 448; *Mallalieu v Drummond (Inspector of Taxes)* [1983] 2 AC 861.
2 *McKnight (Inspector of Taxes) v Sheppard* [1997] STC 846, CA.
3 *IRC v Warnes & Co Ltd* [1919] 2 KB 444; *IRC v Alexander von Glehn & Co Ltd* [1920] 2 KB 553; *McKnight (Inspector of Taxes) v Sheppard* [1996] STC 627 (this last case went to the Court of Appeal, see [1997] STC 846, but not on the question of deductibility of fines).
4 The trading purpose must be the sole purpose of the expenditure. A mixed motive is insufficient. Where a company made substantial payments in sponsorship of a stock of horses and horse box which had the effect of affording benefits to the wife and children of the majority shareholder and director, the Special Commissioners held that a non-trade purpose (benefiting the equestrian interests of the wife and children) was a conscious motive. In any event, the non-trade result was so inevitably and inextricably involved in the sponsorship activity that the result must have been a purpose of the activity. The expenditure did not qualify for a deduction: *Executive Network (Consultants) Ltd v O'Connor (Inspector of Taxes)* [1996] STC (SCD) 29.

Business entertaining expenses incurred in connection with a trade (such as those incurred in the provision of hospitality to customers at sports events) are not deductible[5].

Pools payments to the Football Trust for football ground improvements, in consequence of the reduction in pool betting duty effected in 1990, are deductible in computing for tax purposes the profits or gains of a trade carried on by the person making the payment[6]. Payments from the pools promoters to their Foundation for Sports and the Arts for the support of athletic sports and games are similarly deductible[7].

Although in general the cost of gifts is not an admissible deduction in computing profits chargeable under Schedule D, business donations to registered charities are deductible[8] (provided the deduction would otherwise be allowable), as are gifts for the benefit of a local body or association of persons established for recreational purposes, not restricted to persons connected with the donor, where the gift is reasonably small in relation to the scale of the donor's business[9]. Charities are further dealt with below.

Depending on the nature of the trade and of the organisation, it may be possible to negotiate with the Inland Revenue the allowance of some apportioned part of the overall costs of running the organisation.

Capital allowances

Where a person carrying on a trade incurs capital expenditure on the provision of machinery or plant wholly and exclusively for the purposes of that trade, the expenditure will, if the machinery or plant belongs or has belonged to him, rank for a capital allowance, currently providing a writing-down allowance against trading income at the rate of 25% per annum on a reducing balance basis (that is, 25% of a sum equal to the cost of the asset less the amount of allowance already given)[10]. The allowance extends to machinery, equipment and apparatus of all kinds, fixed or unfixed. It does not extend to buildings or certain structures but there is special provision preserving the capital allowance for expenditure on the provision of swimming pools and their equipment.[11]

---

5   ICTA 1988, s 577. Thus a sponsor, who could otherwise claim a deduction in respect of sponsorship fees paid out, would not be permitted to deduct the notional cost of any tickets etc which he might receive as sponsorship benefits and use for entertaining his customers. Business entertainment has occasionally been considered by the courts in relation to VAT, as to which see below.

6   Finance Act 1990, s 126.

7   Finance Act 1991, s 121.

8   ICTA 1988, s 577(8), (9).

9   Extra Statutory Concession B7.

10 Part II Capital Allowances Act 1990 (see s 24). In his 1997 Budget the Chancellor of the Exchequer announced that the allowance was to be doubled for small and medium-sized firms for a temporary period of 12 months ending 1 July 1998.

11 Section 83(7) and Sch AA1 of the Capital Allowances Act 1990, inserted by Finance Act 1994, s 117(1). The present rules excluding certain expenditure from the expression 'expenditure on the provision of machinery or plant' have effect in relation to expenditure incurred after 29 November 1993, other than expenditure relating to binding commitments made before that date where the expenditure is incurred before 5 April 1996. In other cases, the relevant question is whether buildings or structures (used for the purposes of the business) function as premises or as plant: *Wimpy International Ltd v Warland (Inspector of Taxes)* (1988) 61 TC 51, [1989] STC 273; *Attwood (Inspector of Taxes) v Anduff Car Wash Ltd* [1997] STC 1167. 'Plant' does not include the premises or place in or on which the business was conducted and so did not include a football stadium: *Brown (Inspector of Taxes) v*

Special provision is made for capital allowances for expenditure on safety at sports grounds[12].

CHARITABLE STATUS

The achievement of charitable status will enable a sporting organisation to save tax by qualifying for many reliefs from tax where the relevant income forms part of the income of the charity or is applicable (and applied) for charitable purposes only[13].

Charitable status is not achieved by being dedicated to the pursuit of sport. Charitable status may be achieved if the objects of the organisation (which may, but need not, be a trust) are properly 'charitable', namely for relieving poverty, advancing religion or education or for other purposes 'beneficial to the community'[14]. The preamble to the Statute of Elizabeth, 43 Eliz 1 c 4, 1601 has formed the starting point for the courts in determining the legal meaning of charity, though it was repealed in 1888. The concept of charity has passed through a process of extension 'to cases analogous to cases which have been adjudged to be analogous'[15].

The provision of prizes for sport at an educational establishment[16], for chess[17], and the provision of facilities to enable school students to play sports[18] have all been held to be charitable. In the last of these cases, while the Football Association Youth Trust was held to be charitable as being for the advancement of education, the House of Lords left undecided the question whether a gift for physical education, not associated with persons of (or just above) school age would be charitable. It has been said that

> 'Healthy and manly sports are certainly in fact beneficial to the public, but apart from special concomitants are not generally entitled to qualify as charitable objects'[19].

Burnley Football and Athletic Club Co Ltd (1980) 53 TC 357, [1980] STC 424, nor an inflatable cover for tennis-courts: *Thomas (Inspector of Taxes) v Reynolds and Broomhead* (1987) 59 TC 502, [1987] STC 135. It did include a swimming pool at a caravan park: *Cooke (Inspector of Taxes) v Beach Station Caravans Ltd* [1974] 1 WLR 1398.

12 Capital Allowances Act 1990, s 70. The allowance applies to expenditure in respect of certain sports grounds and regulated stands (see the Safety of Sports Grounds Act 1975 and the Fire Safety and Safety of Places of Sport Act 1987) in meeting the requirements of a relevant safety certificate or in taking the steps set out by the relevant local authority in a letter or other document as steps the taking of which would be taken into account in deciding what terms and conditions should be included in a present or proposed safety certificate. Where the allowance is available, the expenditure is treated as capital expenditure incurred on the provision of relevant machinery or plant, even if it would not otherwise have so qualified for relief. Section 70 does not automatically give relief for expenditure incurred in meeting requirements imposed under the Football Spectators Act 1989, or other requirements, but such expenditure may qualify independently of this provision.

A subsidy from the Football Trust in respect of capital expenditure on improving the safety or comfort of spectators does not have to be taken into account in reduction of expenditure ranking for a capital allowance: Finance Act 1990, s 126(4), disapplying s 153 of the Capital Allowances Act 1990.

13 See ICTA 1988, ss 505, 506.
14 *Income Tax Special Purposes Comrs v Pemsel* [1891] AC 531 at 583 per Lord Macnaghten.
15 *IRC v Yorkshire Agricultural Society* [1928] 1 KB 611.
16 *Re Mariette, Mariette v Aldenham School Governing Body* [1915] 2 Ch 284.
17 *Re Dupree's Deed Trusts, Daley v Lloyds Bank* [1945] Ch 16.
18 *IRC v McMullen* [1981] AC 1.
19 *National Anti-Vivisection Society v IRC* per Lord Wright, [1948] AC 31 at 41; sub nom *IRC v National Anti-Vivisection Society* (1947) 28 TC 311 at 353.

Nonetheless, a testamentary bequest to promote sport in the testator's old regiment (where 'sport' was defined to mean only shooting, fishing, cricket, football and polo) was held to be charitable, as being for the worthwhile purpose of promoting the physical efficiency of the army[20].

The provision of prizes for yacht racing or any sport[1] and restocking the waters fished by an angling society[2] have been held not to be charitable objects. A club providing facilities for instructional and sporting aviation was held not to be charitable[3], as were an Athletic Association for the City of Glasgow Police Force[4] and a bequest to the Surrey County Cricket Club[5].

More generally, the provision of facilities for recreation or leisure time occupation is deemed to be charitable only if the facilities are provided in the interests of social welfare, that is with the object of improving the conditions of life for those for whom the facilities are primarily intended, where they need such facilities by reason of youth, age, infirmity or disablement, poverty or social or economic circumstances, or where the facilities are for the benefit of the members or female members of the public at large[6].

It is the duty of the Charity Commissioners to keep a register of charities in which every charity (with certain specific exceptions) must be registered[7].

The tax exemption available to charities covers interest, dividends and distributions. It also covers tax under Schedule D in respect of the profits of any trade carried on by the charity, if the profits are applied solely to the purposes of the charity and the trade is exercised in the course of the actual carrying out of a primary purpose of the charity[8]. A gain is not a chargeable gain if it accrues to a charity and is applicable and applied for charitable purposes[9]. A disposal of an asset to a charity otherwise than under a bargain at arm's length is treated as being made for a no-gain no-loss consideration if made by way of gift or for consideration not exceeding costs of acquisition, improvement and disposal[10]. A charity has the benefit of favourable treatment in respect of business rates[11]. Charitable status enables additional income to be generated through tax efficient deeds of covenant and the Gift Aid scheme.

Where a charity carries on a trade which is not itself within the relief for trading, it will often be effective for the charity to establish a non-charitable trading subsidiary which covenants its profits to the charity, obtaining a benefit of a charge on income[12], relieving the subsidiary of its corporation tax liabilities and permitting the charity in its turn to benefit from relief

20 *Re Gray, Todd v Taylor* [1925] Ch 362.
1 *Re Nottage, Jones v Palmer* [1895] 2 Ch 649.
2 *Re Clifford, Mallam v McFie* [1912] 1 Ch 29.
3 *Scottish Flying Club v IRC* (1935) 20 TC 1.
4 *IRC v City of Glasgow Police Athletic Association* [1953] AC 380.
5 *Re Patten, Westminster Bank v Carlyon* [1929] 2 Ch 276.
6 Recreational Charities Act 1958, s 1 and see *Guild v IRC* [1992] 2 AC 310.
7 Charities Act 1993, s 3(1).
8 ICTA 1988, s 505(1)(e).
9 Taxation of Chargeable Gains Act 1992, s 256.
10 Taxation of Chargeable Gains Act 1992, s 257.
11 Where a hereditament is wholly or mainly used for charitable purposes, or, if unoccupied, it appears that it will be so used when next in use, the chargeable amount is automatically one-fifth of that otherwise payable: Local Government Finance Act 1988, ss 43(5), (6), 45(5), (6), 64(10). A billing authority may grant discretionary relief (up to 100%) to a charity as well as to a non-profit making recreational club: s 47(2)(a), (c).
12 ICTA 1988, s 338.

available in respect of covenanted income[13]. Payments under such profit-shedding covenants are required to be made after deduction of tax at source[14]. The charity will thus receive income under deduction of tax and will qualify for repayment of the tax if it is otherwise eligible for tax exemption.

Charitable covenants by individuals take effect as charges on income[15]. The covenant must be capable of subsisting for more than three years and not capable of earlier termination without the consent of the persons entitled to the payments[16]. The effect of such a covenant is that the charity is able to reclaim basic rate tax and that the covenantor is entitled to credit in respect of higher-rate tax[17].

In order to minimise cash-flow disadvantages for charities, the Inland Revenue is prepared in appropriate cases to make provisional repayment of tax without awaiting formal verification[18].

Gift Aid

Gift Aid is a tax relief for single cash gifts to charities[19]. For a gift made on or after 16 March 1993 the minimum amount of the gift in order for it to qualify for the relief is £250. The donor makes the gift net of basic rate tax (that is, the basic rate in force in the tax year when the Gift Aid payment is made) provides the appropriate certificate[20], and the charity claims the tax back from the Inland Revenue. Gift Aid income must be used only for charitable purposes.

Charitable fund raising

Bazaars, jumble sales, gymkhanas, carnivals, firework displays and similar activities arranged by voluntary organisations or charities for the purposes of raising funds may fall within the definition of 'trade' in s 832 of the Income and Corporation Taxes Act 1988, referred to above, with the result that any profit would be liable to corporation tax. Tax is not, however, charged on such profits provided all the following conditions are satisfied –

(a) the organisation or charity is not regularly carrying on these trading activities;

(b) the trading is not in competition with other traders;

(c) the activities are supported substantially because the public are aware that any profits will be devoted to charity; and

(d) the profits are transferred to charities or otherwise applied for charitable purposes.[1]

13 ICTA 1988, s 339.
14 ICTA 1988, s 339(7). Covenanted donations made in accounting periods beginning on or after 1 April 1997 and made within nine months after the end of the previous accounting period can be related back to that accounting period, provided that the company is wholly owned by one or more charities: s 339(7AA)–(7AC).
15 ICTA 1988, s 347(2)(b).
16 ICTA 1988, s 47A(7).
17 The Inland Revenue publishes guidance on covenants to charities. See Inland Revenue press release of 20 March 1990.
18 Inland Revenue Statement of Practice SP 3/87. See also SP 4/90.
19 ICTA 1988, s 339 (company donations); Finance Act 1990, s 25 (individual donations).
20 Form 190(SD) for gifts from individuals; form 240(SD) for companies.
1 Extra-Statutory Concession C4.

The Inland Revenue produces a booklet 'Fund-raising for charity', giving guidance on tax treatment of such fund-raising.

Taxation of individuals

EMPLOYEES

Who is an 'employee'?

An employee is an individual who is engaged under a contract 'of service' (in common parlance, a contract of employment)[2], in contrast to one who works under a contract 'for services'. The taxation consequences follow the employment status[3]. The former is taxed under Schedule E, almost invariably collected under PAYE arrangements, and pays Class 1 national insurance contributions (as does the employer in respect of each employee). The latter is taxed under Schedule D and is responsible for his own tax and Class 2 national insurance contributions. The borderline between employment and 'self-employment' is difficult to identify and has been the subject of much litigation[4].

The modern approach is to look at the whole circumstances of the engagement:

> 'The facts as a whole must be looked at, and a factor which may be compelling in one case in the light of the facts of that case may not be compelling in the context of another case'.[5]

The object is to 'paint a picture from the accumulation of detail'[6]. Who has the control over where, when and how the work is to be done? Is the individual in business on his own account? Can he profit from doing the work better or more efficiently? The label applied by the parties to their relationship is not conclusive, but in a case where the relationship is ambiguous, it is appropriate to look to their intention[7].

In the special case where the relationship between the parties is governed exclusively by a written contract, the question must be answered by consideration of the express and implied terms of that contract (construed in its factual matrix) and is a question of law[8]. Generally, however, the question may be regarded as one of fact[9], or mixed fact and law[10].

---

2 The employment may be full or part time. Thus, a person who acts as a gateman only once a week may nevertheless be an employee.
3 *Fall (Inspector of Taxes) v Hitchen* (1973) 49 TC 433 at 439A, [1973] 1 WLR 286 at 293C-F.
4 *Hall (Inspector of Taxes) v Lorimer* [1994] 1 WLR 209; *Barnett v Brabyn (Inspector of Taxes)* [1996] STC 716. See also *McManus v Griffiths (Inspector of Taxes)* [1997] STC 1089, which is discussed further below.
5 *Walls v Sinnett (Inspector of Taxes)* (1987) 60 TC 150 at 164 per Vinelott J, [1987] STC 236.
6 *Hall (Inspector of Taxes) v Lorimer* (1992) 66 TC 349 at 366E-H, [1992] 1 WLR 939 per Mummery J; affd [1994] 1 WLR 209, CA.
7 *Massey v Crown Life Insurance Co* [1978] 1 WLR 676; *Barnett v Brabyn* [1996] STC 716.
8 *Davies v Presbyterian Church of Wales* [1986] 1 WLR 323, *Lee Ting Sang v Chung Chi-Keung* [1990] 2 AC 374, *Narich Pty Ltd v Payroll Tax Comr* [1984] ICR 286.
9 *Lee Ting Sang v Chung Chi-Keung* [1990] 2 AC 374 at 384–386 per Lord Griffiths.
10 *Hall (Inspector of Taxes) v Lorimer* (1994) 66 TC 349 at 373C, [1994] 1 WLR 209 at 214B-C, [1994] STC 23 at 26j per Nolan LJ.

The importance of addressing the question, and getting the answer right, is exemplified by *McManus v Griffiths (Inspector of Taxes)*[11], where a golf club engaged a steward and stewardess under a joint 'contract of employment' whereby the stewardess was responsible for the catering, kept all the income and paid the expenses of food and catering staff. It was held in the High Court that, while the steward was an employee taxable under Schedule E, in relation to the catering arrangements the stewardess (despite the contractual description of 'employment') was in business on her own account and therefore taxable under Schedule D.

PAYE and National Insurance

An employer has an obligation to deduct tax (and earnings related national insurance contributions) from any payment of, or on account of, any income assessable to income tax under Schedule E[12].

Class 1 earnings related national insurance contributions are payable in respect of an 'employed earner' and are made up of a primary element paid by the employed earner and a secondary element paid by his employer[13]. An employed earner is defined in part as a person

'gainfully employed in Great Britain [...] under a contract of service [...] with emoluments chargeable to income tax under Schedule E.'

A self-employed earner means a person who is gainfully employed in Great Britain otherwise than in employed earner's employment[14]. In cases of dispute the Secretary of State determines what is the individual's employment status, subject to appeal to the High Court on a question of law[15].

The burden rests on the employer to make the appropriate deductions and, if they are not made, the primary liability rests on the employer to account for the sums which should have been deducted[16]. Where the Board of Inland Revenue is of the opinion that an employee has received emoluments knowing that the employer has wilfully failed to deduct, it may direct that the relevant amount of tax be recovered from the employee as well as (or instead of) the employer[17]. In practice, however, recovery is generally sought from the employer.

Bonuses, benefits and signing-on fees

Questions have occasionally arisen as to the tax status of one-off payments made to employed sportsmen whether as bonus, the proceeds of a benefit match, or as inducements to enter into contracts. An individual who is a self-employed trader or professional taxable under Schedule D in respect of sporting activity is likely to find that any such payment forms part of his taxable profits. Where the individual receiving the payment is taxable under

---

11 [1997] STC 1089.
12 ICTA 1988, s 203; Income Tax (Employments) Regulations 1993 (SI 1993/744); by Reg 46 and Sch 1 of the Social Security (Contributions) Regulations 1979 (SI 1979/591), that regime is applied to the collection of national insurance contributions.
13 Social Security Contributions and Benefits Act 1992, s 6 (SSC&BA 1992).
14 Section 2(1)(a) and (b) SSC&BA 1992.
15 Social Security Administration Act 1992, ss 17 and 18.
16 Regulation 49 of the Income Tax (Employments) Regulations 1993; SSC&BA 1992, Sch 1, paragraph 3(1); Social Security (Contributions) Regulations 1979, Sch 1 paragraph 28.
17 Regulation 42(3) of the Income Tax (Employments) Regulations 1993. For national insurance contributions see reg 50 of the Social Security (Contributions) Regulations 1979.

Schedule E the payment is taxable if it is made to him for acting as, or being, or becoming, an employee. Accordingly, where payments were made to Peter Shilton, the England international goalkeeper, to induce him to agree to transfer from Nottingham Forest Football Club to Southampton Football Club, the respective payments by the club from which he was transferring and by the club to which he was transferring were held to be indistinguishable in nature and both were taxable as emoluments from his employment with the transferee[18].

By contrast, a cricketer successfully resisted the Inland Revenue's attempts to tax the proceeds of a benefit season where the cricketer was paid the gate money of one of the home matches. It was held that the payment was a personal gift in circumstances where the cricketer had no right to a benefit season, and was not an emolument from employment[19]. The exceptional nature of the testimonial was significant in distinguishing a gift from a taxable emolument. If, despite the absence of a formal contractual arrangement, there had been an expectation arising from the regularity with which such benefits were made available, it is more than doubtful that the decision would have been the same[20]. In contrast, therefore, where a professional cricketer was contractually entitled to have a collection taken for him, the proceeds of the collection were taxable[1]. Similarly customary presents given to a huntsman at Christmas by members of the hunt were held to be chargeable to tax[2].

Payments made to mark England's victory in the World Cup in 1966 were held not to be taxable[3]. It was said (perhaps a little pessimistically) that the payment 'had no foreseeable element of recurrence' and that there was no element of reward (because the employee had been unaware of the impending payment until after he had qualified for it). Having regard to the character and functions of the Football Association, the payment was to be construed as 'applause for the victory' rather than as a reward for services rendered by employees. Those engaged in the modern business of sport may think that it would be safe to proceed on the working assumption that payment of lump sums by way of 'applause' would not be effective as a means of tax avoidance.

Signing-on fees may escape tax because they do not arise from employment, that is to say, from acting as, or being, or becoming an employee. Such cases are likely to be rare since *Shilton v Wilmshurst*[4]. A signing-on fee which was properly to be regarded as compensation to an amateur rugby player for loss of his amateur status has been held not to be taxable[5]. Where the

---

18 *Shilton v Wilmshurst (Inspector of Taxes)* [1991] 1 AC 684.
19 *Seymour v Reed (Inspector of Taxes)* [1927] AC 554.
20 So, in *Corbett v Duff (Inspector of Taxes)* [1941] 1 KB 730 a footballer's benefit payment was held to be taxable where, despite the absence of formal contractual arrangements, the payments 'though not obligatory, are expected, are generally asked for, and are usually accorded'. See also *Davis (Inspector of Taxes) v Harrison* (1927) 11 TC 707 (payment taxable where made 'in lieu of' accrued share of footballer's contractual benefit).
1 *Moorhouse (Inspector of Taxes) v Dooland* [1955] Ch 284. See also *Blakiston v Cooper (Surveyor of Taxes)* [1909] AC 104 where Easter offerings to a vicar were held to be taxable emoluments.
2 *Wright v Boyce (Inspector of Taxes)* [1958] 1 WLR 832.
3 *Moore v Griffiths (Inspector of Taxes)* [1972] 1 WLR 1024.
4 Above.
5 *Jarrold (Inspector of Taxes) v Boustead* [1964] 1 WLR 1357.

payment was made in consideration of the player serving the club in the future, it was taxable as an emolument[6].

Sporting and recreational facilities provided for employees

No charge to tax arises under Schedule E in respect of the provision of a benefit consisting in, or in a right or opportunity to make use of, any sporting or other recreational facilities provided so as to be available generally to, or for use by, the employees of the employer in question[7]. This exemption does not extend to the use of cars, overnight accommodation, facilities on domestic premises, facilities available to members of the public generally, or to facilities not used wholly or mainly by persons whose right or opportunity to use the facilities derives from employment.

THE SELF-EMPLOYED

A self-employed individual carrying on the trade or profession of sport will be subject to Schedule D tax on prize money, sponsorship and appearance money[8]. There is no general obligation to deduct tax at source from such fees.

Special provisions govern the treatment of certain payments to entertainers and sportsmen who are not resident and ordinarily resident in the United Kingdom[9]. Tax at basic rate must be deducted from payments (which includes connected payments and would extend to cover fees and prize money) and accounted for in respect of transfers (such as loans and transfers of rights and including connected transfers). This applies to such payments and transfers in excess of £1,000 in total in the tax year made in respect of appearances in the United Kingdom as such an entertainer or sportsman on or in connection with a commercial occasion or event, including promotional appearances and participation in live or recorded television and similar transmissions. The relevant activities are treated as part of a trade, profession or vocation exercised within the United Kingdom, except where they are performed in the course of an office or employment. The profits or gains are charged to tax on a current year basis; regulations provide for deduction of losses and expenses.

PENSIONS

Tax relief is available for contributions from relevant earnings by individuals to personal pension schemes approved under Chapter IV, Part XIV of the Income and Corporation Taxes Act 1988. Such approval is subject to certain restrictions. In particular, the personal pension scheme must provide for the payment of an annuity or income withdrawals[10]. The annuity must not,

6   *Riley (Inspector of Taxes) v Coglan* [1967] 1 WLR 1300.
7   ICTA 1988, s 197G.
8   Even if not carrying on the trade or profession of journalist or author taxable under Sch D, Case I or II, such an individual may suffer a charge to income tax under Sch D, Case VI on providing his life story to a newspaper: *Hobbs v Hussey (Inspector of Taxes)* [1942] 1 KB 491.
9   Part XIII, Ch III of the ICTA 1988 (ss 555–558); Income Tax (Entertainers and Sportsmen) Regulations 1987, SI 1987/530.
10 Section 633(1)(a).

generally, commence before the member attains the age of 50 unless the Board is satisfied that the member's occupation is one in which persons customarily retire before that age[11]. Sportsmen and women are obvious candidates for retirement before the age of 50.

The Inland Revenue has approved a list of occupations with customary early retirement ages[12]. The earlier pension age there shown applies only to pension arrangements funded by contributions paid in respect of the relevant earnings from the relevant occupation or profession. Furthermore, the earlier retirement ages for professional sportsmen apply only to arrangements made in respect of relevant earnings from activities as professional sportsmen (such as tournament earnings, appearance and prize money) and do not apply to relevant earnings from sponsorship or coaching.

Separate pension arrangements have to be made in respect of any other sources of relevant earnings.

Value Added Tax

Value Added Tax is a tax levied upon certain persons (whether corporate, individual or otherwise) engaged in business on their own account. It is charged on the supply (and deemed supply) of goods and services in the United Kingdom at the (standard) rate of 17.5% of the value of the supply[13]. A taxable person for the purposes of VAT is someone who is registered, or is required to be registered, for the purposes of the Value Added Tax Act 1994[14]. The registration threshold is £48,000 (of taxable supplies, which excludes exempt supplies) and the deregistration threshold is £46,000 per annum[15]. A taxable person is entitled to credit in respect of 'input tax' (the VAT payable by him on the supply to him of any goods or services used, or to be used, for the purpose of any business carried on, or to be carried, on by him)[16].

An exempt supply is not chargeable to VAT[17]. Since 1994 the businesses of sport, sports competitions and physical education have had the benefit of a significant exemption from the scope of VAT. The following are exempt supplies:

> '1. The grant of a right to enter a competition in sport or physical recreation where the consideration for the grant consists in money which is to be allocated wholly towards the provision of a prize or prizes awarded in that competition.

---

11 Section 634(3)(b).
12 Those occupations and ages relevant to this work are:
   Athletes (35 years), Badminton Players (35), Boxers (35), Cricketers (40), Cyclists (35), Dancers (35), Footballers (35), Golfers (40), Ice Hockey Players (35), Jockeys (Flat, 45) (National Hunt, 35), Motor Cycle Riders (Motocross or Road Racing, 40), Motor Racing Drivers (40), Rugby League Players (35), Rugby Union Players (35), Skiers (Downhill, 30), Snooker/Billiards players (40), Speedway Riders (40), Squash Players (35), Table Tennis Players (35), Tennis Players (including Real Tennis, 35), Trapeze Artistes (40), Wrestlers (35).
13 Value Added Tax Act 1994 ('VATA 1994'), ss 1–5.
14 VATA 1994, s 3, Schs 1–3.
15 Schedule 1, paragraphs 1 and 4. From 1 December 1997 the limits are £49,000 and £47,000 per annum respectively.
16 VATA 1994, s 24(1).
17 VATA 1994, ss 4, 31, Sch 9.

2.   The grant, by a non-profit making body established for the purposes of sport or physical recreation, of a right to enter a competition in such an activity.

3.   The supply by a non-profit making body to an individual, except, where the body operates a membership scheme, an individual who is not a member (three months or more) of services closely linked with and essential to sport or physical education in which the individual is taking part.'[18]

The effect of this important provision is to exempt (in relation to non-profit making sports organisations) subscription and joining fees of playing members and hire charges for equipment and facilities (such as pitches and courts).

Nonetheless, the VAT regime has a substantial effect on those engaged in the business of sport. Items of income liable to VAT will include subscriptions for non-playing membership, visitors' fees, bar sales, income from sponsors (other than patrons) catering and vending machine income and profit-making competitions.

A supply for no consideration may nonetheless attract a liability for VAT[19]. But where trophies were given away at a dinner for professional footballers (who had paid for their tickets) VAT was not payable on the cost of the trophies[20].

VAT may be payable even if the income is not received directly by the person providing the facility[1].

The letting for 24 hours or less of an entire football stadium complete with spectating and other facilities, for the playing of a football fixture, was a standard-rated supply. Similar supplies by owners of other outdoor and indoor sporting facilities are taxable at standard rate rather than exempt where the letting is for 24 hours or less[2].

Where a taxable person provides 'business entertainment' (that is, hospitality in connection with a business carried on by him) such as by inviting his valued customers to sports events as his guests, the input tax on the cost of the hospitality is not deductible[3].

By concession, input tax is deductible where necessarily incurred on the provision of accommodation and meals for amateur sports persons selected by recognised representative sports bodies[4].

---

18 VATA 1994, s 31, Sch 9, Group 10. This exemption was backdated to 1 January 1990: VAT (Sport, Physical Education and Fund-Raising Events) Order 1994, SI 1994/687. Refunds of VAT as a result of that exemption are treated by the Inland Revenue as not taxable for corporation tax purposes, and (where returned to members pro rata to the VAT originally paid by them in the relevant period) as not giving rise to a distribution for tax purposes. Interest on the repayments is treated as chargeable to corporation tax. Revenue Interpretation RI 109 (April 1995).

19 VATA 1994, s 5, Sch 5, paragraph 5, Sch 6, paragraph 6.

20 *Customs and Excise Comrs v Professional Footballers Association (Enterprises) Ltd* [1993] STC 86, [1993] 1 WLR 153.

1   *Lord Advocate v Largs Golf Club* [1985] STC 226 (golf club providing facilities on course owned by trust, to which playing members of club made payments for purchase of units in the trust; golf club liable to account for VAT in respect of the facilities it supplied).

2   *Queens Park Football Club Ltd v Customs and Excise Comrs* [1988] VATTR 76. Press Notice No 72/88, 20 September 1988. VATA 1994, Sch 9 Group 1, Item 1 exception (m).

3   VATA 1994, s 25(7) (formerly VATA 1983, s 14(10)), Article 5 of the Value Added Tax (Input Tax) Order 1992, SI 1992/3222. See *BMW (GB) Ltd v Customs and Excise Comrs* [1997] STC 824 (no deduction of input tax by car importer and distributor in respect of golf events, clay pigeon shoots and curling provided for independent dealers and their customers).

4   Extra Statutory Concession No 16 (Notice No 748).

Index